D0915893

Xhosa Beer Drinking Rituals

Xhosa Beer Drinking Rituals

Power, Practice and Performance in the South African Rural Periphery

Patrick A. McAllister

UNIVERSITY OF CANTERBURY,
CHRISTCHURCH, NEW ZEALAND

CAROLINA ACADEMIC PRESS
Durham, North Carolina

Library of Congress Cataloging-in-Publication Data

McAllister, P. A.
  Xhosa beer drinking rituals : power, practice, and performance in the
South African rural periphery / by Patrick A. McAllister.
     p. cm.
  Includes bibliographical references.
  ISBN 0-89089-021-8
  1. Xhosa (African people)--Alcohol use. 2. Xhosa (African people)--Rites
and ceremonies. 3. Beer--Social aspects--South Africa. 4. Drinking customs--
South Africa. 5. South Africa--Social life and customs. I. Title.

  DT1768.X57M35 2005
  305.896'3985--dc22

                                                           2005012709

Carolina Academic Press
700 Kent Street
Durham, North Carolina 27701
Telephone (919) 489-7486
Fax (919) 493-5668
www.cap-press.com

Printed in the United States of America

For Kerry Anne and Brendan

Contents

List of Illustrations xi
Preface and Acknowledgments xiii
Series Editors' Preface xv
    Endnotes xx
    References xx

1 **Introduction** 3
    Why beer drinking rituals? 5
    Fieldwork in Shixini 7
    About this book 12
    Endnotes 17

2 **Beer, Colonialism and Social Change in Southern Africa** 19
    Beer in southern Africa: An overview 20
    'Nocturnal jollifications': Beer among Xhosa speakers, 1800–1950 25
    Agrarian change and the development of co-operative work 31
    Endnotes 41

3 **Power, Practice and Performance—A Theoretical Orientation** 43
    Bourdieu—habitus, capital and field 45
    The struggle for labour 49
    Red and School Xhosa 51
    The anthropology of performance 67
    Endnotes 80

4 **Characteristics of the Rural Field** 81
    Physical features and settlement 84
    Migrant labour and agriculture 89
    Land and livestock 91
    Co-operative work 95
    Endnotes 103

5   Ritual Beer Drinking, Other Drinks and Other Rituals   107
    Beer drinking rituals—a distinctive genre?   111
    Types of beer drinks   117
    Endnotes   121

6   Going to War: Rituals of Labour Migration   123
    Departure and return   124
    The *umsindleko* beer drink   127
    Ndabanduna and Ndlebezendja   129
    Umsindleko for young men and unsuccessful migrants   136
    Oratory and the performance of *umsindleko*   146
    Endnotes   150

7   Snakes, Blood, Money and Migration   153
    An old custom of Hintsa's?   153
    Relations of production and ritual change   157
    Danger in the margins   161
    Habitus, change and performance   163
    Endnotes   167

8   Brewing, Beer Talk, Preparations and Preliminaries   169
    A beer drinking register   170
    Brewing and preliminary beer distribution   173
        (i)   *Umlumiso*   175
        (ii) *Intluzelo*   175
    Endnotes   179

9   Space and the Social Order   181
    Structuralist approaches—a critique   184
    Domestic space and territorial organization   189
    Individual and community   195
    Endnotes   199

10 Beer Distribution and Consumption   201
    Beer prestations (*iminono*)   202
    The *injoli*—master of ceremonies   205
    Customary allocations (*amasiko*)   207
        (i)   *Iimvuko* (awakening)   208
        (ii) The sub-headman's beaker   210

(iii) *Intluzelo* and *isikhonkwane* 211
(iv) *Umcakulo* (the first dip) 211
Intselo—the main drink 211
(i) *Ukugabu* (to allocate by numbers) 211
(ii) *Ukulawula* (to allocate by social groups) 212
Ukurhabulisa—informal sharing 214
Women's allocation 219
Emptying the pot (*ukuqwela*) 220
Drinking and the social order 222
Endnotes 224

11   Modification and Improvisation 227
Work party beer 229
Practice, interest and strategy 231
Local history, practice and the meaning of beer 235
Beer for sale 239
Endnotes 242

12   Speech, Practice and Performance 243
Explanation and consensus 246
Constructing harmony 249
Argument and dispute—negotiating meaning 252
Oratory and transformation 258
Endnotes 261

13   Beer Drink Oratory and Social Reproduction 263
Beer for a new homestead 263
Thwalingubo's *ntwana nje* beer drink 265
Public reflexivity and the rural Xhosa habitus 272
Endnotes 279

14   Power and Gender 281
Patriarchy and the widow's fate 281
Nowinile and Nosajini 285
(i) Nowinile 285
(ii) Nosajini 289
Performance, power and the homestead 290
Endnotes 297

15   Conclusion   299
       The problem of 'misrecognition'   303
       The morality of beer drinking   306

Appendix 1   Brewing Beer (*Ukusila*)   309
Appendix 2   Mbambaza's Addresses to Nowinile and Nosajini   315
       Endnotes   323
References   325
Index   343

List of Illustrations

Maps

1. South Africa—Provinces   4
2. Eastern Cape Province   4
3. Shixini sub-wards and Folokhwe sub-ward sections   82

Tables

1. Distribution of *iminono* gifts   203

Figures

1. Spatial dimensions of a Xhosa homestead   190
2. Allocation of seating places within Folokhwe sub-ward   193

Illustrations

1. Shixini women with pipes   83
2. Homesteads   86
3. Homestead with byres and gardens   87
4. Storing maize   93
5. Harvesting   94
6. Work party   97
7. Drinking beer   109
8. Speaker at beer drink   147
9. Grinding maize for beer   174
10. Division of beer into portions   178
11. Men in hut   182
12. Women in hut   182
13. Drinking outside   192
14. Women outside near woodpile   198
15. Distribution to men's groups   207
16. Calling others to drink   215
17. Women called in to drink   218
18. Workers drinking in a field   231
19. Listening to an announcement   247

Preface and Acknowledgments

The material in this book is based on many hours spent at beer drinking and other rituals in Shixini, an administrative area in the coastal part of Willowvale (Gatyana) district in South Africa's Eastern Province. Without the tolerance, generosity and good humour of the people of Shixini this would not have been possible. They shared their time, their knowledge and their beer with me. My particular debt is to the people of Komkhulu section of Folokhwe sub-ward, where I was based and among whom I lived as a resident at the homestead of Nothusile and Mzilikazi Tshmese. To Mzilikazi and Nothusile (both now dead), their immediate family, other kin and neighbours, especially Masilingane Tshemese, I am extremely grateful for friendship and hospitality. I am also grateful to Shixini's chief and headman, Chief Mandlenkosi Dumalisile, for allowing me to work in the area and for his assistance and hospitality. Similarly, successive sub-headmen in Folokhwe sub-ward, particularly Kenedi Balile, facilitated my work there.

Most of my research in Shixini was conducted while I was employed at Rhodes University Grahamstown, South Africa, first as a member of the Department of Anthropology, from 1981 to 1990, and later as Director of the Institute of Social and Economic Research (ISER), from 1991 to 1996. I would like to acknowledge the support I received from the Board of Management of the ISER, and the role played by my former colleagues in the Department of Anthropology, particularly Michael Whisson, whose encouragement and support were important in enabling me to maintain my involvement with Shixini people over the years.

Some of the ethnographic material presented in this book has appeared in other forms, and I am grateful to the following publishers for permission to use sections of earlier published work: African Studies Centre, Leiden; Institute of Social and Economic Research, Rhodes University; *Ethnology* (University of Pittsburgh); Taylor and Francis (U.K.).

For research funding received at various times I would like to acknowledge the Chamber of Mines of South Africa, the Human Sciences Research Council of South Africa, the Council of Rhodes University, the South African Council for Scientific and Industrial Research, the Anglo American and De Beers Chairman's Fund, and the Deagrarianization and Rural Employment Programme of the African Studies Centre, Leiden. A number of Xhosa-speaking field assistants have been of great help to me, most recently Cecil Nonqane of the Albany Museum, Grahamstown, and Richard Mali of Willowvale, in earlier times. Others are mentioned in chapter one, below.

Finally, I would like to thank the editors of this series, Andrew Strathern and Pamela Stewart, for their careful reading of the manuscript, and for their helpful comments.

Series Editors' Preface

Andrew Strathern and Pamela J. Stewart

Patrick McAllister's study of Xhosa Beer Drinking Rituals provides a link for our Ritual Studies Monograph Series with a long tradition of detailed and insightful work on African themes that characterized British social anthropology in the post World War II context. While much of this work was done in the synchronic analytical mode of the mid-twentieth century, a vigorous tradition of historically informed work grew out of the applied studies conducted through the Rhodes-Livingstone Institute in Northern Rhodesia (Zambia) and by other anthropologists coming from, or working in, Southern Africa in general (See Schumaker 2001 for a history). McAllister's own work grew out of the earlier ethnographic work among the Xhosa people by Philip Mayer. As McAllister explains, it was Philip Mayer who first suggested to him the 'location' of Shixini in Willowvale District among the people historically known as the 'Red Xhosa', i.e., those who had maintained a mode of life that they themselves considered to be 'traditional', by contrast with the 'School Xhosa' who had embraced an urban and 'modernizing' strategy.

Philip Mayer established this contrast in the ethnographic literature with his study of *Townsmen or Tribesmen*, published in 1961. The contrast became classic, expressing the dilemmas, struggles, and divisions in many areas subjected to the imperatives and opportunities of colonial and post-colonial existence (see, for example, Brookfield 1973; Brown 1995, both on the Chimbu [Simbu] people of Highlands Papua New Guinea). John Comaroff and Jean Comaroff (1992) have aptly dubbed the compromise social configurations that arise out of such struggles as 'neo-traditional'. It is just such a neo-traditional context that McAllister has deftly explained in the present book, pointing out that categories such as 'traditionalist' and 'modernizing' should not be over-essentialized as representations of reality, but should rather be regarded as intertwined nuances or tendencies in the fabric of social processes (see Strathern and Stewart 2004 for another discussion of these topics as viewed from ethnographic materials on Papua New Guinea).[1]

With this perspective McAllister succeeds in updating Philip Mayer's earlier work, both in empirical and in theoretical terms. The Xhosa with whom McAllister worked have been engaged in the kind of delicate and sometimes fragile balancing act that encompasses the lives of many people incorporated into the capitalist world: trying to gain what benefits they can while trying also not to pay too high a cost for those benefits. Their lives become simultaneously 'traditional' and 'modern'; but these two categories are still in many ways cognitively opposed and must be kept separate in people's perceptions. The ritual beer drinks accomplish this separation and mediation of opposites.

McAllister's study shows in fine-grained detail the working-out of a neo-traditional texture of local life in a social formation characterized by the predominant practice of labor migration, a pattern earlier set in hand by the exigencies of colonial demands for labor in South Africa, counterbalanced against the Xhosa drive to maintain their own forms of social life and values. The result of these contradictory forces is their mediation through ritual: the rituals of departure and return for the mostly young and male migrants who leave Shixini for work elsewhere and who are reminded on their departure of the expectation that they will work hard and return later, and on their return are greeted and formally reintegrated back into their local area. Both departure and return are 'rites of transition', in which the migrant is seen as exiting from one social world and entering into another. (In similar contexts of migrant work in Papua New Guinea we have termed these transitional processes or movements 'trans-placements', see Stewart and Strathern 2004a.)

The rituals that are detailed here punctuate this process, stressing the normative view that the migrant's own community of origin is the really important social context; and the rituals of beer drinking performed for a returning migrant emphasize aspects of rank, etiquette, precedence, and placement within a gendered social universe, acting as a mnemonic 'refresher course' on what life in the settlement is about. The 'calling out' to recipients to accept a drink parallels the actions at pig-killing festivals in the Pangia area of Papua New Guinea at which the killer of a pig distributes its parts, loudly calling out to kinsfolk and partners, and runs to each recipient in turn, speeding across the communal ceremonial ground to deliver an individual gift (Strathern and Stewart 2000a). The gift is individual; but the context is communal and public, and there are always interested spectators.

While rituals act to partially stabilize and reframe the processes of social action and events in general, McAllister's focus on ritual does not mean that he simply anchors his account in the idea of continuity. Far from it. The rituals he discusses are themselves evidence of historical changes and further affect the pathways of such changes. McAllister's theoretical concerns lead him to relate beer drinking to its historical transformations and to delineate a shift from a kin and family based system of agricultural work to an emphasis on the wider neighborhood as a source of help with ploughing and other tasks. This shift, itself caused by labor migration, is made central to McAllister's analysis: beer drinking occasions reaffirm the importance of neighborhood ties and therefore help to maintain co-operation across kin and household divides.

At the same time, we may note that senior kin are pivotal in these rituals: for example the relationship between a father and his sons is often highlighted. Sibling relations are also at work: the initiator of a 'beer drink' for a returnee may be a younger brother as well as a father; or it may also be a wife. Women in any case carry out the work of brewing the beer. Sons-in-law and affines are favored in the distribution, and on the occasions themselves close kin usually speak first. While, therefore, beer drinks emphasize the neighborhood, they do not deny or obliterate kin ties but incorporate these into a wider emergent structure of relations.

McAllister carefully explains the context of beer drinking in general among the people he worked with. Women brew the beer, and their labor in doing so is essential to the ritual use of beer, even though on many (but, significantly, not all) occasions men appropriate control of it for distribution. Its alcoholic content is not high, and it is regarded as a form of nourishment rather than primarily as a means of intoxication. It is domesticated, belonging to the locality as one of the locality's products, and it is therefore suitable for communicating and embodying aspects of local 'morality'. All this must surely be in contrast with the contexts in which migrants consume alcohol in the towns where they go to work.

In the Papua New Guinea Highlands there was in the pre-colonial past (prior to the 1930s) no tradition of brewing home-made alcohol. Consequently when alcohol consumption was permitted from the 1960s onward by the Colonial Australian Administration, the results were devastating, with excessive consumption, aggression, and disorder, only partially muted through the incorporation of cases of beer into inter-group ceremonial exchanges (Strathern and Stewart 2000b, see also Strathern and Stewart 2003).

The situation among the Xhosa (and many other African peoples) is closer to the place of millet wine in the traditions of the Austronesian-speaking indigenous people in Taiwan, where the ability to drink quantities of wine seems to have been a part of male 'initiation' rituals, nowadays represented in performances as a part of 'cultural revival' movements (see both Stewart and Strathern 2005, and Strathern and Stewart 2005 on these movements).[2] Millet wine use among these indigenous Taiwanese groups was, and remains, also important in libations to the ground and in blowing it to the air for spirits to partake of during ritual ceremonies.

McAllister mostly stresses the reintegrative social purposes of beer drinking rituals; but an aspect of communication with spirits, as a part of the reintegration itself, is present. He makes this clear when he notes that beer drinks may be intended to thank or appease ancestors, for example at harvest; or to ensure good luck for a migrant setting out to work elsewhere. The favor of the ancestors was, and is, seen as important for success in all kinds of work. And when McAllister asked if the beer used in the *umsindleko* ritual was for the ancestors or the living people, one man told him, with that expressive flair that is so often met with in the context of such discussions: "I bind them both with one rope". The image of the 'rope' here is one that translates well into Papua New Guinea contexts that we are familiar with. In Mount Hagen, for example, a ritual to pull back the spirit of a sick person and bring them again into the world of the living was called *min kan karemen*, "they straighten the rope of the spirit", in the local Melpa language.

McAllister explains that *umsindleko* is the term for a ceremonial beer drinking to welcome back a returning migrant. The term is similar to *umhlinzeko*, referring to the earlier custom of the sacrificial killing of an animal (a goat or ox) for the same kind of occasion, accompanied by an address to the ancestors. This sacrifice was a relatively private affair, centering on agnatic kin and the cattle byre. *Umsindleko* are much larger affairs, reflecting the shift from extended homesteads centered on kin to smaller extended homesteads linked in neighborhoods. The ritual change thus reflects a historical change in social morphology, exogenously induced; while it also recaptures and carries forward the feature of communication with ancestors. This combination of continuity and change is mirrored at the linguistic level by the similarity between the terms *umhlinzeko* and *umsindleko*, coupled with their differing etymologies, the former referring to 'slaughtering', the latter to 'having a narrow escape' (i.e., from the dangers of leaving home to work elsewhere).

The dangers involved in migration seem to cut two ways. There is first the danger to the migrant himself, that he might fail at his work or suffer misfortune. Second, there is the danger that the migrant might be changed, and bring back 'a snake', i.e., a form of witchcraft that could be dangerous to his own father—a dramatic representation of the potentiality for inter-generational conflict resulting from the son's role as an earner of money and the father's authority in the home context (for a recent review of contemporary notions of 'witchcraft' ideas in Africa see Stewart and Strathern 2004b). Beer drinks dissolve that potentiality for conflict through the medium of ritual expenditure. Since in some ways beer and money are thus opposed, it is easy to understand why there is ambivalence toward the practice of selling beer for money. In other social contexts of this kind around the world money itself becomes domesticated through its incorporation into ceremonial exchanges, such as in Highlands New Guinea (Strathern and Stewart 1999); or money is used to purchase beer, which is then used to promote social relations. (We were particularly struck by customs of beer drinking and toasting on convivial occasions in academic circles on a lecturing trip that we made to Mainland China in October 2004.)

In addition to his rich ethnographic analysis, McAllister provides important theoretical perspectives on his materials. We mention two of these perspectives here. One is his use of performance theory; the other is practice theory. For the first, McAllister's starting point is Victor Turner's concept of the social drama; for the second, Pierre Bourdieu's concepts of habitus and field. The social drama is an arena of performance, the making public of versions of social reality in situations of conflict, supporting, resisting, or subverting the status quo. McAllister points out that Turner's approach breaks out of a functionalist framework by recognizing ambiguity and uncertainty in outcomes. Process is the key concept here, since process is not chaotic, but it is also not over-determined, and allows room for the expression of agency. McAllister brings these ideas interestingly into the same frame of analysis as Bourdieu's concepts by pointing out that Turner was essentially moving toward practice theory. He also stresses, contra some critics of Bourdieu, that Bourdieu's notion of habitus is flexible and does allow for the consideration of change.

Applying these synthetic ideas to his ethnographic findings, McAllister goes on to stress the performative capacities of rituals to recreate order, not necessarily by denying change, but by embracing it. The beer drinking ceremonies do this by creating a social context for the reincorporation of migrants back into neighborhood life; and historically they have been instrumental in change though the shift from animal sacrifices to communal consumption of beer. The common element that is preserved is the sense of danger. Migrants are said to be going out to war. 'Analogical transfers' in ritual contexts are thus ways of mediating change. This useful concept can be applied also to contexts of religious change such as are involved in religious conversion processes.

Part of the performative work in beer drinking rituals is done by oratory, and McAllister provides interesting examples of eloquent speeches made on these occasions. Speakers point out that actions are not enough, and they use speeches to 'explain things properly'. While the mouth consumes beer, the most important thing is that it can produce words. And consensus is not automatic, but negotiated and provisional. Words are also used to contain conflict. As one speaker said, "Boys settle things with violence, men with words".

The Xhosa view here resonates strongly with the idea of speech in Highlands New Guinea. In the Hagen area, for example, in the 1970s, leaders would say that people should eat first at feasts, but after this they should talk. And pre-eminent leaders, known for their dispositions of wealth, would nevertheless stress that their power lay in their creative control over talk (see for example, Strathern and Stewart 2000b).

Patrick McAllister has certainly exercised a creative control in his absorbing presentation of materials in this book. The book will be of particular interest to scholars in ritual studies, religious studies, cultural anthropology, African studies, and colonial and post-colonial studies.

March 2005
Pittsburgh, PA, USA

Endnotes

1. Much of our own research work, over many years, has been conducted in Highlands Papua New Guinea in the Hagen area among the Melpa-speaking people, in Pangia where the language is Wiru, and in the Duna area where the language is Duna.

2. Since 2000 we have had an active research program in Taiwan, returning regularly for further work.

References

Brookfield, Harold (ed.) 1973. *The Pacific in transition*. New York: St. Martin's Press.

Brown, Paula 1995. *Beyond a mountain valley. The Simbu of Papua New Guinea*. Honolulu: University of Hawai'i Press.

Comaroff, John and Jean Comaroff 1992. *Ethnography and the historical imagination.* Boulder, CO: Westview Press.

Schumaker, Lyn 2001. *Africanizing anthropology.* Durham, N.C.: Duke University Press.

Stewart, Pamela J. and Andrew Strathern 2004a. Body and mind on the move: Emplacement, displacement, and trans-placement in Highlands Papua New Guinea. Paper presented in the session "Transformation and Trans-placements: Mobilities in Pacific Islands" organized by P. J. Stewart and A. Strathern at the International Association for Historians of Asia conference held at the Institute of Ethnology, Academia Sinica, in Taipei, Taiwan, December 6–10, 2004; forthcoming in 2005 in Asia-Pacific Forum.

Stewart, Pamela J. and Andrew Strathern 2004b. *Witchcraft, sorcery, rumors, and gossip.* For New Departures in Anthropology Series, no. 1, Cambridge: Cambridge University Press.

Stewart, Pamela J. and Andrew Strathern 2005. Introduction: Ritual practices, "cultural revival" movements, and historical change. In Pamela J. Stewart and Andrew Strathern, eds. *Asian ritual systems: Syncretisms and ruptures,* Special Issue of the Journal of Ritual Studies 19.1: i–xiv.

Strathern, Andrew and Pamela J. Stewart 1999. Objects, relationships, and meanings: Historical switches in currencies in Mount Hagen, Papua New Guinea. In David Akin and Joel Robbins, eds. *Money and modernity: State and local currencies in Melanesia.* Association for Social Anthropology in Oceania, Monograph no. 17, Pittsburgh, PA: University of Pittsburgh Press, pp. 164–91.

Strathern, Andrew and Pamela J. Stewart 2000a. Dangerous woods and perilous pearl shells: The fabricated politics of a longhouse in Pangia, Papua New Guinea. Journal of Material Culture 5(1): 69–89.

Strathern, Andrew and Pamela J. Stewart 2000b. *Arrow talk: Transaction, transition, and contradiction in New Guinea highlands history.* Kent, Ohio, and London: Kent State University Press.

Strathern, Andrew and Pamela J. Stewart 2003. Conflicts vs. contract: Political flows and blockages in Papua New Guinea. In Brian Ferguson, ed. *The state, identity and violence: Political disintegration in the post cold-war world.* London and New York: Routledge, pp. 300–17.

Strathern, Andrew and Pamela J. Stewart 2004. *Empowering the past, confronting the future.* For Contemporary Anthropology of Religion Series, New York: Palgrave Macmillan.

Strathern, Andrew and Pamela J. Stewart 2005. Introduction: Expressive genres in historical change. In *Expressive genres and historical change: Indonesia, Papua New Guinea, and Taiwan*, eds. Pamela J. Stewart and Andrew Strathern. For the Anthropology and Cultural History in Asia and the Indo-Pacific Series, London: Ashgate Publishing.

Xhosa Beer Drinking Rituals

1 Introduction

When I first went to Willowvale (Gatyana), in South Africa's Eastern Cape Province in 1976 (Map 1), it was with the intention of examining the relationship between labour migration and ritual among the Xhosa-speaking residents of the district. The district was then part of the Transkei, a 'homeland' created in terms of the apartheid ideology, and this was a dramatic time in South Africa's history. In the winter of 1976 there was an explosion of resistance, riots and protest ('the Soweto uprising') against white minority rule in South Africa, and this was also the year of Transkei's notional 'independence' under the apartheid strategy of black self-rule. At the time I was part of a fairly loosely co-ordinated team of six anthropologists involved in a large research project aimed at examining various aspects of migrant mine labour, being conducted by the Institute of Social and Economic Research at Rhodes University, led by Philip Mayer, and funded by the Chamber of Mines of South Africa. Initially the funders were motivated by the question of labour supply and the difficulty in attracting migrant workers from within the borders of South Africa, including its supposedly autonomous (though controlled from Pretoria) 'homelands'. Almost as soon as the project got underway, however, in 1975, and with the funding having been committed, the labour issue was resolved by a significant increase in the wages being offered to mine workers. The result was that the researchers on the project were able to think much more broadly about the topic, freed from the constraints surrounding the original motivation of the funders.

At the start of the project I had conducted a pilot survey in three Transkei districts—Elliotdale, Umtata and Ngqeleni—exploring various aspects of migratory mine labour from these areas. In the course of these two months I learned that Xhosa-speaking migrants would occasionally time their trips home to co-incide with some important ritual, that misfortune at work might drive a worker home to fulfill some outstanding obligation to the ancestral shades, and that newly circumcised youths were expected to go out to work 'to change the khaki', as it was put, referring to the khaki-coloured clothing that was worn by newly initiated young men, signalling that they were in the last phases of transition from boyhood to manhood. These things indicated that labour migration and ritual life were to some extent connected, and it was this connection that interested me. In order to pursue this topic I decided to work in a conservative area, where the ancestor religion was still strong and

3

Map 1   South Africa— Provinces

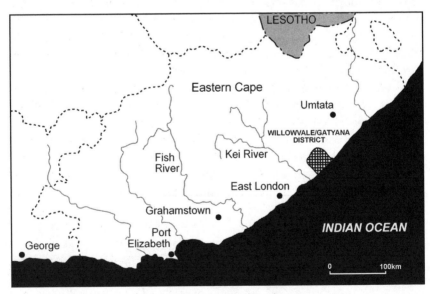

Map 2   Eastern Cape Province

where mission churches had not had much influence. Philip Mayer suggested Shixini 'location' in Willowvale district (Map 2), where he had worked fifteen years earlier. After having a look at a number of alternative coastal locations in the district, the areas where modernity appeared to have made the least in-roads into life and where Xhosa traditions seemed to be strongest, it was to Shixini that I went.

For the first six weeks in Shixini my two assistants and I pursued the question of the relationship between ritual and labour migration. We questioned people, attended rituals and spoke to the participants, sought out those who were regarded as knowledgeable or who had recently performed rituals, and interviewed migrants who had recently returned home. We collected a fair amount of information, but there was something missing; the data we had obtained seemed dull and lifeless. One of the reasons for this was that it con-sisted of disconnected bits and pieces; another was that it was based mainly on interviews. During this period we did learn about the area and its people, about matters pertaining to politics and kinship, the composition of home-steads, and so on, but the bulk of the information collected by means of in-terviews and on the basis of our preconceived ideas was unusable. In asking: 'How do migrant labour and ritual affect each other?' I had placed in a cen-tral position an issue that was only of peripheral interest and importance to the people themselves. What we ought to have been doing was to allow the focus of our study to be determined by what was happening, by what people were doing and talking about in relation to migrant labour, rather than to ask questions.

Why beer drinking rituals?

The signs were there although I did not recognise them. Firstly, during the initial six-week period in the field there was frequently a beer drink being held in the immediate vicinity. Often our inquiry for a person whom we wished to speak to was met with the response *usetywaleni* ('he/she is at a beer drink').[1] Since I did not think that beer drinks qualified as ritual, we did not bother to attend. The conventional wisdom (implied in terms like 'beer parties' rather than explicitly stated) was that beer drinks might be fun, but not really wor-thy of serious study. Philip Mayer told me that he had ignored them during fieldwork because he thought that they were a new thing, not 'traditional'. Al-though he was partly right (see chapter 2) the ethnographic literature on

Southern African peoples made it clear that beer drinking featured in ritual, but it usually did so in passing and without a great deal of analysis. It became apparent to me later that very few observers had addressed this issue directly or in detail. Later, we naively thought we might be able to pursue our inquiries concerning ritual and labour migration by attending beer drinks and questioning people there, but on our first attempt were politely told that such things (concerning the ancestors) were not discussed at beer drinks.

Secondly, two weeks after arriving in Shixini I recorded in my diary that a beer drink had been held "by a man who has just returned from work". A fortnight later I learnt that it was required that a beer drink be held for a returned migrant by his close kin. It was also clear that returned migrants were expected to distribute bottles of brandy and other gifts, and one protracted dispute concerning such distribution indicated that people took this practice seriously. The implication of these events, however, escaped me, at least until after I had spent a month at home in Grahamstown going through and thinking about the material we had collected, before returning to Shixini. Shortly after returning I was told that a beer drink called *umsindleko* was about to be held for a returned migrant. Slowly it dawned that there were ritual and symbolic activities integral to the departure and return of migrants, and that I should be attending these instead of running around conducting interviews. I had made the transition from what Fabian (1990) later called 'informative' to 'performative' ethnography. Attendance at this *umsindleko* made me realise that there were rituals *of* labour migration in Shixini, and I spent the next five months examining these.[2]

The rituals of labour migration that I studied in Shixini included three different kinds of beer drinks, as well as a variety of other ritual actions. After realizing something of the significance of beer drinks I started to attend them more regularly on subsequent fieldwork trips and I decided, after joining the teaching staff at Rhodes University, to make them the subject of my doctoral dissertation. When this was completed in 1986 I continued to visit the Transkei regularly, and became involved in a variety of other research projects, but I continued to attend and monitor beer drinking rituals right up to my most recent fieldwork in 1996–1998. What emerged initially was that there was a wide variety of kinds of beer drink rituals, held for a variety of purposes and frequently named accordingly. In addition, regular attendance at beer drinks made me realise that what seemed at first to be noisy, chaotic and unstructured affairs, a sort of elaborate Xhosa version of Friday night at the local pub, were in fact orderly and carefully regulated. Clearly, to make sense of beer drinks I had to identify how they were constructed and regulated, which seemed to be linked to the particular reason for brewing. Thirdly, beer drinks were marked by much talking, debate, discussion and other kinds of verbal

activity. There were frequently long and heated arguments which the participants appeared to enjoy immensely, and also more orderly speeches which obviously provided senior men with an opportunity to display their oratorical
skills. At first I was interested mainly in the content of what people said, as an
aid to my understanding of what was going on at beer drinks. Later I started
to realise that why and how people said things, and who the people were who
said them, were important independently of what was actually said.

Beer drinks were so common in Shixini and of such obvious importance
in everyday life (however long it took me to realise this) that they could not
be ignored. Later, I found that published work on the topic was scarce, but
that there were certain indications of their significance. Hunter (1936 *passim*)
had a fair amount to say about beer drinking in Pondoland and Davies (1927)
had published a three page article on Bomvana beer drinking customs, a topic
dealt with also by Cook in his book on the Bomvana (1931, 26–30). As far as
other South African Bantu-speakers were concerned an article by Krige (1932)
was the only publication I could find dealing specifically with the social significance of beer. Although virtually all the ethnographies mentioned beer and
its importance in social life, especially its role in ritual and its use as a reward
for participants in work parties, it was apparent that beer drinks or 'beer parties' was a neglected field of study.

Fieldwork in Shixini

At the time when I started work in the Transkei researchers had to get written permission from the central government in Pretoria to enter and reside in
any of the 'homelands'. The permit came with a long list of prescribed and
prohibited activities. Among the latter were prohibitions against living in 'a
Bantu homestead' and against 'interfering in Bantu activities'. The South
African police had a large network of informants in Transkei, and within a
week of my arrival in Shixini I was visited by local security-branch personnel
who asked to see my permit and what my business was. As a result I was forced
to start my fieldwork in a caravan, an incongruous sight parked out next to
thatched rural homesteads, but after Transkei's supposed independence in late
1976 I was able to get around this restriction and to live with a family in one
of their huts. In Shixini I lived at first at the homestead of Bavumile Kenkebe,
the highly respected and powerful sub-headman of Ndlelibanzi sub-ward at
the time, and after a few months I moved to the homestead of Mzilikazi and
Nothusile Tshemese in Folokhwe sub-ward, encouraged by a gift of sweet potatoes from Nothusile to mark the first time, she said, that a white person had

ever entered her home. It was this homestead that I continued to frequent for the next twenty two years.

As a member of this homestead I was associated with Mzilikazi's clan group, the Cirha clan, which was prominent in the area. I was referred to by my 'adopted' clan name by other residents, called by other clan members to events such as important rituals, and required to participate in the ritual tasting of special portions of meat and beer by the clan and other kin at these events. I found this ready acceptance and incorporation of a white stranger among people who had long suffered the injustices and indignities of apartheid to be quite remarkable. As a resident in Mzilikazi's homestead I was also part of the local neighbourhood group and was thus called to other neighbouring homesteads, at all times of the day or night, to partake of beer and other alcoholic drinks when migrants returned home or on other small neighbourhood occasions, such as those preliminary to public beer drinks.

Folokhwe is a relatively small area, consisting of around 80 homesteads (the exact number varies slightly from year to year). This meant that I was able to get to know virtually all the adult members of the sub-ward, as well as many of those from adjoining sub-wards. The advantage of this was that I was eventually able to identify most people present at a beer drink and to record who sat where, who spoke, who was allocated beer, who called who for a drink, and so on. Folokhwe was also small enough for me to correlate such observations with others in the political and economic sphere, such as the composition of work parties. I also attended beer drinks and other events in other wards such as Ntlahlane, Mhlahlane, Jujurha and Ngxutyana as well as in other sub-wards of Shixini—principally Ndlelibanzi, Nompha, Jotelo, Mngwevu, Mtshayelo and Mandluntsha.

I spent nine months in the Transkei between May 1975 and August 1977, seven of these in Shixini, and undertook a number of shorter visits, of up to six weeks duration, at regular intervals after that, my last visit being in 1998. Most of my information was obtained first hand by attending and taking part in beer drinks and other events, and by recording what was said for later transcription and translation. After the first six weeks I did little formal interviewing except during my last two spells in the field. I administered no questionnaires except for an initial household census and repeated this in 1990 and again in 1998 for comparative purposes. In all, I attended well over fifty beer drinks, and made detailed notes and audio tape recordings at thirty of these. As time went on I became more and more aware of the importance of the public speaking that took place at beer drinks, and of the need for detailed recordings and accurate transcriptions. Recordings were transcribed and translated in the field or later, an assistant and I collaborating in this task.

Often it was necessary to play the recording to the speaker or a local person to obtain an accurate transcription and to inquire into the meaning and significance of what was said. Such inquiries often led to long discussions on related topics, and turned out to be a fruitful way of asking questions without resorting to an interview as such.

I also attended many other kinds of ancestor rituals and public events, such as mortuary rituals, male and female initiation ceremonies, meetings of the sub-ward court or moot (*ibandla*), Tribal Authority meetings, and so on. This enabled me to compare beer drink rituals with other kinds of events and to determine their specific characteristics. I was usually accompanied by a Xhosa-speaking assistant, who was always someone from outside the area. A fair amount of information was obtained simply by walking around the sub-ward, talking to people on an informal basis, observing (and occasionally taking part in) everyday activities such as work parties. In addition, people came to know that I lived in Mzilikazi's homestead and frequently dropped in to say hello and to chat, often after a beer drink that I had been present at, sometimes on their way to and from other events. They came, they often said, to see that I was not being troubled by anything, that I did not have *isithukutezi* (anxiety, loneliness).

Beer drinks as a subject for participant-observation have many advantages because it is practically impossible *not* to be a participant. The beer is nutritious and refreshing and one soon develops a taste for it, though I found it hard to drink large quantities at first because of the bloated sensation that it produced. Even people who do not drink beer, however, attend beer drinks, and are offered the beaker, which etiquette demands they may not refuse, but pass on to a friend or relative. Everyone present is allocated a formal seating place and is included in the allocation of beer. There is simply no such thing as an observer at a beer drink, though of course it was possible to observe and record as well as to take part. I was sometimes given large beakers full of beer and had to decide who to call for a drink, or who to pass the beaker to after I had received and drunk from it. Shixini people were more than willing to instruct me in the correct etiquette involved in giving and receiving beer and constantly remarked on my willingness to participate. At *imbarha*, where the beer is sold, I was able, like others, to buy beer for people to whom I was indebted or with whom I wanted to maintain good relations. As a resident of Mzilikazi's homestead I was regarded, for the purpose of the seating arrangements at beer drinks, as a member of the sub-ward section that Mzilikazi belonged to, called Komkhulu, and on one occasion when my assistant and I were present at a beer drink in another part of the sub-ward and Komkhulu men were occupied elsewhere eating an ox that had been slaughtered due to old age, it was considered by the hosts that Komkhulu was present and that the beer could thus be given out. No doubt this was because the men present were thirsty and wanted to get on with it, but it seemed at the time also to be a sign of a degree of acceptance.

It would be naive to claim that my presence at beer drinks did not affect the proceedings in any way. Apart from the above mentioned factors there were times when the presence of an audio recorder influenced speakers. On one occasion an elder brought some light relief during an argument by turning to me in the course of his speech, pointing to the recorder, and commanding: "Don't write this down Pat!" On another a speaker said that he had risen to speak because there was "a machine to be filled up." The same individual was once told to be quiet and sit down by others because it was clear that he was talking for the recorder. In general, however, I am confident that most people simply forgot about or ignored the recorder, and behaved as they would have had I not been present. I attended a number of beer drinks without notebook and tape recorder and noticed no difference in the proceedings or character of the speeches.

My presence did at times influence the proceedings in small ways, as when I was called for sips by others or given a gift of beer. On one occasion at a beer drink in Elwandle section of Jotelo sub-ward, which I was visiting for the first time, the homestead head and host placed my assistant and myself with his own (Elwandle) group when the seating places were allocated. Dlathu, the man with whom we had gone to Jotelo, was also put with Elwandle, because there were no other Folokhwe people present. Soon afterwards, some other Folokhwe men arrived, Folokhwe was given its proper seating place, and Dlathu joined the others there. However, my assistant and I were told by the host to remain with Elwandle, because as distinguished visitors "from the government" we should be given respect (*imbeko*) by being seated with the host section. There was some disagreement about this and both Folokhwe and Jotelo men pointed out to the host that we had been attending beer drinks for some time and should be seated with Folokhwe. This placed me in something of a dilemma, since Folokhwe people treated me as a member of one of their sections at beer drinks in Folokhwe, and I was not keen to seem to want to sit apart from Folokhwe people here. At the same time I did not want to offend the host by saying that I did not want to sit with his group and accept the *imbeko* being offered. The problem was whether to remain silent, a non-participant, and allow the argument to run its course, or whether to participate, as a local man might have done in a similar situation (or so I thought). Since members of the host's own section disagreed with him, and it was not the only occasion in the course of the beer drink that this was the case, I decided to speak in order to identify myself with Folokhwe and to correct the impression that I was associated with the government. I did so and, after further argument, Elwandle people as a group overruled the individual host/homestead head, and decided that we should go and sit with Folokhwe, saying that we should "go to our home". The host objected, but as one of the Elwandle men put it: "It is the *ilali* (Elwandle section) which is releasing them, it is not up to you." Had I been longer in the field, however, I would have realized that the polite thing to do would have been to remain quiet and that staying with the hosts would have gained me access to much more beer than I would have in moving to Folokhwe's place, where my assistant and I simply added to the number that had to eke out a rather small beer allocation. Folokhwe men were, therefore, not all that impressed with my attempt at identifying with them, though I sometimes heard them recalling this event years afterwards.

Despite the overall political climate in South Africa in the 1970s and 1980s, I never felt anything but welcome, secure and comfortable in Shixini over the long period of my association with it. By any standards Shixini people are very poor in material things, but they gave generously of their time and hospitality. Certainly, there were sometimes the kinds of difficulties and demands faced by most fieldworkers; requests for money and liquor, a ride into town (I usually had a vehicle with me), or to convey people to visit sick relatives or to take ill people to the nearest hospital (a three hour round trip to Kentani, the adjoining district). I helped where I could, especially with regard to health issues. Mostly I reciprocated with groceries, gifts of clothing, maize, fruit, schoolbooks and pens, or by bringing things from the city which could not be easily obtained locally. In the late 1980s I also got involved, at the urging of many (but not all!) Shixini people, in an attempt to prevent the imposition of a state-sponsored agricultural 'Betterment' scheme of the kind that had brought social and economic misery to many communities in the Transkei and elsewhere in southern Africa. This took place from 1985 to 1993 and has been documented elsewhere (McAllister 1994). It involved working with the local acting chief to develop an alternative to Betterment and to bring the pitfalls and inadequacies of the latter to the attention of Transkei government authorities in an attempt to get its implementation suspended. In this we were largely successful, and although it made a few enemies for me among the educated and political elite in the area (none of whom lived in Folokhwe or adjoining sub-wards), it helped to cement my acceptance by Shixini's conservative majority, who were dead set against Betterment and the forced residential relocation and re-organization of land-use practices that it entailed.

I worked with a variety of Xhosa-speaking assistants. One of these was the late Percy Qayiso, who had in the past worked with Philip Mayer and with

David Hammond-Tooke, both prominent South African anthropologists. He proved invaluable during the time that he assisted me, though there were also difficulties. Others who assisted at various times over the next twenty years were, in chronological order, Buyiselo Dyantyi, Mlungisi Nduna, Songo Mlotywa, Richard Mali, Anthony Plaatjie, Timothy Zita and Cecil Nonqane. Despite the efforts of gifted Xhosa language teachers when I was an undergraduate at the University of Cape Town, my Xhosa language skills were rudimentary when I first started fieldwork, but I eventually reached the point where I was competent enough to understand most of what people said to me in Xhosa and sometimes to visit the field by myself to pursue inquiries without an assistant, though I still used a helper when transcribing and translating tape recorded material. In Shixini I was sometimes assisted on an ad hoc basis by Masilingane Tshemese, a Folokhwe neighbour who speaks no English but who nevertheless was of great help in facilitating my work, and who became a good friend.

About this book

It was not long after I decided to study beer drinking rituals that I started to realise that they were very elaborate affairs, highly structured, governed by a complex set of conventions, procedures or customs (*imithetho*), held for a wide variety of significant purposes, accompanied by lengthy debates and discussions as well as by artful oratory, and of obvious importance for anyone attempting to get to grips with the nature of rural Xhosa identity, social life and culture. In the chapters that follow I attempt to illustrate their importance and their complexity through a number of interrelated approaches. In chapter two I briefly survey the role of beer in southern Africa as a whole, primarily from a historical perspective, before turning to the historical emergence of beer drinking as a major social phenomenon in the Transkei, where my study area is located. Although beer drinking is known to have featured among Xhosa-speaking people well before colonial times, it was during the latter part of the nineteenth and the early part of the twentieth centuries that it became extremely noticeable and widespread in the Transkei. This was due, I argue, to the changing nature of rural production and other features of the colonial context to which rural people had to adapt. I then trace the impact of these changes on Xhosa people in terms of their reactions to colonialism and apartheid, which shaped everyday life in Shixini in the late twentieth century, the period during which I did fieldwork, and which help to explain why and how beer drink rituals are firmly embedded in the political economy of the area. The argument is simply that beer drinks are a crucial aspect of a rural Xhosa attempt to maintain homestead production and an agrarian lifestyle in the context of apartheid rule, a context that lingers on despite the formal disappearance of the apartheid state. The approach, then, is that beer drink rituals are a form of political and economic practice which must be historically situated and understood in terms of practice theory.[3]

After setting the scene, the book's primary theoretical orientation is outlined in chapter three. It is derived largely from Bourdieu's practice theory in conjunction with the anthropology of performance. This places the historical and contemporary material (which comes next) within a wider theoretical framework, and provides the conceptual basis for the close analysis of beer drinking rituals that follows in subsequent chapters. Prior to this, the nature of beer rituals as a particular ritual genre within the context of a larger complex of ancestor rituals and rites of passage, is outlined (in chapter five). To illustrate how the theoretical perspective adopted may be applied, and to further illustrate its relevance in the analysis of both historical and contemporary realities regarding beer drinking, in chapters six and seven I turn to a detailed analysis of the beer ritual called *umsindleko*. This event is associated with the oscillation of Shixini men and boys to and from the mines and other industries of South Africa as labour migrants. The analysis serves to illustrate and confirm the contemporary relevance of the historical development of beer rituals and the factors that surrounded this, as outlined in chapter two, and also to show how the impact of these changes on contemporary life in Shixini (detailed in chapter four) are expressed and developed in ritual form. The analysis of *umsindleko* also serves to illustrate how the theoretical themes of the book are applied to individual beer rituals but tied analytically to processes of historical change and development.

I then turn to a general analysis of how beer drinking events are organized and how they proceed, in chapter eight, which deals with the brewing process and other preparations, and in chapters nine and ten, which provide a detailed account of the ways in which these rituals are structured and organized. Chapter nine concentrates on the spatial dimensions, chapter ten on the distribution and consumption of beer. The latter is largely descriptive and should be skipped by readers not interested in the empirical detail of how a beer drink is conducted. In these two chapters, the formal principles in terms of which beer drink rituals are organized and held are outlined, but it becomes clear that particular events need to be understood in terms of social context, where preceding and forthcoming events, interest, improvisation and strategy are crucial aspects in interpreting the meaning of the rituals. This is taken further in chapter 11, examining the relationship between beer drinks and social practice, linking contemporary beer drink rituals (including those associated with co-operative work) to the social, political and economic realities that impinge on daily life, and to the personalities, goals and interests associated with individual homesteads.

At this point a diversion is necessary (in chapter 12) to consider the role and significance of speech at beer rituals, which are associated with elaborate oratory and other kinds of speaking, and to assess the place of speech within the larger theoretical framework guiding the analysis as a whole. The following two chapters develop the themes associated with formal beer drink oratory, in association with the general theoretical orientation revolving around practice and performance, by looking at two kinds of beer ritual associated with individual transitions—the establishment on a new homestead (chapter 13) and the transition that a woman undergoes at the end of the mourning process for a dead husband (chapter 14). These cases also further illustrate how the general principles on which particular beer rituals are based are both applied and modified in relation to particular circumstances. Chapter 15 concludes the volume and attempts to draw together some of the main themes emerging from the analysis as a whole.

I do not intend to provide a survey of alcohol studies in anthropology. This has already been done in a comprehensive manner by Heath (1987, 1987a) and Douglas (1987). Nor will I review the published work on beer drinking, much less on beer or alcohol in Africa, though I will refer to relevant work as and when appropriate. Recent surveys of the latter kind may be found in Lentz (1999) and Bryceson (2002). There are many journal articles devoted to the topic of alcoholic drink (including beer) in Africa, and a variety of other writers refer to beer drinking in Africa in the course of a larger study of something else. I cite from these works as and where relevant. However, I have not yet come across detailed work on beer drinking, or a full length monograph on this topic, with the exception of Colson and Scudder (1988), though like many other writers on alcohol in Africa they are concerned with increased beer drinking through its commercialization and sale, and with the problem of increased alcohol consumption generally, rather than with the beer drinks held in association with work parties, rituals, and the like, though the latter are mentioned in their book. The gap that the present book tries to fill is the one described by Hagaman (1980, 203), when she wrote that fieldworkers in Africa have yet to pay attention "to the place that beer…holds in the total socioeconomic and ritual life of its brewers and drinkers."

Mary Douglas' view is that alcohol studies need to pay attention to a number of different aspects of consumption—the religious, the political, and the economic (Douglas 1987). I would add the historical, as a crucial dimension that needs to be accounted for. In this respect I would highlight a perceptive comment by Lentz, who re-iterates Douglas' view, but who adds that "it is precisely the study of the historical changes in alcohol consumption…which requires the consideration of both the symbolic-ritualistic and the political-economic aspects" that enables us to grasp its full significance (Lentz 1999, 155). A major aspect of my study revolves around the economic, but that this is insufficient by itself is illustrated by some earlier work on the economic role of beer drinking in Africa, conducted from a neo-Marxist perspective (O'Laughlin 1973; Donham 1985). O'Laughlin's main concern (in an unpublished PhD thesis) is the economic significance of Mbum beer feasts and their link with co-operative work groups. Access to labour was "the central economic problem" (1973, 27) and it was in this context that beer was significant. Thus little attention is paid to other (non-work group) beer parties, though they are mentioned in passing and it is clear that beer was used in many other, including ritual, contexts (ibid., 125, 189–90). Donham (1985), similarly, looks at beer drinking in Maale in relation to co-operative labour but his emphasis is on forces and relations of production rather than on beer drinking itself. It seems that a neo-Marxist paradigm leads to a concentration on labour processes and a neglect of beer drinking in other contexts. In the Xhosa case, ironically, it is these other contexts together with an understanding of work-party beer, that enables one to provide a full and contextualised understanding of labour processes. As I have indicated in an earlier, detailed study of co-operative work and its relationship with beer drinking in Shixini, it is necessary to place labour and production within a wider system that includes consumption of the product in the form of beer drinks that, on the surface at least, might seem to have nothing to do with labour (McAllister 2001).

   Where O'Laughlin does, however, provide an important indirect lesson is in showing that Mbum beer parties and co-operative work are organized on the basis of kinship, through whose structures society is reproduced. Therefore kinship expresses the social relations of production on which economic life depends, fusing social and economic reproduction into a single system. This study, similarly, is concerned with social reproduction, but the approach I take, dictated by the empirical material, is different. In Shixini it is the beer drinking rituals themselves that play the key role in social reproduction, and this has rather little to do with kinship, and more with territory and neighbourhood. In this respect, beer drinking in Shixini has something in common with beer drinking in pre-industrial Britain, where drinking rituals served to affirm and reproduce the social relations that formed the basis of community and society, with the exchange of alcohol establishing and maintaining reciprocal relations and obligations among peasant and artisan workers, as well as sometimes functioning as a way to raise funds for a member in need. As Adler puts it, in Britain "the ritual occasions for drinking served to reaffirm principles for the organization of social relations of exchange in a pre-capitalist economy." Drinking practices were "embedded in the social relations that bound men into relations of exchange and production..." and affirmed "communal values grounded in the process of symbolic exchange..." (Adler 1991, 388–89). However, the transformation to capitalism marginalized these principles, though they remained "counter-hegemonic themes in a society whose organization was overwhelmingly governed by a different order." (ibid., 382). In Shixini, I argue by contrast, beer drinking rituals emerged precisely as a 'counter-hegemonic theme' in the context of colonialism, apartheid and capitalism and were based on principles opposed to that order.

This makes Xhosa beer drink rituals political, in common with feasts in general which are "a fundamental instrument and theatre of political relations" through which people "negotiate relationships, pursue economic and political goals, compete for power, and reproduce and contest ideological representations of social order and authority." (Dietler 2001, 66). As Dietler indicates, a practice approach lends itself to an analysis of such events because it "approaches ritual as an instrument of both domination and resistance, as an arena for the symbolic naturalization, mystification and contestation of authority." (ibid., 71). Beer drinks, like feasts in general, have to do with power relations and competition for power, not necessarily of the overt or aggressive kind that the word 'competition' evokes, since Xhosa beer drinks do not involve openly competitive brewing and drinking of the kind found among the Mambila (Rehfisch 1987). Rather, competition may be subtle and understated, and political not in the sense of a trying to gain prestige and power at the expense of others but simply being a matter of maintaining a particular status position within a group (Dietler 2001, 77).

An illustration of this may be found in developments in Sardinia similar to those recorded by Adler. Counihan points out that many rural Mediterranean regions have, during the twentieth century, undergone a process of "modernization without development", characterized by "the stagnation of local production and the increasing emulation of Western industrial consumption patterns...accompanied by changes in social relations...[including] a process of individualization" (Counihan, 1997, 283) and the weakening of community ties and a sense of community. She illustrates this by looking at the production, distribution and consumption of bread, the staple food and symbol of life, which formerly tied rural Sardinian people together in relations of reciprocity and mutual interdependence, and which was made from grain produced through co-operative labour. Bread was exchanged on a regular, reciprocal basis among kin, friends and neighbours, and consumed at feasts symbolizing the ties that were important in subsistence production. Through a combination of factors, subsistence wheat production ceased and people became more dependent on the market, having to buy grain and, later, bread. Reciprocal economic relations between households thus weakened as individualization set in and relationships became more atomized. The redistributive feasts through which community solidarity and mutual interdependence were acted out have declined and survive only in the less modernized areas. Again, my study shows the development of a trend in a rather different direction, with Xhosa beer drinking emerging as a redistributive form closely tied to an attempt to resist the kinds of modernizing forces that Counihan reports, but simultaneously adjusting to them.

At the same time, a political and economic approach to beer drink rituals is perfectly compatible with the classic one in anthropology, developed from Robertson-Smith and Mauss onwards, that focuses on reciprocity and the exchange of food as linked to the creation of social alliances (Meigs 1997), because the exchange of maize-beer produced through the labour of others in intense and highly structured forms of commensality is directly linked to the exchange of selves in the form of labour and other forms of support, through which maize and other products are created. This is why people who do not drink nevertheless themselves brew for beer drinks and attend those held by others, and why they accept the beaker when called for a drink, and themselves call others when the beaker gets to them. It is because in drinking beer people are making and re-making reciprocal social connections with each other, connections which are of extreme social and economic significance in the context of everyday life. It is this theme that runs throughout the chapters that follow.

Endnotes

1. The Xhosa personal prefix, *u-*, does not discriminate between male and female.
2. This study formed the basis of my Master of Arts thesis (McAllister 1979).
3. For a review of the move from social structure to practice as the primary framework for ritual studies in anthropology see Kelly and Kaplan (1990).

2 Beer, Colonialism and Social Change in Southern Africa[1]

…they make a bitter sort of (drink from) grain purposely to make merry with; and when they meet on such occasions, the men make themselves extraordinary fine with feathers stuck in their caps very thick.

Dampier's Voyages, 1690[2]

Beer, an alcoholic drink containing ethanol and produced from fermented grain, has been an important part of the ritual and social life of human beings for millennia. There is evidence for its production nearly six thousand years ago in Mesopotamia, where documentary verification of beer brewing is dated around 3500 B.C., and the Code of Hammurabi includes rules concerning the making and serving of beer. In Ancient Egypt, evidence of the brewing and serving of beer, and of its connection with the deities, goes back to around 5000 B. C. (Katz 2003, 171–73).[3] In Africa in general, brewing is of ancient origin and widespread, as indicated in ethnographic reports from almost every part of the continent. Among southern Bantu it is universally made (Shaw 1974).

In this chapter the historical and contemporary use of beer among southern Bantu-speakers is surveyed briefly, with occasional reference to people living further north in order to indicate that the data presented represent only part of a much more widespread phenomenon. The objective is to introduce and illustrate the social importance of beer and to contextualize the material on contemporary Xhosa ritual beer drinking that follows later. The second and major part of this chapter deals with fluctuations in the availability and use of beer among Xhosa speakers over a period of approximately 150 years (circa 1800–1950). The reasons for these fluctuations are explored and form an essential historical background for understanding the significance of beer drinking rituals among rural Xhosa people today. What emerges from this is that beer making and drinking cannot be regarded merely as an interesting African custom of a 'traditional' kind. Instead, it becomes clear that fluctuations in the manufacture and use of beer are linked to the strategies used by people to react to, or come to terms with, circumstances beyond their control, such as environmental or political changes. This means, in turn, that the significance of Xhosa beer drinking rituals today has to be understood in both historical and contemporary terms. The theoretical perspective brought to bear on this is outlined in the following chapter.

Beer in southern Africa: An overview

In southern Africa the first evidence of beer brewing comes from the many accounts of shipwrecked sailors and early European travelers. For example, Portuguese survivors from the wreck of the Santo Alberto reported that the indigenous inhabitants of the country made 'wine' from millet, which they consumed "with great enjoyment" (Theal 1898 II, 293). Others wrote of a drink called *pombe* "which is very strong and intoxicating" (Theal 1898 Vll, 190) and gave a description of its brewing, recognizable to anyone familiar with the brewing of maize or millet beer today (ibid., *passim*). The historical sources indicate regional variations in the preparation of beer, its uses, and in the sheer quantity available. Beer featured in folktales, songs, myths of origin and proverbs.[4] It was of political importance, and was given as tribute to political leaders, who were required to sanction its production (Monnig 1967; Krige and Krige 1943). Accounts of the Zulu kingdom in the period 1830–1850 indicate that beer was in plentiful supply there, particularly at the King's kraal, from where it was redistributed at his behest (Bird 1885 I, 77, 206; Krige 1936, 265). Gardiner (1836, 54–55) refers to the serving of beer to Dingane's warriors, and states that "the whole food of the soldiers, consisting of outchualla [*utshwala*] in the morning, and beef in the evening, is provided at the King's cost, and partaken of in public. It is no infrequent thing to see a string of thirty or forty women proceeding to the Issigordlo [*isigodlo*—section of the king's kraal where the wives, children and certain servants of the king lived] with bowls of outchualla on their heads, singing as they go".[5]

The reason beer was given to Zulu regiments was because beer, grain and meat were regarded as 'hard' or 'strengthening' food (Krige 1936, 265), and everywhere in southern Africa beer was not just a drink but also a nourishing or even essential food, in the opinion of both indigenous people and ethnographers (e.g. Krige 1936, 58; Soga 1931, 399). Cetywayo told the 1883 Commission on Native Laws and Customs that "beer is the food of the Zulus; they drink it as the English drink coffee" (Cape of Good Hope 1883 I, 529). Similar accounts come from other parts of Africa.[6] In many parts of the continent beer remains an important foodstuff, and in some areas (such as West Africa) it is estimated that one half of the annual consumption of grain is in the form of beer.[7]

As an important and nourishing foodstuff, beer is rich especially in B vitamins otherwise lacking in the diet (Heath 2000). Fox (1938) surveyed various studies of the nutritional value of what used to be called 'Kafir Beer' in South Africa and concluded that the view of beer as foodstuff rather than alcoholic drink was justified. Beer contained between five and seven per cent solids, significant quantities of vitamins B and C, mineral salts, and proteins. The alcohol content was between two and four percent (see also Bryant 1949, 276) but this was not necessarily related to the degree of intoxication that it produced, which was low.[8] Brewing had the added advantage that grain not suitable for consumption such as musty maize or 'rusted' sorghum, could be turned into beer and thus saved (Ashton 1952, 129). Brewing was (and is) also a means of redistributing food within the community and thus evening out, to some degree, differences in household production. People's reputations depended on the regular brewing of beer, and among Lovedu beer was part of the institutionalized gift exchange system (Krige and Krige 1943, 288).

That beer was food rather than an alcoholic drink is also indicated by the fact that it was possible to subsist on it for days on end and that in the past it formed the bulk of the diet of certain people, such as old men, councilors and chiefs.[9] The low alcohol content and the etiquette of beer drinking, which limited the amount consumed and spread consumption over a long time period, made intoxication uncommon. There were, however, ways of increasing its potency, and variations in potency from place to place. Champion regarded the Zulu king's beer as too strong "for any man to drink much of" (Bird 1885: 206).[10] Lovedu made two types of strong beer through a process of double fermentation. These were drunk privately or in small groups, and not used in beer parties and beer exchanges (Krige 1932, 345).[11]

Apart from the common beer, *utywala* in Xhosa,[12] made nowadays from maize,[13] a variety of similar beverages were made. These include non-alcoholic drinks such as *marhewu*[14] (Xhosa), which are fermented drinks made from maize meal; *umqombothi* (Xhosa), immature beer with no alcoholic content,[15] and *mabudu* or *mapoto* (Lovedu) which is light beer. In the 1920s it was thought that there were more than fifty varieties of 'Native beverages' in South Africa "which take cover under the general name of Kafir beer" (Bud-Mbelle 1926, 131).

However, beer was also much more than simply food. Dos Santos noted in 1609 that beer was used in feasts and in rituals conducted in honour of royal ancestors (Theal 1898 VII, 196). All southern African ethnographies indicate the ritual and religious importance of beer, sometimes referred to as 'food of the gods', and "no occasion, whether social or ritual or economic, is complete without beer" (Krige and Krige 1943, 288). The ritual significance of beer, common throughout Africa, seems to have been greater among Sotho and Venda people than among Nguni. Among Pedi "beer is nearly always the medium of sacrifice" though it was sometimes accompanied by a beast (Monnig 1967, 61). Beer offerings were the usual way of propitiating the ancestors among Lovedu, where blood sacrifice was rare (Krige 1932, 355).[16]

Along with animal sacrifice, beer played an important part in Zulu, Mpondo and Xhosa rituals, and still does so. Among traditionalist Zulu beer was 'the food of men' (including both the living and the ancestral spirits or shades) and communication with the shades through ritual beer drinking was common (Berglund 1976, 209). Beer was used in all life-crisis rituals,[17] and was brewed as part of the now extinct first fruits ceremonies (Krige 1936, 253; Hammond-Tooke 1962, 192). Often, brewing took place in conjunction with the killing of a beast, though beer could be used on its own or as a substitute for a ritual killing (Berglund 1976, 207).

Beer was widely used in rituals of affliction where the cause of misfortune was thought to be the anger of the ancestors (Hunter 1936. 253). Beer was also brewed in gratitude for favours received from the shades, manifested as good harvests, a narrow escape from danger, safe return from work or continued health and prosperity.[18] Among some groups beer, substitute beer or beer residue was at such times poured on to ancestral shrines or left at places closely associated with the shades, such as the graves of dead members of the kin group (Junod 1927 II, 341; Hammond-Tooke 1981, 144). Zulu poured beer on to the back of a sacrificial cow while calling on the shades, and kept fermenting beer at *umsamo*, the far back of the hut associated with the ancestors (Berglund 1976, 102, 205). Lovedu also poured beer onto an ancestral shrine and beer was important in the consecration of the 'ox of the spirits' which was made to drink beer in cases of human illness (Krige 1932, 356).[19]

As indicated here, beer has strong religious associations even when brewed outside strictly ritual contexts. Berglund noted that the differences between beer brewed for ritual purposes and beer for household consumption were minor, and denied by some Zulu. This was evident, for example, in the preparation of beer: a woman could not be 'hot' (ritually impure) when she prepared beer, lest the shades be offended; the grinding had to take place near the hut's doorway or near the back, both places closely associated with the shades, and the water used for brewing should be living water from a running stream (Berglund 1976, 210).[20] Hunter (1936, 253, 358) felt that it was difficult to distinguish beer brewed "to drink with friends" from that brewed for ritual purposes, but she later distinguished beer brewed for the ancestors from beer made "just to drink", beer for work parties, and beer for sale. Cook (1931, 27–28) made a similar distinction for the Bomvana. Among contemporary rural Xhosa speakers, as we shall see, there is no occasion when beer is not to some extent religious.

All over Bantu-speaking Africa beer was associated also with sociability, commensality, communal harmony and neighbourliness. For this reason rituals aimed at effecting reconciliation between quarrelling or disputing parties frequently involved beer drinking as a symbol of the re-establishment of friendly relationships and the ending of feuds and disputes. To Gwembe Tonga, Beer was 'communion' because it was never consumed alone, and "the sharing of beer underwrote the importance of community" (Colson and Scudder 1988, 66). Generally, whether brewed for ritual purposes or not, beer was regarded as communal rather than as private food and every householder was expected to brew beer for public consumption at regular intervals. A person's reputation for generosity and neighbourliness depended on the fulfillment of this social obligation and one who failed to brew was frowned upon. Tyler (1891, 121) claimed that Zulu homesteads took it in turn to brew "for parties of forty or fifty men, whose time is chiefly occupied in going about searching for that *sine qua non* of comfort". Beer drinking was the "favourite pastime" of Tsonga men (Junod 1927 I, 34) and in Pondoland after the harvest "men and *amadikazi* [unattached women, usually widowed or separated] often go on from one beer drink to another, sometimes not returning to their homes for a week" (Hunter 1936, 357).

Ashton (1952, 95) speaks of small, private beer drinks among Sotho speakers and Soga (1931, 400) says that although beer was seldom made for private use among Xhosa speakers, a small brewing for household consumption was "facetiously called *ama-rewu*" to indicate its private nature. Even where beer drinks were held for specially invited guests, other members of the community could attend and received something to drink (Richards 1939, 81). Reader (1966, 148–49) mentions Makhanya beer drinks held exclusively for members of a descent group or a section of such a group to discuss matters of common interest. This type of beer drink is the exception rather than the rule, which was that beer was communal food to which all members of the local community should have access, even though it was brewed by an individual household.

Beer was also the common form of recognition for assistance with economic tasks whether this involved a small group of neighbours or a larger, more formally constituted work party (Reader 1966; Kuckertz 1984). As Hammond-Tooke (1962, 145) put it, "beer is the sanction par excellence for work parties", though it is not regarded as a payment. Beer brewed to reward members of a work party was also consumed by others (non-workers) though sometimes under the control of the workers. At a Mpondo work party for ploughing, for example, "the beer is not distributed until the ploughs have returned at midday, and then a pot is set before each owner of a span of oxen which has worked and he distributes it among his friends" (Hunter 1936, 89). If one is to regard such beer as payment it is hard to understand why it was distributed to all and sundry, unless by payment we include the social recognition and elevation of the workers. Reader (1966, 42) thus suggests that it should be regarded as "a social recognition of, rather than a reward for, the voluntary communal labour performed". Krige and Krige (1943, 288) put it similarly; one pays for something with money, but thanks with beer. In the Lovedu case beer was the basis for a group of people "composed largely of kin and neighbours who often cooperate in economic activities: this group cuts across the lines of the district...and the main obligation of its members is to call fellow members to any beer that is available" (Krige and Krige 1943, 288). This seems neatly to reverse the usual relationship between economic assistance and beer, for it implies that assistance was given in recognition of a relationship that hinged on calling each other for beer.

Beer was usually consumed with some formality and according to rules of etiquette which determined how it should be apportioned and drunk. Frequently mentioned in this regard are divisions according to sex, age and territory. Men and women tended to receive beer separately and in different proportions, and to consume it in different places (for instance in different huts); older people received more beer than younger and were the first to drink; groups of people were allocated beer according to their territorial or political affiliation. People of high rank were served before ordinary people and important kin or distinguished visitors were given a special pot (Junod 1927 I, 341). Among rural Xhosa, the distribution of beer can be extremely complicated and is of great social significance, as we shall see. As the survey above shows, much attention has been paid to the functions fulfilled by beer and beer drinking, very little to the specific manner in which it is actually consumed (one exception to this is Kuckertz 1984).

Beer drinking in Shixini and other parts of the former Transkei is consistent with the trends summarized above, and many of the observations recorded above apply there today. Brewing is socially obligatory, and its consumption is highly regulated and formalised. Its economic significance lies in its role as an important item of exchange between households, and it is also closely connected with co-operative work. Beer features as part of most important rituals and there are a variety of rituals which are defined in terms of beer consumption. Even when beer is brewed 'just to drink', as people say, it is always to some degree religious.

However, as the following section indicates, this should not be seen simply as something that is 'customary' in Africa, or as a continuation of 'age-old' patterns. What emerges below, from a look at beer drinking among Xhosa speakers in the colonial period, particularly between 1880 (shortly after the annexation of most of their territory) and about 1930, is that significant changes in patterns of brewing and beer consumption took place, changes that were of considerable concern to the colonial authorities but which are of vital significance in grasping the nature and significance of beer drinking in rural Transkei today.

'Nocturnal jollifications': Beer among Xhosa speakers, 1800–1950

Some of the survivors of the Stavenisse, wrecked 100 km. south of Durban in 1686, spent nearly three years among Xhosa speakers who, they reported, brewed beer "both small and strong, which is not unpleasant in taste" (Bird 1885 I, 32). Observers such as the missionaries Van der Kemp (1804, 438) and Brownlee (1827, 360) also mention beer, though according to Alberti (1969, 24), who traveled among the Xhosa between 1803 and 1806, it was drunk "only seldom, and more for the sake of giving themselves a treat". Kay (1833, 109, 123–24) claimed that Xhosa speakers were not acquainted with intoxicating liquors, although they made a drink from wild honey. In Pondoland however, he noticed that people made large quantities of beer and used it on all festive occasions. This evidence seems to indicate that Xhosa speakers, unlike their Mpondo and Zulu neighbours to the north, did not make great quantities of beer in the early nineteenth century, or made it only rarely. Fifty or sixty years later the picture is rather different, as indicated in the following extract from the evidence of Rev. J. A. Chalmers before the 1883 Commission on Native Law and Customs:

> The drink of Kafir beer has changed within the last few years, and it is no longer what it used to be...Only old men were allowed to drink it in olden time, and there were no such immense gatherings as there are in the present day. Up to within a few years milk was the one great beverage at all feasts...(Cape of Good Hope 1883, 136–37).

What sort of explanations could there be for geographical and temporal variations of this kind? One possibility, as Chalmers implied, is that when cattle were plentiful and sour milk the staple diet, beer was not frequently made. In the 1830s, as indicated in the following extract from Gardiner, beer consumption rose when there was a shortage of milk:

The Amapondas having suffered so severely in their wars with Charka have, in consequence, become great beer drinkers; and even now that they are recovering their losses by the increase of their cattle, still I fear this baneful habit, induced by the scarcity of milk, is likely to be of long continuance. When reproached for their frequent inebriety (for they often meet in large parties, and drink until they are stupefied) they archly reply, 'what can we do, we have no cattle, this is our milk'. Even [Chief] Faku...is said to have been frequently found sealed in a torpor induced by outchualla. (Gardiner 1836, 266).

The production and consumption of beer was also directly related to the availability of grain. Beinart (1982, 52) states that in Mpondoland a glut of maize "tended to result in increased consumption" in the form of beer parties. Hunter, working in Pondoland in the 1930s, pointed out that more grain was available than previously, owing to larger areas being cultivated, and that older people were "emphatic that far more beer is drunk than when they were young" (Hunter 1936, 357). In adjoining Bomvanaland the frequency of beer drinks had increased greatly in the 1920s and this was a cause of "great concern" among older men (Cook 1931, 26). Similar reasons for fluctuations in beer supply occurred in other parts of South Africa (Krige and Krige 1943, 41; Berglund 1976, 207).

These accounts point to the brewing of beer as a social, political and economic resource, the fluctuating use of which must be understood within a wider context of events and circumstances. Changes in beer drinking habits also occurred owing to factors such as government regulations prohibiting brewing and missionary influence. Converts to the mission churches were not allowed to attend beer drinks (Tyler 1891, 122; Bigalke 1969, 15), which were associated with paganism. Rev. J. Harper, for example, who regarded heathens as "dreadfully immoral", felt that although beer itself was no great evil, beer drinks should be suppressed (South Africa 1905 II, 693; 1905 III, 853). The association between beer drinking and traditionalism is long standing. A song composed by a Bhaca teacher about three kinds of Bhaca—Christian, pagan and neo-pagan—refers to the pagans as "people of beer and beer alone" (Hammond-Tooke 1962, 65).

Excessive beer drinking in Eastern Cape districts in the late 1880s was frequently mentioned in the Blue Books on Native Affairs and was linked by officials to crimes such as assault and stock theft. In some areas, such as Grahamstown and King William's Town, it was reported that more potent beer was being made and beer mixed with Cape brandy, leading to disorder and fighting (DNA 1887, 5). It was felt that legislation was needed to prevent this. Official reports indicate that beer brewing and selling led to "carnivals of booze and demoralization" and was symptomatic of the appalling conditions under which displaced people in urban areas had to live (DNA 1883, 88; 1887, 34;

1904, 27). But even in rural areas, good harvests resulted in increased beer drinking "to the utter demoralisation of the tribes" (DNA 1904, 32. See also DNA 1884, 30–31; 1886). The contradictory statements and observations of colonial administrators indicates that it is likely that some of these reports were exaggerated and based on misconceptions about the nature of beer and its consumption. This is also suggested by evidence from other parts of colonial Africa. For example, the incorporation of central Kenyan communities in a colonial economy "undermined the stability of established drinking practices" and led to greater consumption than before, and in the eyes of colonial administrators, to high rates of alcohol consumption among youths, social disorder and an "epidemic of drunkenness" (Ambler 1991, 168). In fact, Ambler argues, while there were undoubtedly changes in drinking patterns, colonial administrators tended to misunderstand drinking behaviour (and also dancing) and to exaggerate the problems.

Fluctuations in the brewing of beer were also linked to Xhosa resistance to white domination. Many of the complaints about drinking by government officials and farmers in the late nineteenth century (and voiced before the South African Native Affairs Commission of 1903–1905) may be seen in this light, since this was a time during which good harvests allowed rural Xhosa to both resist work for low wages and brew more beer.

In the late 1860s and early 1870s resistance to oppression by white farmers in the Eastern Cape led to the development of informal associations of Xhosa farm workers and tenants, organized around beer drinks and dances (Crais 1985, 31), and Lewis (1985) has shown how people in the Eastern Cape were able to use beer as a resource with which to resist both exploitative grain prices and the necessity of labour migration. When maize was plentiful Xhosa producers were offered very low prices, so they brewed beer with their surplus maize instead, and sold some of it.

With plenty of food and beer available the supply of labour to the mines and farms fell dramatically. The festive occasions at which beer was normally consumed (for instance, the feasts held in association with initiation and marriage) were lengthened to accommodate the larger quantities of beer available. Reports to the Department of Native Affairs and evidence given before the 1903–1905 Commission include a number of references to farmers' complaints about the effects of beer drinking on their workers. R. P. Edwards, who gave evidence before the Commission, said that he had tried to prohibit the holding of beer drinks on his farm, but had been unable to do so otherwise people would not work for him. His workers went to beer drinks on neighbouring farms almost every weekend and "were anxious to be allowed to return the hospitality of others" (South Africa 1905 II, 766–67). Beer drinks were held over weekends with the result that workers frequently did not turn up on Mondays. When harvests were good in the labour-supplying areas beer drinks were plentiful and it was difficult to get labour at all. When grain was abundant the period of seclusion for boys undergoing initiation (the *abakwetha*) was lengthened. It was reported from Middledrift in 1886 that the recent good harvests had led to "a beer and bakweta orgie, with its inevitable attendant immorality, lasting six months...in almost every location throughout the land" (DNA 1887, 35). Complaints about this eventually led to the passing of the Abakwetha and Intonjane Dances Prohibition Act (No 19 of 1892) by the Cape Parliament.

In the Transkei during this period beer drinking seldom featured in reports to the Department of Native Affairs. Here too, however, good harvests led to lots of brewing, and local officials sometimes associated this with problems such as crime and immorality (DNA 1904, 83, 95). In 1908 it was claimed that beer drinks were on the increase and that they were being attended by children. Some councilors wanted to prohibit beer drinks altogether, to tighten control over "these customs of heathendom" (UTTGC 1912, 51). However, various attempts to regulate brewing and drinking more strictly were largely unsuccessful.

Comments in the Council indicate that there were undoubtedly important changes to beer drinking practices although the way in which this was portrayed was probably somewhat exaggerated. Contrary to the past "it was now the custom to brew beer in large quantities...[and] a whole location would brew beer at the same time" (UTTGC 1914, 109). The Sunday Observance Law was being flouted by holding beer drinks and dances on that day and beer drinks were being attended by women, young men and girls. During discussion of the issue in the Council, an interesting observation was made by Councillor Mamba (who was from the district of Idutywa, which adjoins Willowvale). In proposing a motion for stricter legal control over the holding of beer drinks, he referred to:

> ...the barrels of beer which were being made in the locations. This was practically a new custom...but it was a growing one. Their mothers and ancestors made their beer in small clay pots...Nowadays it was beer everywhere...[This] was not according to the state of things in days gone by...[and there were] *new kinds of beer drinks now...* (UTTGC 1914, 109; emphasis mine).

The Select Committee on Kaffir Beer Drinking and Dances, however, came to the conclusion that existing legislation was adequate for the control of these events. Many council members were opposed to stricter control and worried about passing regulations which could not be enforced (UTTGC 1916, 40–41). These issues were raised again and again over the next five years, with further unsuccessful attempts being made to control what came to be known as 'nocturnal jollifications' (sic) or 'night merriment' (UTTGC 1918: 67).

It is clear, however, that beer drinking had become more frequent in the first decades of the nineteenth century, in response to increased maize yields and a shortage of milk as a result of the loss of large numbers of cattle, owing to East Coast fever. In the period 1927–1928 the attempt to regulate beer drinking was taken up with renewed vigour and the list of evils associated with beer grew dramatically. The two basic principles of Xhosa life, seniority and patriarchy, were seen as under threat. It was because of beer, it was claimed, that people did not obey the government, that taxes were not paid, that the country's jails were full, and that men would not go out to work (UTTGC 1927, 62). Children were being fed on beer, drinking with their fathers and not attending school. Women were never at home because they were out looking for beer and young children were being neglected. It was due to the presence of women that fighting supposedly took place at nearly every beer drink and these disgraceful things were ruining people's good names and "keeping them back as a nation" (UTTGC 1928, 58). When magistrates tried to meet with their district headmen they were unable to do so, because headmen, too, were at beer drinks all the time. There were so many beer drinks being held that people were doing no work and neglecting to plough their lands (UTTGC 1928, 56).

It would seem then, in the eyes of the authorities at least, that people were drinking beer with an almost millenarian frenzy, and beer drinking may well have been associated with rural resistance during certain periods. In the Transkei, the years 1913 to 1917 were characterized by fairly widespread resistance to cattle dipping (Beinart and Bundy 1980) and it is possible that beer drinks provided a forum for the expression of anti-dipping views and for organizing resistance to the dipping laws. Present-day beer drinks provide a forum for just about any burning issue and it is thus more than likely that dipping was discussed then. It is possible that beer was brewed with the express purpose of bringing people together to discuss or facilitate resistance to the dipping laws but there is no evidence on which to base such a claim.

It was also said in the Council, however, that beer drinking was associated with the millenarian movement founded by Wellington Buthelezi which, along with other similar movements, became active in the Transkei in the late 1920s. Buthelezi preached that a day of judgement would arrive when believers would be freed from white oppression; Afro-Americans would arrive in airplanes bearing goods such as clothing; taxes would be abolished and factories established. Allegiance to the movement was characterized by hostility towards the authorities and the institutions of government (Beinart and Bundy 1980). There is also some evidence to indicate that increased beer consumption was a feature of the earlier, 1857 cattle-killing episode, the so-called 'national suicide of the Xhosa', which involved not only the destruction of cattle and grain but also much feasting and dancing. At least some of the animals killed were eaten and grain was cooked and turned into beer (Long 1949, 192–93).

Again, although there seems to have been a link between the Wellington movement and beer drinking, with beer drinks possibly functioning to assist in spreading the teachings of the movement, attempts to control beer more strictly were not successful. Some councilors pointed out that beer was the national beverage and beer drinking a national institution which ought not to be legislated against (UTTGC 1927, 62). Existing legislation was thought to be adequate and Proclamation No 246 of 1929 consolidated this.

Another example of the strategic use of beer to adapt to changed circumstances is the brewing of beer for sale, a common practice in other parts of Africa (Bryceson 2002) and in urban areas (Hellman 1934; De Haas 1986). Beer was brewed for sale amongst Xhosa speakers at least as early as the 1880s and this practice continues today, though it has never reached the scale, in rural parts of Transkei, at least, that it has in other African countries. Colonial Officials were keen to put a stop to it but were unable to do so (DNA 1887, 7; South Africa 1905 II, 863). The prohibition on the sale of liquor to Africans (Act No 30 of 1928) was applied in the Transkei in the form of Proclamation No 53 of 1933. 'Kaffir beer' was defined in the Act as containing not more than 2% alcohol, and was permitted on farms and in the reserves but not in urban areas. Techniques for increasing the potency of maize or sorghum beer quickly found their way to the reserves, where such beer was brewed and sold. In 1945 the UTTGC passed a motion limiting the alcoholic content of beer so that "our national drink, Kaffir beer…should not be adulterated by concoctions brought from other countries" (UTTGC 1945, 40). Attempts were made also at other times to tighten up control over the selling of beer in the Transkei but with little success (UTTGC 1945, 24, 96).

In conclusion, then, it seems that the manufacture and consumption of beer in the Transkei has long been subjected to political, economic and other (for instance religious) pressures, the nature of which change over time. Beer drinking, although 'traditional' in the sense that it has been around for a long time, is also a means through which people can give expression to the social changes to which they are subject and over which they may have little control. Thus how, when, and in what quantities beer is consumed forms part of a conscious or unconscious strategy to adapt to change and must, at least in part, be related to the wider factors affecting those involved, which are sketched in the following section. This leads to a view of beer as not just a material artefact, but also as an important cultural resource.

Agrarian change and the development of co-operative work

This question now needs to be examined in relation to other historical factors in the Transkei. It has already been established that there was a great increase in the amount of beer brewing and drinking in the first two or three decades of the 20th century. But what brought this about? What is the larger historical picture in which we need to situate this? And what were the consequences for the nature and practice of Xhosa ritual?

The increase in beer drinking that the UTTGC and others were so worried about was merely one aspect of a number of changing conditions of rural life in Transkei. These involved, firstly, changes in homestead size and composition, which were related in turn to factors such as the institutionalization of labour migration and a modification of land tenure and agricultural practices. These contributed to consequent changes in the social organization of production and a range of other institutional adaptations which in some ways altered the nature of rural Xhosa speaking society in the early decades of the twentieth century. The evidence for this is presented in what follows, and is extremely important because it provides key aspects of the overall historical context for an understanding of contemporary beer drinking and associated factors in Shixini. It is drawn from various parts of the Transkei, and from various sources, including William Beinart's detailed analysis of the changing nature of rural production in Pondoland, in the north-eastern part of the Transkei, between 1860 and 1930. The Transkei is culturally and historically (at least since annexation) relatively homogenous. The coastal districts, which include parts of Pondoland as well as Willowvale and other more southern districts, are also fairly homogenous in ecological terms. Beinart's historical analysis, which concentrates on but is not confined to the Pondoland districts, is supported in many respects by Hunter (1936), and its relevance to other parts of the Transkei finds confirmation in some of the findings reported by Wilson et al (1952), Wilson (1971), and Hammond-Tooke (1962; 1975).

In the pre-colonial period, indigenous settlement in the Transkei was determined largely by the nature of the environment, which was characterized by "small-scale repetitive configurations that contained a variety of natural resources" (Sansom 1974, 140). Each small area within a tribal territory was similar, containing within it the resources needed for subsistence according to the southern Bantu pattern—primarily arable land, grazing for livestock, perennial water, fuel, an area within which to hunt and gather, and access to resources such as thatching grass. Sansom has characterized this as the Eastern (primarily Nguni) ecological adaptation, found right across southern Africa's eastern seaboard, between the escarpment of the Drakensberg and the sea, and he refers to the economy associated with it as one of "contained investment" (ibid., 135). Settlements were dispersed over the tribal territory; homesteads were widely scattered and not concentrated into villages, and subsistence activities were confined to the areas near the homesteads. The Eastern unit of exploitation was "a small, concentrated area, containing the full range of natural resources that individuals wished to exploit" (ibid., 139). Economic relationships were similarly concentrated. The inhabitants of each local area pursued their subsistence activities more or less independently of those in other areas. As we shall see below (chapter four), the contemporary organization of agriculture and of co-operative work in Shixini still follows this pattern to a certain extent, while at the same time being a response and adaptation to the position of the area within the wider South African socio-political and economic context and the historical factors impacting on it within this.

The Eastern form of adaptation was associated with a decentralized political, judicial and administrative system, and with a high degree of local autonomy. Although each tribal area was under the overall authority of a chief, ecological conditions were suited to local regulation of resources. The chiefdom was divided into economically self-sufficient districts under sub-chiefs or headmen, the boundaries between districts being natural markers such as streams and rivers. But even within a headman's area further decentralization was possible, because "repetitive configurations allowed definition of tiny areas associated with neighbourhood groups or kraals within a district." (ibid., 140). In the past, such groups often consisted of close kin, under the leadership of a senior agnatic kinsman. Rights to grazing, arable land and other resources were allocated on the basis of membership of the local group, though ratified by the headman and, ultimately, by the chief. In many parts of the Transkei today, a local group is called *ummango* (plural: *imimango*), literally a 'ridge', and consists of a group of homesteads occupying a small local area. Homesteads were usually located on hilltops or ridges, often on land not particularly suited for cultivation, overlooking or near to their arable lands situated in the river valleys below, or on sheltered hill slopes (Shaw and van Warmelo 1981, 229–34). Typically, grazing was also found nearby, the cattle going out to graze each morning, and returning to the byres adjoining homesteads each evening. Socially and economically, this produced a kind of inwardness in terms of exploitation of basic resources (Sansom 1974, 141). There are clear resonances of this pattern of co-operation in places like Shixini today, as we shall see in chapter four.

The crops grown included sorghum and a variety of pumpkins and gourds. However, milk was the staple diet rather than grain, and the natural environment was able to support a relatively dense livestock population, especially in higher rainfall areas. This made possible differences in wealth, and also a complex network of social ties and obligations based on debts in livestock, since cattle were needed for bridewealth and for other purposes such as ritual, transport and food. Conflicts caused by incidents such as cattle trespassing into arable land were resolved at the local level, between neighbours, though recourse to the local headman's, and ultimately the chief's, court was possible. Even the rituals associated with the seasons were celebrated locally and not synchronized at the tribal level, as with Sotho and Tswana speakers in the interior of the country.

In addition to the low-lying fields, some homesteads also had small, fenced gardens nearby, often on a fertile old kraal site, in which crops such as tobacco were grown. The fields, too, were fenced to keep out wild animals, but such fences were taken down at the end of the harvest, the lands effectively reverting to commonage, with cattle allowed to graze on the grain stubble in the winter months (Shaw and van Warmelo 1981). Soils were relatively infertile, and old land was fallowed after a number of years and new fields established. This practice both maintained productivity at the desired level and prevented serious damage to the environment. From time to time homesteads split as sons moved out to establish their own homesteads nearby, sometimes on virgin territory. The political system as a whole was one "geared towards expansion", and the sons of chiefs often broke away with their followers to establish a new chiefdom on new land (Peires 1981, 53). People were able to cultivate as much land as available labour made possible, the right to such land being obtained simply by breaking the soil (Shaw and van Warmelo 1981). Most of the agricultural work was done by women; men being involved primarily in clearing the bush off new lands.

Much of the above description still appears to apply in Shixini, but only to some degree, and we have to be careful not to mistake superficial appearances for continuities in lifestyle, and to come to grips with the historical changes that have taken place and how they have affected economic life, in particular. For one thing, there have been important changes in family size and structure. In pre-colonial times in Transkei, homesteads were large and polygynous, consisting of between ten and forty huts. A homestead was made up of an extended family, under the control of a patriarch whose wives were associated with different 'houses', each house holding property allocated to it by the head and to which it had a right, including livestock and lands (fields and gardens). Labour was provided by members of the household—primarily the head's wives, their children, and his son's wives (Wilson 1969, 111). Homesteads were normally large enough to provide their own labour needs, with occasional exceptions. Smaller homesteads in the same local area co-operated with each other economically when required, with labour offered on a reciprocal basis, though production was the business of an individual homestead. When work groups from a number of homesteads were needed for large tasks (e.g clearing new land for cultivation) the workers were rewarded with food and/or drink by the host homestead, as was common elsewhere in the region and in Africa in general.

In the extended family homestead, sons were dependent on the father for their subsistence and for wives, since he controlled the cattle holdings, and cattle were required for bridewealth. Sons remained at the father's homestead until he died or until they were senior men. Hunter says that "old [Mpondo] men lament the days when 'grey-headed men lived in the *umzi* [homestead] of their father, obeying him in all things, as if they were children.'" (1936, 25). While obviously an idealization of the past there is little doubt that Mpondo homesteads had declined in size by the 1930s (ibid., 15; Beinart 1982, 94 ff.), and this trend occurred amongst all Xhosa speakers.[21]

Homesteads became smaller and closer together than they were in the past, due to a number of related factors. Land shortage and increased population pressure as a result of the colonial appropriation of Xhosa land was one of these. Since a man with his own homestead would have had a greater claim to a field than one living in his father's home (as is the case in Willowvale today), it was to the advantage of the family for sons to establish independent homesteads soon after marriage. It is possible that homesteads also became smaller because there was no longer any need to concentrate for defensive purposes, a function fulfilled by the traditionally large *umzi* (Hunter 1936, 59). This was a result of the decline of chiefly power (chiefs organized raids and warfare) and of the incorporation of formerly independent chiefdoms into the colonial system, with its magistrates and police force. Hammond-Tooke (1962; 1975) suggests that the reduction in chiefly power and the introduction of the concept of individual property, along with increased independence as a result of migratory labour opportunities, allowed for greater individualism. He indicates that the change in homestead size and distribution was already marked as early as 1883 (1975, 82–83) but the process continued until at least the 1960s, as the figures for homestead composition from various parts of the Transkei over the period 1934–1963 indicate (ibid., 111). This was a widespread trend among rural Xhosa speakers in general.[22]

Migrancy was also partly responsible for the decline in homestead size. As early as the 1920s in Pondoland, slightly earlier in other parts of the Transkei, maintaining rural production came to depend partly on access to cash through migrant wages. Diseases had wiped out most of the cattle, and wage-earnings were needed to replace them. There were other cash needs also, e.g. for taxes, and for manufactured goods, as rural homesteads got drawn into the developing capitalist economy. It became common for one or more of the young men in each homestead to spend some time on the mines and other industries earning a cash wage. By 1936 already, in Pondoland, the large majority of homesteads had at least one migrant, and 45% of men between 15 and 45 years of age were absentee wage earners. This rate was even higher in other parts of the Transkei (Beinart 1982, 94–95). Migrancy led to tensions between older and younger men in the homestead, largely over the control of the migrant's wages and the cattle purchased from it. Migrancy provided sons with an alternative source of cattle (through wages) and as they became less economically dependent on their fathers, this allowed them to establish independent homesteads earlier in life (Hunter 1936; Wilson et al 1952; Hammond-Tooke 1962; 1975). In this they were probably encouraged by their wives, who wanted to be freed from the control of their mothers-in-law, and who desired a greater claim to their husbands' cash earnings. Like migrant labour, the establishment of an independent homestead involves greater independence for the son as well as for his wife, and a slackening of parental control. Growing individualism due to education and contact with missionary ideas also contributed to a change in the relationship between fathers and sons, and sons started to establish their own, independent homesteads earlier in life than before. The senior generation also started to play less of a role in land allocation as population pressure grew and land became scarce and this task fell to the headman of the location, acting in conjunction with the men of a neighbourhood as a group. Since land was allocated to homestead heads, having their own homesteads made it easier for the younger men to get fields.

It is possible that the tendency for young people to move into their own homesteads earlier than before is exaggerated by a change in the age of marriage. Wilson et al (1952, 89) state that the age of marriage for males increased from 24 years in the pre-1890s to 30 years in the period 1940–50. Obviously, the older the son is when he marries, the less time he will spend in his father's homestead as a married man. Homesteads also became smaller due to a decline in polygyny, which was probably related to land shortage and increased population and also to a decline in cattle holdings.

New technology, principally the plough and the introduction of ox-draught, enabled the smaller homestead to cope. The migrant became both wage earner and independent homestead head. Although this meant a loss of power to the seniors it was not always opposed by them, partly because it freed them from responsibility for civil liabilities incurred by their sons, since the latter were homestead heads in their own right and therefore fully responsible for their own affairs (ibid ., 97). Under conditions of land shortage, fathers may well have encouraged their sons to establish independent homesteads nearby, hoping nevertheless to retain some authority over them.

This move towards smaller homesteads had important implications for the organization of agricultural production and for relationships between homesteads. Most importantly, it encouraged the widespread production of maize which gradually replaced sorghum as the staple crop. Sorghum is vulnerable to birds and needs to be protected as it ripens, and the smaller homestead did not have the labour to do this because children were too young or in school and the husband was sometimes away at work. Maize develops within the protection of a sheath and does not require labour to guard it from birds. It is also more amenable to intercropping. In pre-colonial times, vegetables and grain were cultivated separately, with vegetables being grown in gardens near homesteads and grain in more distant fields. Under the new system the smaller homestead became associated with only one field and inter-culture became the norm; maize was widely spaced in fields and other vegetable crops grown between the maize stalks. These other crops, such as pumpkins and sweet potatoes, filled the spaces between the plants and made weeding unnecessary after the first or second lot of weeds had been removed and the secondary crops had started to develop. This lessened the need for a daily labour input, and it was no longer necessary to hoe throughout the growing season. Intensive labour inputs, including ox draught, were needed at a number of widely spaced points of the agricultural cycle—ploughing and planting the maize seed, once or twice during the growing phase to remove weeds, and again at harvest time. The smaller household could manage the rest of the day-to-day labour, now concentrated in a single field.

These intensive inputs of labour could not be supplied from within a single homestead and were provided by forms of mutual assistance or co-operative work in which the members of different households collaborated to plough and plant each other's fields in rotation and, later in the season, to assist with weeding and harvesting. Individual homesteads pooled their resources in order to perform the required tasks and work parties and co-operative ploughing groups became very important. Both the general decline in homestead size and the reduction in cattle holdings meant that each individual homestead depended on the labour power and oxen of others. Hunter (1936, 87) recognized this development in the 1930s during fieldwork in Pondoland. In large homesteads where there were a number of 'houses', with each wife being responsible for her own field, the women of the homestead as a whole assisted each other in cultivation. In the case of the smaller homesteads, neighbours (who might also be kin) assisted each other.

Similar developments have been noted in other parts of the region (Shaw 1974),[23] and in other parts of Africa (Swindell 1985, 136). Among the Gwembe Tonga, as homesteads fragmented, reciprocal work parties came to provide the labour that had come from an extended family household and from slaves in large households (Colson and Scudder 1988, 72). Later, in the early 1960s, work parties (and work party beer) again became very frequent after resettlement (because of the development of the Kariba dam) due to the changed agricultural circumstances in the new village areas, then became less frequent in some areas largely due to the development of cash-cropping and the ready availability of beer for sale (ibid., 78). In south-western Nigeria, Painter (1986, 208) attributed new and changing forms of co-operative labour to a pattern of younger males establishing their own independent homesteads earlier than before, leading to a decline in the availability of household labour. In Zimbabwe, too, expanded rural production and the institutionalization of migrant wage labour had important consequences for the nature of rural households and the social relations between them, including those involving rural labour (Worby 1995). In Cameroon, new forms of co-operative labour developed in association with cash-cropping (Geschiere 1995). In the Transkei case, state segregationist policy that favoured whites over blacks and the emerging capitalist economy had rather different effects, the primary one of which was to retard and handicap, rather than to foster and support, the development of black rural farmers. In the process, conditions for the emergence of co-operative work were created—a society consisting of small, poor and relatively undifferentiated land-holding homesteads with low cash incomes and no opportunities for cash-cropping (see Moore 1975, 281), but with a determination to maintain homestead production.

In the Transkei, co-operative work groups were not necessarily a totally new development. Beinart found no evidence of their existence in earlier times, though they certainly became more important and more widespread, and used for new purposes, in the period under review. However, the existence of a specialized lexicon relating to co-operative work and the beer drinking associated with such labour in Kropf's dictionary, first published in 1899, testifies to the relative antiquity, if not the importance, of these institutions (Kropf 1915).

The change in the nature of rural production also depended on involvement in the migrant labour system. Firstly, the cash earned at work was important to the agriculture of the home area, because it allowed people to buy ploughs, fertilizer, and other inputs. Purchase of oxen provided the homestead with bargaining power in its co-operative economic relationships with other homesteads and also contributed to the welfare of the community as a whole. Secondly, as homestead heads became increasingly involved as migrants, dependence on neighbours grew in areas other than agricultural production. The head's absence meant that someone had to be delegated to act in his place (especially if he had no grown sons), to make decisions on his behalf and look after the affairs of the homestead. This task usually fell to a neighbouring agnate, but any good neighbour would do. In Willowvale district this led to the institutionalization of the 'caretaker' (usipatheleni) who could be a kinsman, if he lived nearby, or an unrelated but trusted neighbour (Heron and Cloete 1991). The general dependence on occasional intensive co-operative inputs and the importance of labour migration in both contributing to rural agriculture and the increasing general dependence on neighbours may explain the emphasis among Shixini people on good neighbourliness, the increasing importance of this principle in social organization, and, as we shall see below, a change in the nature of certain rituals. It can be seen that the above process involved a paradox. The growth of individualism and increased economic independence, accompanied by increased labour migration and the change in rural production, led to a greater dependence on other homesteads and neighbours, on the community as a whole.

Whether neighbours were or are in fact kin or not is immaterial, for the change that took place was both structural and ideological. The ideology associated with a closely knit economically independent extended family based in one homestead gave way to one of greater individualism, of smaller autonomous homesteads which were dependent on one another. Adjoining homesteads, now closer together than when homesteads were larger, provided the basis of socio-economic interaction. Those congregated within a particular geographical area became important as such, as neighbours, as independent homesteads which were involved with each other in the productive process, rather than as kinsmen. It was evident among the Mpondo that "the more imizi [homesteads] subdivide the more kinship bonds tend to be replaced by ties binding neighbours." (Hunter 1936, 60; cf. Meillassoux 1972; 1973). This is why Shixini people today say that ploughing, for example, has nothing to do with kinship, although in practice ploughing companies are composed largely of agnatic kin (chapter four). It is important to emphasize that I am not suggesting that neighbourliness arose as a new social principle, but that it became relatively more important as the kinship system weakened with the decline in homestead size and other related factors.

Other important changes relating to increased grain production, and thus the increased availability of beer, also need to be considered. Bear in mind that the changes we have been looking at took place more or less simultane-ously with the increase in beer drinking noted earlier. In pre-colonial times cultivation was almost entirely in the hands of women while men were occu-pied with the high status task of tending cattle. The basic foodstuff was sour milk rather than grain, though grain and other vegetables, as well as hunting and gathering, made an important contribution to the diet. Women cultivated the soil with a short digging stick, the point of which was flat and a few inches wide. They worked in a squatting position, and the amount of land cultivated was not large. The introduction of the plough and of steel bladed hoes made it possible to cultivate much more land than the earlier techniques of hoe cul-tivation. By the early twentieth century steel ploughs and hoes were wide-spread, the amount of land being cultivated had increased considerably as a result, and large amounts of maize, sorghum and other products were being produced and marketed by Xhosa speakers. By this stage population had grown, much land lost to the colonial forces, wild game drastically reduced and the bulk of the Xhosa cattle destroyed in the millenarian movement of 1857 (the 'cattle-killing') and in subsequent epidemics. Grain had therefore become much more important as a food supply, and it was also being mar-keted to obtain money for taxes and to purchase goods. Individual land hold-ings had become larger, fixed and more valuable.

The amount of land under cultivation in Pondoland and in other parts of the Transkei continued to increase considerably in the early 1920s and 1930s, however, due to previously uncultivated areas being brought under the plough, and was reflected in increasing maize yields (see appendix in Beinart 1982; Hunter 1936, 357), although this was later neutralized by rapidly increasing population. For the smaller homestead this meant that acquiring implements and building up a herd of cattle were vital, and the primary means of achiev-ing these objectives was through migrant labour. Ox-draught, however, put much of the important agricultural work in the hands of men. Women were forbidden to work with cattle, but their total labour input probably increased due to the much larger amounts of land being cultivated, since they were still responsible for tasks such as weeding and harvesting. Ox-draught may well have contributed towards entrenching patriarchy and lowering the status of women, however, because it deprived them of sole charge of garden produce and placed cultivation under the control of men. As Heron (1990, 131) puts it:

> The impact of the plough on 'traditional' Xhosa society was vast. It created new wealth differentials while at the same time reinforcing old ones; altered the division of labour; increased men's power over women; changed the ecology of the area because of greater areas under cultivation; pushed people towards a more sedentary way of

life; and brought cattle into agriculture. This also meant that the economic importance of cattle increased. They were now essential for use as draught and they were also a source of manure—a replacement for ash in the old slash and burn system.

At the same time, labour co-operation between homesteads became vital to solve the labour shortages created by migrancy and declining homestead size. In this way, despite the difficulties and contradictions "the evidence suggests that total and perhaps even *per capita* output may have continued to increase during the decades when mass migrancy became institutionalized" (Beinart 1982, 100).

Maintaining homestead production in Transkei also needs to be understood in the context of the development of racist and segregationist policies from the time of annexation through to the development of apartheid. How this affected Xhosa speakers is dealt with in more detail in the next chapter, and needs only brief mention here. Colonial rule and apartheid deprived rural blacks of land and freedoms, discouraged them from urbanizing, and forced them to attempt to conserve and maintain household production as far as possible. In Pondoland, households "had been blocked from access to external markets for their grain and stock and were intent on protecting their natural resources for communal purposes." (ibid., 100). This ability was eroded over the years, especially by increasing land shortage and agricultural 'Betterment' schemes, but in areas like Shixini where Betterment was successfully resisted and where land availability and lack of population pressure made it possible, homestead production remained important, though after about 1940 it was seldom more than a supplement to wage labour for the majority of homesteads in many areas. The question of maintaining homestead production as both practice and ideology remains crucial to understanding beer drinking in Willowvale, as we shall see.

As Beinart points out, in Pondoland the new style of agricultural production could not continue to meet household food needs for long after the 1930s, as population pressure and land scarcity grew, and as lands became infertile due to over use and erosion. These problems were partly resolved in Willowvale district and adjoining areas of the Transkei, by yet another adaptation, a switch from field to garden cultivation and the expansion of gardens to make up for the declining fertility of fields (see chapter four). The persistence of homestead production in South Africa was, as historians have commented, combined with a flexibility which allowed it to survive in diverse circumstances (Marks and Atmore 1980, 10–11) and this flexibility has persisted for far longer than is commonly thought, at least in certain areas.

What has all this got to do with beer drinking rituals? Clearly, the larger amounts of grain which became available in the first decades of the twentieth century, as a result of the factors outlined here, and combined with increasing population and a shortage of livestock and therefore of milk, led to increased beer drinking. But it was not simply a matter of increased beer drinking; there were also, as was noticed in the UTTGC, "new kinds of beer drinks" developing. In some cases this was a matter of existing rituals being modified to take the form of a beer drink rather than that of a ritual killing of a goat or ox (see chapter five) and which may be explained in terms of shortage of livestock. However, the implications of substituting a beer drink for a ritual slaughtering are significant, in that they co-incide with and give symbolic and supernatural support for a change in the nature of the worshipping group from one based primarily on kinship to one in which neighbourhood is very important. These substitutions, explored in more detail in subsequent chapters, developed in tandem with a changing mode of production, where the reliance on kinship-based labour within the extended family household was largely replaced with a reliance on neighbours and co-operative work based on spatial rather than kinship principles.

Endnotes

1. The first two sections of this chapter are a condensed version of McAllister (1993).
2. Cited in Bird (1885 I, 58).
3. See also Mandelbaum (1979).
4. Survivors from the Stavenisse reported that the Xhosa "deduce their origin from a certain man and woman, who grew up together out of earth, and who taught them to cultivate the ground, to sow corn, to milk cows, and to brew beer", although they had "not the slightest trace of religion" (Bird 1885 I:45). The Zulu sky-princess, Nomkhubulwana, is said to have taught men to plant millet and to brew beer from it (Bryant 1949, 57). See also Junod (1927 II, 238), Junod and Jaques (1957), Hammond-Tooke (1962), Broster (1976), Mesatywa (1954) and Nyembezi (1954).
5. Revd. F. Owen made a similiar observation (Bird 1885 I, 336).
6. The LoDagaa called beer and porridge by the same name (Goody 1982, 72–73); the Uduk compared beer to mother's milk, "and the point of comparison lay in its nourishing goodness" (James 1972, 22). Basotho identify beer with life and beer brewing with the making of a human being (Bosko 1981).
7. Colson and Scudder (1988), citing Saul (1981).
8. Some of the illegal urban brews found in South Africa in the 1930s and 1940s (isikokiyana, for example) had similar alcohol levels but were much more potent because of the ingredients (carbide, brown bread and suchlike) that went into them.
9. See Tyler (1891, 121); Schapera and Goodwin (1937, 133); Richards (1939, 77).
10. This may have been impoba, a strong brew distinguished from the usual utshwala (Krige 1936, 59).
11. Doke refers to Lamba beer as "very intoxicating" and Bemba beer, though low in alcohol, was drunk hot, thereby possibly increasing its potency (Doke 1931, 107; Richards 1939, 77).
12. Also known as utshwala (Zulu) or bjalwa (Sotho), bojalwa (Tswana), bjalwe

(Kgaga), *byaloa* (Lovedu), *halwa* (Venda), *umbwalwu* (Bemba) and *ubwalwa* (Lamba).

13. Nowadays beer is made from maize in most parts of the country, though in the past it was made mainly from millet (sorghum, quinea corn, Kaffir corn). Bryant (1949) says that Zulu beer was made originally from eleusine (*upoko*) and pennisetum (*unyawoti*) while sorghum was used primarily as a (hard) foodstuff. As maize replaced sorghum as the main food crop the latter came to be used primarily for beer.

14. *Marhewu* has been called "Christians' beer" because it is non-alcoholic. The word is probably derived from the Afrikaans *gou* (quickly) because it is quick to prepare (Bud-Mbelle 1926, 131).

15. Kropf (1915, 358) refers to *umqombothi* as light beer. Among contemporary Xhosa speakers it has become synonymous with *utywala* (beer). Among Xhosa speakers *utywala* is also the generic name for alcoholic drink.

16. This was also the case among central Bantu-speaking groups such as the Shona, Bemba, Nyakyusa, Ndembu and Lamba (Gelfand 1959; Richards 1939; Wilson 1957; Turner 1957; Doke 1931). Among Gwembe Tonga the ritual use of beer was extensive and beer was associated with "almost everything that Gwembe people thought important" (Colson and Scudder 1988, 65). Here, beer remained ritually important even after the rapid development of beer for sale from the early 1960s onwards.

17. For example, beer was brewed to mark the end of the isolation period for a mother after the birth of a child (Krige 1936, 69; Hunter 1936, 155); it was used in name-giving ceremonies to introduce a child to the ancestors (Monnig 1967, 106); and in the initiation ceremonies of both boys and girls (Ashton 1952, 53; Hunter 1936, 365; Monnig 1967, 120; Krige 1936, 91-92). Beer was an important element in marriage rituals (for instance Bird 1885 I, 477; Junod 1927 I, 117; Krige 1936, 131-34) and in mortuary rites (for instance Kuper 1947, 186; Gelfand 1959; Wilson 1957, 41–42).

18. Berglund (1976, 210–12) describes the ritual brewing of beer in gratitude for a boy's narrow escape from death after having been gored by an ox. The circumstances, the form of the ritual, the procedure followed, and the symbolism, are in many ways virtually identical to *umsindleko*, a beer drink held to mark the safe return of a migrant worker in the Transkei, which is discussed in chapters six and seven.

19. Similiar ritual uses of beer are recorded from other parts of Africa. The Nuer, for example, held a ceremony called "the bathing of the cow in beer", in which beer was poured over the peg to which the cow was tethered (Evans-Pritchard 1956).

20. Similiar prescriptions existed among other Bantu-speakers — the Nyakyusa, for instance (Wilson 1957, 138).

21. See Hammond-Tooke 1962, 35–36; Wilson et al 1952, 52–59; Wilson 1971, 63; Wilson 1981.

22. See Hunter (1936, 25); Wilson et al (1952, 52–59); Hammond-Tooke (1962, 35–36); Wilson (1971, 63); Hammond-Tooke (1975, 82–83).

23. In Southern Africa the evidence indicates the primacy of neighbours in co-operative labour though territorial units are seldom formally used to define the boundaries of work groups, and precisely which neighbours are asked or invited to work is less clear but of obvious importance (Kuckertz 1985). Marwick (1940, 166) says that a Swazi man organizing a work party sends word to his "more industrious neighbours" asking them to come and help. In Lesotho, people invite their "close friends and neighbours" (Ashton 1952, 131).

3 Power, Practice and Performance—A Theoretical Orientation[1]

In the analysis of Xhosa beer drinking rituals presented in this book I make use of a number of theoretical perspectives that involve the question of social 'practice', in the sense that it is used by practice theorists, and its relationship to other aspects of social reality. A major part of my approach derives from the work of Pierre Bourdieu,[2] and I attempt to link this to a current of anthropological writing in an area known as the 'anthropology of performance', exemplified particularly in the work of Victor Turner and his followers, as well as in the related work of a number of other anthropologists whose ideas and styles of analysis may be placed within this broad category. This provides the basic theoretical framework for my analysis, into which are woven a number of other threads linked to specific aspects of beer drinking or to specific types of beer drink rituals. Linking the anthropology of performance with Bourdieu may seem at first glance to be an ambitious undertaking, particularly in view of the fact that the latter pays relatively little attention to change while performance is often closely linked to issues of change and transformation. However, they are both clearly related to the question of process and to social reproduction, and there are certain other compatibilities, as we shall see, that may make the attempt worthwhile. I will suggest, in fact, that a performance approach may help to specify part of the mechanism for change absent in Bourdieu's work.

I take the anthropology of performance to be a particular approach within the broader body of practice theory. This is implicit in the work of others who have taken a practice approach to ritual, such as Bell (1997) who, despite her criticisms of a performance approach in an earlier work (Bell 1992), feels that performance theory is particularly useful for a study of the role ritual plays in situations of social change and uncertainty because it suggests that people are actively engaged in constructing and reproducing their socio-cultural reality (Bell 1997, 73). This is precisely one of the points I wish to make about Xhosa beer rituals.

However, there have been few studies which have made explicit links between performance theory and practice theory or attempted a fusion between them, despite the affinities between the two approaches, as noted, for example, by Drewal (1991) and Schieffelin (1998). Kapferer's (1986) application of a performance approach to his understanding of Sinhalese exorcism rituals indicates a very close relationship between performance and practice without explicit reference to practice theory, while Sax (2002) combines elements of Bourdieu's theory with a performance approach in his study of the ritual construction of the self in the North Indian Himalayas, but without explicitly discussing the divergence and possible convergence between the two. Bloch's approach to ritual has some affinities with a performance approach, in that he draws on speech act theory and examines the role of ritual speech, song and dance in establishing relations of hierarchy and domination in society (Bloch 1974, 1975), and in this way it bears some resemblance to practice theory. However, his overall theoretical framework is a neo-Marxist one. His conclusions have been both supported (e.g. Rappaport 1999, Brison 2001) and refuted (e.g. Werbner, 1977; Bourdillon, 1978, Schieffelin 1985, Gellner 1999). Others who have adopted a practice approach to ritual have not, by and large, drawn on the anthropology of performance in their analysis (see Bell 1997), though I do share with these approaches a concern with ritual as part of a historical process and social change, a focus on what rituals do and how they do it (their performative effect and efficacy), and on the relationship between ritual and other forms of practice.

My approach is therefore compatible with other varieties of practice theory, such as that of Sahlins (1985) and Ortner, who has characterized practice theory as being explicitly concerned with history and change:

> [Practice theory]…is a theory of how social beings, with their diverse motives and their diverse intentions, make and transform the world in which they live.…Why does a given society have a particular form at a particular moment—that form and not some other? And how do people whose very selves are part of that social form nonetheless transform themselves and their society? (1989, 193).

Bourdieu's project, as often stated by him, is largely to overcome the divide between subjectivist and objectivist positions in social science and to avoid the pitfalls of debates relating to the relationship between structure and agency, or between society and individual (Bourdieu 1977, 3–5). The very term 'practice' refers to this fusion of objective and subjective dimensions as they are brought together in the acts of human agents operating within a set of normative constraints and possibilities. In this sense one object in making use of Bourdieu's approach in this book is to bring together in a single analytical framework the subjective experiences of a group of rural Xhosa (not *all* rural Xhosa)—their beliefs, values, understandings, orientations, judgements, relationships and actions in terms of which their social life is made meaningful and may be characterized — and the wider circumstances ('objective conditions' to Bourdieu) in which their subjective experience is constructed and on which it is brought to bear, namely the cultural, economic and political structures that impinge on them, both during my period of fieldwork in Shixini and historically. In other words, the analysis of beer drinking rituals attempts to show how people on the ground constitute and understand their reality, the historical conditions impinging on this, and the contemporary external conditions that emerge from this and which relate to how this reality is made. My use of Bourdieu's concepts here conforms to the spirit in which they were conceived, that is as flexible concepts that need to be deployed in relation to a particular empirical setting (Swartz 1997).

Bourdieu — habitus, capital and field

The three main concepts that Bourdieu uses are habitus, capital and field, and it is in terms of the relationship between these three that social action or practice needs to be understood. None of these concepts are particularly straightforward and the relationship between them is complex.

One of Bourdieu's definitions of habitus is "a set of dispositions which incline agents to act and react in certain ways" and which "generate practices, perceptions and attitudes which are 'regular' without being consciously co-ordinated or governed by any 'rule'" (Thompson 1991, 12). Dispositions are inculcated during socialization and they become attitudes and ways of perceiving that are second nature and that predispose agents to certain kinds of experience and action in which the dispositions of the habitus are embodied. They are structured, reflecting the 'objective conditions' in which they were acquired, and 'durable' in that they are ingrained and not generally amenable to conscious reflection and modification. This does not, however, mean that they cannot change. The habitus is shared within a group, provides people with largely unconscious guidelines on how to act in daily life, orients their actions without determining them, and gives them a sense of what is appropriate, a 'practical sense' of how to go about the business of living. The notion of habitus is derived from Mauss' analysis of 'body techniques' (Mauss 1979) though Bourdieu uses the notion of an embodied habitus in a rather broader and more encompassing way than Mauss did, since to him the habitus is in the mind and is found in cognitive structures as well as being manifest in movement and posture. It consists of "mental dispositions, schemes of perception and thought, extremely general in their application" (1977, 15).

Habitus refers to the fact that the structures of society are incorporated into the body in the form of what he calls a bodily hexis, turned into "a durable manner of standing, speaking and thereby of *feeling* and *thinking*" (Bourdieu 1977, 93–94, emphasis in the original).

Bourdieu's general theory is largely a theory of social reproduction within a context of a structure of power relations marked by inequality and domination. The habitus arises out of the basic structural conditions of existence (material, cultural, political) within which a group lives and which determine life chances and possibilities, which become incorporated into dispositions, which in turn have a structuring effect. These are 'objective conditions' in the sense that they are the context within which subjectivity is constructed, not in the sense that they are free of interest or apolitical. Action is not rule governed but follows from the intersection between dispositions and the opportunities or constraints of a given situation in which action takes place and which allow for a variety of responses in terms of the dispositions inculcated by the habitus.

Dispositions are 'generative' and 'transposable', i.e. they are able to generate a multiplicity of practices and perceptions in areas of action (fields) other than those in which they were originally acquired. Different strategies or courses of action are possible in most situations, allowing the agent to choose according to unconscious notions of appropriateness or an intuitive feel for the 'rules of the game'. Putting strategies into practice successfully reproduces the habitus and the conditions which generate it.

According to Swartz (1997, 101) Bourdieu's various formulations of the concept of habitus:

> …all evoke the idea of a set of deeply internalized master dispositions that generate action. They point toward a theory of action that is practical rather than discursive, prereflective rather than conscious, embodied as well as cognitive, durable though adaptive, reproductive though generative and inventive, and the product of particular social conditions though transposable to others.

So, the habitus predisposes people to act in certain ways given the historical circumstances of its development, but it is not the only determinant of action. Action always takes place in specific contexts or fields and in accordance with the interests, broadly defined, of the actors, which arise out of the habitus and together with it affect their actions. Interests, which may be conscious or unconscious, short or long term, and which cannot be reduced to the utilitarian, have to be determined "through a careful empirical or historical inquiry into the distinctive properties of the fields concerned" (Thompson 1991,

16) and in terms of the relations between different fields. Practice thus occurs in fields, in which there are a number of groups of actors who are in different positions (often opposing and competing) in relation to each other, and who possess differing amounts and kinds of capital (see below). The field is constructed by historical conditions that embodies the actions of past agents and re-constructed by the actors through their practice.

Within fields there are various forms of 'capital', which are resources and also forms of power. The forms of capital that most concern Bourdieu are economic (land, labour), social (networks, reciprocal relationships), cultural (religion, education, art) and symbolic capital. Symbolic capital relates to power and refers to the authority and legitimacy conferred on and secured by people through their relations with others and their possession of other forms of capital, since the various forms of capital can be converted into each other. Individuals and groups attempt to maximize capital in terms of their particular positions within a field. In a differentiated society a field is usually a site of struggle between groups over the definition of and control over the various forms of capital and over the power to define the nature of the field, or the nature of social reality, in which dominance and resistance to dominance co-exist as part of the structure of the field (Swartz 1997, 122). Struggles for position within a field are thus also struggles for authority, legitimacy and power. The struggle within the field takes on an oppositional character, the dominant and the dominated taking on opposing strategies which are dialectically related, the one being derived from and indexing the other. The 'logic of practice' within the field is thus determined by the struggles over capital and the power to define capital. There may also be struggles *within* particular groups within a field (based on factors such as gender or age), and these too have to do with a struggle for the definition and control over forms of capital. The existence of a group habitus does not imply homogeneity and lack of difference within the group. Habitus is a fairly flexible and relative concept, and may be applied at various levels of aggregation based on factors such as age, gender, class, region, and so on.

The legitimacy of particular forms of capital are closely linked to the nature of the habitus of the actors within the field. To express this slightly differently, the identity, lifestyle and political position of a group are linked to the nature of its material and cultural resources and the power derived from these (Swartz 1997, 137). Practice arises out of the nature of the habitus in relation to a particular power position occupied by a group within a field and the group's cultural capital. Practice is thus a relational concept, "the outcome of a relationship between habitus, capital, and field." (Swartz 1997, 141). It is due to habitus that actors display similar characteristics across a range of fields, connecting and partially unifying these, helping to make them structurally homologous and blurring the boundaries between them. Fields are not fully autonomous also in the sense that capital gained in one may be transferred into another.

Bourdieu has been criticised for producing a theory of social reproduction characterized by a structural determinism that is unable to deal with the question of change (Jenkins 1992). Overall, Bourdieu's theory of social change does appear weak and undeveloped, even though the charge of structural determinism brought by his critics can be rejected (Swartz 1997, 211–17, 289–90). In addition, he neglects the question of contradictions between fields and the crises and consequent changes that could result from this (ibid., 292). The charge of determinism rests largely on Bourdieu's discussion of habitus as both emerging from and generating structure, as having a tendency to reproduce the objective structures to which it owes its genesis. However, as is illustrated above, his theory of practice holds that action is the outcome of an *interaction* between habitus and field in which people vie for various forms of capital through which to secure power and control within the field. Fields constitute the structure, or the social, political and economic conditions in terms of which the habitus develops. The habitus is adjusted as agents develop new orientations as these conditions change (Bourdieu 1977, 78). The impact of colonialism on indigenous people is one of the prime contexts for such changes, and Bourdieu states that: "There is no doubt that uprooting from the traditional order and an often brutal entry into the world of the modern economy bring about and presuppose systematic transformations of the habitus." (1979, 32). Bourdieu has been quite explicit about the question of change, stating that the habitus is not permanent but "long lasting" and "a fate, not a destiny", adding that: "The model of the circle, the vicious cycle of structure producing habitus which reproduces structure *ad infinitum* is a product of commentators." (2002, 27–30). Habitus is a product of history and it can change when circumstances change, when people are subject to new structures or objective conditions, where old practices are no longer feasible and new strategies have to be developed. Habitus "may be *changed by history*, that is by new experiences, education or training..." (ibid., 29 emphasis in the original).

In any case, however, not *all* behaviour is determined by habitus—conscious strategizing may be required in times of crisis or change (Swartz 1997, 113), the strategies developed becoming habituated in future generations. For Bourdieu, in fact, as commentators such as Swartz have pointed out, the concept of field comes more and more to replace the notion of habitus as he turns to complex, differentiated societies rather than traditional societies. Overall, however, Bourdieu argues that it is the habitus in conjunction with the field and the struggle within it that generates particular forms of action. Thus as the field changes, perhaps as new actors enter it and power relations change (e.g. colonialism), so does action as the habitus reacts and changes, though there is usually a lag here. The relation between field and habitus thus changes over time as each influences the other through mutual feedback and adjustment. Thus "practice cannot be deduced either from the present conditions which may seem to have provoked them or from the past conditions which have produced the habitus..." but from their interrelationship (Bourdieu 1991, 56). This is the key to understanding Bourdieu's theory of change and his view of the habitus as being inventive, characterized by innovation as well as simply reproductive. It means that "each state of the social world is thus no more than a temporary equilibrium, a moment [in the struggle for power]" (ibid., 1991, 141).

Change arises out of the struggle for capital and power, from attempts to defend or improve a particular position. New orientations are developed to this end, drawing on the particular resources, interests and knowledge of the actors and the particular positions that they occupy in the field. Such change may involve creativity and cultural production, which involves adjusting a group's position in relation to others in the field, and can transform the forces operating within it as the positions of different actors or groups change, with consequent changes to the habitus. Such changes in the habitus can occur between or within generations in conditions where there are significant changes to the material and social environment, in terms of which dispositions are inculcated.

How does this rather abstract discussion relate to the South African situation and the empirical material that is the concern of this book?

The struggle for labour

Firstly, fields exist within a 'social space', and in this case the social space is one defined and structured largely in terms of colonialism (and, later, apartheid) which unified parts of southern Africa into a single political economy characterized by a particular structure of power relations in which colonial-settler and indigenous components occupied very different positions in relation to different kinds of capital and access to capital. It is not possible or appropriate here to outline and analyse this in terms of the South African social space as a whole, but because of the prominence of capitalism in the relationship between dominant and dominated in South Africa one can start with the field of economic production, and with labour as a form of economic capital, and then broaden this out somewhat to touch on the other fields and forms of capital that are of relevance for an analysis of the social position of Shixini people and their beer drinking rituals. In what follows, then, I start with a sketch of the nature of this field as it developed under colonialism in South Africa, before turning to the impact of entry into this field on the Xhosa speaking people of the Eastern Cape. The position of Xhosa within this field is then examined in the theoretical terms outlined above.

The impact of the British colonial state and of the demands for cheap wage labour brought about by mining, settler farming and industrial production in colonial South Africa (from about the 1850s onwards, before and after unification of the four settler states in 1910) has been thoroughly documented by historians and only the key elements need to be mentioned here. There was a general pattern of incorporation of indigenous peoples into the colonial polities and the post-colonial state and into the field of capitalist production, though the details varied considerably. Khoisan peoples (so-called 'Bushmen' and Khoikhoi) were practically wiped out early on by various means, their remnants settled on farms and in the towns and cities. To the majority of other native peoples, who spoke a variety of Bantu languages, colonisation was usually associated with the assertion of control by military might and the armed subjugation of indigenous chiefdoms.[3] This was followed by loss of autonomy through the imposition of colonial rule, land alienation, the displacement and absorption of groups of people, and confinement of many to what ultimately became the 'native reserves' and then 'homelands'.

The development of industrial capitalism from the late 1860s onwards, together with successive regimes based on keeping blacks socially and territorially separate and disenfranchised, changed the nature of the areas occupied by black people in a variety of ways. Chiefly, it transformed many of them into 'labour reservoirs' providing cheap migrant labour that served the needs of mining, manufacturing and commercial farming, controlled by white settlers or their descendants. Merchant capital penetrated the reserves in the form of traders, and most rural areas had long also hosted missionaries, many of whom established educational institutions. Urbanization of black rural dwellers was discouraged and later prohibited, and under apartheid most black people in urban areas were viewed as temporary sojourners (even if born there) and destined ultimately to return to their 'homelands'. Indeed, many were forcibly removed and re-settled in remote areas during apartheid rule, particularly in the 1960s and 1970s.

Red and School Xhosa

The effects of being drawn into the capitalist economy were uneven. In the Xhosa case there were two very different political responses, manifested in the development of what were labeled two distinct sub-cultures called Red and School. These sub-cultures emerged out of the history of uneven contact between Xhosa and whites, and lasted from around 1850 to 1970. Many have seen this distinction as basically a conservative/progressive division, deeper and more enduring in the Eastern Cape than elsewhere in Africa and representing a degree of resistance to change unprecedented south of the Sahara (Mayer 1980, 1). However, placing the development of these two ideologies within a Bourdieu-ian framework illustrates that the division was not as simple as this, and that the characterization of Red people as 'conservative' is probably inaccurate. The categorization of Red and School, particularly in Mayer's initial work (1961), tended towards essentialism and dualism though it did not imply an evolutionary trend from one to the other. Later, however, Mayer (1980) characterized them as subordinate 'ideologies of resistance' to white domination, as variations within a common political and economic framework. In some ways this usage conforms to what Ferguson (1999) prefers to term cultural 'styles' or 'modes', in referring to a similar distinction in Zambia, and although he distinguishes cultural style from Bourdieu's habitus because he feels that 'style' is not as all-encompassing as habitus, there is considerable affinity between the two, particularly in his emphasis on cultural style as "practices that signify differences" (ibid., 95) or "a capability to deploy signs in a way that positions the actor in relation to social categories" (ibid., 96). Bourdieu has indicated that this is precisely what habitus is about (1998, 8–9). Habitus is a shared quality of groups and of individuals, a system of dispositions guiding action, "a kind of affinity or style, like the works of the same painter…" Bourdieu (2002, 28). This does not mean that there are no variations, inconsistencies or contradictions—the term 'style' or 'lifestyle' refers to a "practical unity" (ibid., 28–29). He uses the concept habitus "to account for the unity of style which unites the practices and goods of a single agent or a class of agents" (1998, 8).

Red and School ideologies, wrote Mayer, "represented comprehensive patterns of belief, laying down precepts for most aspects of life, including economic behaviour", elaborated with "meticulous attention to detail" (1980, 2–3), which adjusted to the changing economic and social environment over time. Both were born out of the material and socio-political conditions of colonial incorporation which presented Xhosa with "a particular structure of objective probabilities—an *objective future...*" which generated "determinate dispositions" towards the future (Bourdieu 1979, vii). These dispositions form the habitus, "structured structures which function as structuring structures, orienting and organizing the economic practises of daily life..." (ibid., 1979). Given their common origin in the same historical conditions, and that they were both Xhosa, there was considerable overlap between Red and School in terms of their interests, objectives and activities, but there were also important differences arising from the different ways in which different groups of Xhosa had been incorporated, differences in exposure to education, missionary influence, wage labour, and so on, which led to different perceptions of the overall situation and thus to the development of different dispositions and practices. As Bourdieu insists, habitus is produced "...by conditions of existence which, in imposing different definitions of the impossible, the possible, and the probable, cause one group to experience as natural or reasonable practices or aspirations which another group finds unthinkable or scandalous, and vice versa." (Bourdieu 1977, 78).

It is evident, then, that this represented division, that for the Xhosa as a whole there occurred a change from doxa to orthodoxy and heterodoxy (Bourdieu 1977, 164–69); from an implicit acceptance of the world as a given state of affairs to one which had lost its arbitrariness and homogeneity, and which required justification and rationalization. A wider range of choices became possible, produced not only by the colonial presence but also by the differential nature of incorporation. Most School people aspired to equal status with whites and accepted the trappings of colonial life, including education, Christianity and wage labour. Many had benefited from education, the church and the limited employment opportunities available; they saw a possibility of incorporation as full citizens, and this affected the dispositions that they developed towards the situation and towards their future (Bourdieu 1979, 64). Red people, on the other hand, actively re-invented and asserted their African identity and implicitly rejected involvement in the colonial state. Both denied the legitimacy of white domination and expressed opposition to it. School people 'argued and prayed' for change, and strove to meet whites on their own terms, while Reds turned their backs on whites and things associated with them and designed ways of insulating themselves, which they justified in terms of the actions of both the dominant whites and the traitorous actions of the colonists' Xhosa allies in times of war. The Red orientation was still fairly prominent in Shixini in the 1970s, when I commenced fieldwork there, though diluted "by the spread of a new, secular, urban-influenced culture" (Mayer 1980, 2) which gradually became more widespread over my period of association with the area.

The history of the Xhosa people of the Ciskei and Transkei falls into two periods. During the first, as Mayer put it, they fought the whites; during the second, they laboured for them. This transition, and the roots of Red and School, go back to the early 1800s when the Eastern Cape first received significant numbers of British settlers, who joined the Afrikaner (Boer) farmers who were already there. Encounters between Xhosa and colonists became more commonplace. Self-sufficient, relatively well organized and not depending greatly on what the white colonists could offer them (though there was considerable trade), Xhosa at first successfully limited their involvement with the colonists, and later defended at least part of their territory through a hundred years of frontier wars. However, they gradually lost much of their land and cattle to the colonial forces, and were pushed further and further back into a fraction of the land that they had once occupied.

Initially, resistance to the colonists was associated with resistance to the missionaries, whose attempts at conversion were not very successful, except with displaced people and a few chiefs. Converts came to be seen as traitors by other Xhosa and were called by the derogatory term *amagqoboka*, since they were prone to joining the colonial forces against their fellow Xhosa.[4] (Shixini people still use this term to refer to the missionized and well educated.) The colonists found ready allies particularly among those of Mfengu origin, whose structural position in relation to both Xhosa and the colonists provided the objective conditions facilitating adaption of an earlier habitus and the development of new forms of self-identification. The Mfengu were refugees from Natal who had settled east of the Kei river (Map 2) where they were subordinate to their Xhosa hosts, and who were attracted by the prospects of their own land and economic advancement that the colonists offered. Mfengu sometimes received gifts of land taken from the other Xhosa-speaking tribes by colonial forces, and were resented by many Xhosa. Nevertheless they identified as Xhosa and maintained important aspects of this identity in their later struggle for equality with whites. These were the fore-runners of the first 'School' people. After the 1834–1835 war, 17,000 Mfengu were moved from east of the Kei and settled as a buffer between the colonists and the other Xhosa south-west of the Kei river, where many of them prospered until this became unpalatable to the colonists.

The coming divide into School and Red Xhosa was foreshadowed in 1811–1812 when thousands of Xhosa were driven over the Fish river from their land west of it. Two prophets arose out of this traumatic time. One of them, Ntsikana, preached submission to the will of the Christian God and affiliation with whites. Nxele, on the other hand, claimed that the God of the whites was inferior to that of the Xhosa, and he led Xhosa forces in an unsuccessful attack on the garrison town of Grahamstown in 1819. Further prophecies after the Xhosa defeat in the war of 1850–1853, by a young girl called Nongqawuse and her uncle, predicted the ultimate defeat of the whites and the return of all stolen land and cattle, as well as the return of the dead to assist them, provided that people killed all their livestock and destroyed their grain. This millenarian movement has been described as the 'cattle-killing' or the 'national suicide of the Xhosa', though the foremost historian of this period, Jeff Peires, eschews the latter term, considering the cattle-killing to be "as much a murder as it was a suicide". This is because of the role of the governor of the Cape Colony, Sir George Grey, who "encouraged and then capitalized on the movement" (Peires 1989, 10). Peires states that Grey "trampled on this human wreckage...exiled the starving, crushed the survivors, and seized more than half of Xhosaland for a colony of white settlement." (ibid., ix). Together with the resettlement of Mfengu and further attempts at assimilating Xhosa by the Cape colonial authorities, this was a turning point in the incorporation of both Mfengu and Xhosa (Mayer 1980, 11), increasing conversion to Christianity and driving many impoverished and starving Xhosa out of their homes and into the employ of colonists. The promotion of education and trade, expansion of the areas of colonial settlement, and the deployment of white magistrates to take charge of administration and law (a process that had started well before the cattle-killing) in British Kaffraria, the area between the Kei and the Keiskamma rivers, gave further impetus to the developing School culture.

The cattle-killing episode led to the expulsion of Sarili, the Gcaleka paramount chief (the senior chief of the Xhosa proper) and his remaining followers from the area between the Kei and the Bashee rivers. He was banished to across the Bashee, but in 1865 he was allowed to return to the coastal parts of his former chiefdom, occupying perhaps a third of the land that he had once ruled (Peires 1989, 333). This coastal area, which later became the districts of Willowvale (the site of this study) and Kentani, remained very conservative culturally, and in a sense became the heartland of the Red Xhosa sub-culture, though many of the other Transkeian districts such as Elliotdale and Mqanduli, and certain districts in the Ciskei, were also predominantly Red until the 1970s. In the war of 1877–1878 the Gcaleka made a last effort to stay out of colonial control, but shortly after this the territories across the Kei river were formally annexed and incorporated, and the Cape magisterial system was extended to it, despite various attempts to resist this (Benyon 1974). British Kaffraria was officially annexed in 1865 and by 1884–1885 all the Transkeian Territories had been annexed to the Cape except for Pondoland, which submitted in 1894. The Territories were divided into 27 magisterial districts under three Chief Magistracies (Benyon 1974, 389) and became the United Transkeian Territories, later the Transkei 'homeland'.

Among the educated and missionized Xhosa speakers, including the Mfengu, the early potential for equality with the colonists soon dissipated in the face of the racist orientation of colonial society. Missionaries, influenced by "a Christian version of Social Darwinism…began redefining their educational policies" (Mayer 1980, 12). Notions of paternalism and trusteeship replaced the earlier ideal of assimilation on equal terms. Many Xhosa became economically dependent on white employers, and educational policies sought to further the notion that blacks should be useful to colonial society as labourers (Mayer 1980; Benyon 1974). There was little scope for social mobility or economic development, as markets were closed to formerly successful black peasant entrepreneurs who had been competing effectively with whites. Soon, capitalist employers collaborated with each other and with administrators to secure a ready supply of cheap labour, using various means (e.g. taxes, land alienation) to prevent economic development in the Xhosa-speaking areas and to force men into migrant labour in mines and industry, where they endured harsh conditions and were denied bargaining power.

In the 1940s there were moves on the part of capital and the state to facilitate permanent migration to cities in order to provide for a more stable and skilled urbanized work force. These plans were thwarted by the coming to power in 1948 of the Nationalist party, which soon embarked on the development of the elaborate apartheid ideology, legislation and structures that South Africa became notorious for, including the institutionalization of a system of oscillating labour migration accompanied by strict influx control regulations designed to keep blacks in their rural areas. The native reserves, which were subject to a process of underdevelopment, came to serve the function of labour pools from which men could enter 'white' areas only under contract with an employer.

Forays into migrant labour by Xhosa in the early colonial period were usually sporadic and linked to emergencies such as droughts, livestock diseases, or to particular 'targets' such as the purchase of cattle or guns. People continued to cultivate their land and raise livestock, on which they depended for subsistence. Progressive land alienation, overcrowding and lack of state support for agriculture changed this. Right through the period when the Xhosa-speaking areas were native reserves and then Ciskei and Transkei 'homelands' (from the early to the late twentieth century), only sporadic and ineffectual attempts were made to stimulate agricultural and other economic growth, invariably having little impact on economic realities. Instead, these areas became steadily more impoverished and overpopulated, and making a living through pastoralism and cultivation more and more difficult. This situation has not yet changed in 2005, and the problems of black economic advancement and rural development in places like the former Ciskei and Transkei, now the Eastern Cape Province, are immense and worse than they were ten years ago (Bank 2005, Ainslie 2005).

While nothing more than a general sketch, this gives a picture of the historical process of interaction between Xhosa and colonial power (what Bourdieu terms the 'objective conditions') in terms of which the subjective orientations known as 'Red' and 'School' were constructed in the rural Xhosa-speaking areas. Despite later racism and discrimination, School people developed dispositions that enabled them to accept many aspects of colonial society. Their world view and lifestyle incorporated elements of the new order but also many elements of the Xhosa past, reflecting both their aspirations and their history. School people accepted the desirability of education, Christianity and engagement with western society and the dominant majority on equal terms, but their world view was founded on the disenchantment that colonial racism and apartheid had sowed. The result was the development of a syncretism that incorporated many elements of the Xhosa past into an outlook and lifestyle that accepted the principles associated with education and Christianity. The ancestors remained important and were incorporated into Christian belief, old status distinctions based on marital status, gender and age were given new life through new forms of behaviour and etiquette, and symbolized by means of new items of western style clothing worn in distinctive ways. Church and school remained centres of activity, square houses with sub-divisions into rooms were built, with furnishings based on western styles and pictures adorning the walls. Male initiation and circumcision were retained but given a particular School flavour, and the rural homestead and agricultural production remained important.

Acutely aware of the injustices inflicted on them, School people protested against and challenged discrimination through literary and other means, criticised the double standards of the dominant whites, and strove to show that they were equal to whites in all respects. The more successful were able to enter professions such as nursing and teaching, and wealth provided some basis for internal status differences. Cash was needed to meet material aspirations based largely on western consumer items and wage employment was considered essential. Many school people migrated to cities on a permanent basis before this became impossible or fraught with risk under apartheid, after 1948. There the School sub-culture dissolved into an urban based, proletarian environment.

Rural interests were not paramount and towns offered more opportunities for 'civilized' living (Mayer 1980, 38). As more wage-earning opportunities arose in cities, proletarianization increased also in rural areas. By the late 1970s, the rural School folk culture had disappeared, being replaced by "a culturally much more amorphous population of 'modern' people…strongly influenced by the way of life and values of the urban townships." (Mayer 1980, 39).

To the people who came to be called Red Xhosa, the centre of life was the rural homestead (*umzi*) and the purpose of life was to maintain and develop it to the best of one's ability. The *umzi* contained one's family and was associated with certain material assets—huts, arable land, byres, cattle and other livestock. It was also associated with the ancestors and serving the *umzi* was at the same time service to the ancestors. Ancestral rituals involving animal sacrifice and beer drinking took place in the cattle byre associated with each homestead, and these events required the participation of a wider community of kin and neighbours, so the homestead was also a social centre. Economic, social and religious dimensions were closely interwoven. As homesteads became smaller from the 1850s onwards, due to a variety of interrelated factors (see chapter two), so the institution of collaborative work became more and more important to ensure homestead production and neighbouring homesteads depended on each other for survival. With the entry of men into migrant labour, this dependence grew.

Much of this was also true of School people, except that they were less explicit about the ancestors and disguised the rituals associated with them within new forms compatible with Christianity (Pauw 1975). The distinctive Red subculture arose out of the majority of Xhosa speakers who reacted to colonial intrusion with hostility or, later, by having as little as possible to do with missionaries, educational institutions and colonists, and who re-constructed their Xhosa identity to this end. After defeat and annexation they maintained their distance socially and culturally even though many were forced into wage labour, convinced that there was nothing to be gained from school, church and other aspects of the politically dominant order. When possible, they sold their surplus agricultural produce and livestock to minimize their involvement in migrant labour (Mayer 1980, 15). They strove to maintain Xhosa custom and law, and they practised the ancestor religion "with an orthodox attention to detail" (ibid., 40). The term 'Red' comes from the old Xhosa practice of using red ochre on the body and to dye cloth for clothing, and Reds were called *amaQaba* (the smeared ones) by School people. Older people in Shixini still use this term as a form of self-identification, but when used by non-Reds generally it is a derogatory term connoting uncouthness, lack of sophistication or backwardness. Much of the administration of Red areas was done by local chiefs, headmen and sub-headmen, from whom magistrates sought advice, and communal tenure was retained in many of these areas. In the main, Reds remained loyal to their chiefs until the implementation of the Bantu Authorities Act of 1951, which drew chiefs into a system of local government devised by the apartheid state, made them less accountable to their people and greatly enhanced their powers. The implementation of this legislation, together with the state's enforcement of tenure reform, livestock culling and villagisation under agricultural 'Betterment' schemes, from the 1940s onwards, led to numerous violent outbreaks in the Transkei and contributed significantly to the rebellion in Pondoland in 1960. In their review of rural resistance in the Transkei from 1900 to 1965, Beinart and Bundy (1980, 312) conclude that "from the 1930s onwards, the core of militant resistance…appears to have been provided by traditionalist middle migrants" and that such resistance was symptomatic of the rejection by traditionalists of the dominant culture.

Although soon incorporated into the money economy, Reds spurned the trappings of western civilization such as manufactured clothes, furniture and other consumer items, except for those that were required for the production of the distinctive styles of dress and bodily decoration (mainly beadwork) which signalled their identity and immediately distinguished them from School people. Given the central importance of the homestead, the purpose of migrant labour was to serve it, not to earn money for consumer goods, though items such as steel ploughs and hoes became necessary, and money was useful for re-building herds or obtaining grain after droughts or episodes of disease. Cattle remained of supreme importance since they were essential for marriage (as bridewealth), in maintaining a good relationship with the ancestors, and in the economic development of the homestead where they provided draught power, material products, and status.

When in town or mine for the purpose of wage labour, Red men 'encapsulated' themselves by forming exclusive networks designed to ensure that they remained loyal to their code, reinforce the values associated with the rural *umzi* and counter the many threats to Red identity posed by urban life. These included involvement with 'town women', who would distract the migrant from his primary task and encourage him to abscond (*ukutshipa*) in town and forget his rural family. Engagement in wage labour was limited to what was essential to maintain the rural home, and right up to the 1970s men spent long periods, sometimes years, at home between work spells and retired from migrant work soon after the age of forty when teenage sons were able to start their migrant careers. Going out to work was referred to as going 'to war' (*emfazweni*) or as an unavoidable and dangerous expedition (*itorho*). When at home young migrants were actively engaged in the youth movements where the values that sustained the Red ideology were actively propagated through what the Mayers aptly termed "socialisation by peers" (Mayer and Mayer 1970). These were the *umtshotsho* for uncircumcised boys and girls of equivalent age, and the *intlombe* for young men and women of marriageable age. Red people referred to them as their 'schools'. Here, boys developed their skills at stick fighting, dancing and seduction, sometimes engaging in serious battle with neighbouring groups, and young men inculcated the values of the Red lifestyle in members through an elaborate display of oratorical skills in debates about custom and law, in addition to the dancing and courtship that accompanied their all-weekend gatherings. These movements were extremely important in reproducing the Red Xhosa world view, and they remained strong in many Red areas up to the late 1970s, when a variety of factors started to make the Red way of life difficult to sustain (McAllister and Deliwe 1993). School people, on the other hand, developed forms of socialization and entertainment modeled on church and school—concerts, 'tea-meetings', and sports such as rugby and cricket.

Practice theory, in so far as it is always broadly political, concerned with both continuity and change, and with bridging the divide between the subjective and the objective, would seem to be applicable to the kind of process outlined above. As Ortner (1989, 200) puts it:

> A theory of practice...is a theory of conversion, or translation, between internal dynamics and external forces. One dimension of this concerns how people react to, cope with, or actively appropriate external phenomena, on the basis of the social and cultural dynamics that both constrain and enable their responses...the ways in which a given social order mediates the impact of external events by shaping ways in which actors experience and respond to those events.

In Bourdieu's terms, what this discussion of the historical emergence of Red and School illustrates is that the engagement of Xhosa people with the dominant group in a variety of fields was associated with a struggle for the definition and control over various forms of capital—education, religion, political influence, and so on. In the field of economic production, the struggle turned on control over labour. Wage labour (and its associated economic and cultural capital) as a manifestation of the habitus of various groups under apartheid or earlier colonial conditions was interpreted differently by these groups within the field, with the Red Xhosa interpretation differing considerably from that of employers as well as from that of School people. Labour was the key issue in the structure of objective relationships between

competing groups within the field and in defining the forms of capital that
the different groups strove to accumulate. The struggle was (and is) over various aspects of labour—its price, availability, location, application and
meaning. To the dominant actors in the field (the exclusively white 'captains
of industry' and the colonial/apartheid state) labour served the needs of industry and its appropriation through the application of various forms of
pressure (such as taxes) and the institution of migrancy was seen in these
terms. This was supported by structures framed in terms of the culture and
values of the dominant, by colonial and apartheid legislation and practices
such as those associated with the denial of bargaining power at the work
place and the provision of inferior or inadequate education to blacks. Even
today, more than ten years after the election of South Africa's first democratic government, the dominant actors within the field of production are
drawn primarily from the white minority, who have largely retained their
economic power. In an earlier period Victorian notions about the 'dignity of
labour' and the 'indolence' of the natives provided additional cultural am-
munition for the colonialist-capitalist armoury.

To the dominated, arising out of their interaction with the dominant within
the field of production, the nature and value of labour as a form of capital
varied along the lines of Red and School as illustrated above. To School people, waged work was a mark of status and advancement, a way of demonstrating equality and achievement within the new social order. To Reds, given
both continued attachment to the rural home and the conditions under which
migrant labour was initiated, undertaken and developed, and given their perception of their overall position within the field of power, wage labour became interpreted as a necessary evil, limited as far as possible, and designed
to serve the needs of the homestead and its inhabitants located in rural areas.
In this respect institutions such as the youth movements were 'instruments of
reproduction', linked to a habitus through which the status quo as defined by
Reds was maintained but which at the same time consisted of strategies of subversion, in Bourdieu's sense, which challenged the dominant position of
whites and their power to define the field (Swartz 1997, 125). Resistance of
this kind was not new to Xhosa people, who had a history of 'voting with their
feet' and other measures to rid themselves of unpopular chiefs and headmen,
and of successfully remaining politically independent in the face of threats
from rival chiefdoms (Peires 1981, Wilson 1969).

However, this resistance, like the Red habitus in general, was usually not
consciously formulated in explicit political terms unless their rural interests
were directly threatened (as in the Pondoland revolt). For Red people, the
rural homestead, under migrant labour conditions, became the only possible

source of ultimate security and satisfaction, and their development of a distinctive set of dispositions and practices was a creative and radical response linked to this orientation. Although framed in 'traditionalist' terms, it was a selective and 'defensive traditionalism' (Beinart and Bundy 1987, 12), a product of the colonial encounter but not an explicit political ideology. Migrant labour became one of many forms of labour directed at fulfilling aspirations connected to the homestead which, from the capitalist point of view, competed with these other forms of labour. Reds transformed and recontextualized migrant labour, they incorporated it into their rural economy and social system, remade it to fit into their society, and adapted the latter to facilitate this. This struggle over labour in the field of production was thus one over the time and space in which labour was to be deployed, and over the ends to which it was to be directed. Employers and the state responded with measures designed to ensure a steady supply of workers. Red migrants complied to the extent that they had to, but converted the economic capital so gained into forms of rural capital (economic, social and cultural) designed to build their homesteads. Where possible they withheld labour and maximized social capital by staying at home for as long as possible and 'retiring' early. Labour shortages on the mines, in particular, were a chronic aspect of the industry, which had to be solved by importing labour from outside of South Africa's boundaries.

Further innovative responses among Reds, and which they had in common with School people, arose from important changes in the rural social space, in the ways in which rural social relations were forced to adapt, and in which the question of capital conversions is particularly important. A variety of historical factors arising out of colonisation and operating around the period 1850 to 1920, as we saw in the previous chapter, led to homesteads declining in size and to the necessity for economic and social collaboration between neighboring homesteads. In this situation the utility of non-waged labour as a form of capital to the individual homestead took on a communal dimension through various means, primarily the development of forms of co-operative or communal work. Instead of the homestead consisting of a relatively self-sufficient extended family, it declined in size and came to depend on its social relations with others, through which co-operative work was mobilized. In this sense, the assets of any particular homestead, including its labour and its potential for wage-earning, became something of communal interest. In this struggle with the dominant over the definition and meaning of labour, over the nature and location of its deployment, and over its legitimate product, Red migrants converted potential wage-labour into and maximized social capital by withholding labour from industry and staying at home for as long as possible and 'retiring' as early as possible, applying their labour to the development of their homesteads and to the extension and maintenance of the social networks related to this. Co-operative work that combined the labour power of many homesteads in the service of each developed as a set of strategies, not as something totally new, but as something of far greater importance than in an earlier era. Such work made sense in terms of a changing habitus generated in a situation of radical and complex change in the wider field of production.

Beer drinking rituals, I argue, developed at roughly the same time and in tandem with the institutionalization of migrant labour and other historical social and economic changes affecting homesteads. They became an integral part of the relationship between homesteads on which the new forms of co-operative rural production depended, linked to the negotiation of rural relations of production that emerged as a form of adaptation to these changes. This process is examined in detail in subsequent chapters, where it emerges as a recurring theme. The ability to host beer drinks, too, became a form of rural symbolic capital closely related to the way in which labour was constructed and used, and some of the newly developed forms of beer drinking were directly tied to migrancy. Beer drinks emerged as a form of practice through which people (re-)constructed their lives in relation to both the wider social space of apartheid and the rural social field, encapsulating a set of dispositions acquired in, and strategic improvisations arising out of, the socio-political conditions that structured the rural social field and out of the attempts by actors to accumulate 'capital' with which to position themselves within the field *vis a vis* others. This is also, of course, a simultaneous positioning within the field of capitalist production, which is thus dialectically related to the rural social field. Beer drinking rituals as a form of practice, as we shall see, can be fruitfully analysed as a form of cultural performance along these lines.

In sum, within a particular field of power given legitimacy by the state and capital, but under conditions that made Red Xhosa deny such legitimacy, new forms of habitus manifested in a number of strategies and attempts to legitimise new forms of capital developed, through which people attempted to regulate their relationship with the dominant segment of society (by limiting it) and their relationship with each other, emphasizing the importance of the latter. There is obviously some similarity between this analysis and Bourdieu's understanding of the relation between the Algerian peasantry and the cash economy introduced through French colonialism, where he "emphasizes that the peasant reaction is *not* "purely mechanical and passive forced accommodation" to the new economic system. Rather, the peasants respond with "creative reinvention" to the discrepancy between the demands of the new economic rationality and their customary habits." (Swartz 1997, 102, citing Bourdieu 1979, emphasis in the original).

Although Red people were able to consciously formulate aspects of their outlook and way of life in terms of opposition to white domination and the desire to maximize their rural assets, this formulation was never systematic or comprehensive and, as the evidence from beer drink oratory deployed later indicates, it appears to have dimmed over the years. People in Shixini did not explain their practices as being in explicit opposition to the apartheid state (up to 1994) or, after that, in response to an inept provincial government. Nor do they verbalise an opposition to the employers of migrant labour; it is a largely unconscious operation, an aspect of the 'practical mastery' that people have of their social situation arising out of the Red Xhosa habitus which developed out of the struggle in the field of rural production (as well as within other fields in the social space of apartheid—homologous processes and struggles can be identified in the field of education, politics, health, economic development, aesthetic life, etc.).

What this indicates is that beer drinking rituals (like other aspects of rural social relations) are positioned at the intersection between fields, particularly the two discussed above, and may be seen as attempts at overcoming the contradictions between them. In the case of labour these are basically the contradictions long associated with oscillating migration, and which can be summarized in the need to remove oneself from the rural home in order to work for and develop it. In the first of the two overlapping fields, the field of capitalist production, labour as a form of capital is structured by apartheid and ties rural Xhosa to the wider society, through contracts with employers. In the second, the field of rural social relations (including rural production), also structured by the history of colonialism and apartheid, labour is a form of capital manifested in the homestead and the relations between homesteads which are necessary for production and security.

Other Red strategies make sense in accordance with this. When forced out of necessity to enter the world of wage labour as migrants, by poverty or the need for economic capital in the form of cash, Red Xhosa converted the bulk of their earnings into forms of capital in rural areas that were multi-dimensional; at once economic, social, cultural and religious—cattle, ploughs and other forms of rural assets—in accordance with a habitus arising out of their position in the field of capitalist production. Such conversion was an act of resistance and subversion which signaled the perceived illegitimacy of the existing structure of power in the field (as well as in other fields). But it was also a positive act, aimed at the needs of the homestead and expressing Red people's legitimate position within the rural social field, and which provided them with bargaining power in their relations with other homesteads. Assets like cattle, the homestead, or maize are economic in the sense of being material, but they can be used for social and religious purposes, such as beer drinks and other rituals. In this conversion they are turned into symbolic capital, serving as authorizing and legitimizing agents. Since symbolic capital is the most powerful form of capital the legitimacy of the migrant's waged work came to depend on such conversion being made, to justify engagement with the dominant group in the field of capitalist production. The forms of rural capital that are defined as legitimate are determined in terms of the rural social field and its associated Red Xhosa habitus, not in terms of the field of wage labour and capitalist production.

The development of the Red world view thus involved the development of forms of cultural capital drawing on the habitus—a set of orientations, dispositions and characteristics manifested in the use of ochre, dress, scarification (such as *ingqithi*, the removal of the first joint of the little finger of the left hand), household furnishings, and other material symbols. In other words, it was *embodied* cognitively, physically and in various forms of practice. It was both positive and negative, signaling rejection of western forms of cultural capital such as modern clothes, western religion, formal education, music and dance, and acceptance of certain others—such as cattle, maize and agricultural implements. Cultural capital of a non-material kind, such as knowledge of the ancestor rituals, or oratorical styles, or of custom and law in general, arose out of an earlier Xhosa habitus, but was reconstructed and given new meaning and relevance under apartheid. New cultural forms (such as new kinds of beer drinking rituals, or new practices linked to labour migration which ritualised it—see chapter six) constitute a form of cultural production emerging from the struggle for power in the social space determined by apartheid and its many fields (religion, education, labour, residential location, political rights, and so on) and objectified in the body as well as in other ways, including beer and institutions such as ancestor rituals and beer drinking, which came to be seen as quintessentially Red and barred by Xhosa Christian converts.

One could, of course, have construed the relationship between rural Xhosa and capital in classical class terms; it would be easy to distinguish Shixini people (or Red people in general), in Marxist terms, as members of a rural proletariat who share a common relationship to capital. Indeed, much of South African anthropology in the 1970s and 1980s did just this. To follow Bourdieu's critique of Marxist views on class, this would be to do an injustice to the distinctive features of Shixini, other areas like it, the people who live there, and their distinctive practices such as communal beer drinking and co-operative work groups. These practices provide both a material and a symbolic means of asserting a distinctive world view and lifestyle very different from, say, people with a similar relation to capital from the more overcrowded and modernized parts of the Eastern Cape, or those subjected to agricultural Betterment schemes, which seriously disrupted their social institutions and sense of community and made the continued maintenance of homestead production impossible. The mistake made by many 'neo-Marxist' anthropologists twenty to thirty years ago, in South Africa and elsewhere, was to confuse the theoretical notion of class with real social groups (Thompson 1991, 30).

At the same time, there can be no mistaking the materialist flavour of much of Bourdieu's writing, as well as of the various components of the analysis that I present here.[5] However, I intend avoiding the use of the term class to avoid confusion with Marxist notions of class and because Bourdieu uses it in a variety of different ways that is confusing (Swartz 1997, 154). In the Xhosa case, the Red world view might bear some resemblance to a class ideology in that it developed through a process of political struggle and mobilisation, as a form of resistance against the dominant elements in South African society. However, it was largely an attempt to develop and use cultural capital of a particular kind—that associated with their Xhosa heritage—to provide symbolic power to facilitate a particular kind of relationship with the dominant in the national field of power and to protect their rural economic capital—land and livestock—through formulating a particular vision of the world and their place in it. Their identity as Red and their relationship with the dominant thus had both an objective and a subjective dimension and cannot be essentialised as simply a form of Xhosa traditionalism *or* as a class in terms of their relationship to means of production. Bourdieu's insights in this respect indicate that we cannot speak of Xhosa people, rural Xhosa, black people, or rural black people in South Africa as a class, since there was a range of different responses among black people to colonialism and apartheid—some similar to that developed by Red Xhosa, others very different—depending on circumstances such as location, access to economic and cultural capital, and so on. Those with access to forms of cultural capital such as education, or those in urban residence, or those completely deprived of land (such as farm labourers) responded differently.

In the foregoing pages I have attempted to implement Bourdieu's approach according to the three steps specified by Swartz (1997, 142), viz.:

1. By relating the particular field of practice, in this case beer drinking rituals as an aspect of a habitus linked to the maintenance of the
rural social field, to the field of power in the wider social space that
is South Africa.

2. By identifying the "structure of objective relationships" between
competing groups within the field, and the forms of capital that are
the subject of competition. I have done so largely by looking at labour
as capital in terms of the wider field of power and the field of production, both capitalist and rural.

3. Through an analysis of the habitus of the agents involved in the
struggle and the aims (the 'social trajectory') that they pursue as part
of the struggle in which they are engaged.

The analysis of beer drink rituals which the rest of the book is concerned
with rests on the notion of a habitus guiding the perceptions and actions of
agents acting within the rural social field. Beer drinks may be seen as a symbolic system through which the struggle with the dominant forces of apartheid
(which persist in the post-apartheid era) is fought and social reality constructed in a particular manner by the dominant element of rural society (primarily senior men). This social reality is embodied at beer drinks through the
manipulation of space, time and beer. They attempt to ensure social consensus concerning the nature of this reality and to perpetuate it, enabling the social order to be reproduced in these terms as a strategy aimed at preserving
their autonomy.

This book therefore runs counter to the well established trend in the literature on alcohol in Africa that associates colonialism with a change in the nature of alcohol use that was basically negative, uncontrolled and socially destructive.[6] Certainly there were changes in the frequency and nature of beer
consumption in rural Transkei, as we have seen, but many of these were linked
to an attempt to maintain the rural society and economy by insulating it from
the negative effects of colonial control and, later, the brutality of apartheid.
In this sense it seeks to illuminate processes of change and conflict, as part of
a struggle to resist the forces of the state, rather than being a merely functionalist approach along the lines of other studies of 'traditional' style beer
drinking in Africa, such as those of Netting (1964) and Sangree (1962). It has
to do with the relationship between alcohol and 'disorder' in one of the senses
mentioned by Ambler (1987, 3), namely "discontinuities, tension and conflict
among individuals and groups", and with the attempt by rural people to re-

sist disorder and reconstruct their lives in a way that would allow them to retain a degree of autonomy. They do not do so by drinking, as such, but
through the *performance* of beer drinking rituals. It is to the theoretical implications of this and its connections with Bourdieu's approach that I now
turn. After a brief review of the nature of the field of performance in anthropological work I indicate how a performance approach may contribute to a
practice approach by specifying the mechanisms facilitating change in the
habitus. A detailed analysis of how this applies in the Red Xhosa case is provided in chapter seven.

The anthropology of performance

The notion of 'performance' enjoys wide currency in contemporary social
science, and together with derivatives such as 'performativity' it is used in a
number of different ways, partly in accordance with the writers particular dis-
ciplinary orientation. It is a broad, encompassing concept rather than something that can be succinctly defined (Brown 2003, Bell 1998). To some (e.g.
Irving Goffman, Judith Butler) 'performance' is an aspect of any kind of social action or a way of constructing a particular identity in everyday life. This
is not the way in which I use the term here. In my usage it refers to forms of
action which are spatially and temporally framed or 'set apart' from everyday
life—ritual, theatre, festival, and so on. As such, and as a form of communication, it is aesthetically marked and involves acts "of extraordinary intensity and heightened significance" (Fabian 1990, 16). Even in this sense, however, there have been different ways in which the term has been used in
anthropology, theatre studies, sociolinguistics, cultural studies and folklore
studies. In some ways different approaches have more recently been amalga-
mated under the rubric of 'performance studies' (Schechner 2002) but this has
served to widen the field of application of the term rather than to refine it,
with virtually anything now being fair grist to the performance mill.

Since performance has a variety of meanings and encompasses a variety of
approaches, it is necessary for me to indicate what I understand by 'the anthropology of performance' rather than by 'performance' as such, and how I
intend to apply it to Xhosa ritual beer drinks.[7] There is nothing particularly
novel abut such an application, because anthropologists have viewed ritual as
a form of performance for some time. However, there are different views on
precisely what this means, and on how ritual performance is related to other
aspects of social reality. In this regard too, it has also not always been appar-

ent how performance as a form of social practice is linked to practice theory more generally, even though the close link that has developed between practice theory and the anthropology of performance has been noted (e.g. Drewal 1991, Schieffelin 1998). In what follows I attempt, not a comprehensive review of the field known as the anthropology of performance,[8] but to outline approaches to performance that are relevant to my analysis of beer drinks, and to link these to elements of Bourdieu's theory of practice.

Probably the best known writer in the field of ritual performance is Victor Turner, whose work has been very influential in studies of ritual, theatre and other kinds of performance. Turner's view of performance, ritual or otherwise, developed from the role of ritual as an aspect of the social process in the 'social drama' where it served, in the 'redressive' phase of the drama, as a mechanism for the resolution of conflict and social transformation through a realignment of social relations between individuals and groups. Here, ritual involves an "interpretive re-enactment" of experience (Turner 1982, 104), placing experience within the context of basic values and beliefs, allowing people to reaffirm these and to adjust to changed circumstances. It makes subjective experience intelligible, re-creates sentiments of solidarity and consensus (à la Durkheim and Radcliffe-Brown) but also articulates structural difficulties and the interpersonal conflicts that these give rise to, giving them meaning by "contextualising them in an abiding cosmological scheme" (ibid., 104). In other words, this is done within the context of the script or the text that is enacted as part of the performance, but the performance is always more than simply the enactment of a text. At times the development and outcome of the social drama involves revolution or reformation, developing and implementing new ways of acting and feeling, restructuring the old order if it is successful. Ritual performances are sometimes the agents of change, "representing the eye through which culture sees itself and the drawing board on which creative actors sketch out what they believe to be more apt or interesting 'designs for living.'" (Turner 1986, 24).

As indicated here, performance is closely linked to experience and is itself a particular kind of experience. In Milton Singer's original formulation of 'cultural performance', this notion was present. Searching for an appropriate unit of observation in his study of religion and social change in India, and discovering that "the units of cogitation are not the units of observation", Singer found himself "confronted with a series of concrete experiences" which he called "cultural performances" and which "became for me the elementary constituents of the culture and the ultimate units of observation" (Singer 1972, 70–71).[9] In Turner's formulation, the social drama was a particular type of experience (Turner 1986a, 39), and its third, 'redressive' phase was where the experience of the drama was expressed, reflected upon and made meaningful through ritual performance. The basic assumption is that people express their experiences in ritual performances, thereby reliving experience, making it meaningful and reconstructing culture as part of an ongoing social process. This does not mean that everybody experiences reality in the same way, but that ritual performance enables the commonalities of experience to be articulated and individual experience to be transcended, at least to some degree (Bruner 1986, 11–21).

The emphasis on 'experience' never really took hold, due in part to the difficulties inherent in the term, and due to problems with the subjective nature of experience and its connection with its public representation, noted by many of the contributors to the volume titled *The Anthropology of Experience*, edited by Turner and Bruner (1986). One of these contributors, Bruce Kapferer, makes it clear that it is 'performance' that is the key term rather than 'experience'. Kapferer, very much in line with Turner's approach, argues that what is achieved in ritual as performance is "the universalizing of the particular and the particularizing of the universal" enabling the particular and the universal to be brought together and moulded into one (Kapferer 1986, 191). This has important implications for an understanding of the role of ritual in the construction of a habitus.

Kapferer notes that within ritual there are usually various forms of action, that a ritual is often a 'composition' that interweaves a variety of different phases and media, such as oratory, song, and dance (ibid., 191), These forms of action "manifest in their performance varying possibilities for the constitution and ordering of experience, as well as for the reflection on and communication of experience". It is through these various forms that the particular and the universal are brought together and that experience takes on a communal dimension. (ibid., 191). In addition, performances are scripted; they follow a text but never simply reproduce it, and they have direction, in that they address an audience (though audience may overlap with performers). The enactment of the text by a particular set of performers before an audience brings together structural principles with individual circumstances. The employment of various forms of action which structure the ritual, each bringing with it different meanings and a different definition of reality, enables communication and the construction of meaning and involves the participants in a single experience, transforming individual experience and bringing particular and universal together.

Turner pointed out that ritual is able to play this role largely because of its liminal or 'anti-structural' aspects which often invert the conventional or commonsense order of things, forcing people to critically consider reality. In this process of 'plural reflexivity', social values and categories are made explicit in symbolic form, allowing for reflection and commentary on these, and for a re-generation or re-ordering as well as a questioning of social relationships. Reflexivity refers to the way in which members of a group "turn, bend or reflect back upon themselves, upon the relations, actions, symbols, meanings, codes, roles, statuses, social structures, ethical and legal rules, and other sociocultural components which make up their public 'selves.'" (Turner 1986, 24). This is a crucial difference between Turner's notion of performance and that of Goffman's, who saw all everyday action as performance or acting in the sense of self-presentation. In the liminal phase performance is "more about the doffing of masks, the stripping of statuses, the renunciation of roles, the demolishing of structures, than about putting them on..." (Turner 1984, 26). Turner referred to this as performance's 'subjunctive mood', the expression of supposition, desire, hypothesis and possibility (ibid., 20–21). Liminality and reflexivity are possible due to the fact that ritual as performance is a specially marked form of action occurring within an interpretive frame which is metacommunicative and which influences how communication is to be understood (Bateson 1973). In other words, the performance is 'keyed' in various formal ways, through stylization, formulas and references to tradition, by the temporal and spatial setting in which it occurs, and by the paraphernalia that it requires. Communication is thus given a particular context within which it is to be interpreted and evaluated.

But ritual performance, Turner pointed out, also makes explicit the conflicts and indeterminacies of social life affecting individuals and groups, and works towards a resolution of these. Ritual is part of the regularizing process that attempts to present a particular construction of reality and to resolve the problem of indeterminacy, partly through reflexivity and through the presentation of alternative realities. It is through performance that social reality is defined and acted out by the participants, that established norms, customs and symbolic frameworks are brought into relation with the uncertain and the ambiguous in the search for renewed order, helping to frame communication and action and to create a basis for future action. In the process of working towards order there is always room for maneuver, interpretation, choice and the exercise of interest and agency, and the reconstruction of social order is always temporary, part of an ongoing process that includes future performances, so the problem of indeterminacy is never actually resolved.[10] Hence no performance exists in isolation from previous and future performances of similar (or even of different) kinds.[11] Turner's most explicit discussion of this is in *The Anthropology of Performance* (1986, 72ff.), where the recognition of instability and inconsistency in society, of the lack of harmony and integration, and the emphasis on process and performance, is seen as the hallmark of "postmodern anthropology" (ibid., 73–78). Here, performances are seen as "the manifestations par excellence of human social process" (ibid., 84).

Many of these themes have been developed by anthropologists who have worked on subaltern performance within hegemonic orders, where performance both reproduces aspects of the dominant social order and subverts it at the same time, offering alternative modes of existence in highly developed symbolic codes. In Erlmann's (1992) analysis of Zulu *isichatamiya* dance performances, for example, both accommodation of and resistance to apartheid are evident. Performance reproduces certain practices linked to the apartheid structure but it also comments on, interprets, subverts that order and resists it, and presents an alternative ideal order. At the same time, the construction of an ideal order perpetuates an established asymmetrical, gendered, Zulu order in which males dominate and in terms of which family relations are constructed.

Some commentators regard Turner's approach as functionalist or structural-functionalist and overlook his oft-repeated view of ritual performance as but a stage in an ongoing social process, to which it contributes and out of which further ritual performances arise.[12] The relationship between the two is dialectical. New dramas tend to emerge from the old, they affect and inform each other, and life is a continuous process in which social reality and ritual performance interact (i.e. there is no end product). This is clearly an approach that attempts to integrate structural and subjective phenomena through focusing on practice. It is for this reason that Kapferer, in his preface to the 1996 edition of Turner's classic work, *Schism and Continuity in an African Society*, echoing the Bourdieu-ian approach outlined above, wrote that the book was concerned with how Ndembu villagers "come to participate in the transformations of their own world even as they are caught in the structural processes that are ultimately beyond their control" and that Turner's approach "overcame contradictions in social anthropology between actor-oriented and structure-oriented perspectives..." (1996, ix).

Arising out of but going a step beyond the innovative approach associated with the Manchester School, Turner showed how the location of the Ndembu within a colonial system affected the internal dynamics of village life and generated forces that they attempted to control by drawing on the cultural resources available to them. To Kapferer then, Turner and his colleagues in the Manchester school can be regarded as 'practice theorists' comparable with Bourdieu, though the comparison that Kapferer makes is perhaps overly critical of the latter, whom he incorrectly characterizes as too concerned with the subjective dimensions of action and unable to deal with change (ibid., x–xi).

Of importance here is Turner's notion of the social 'field', "a set of loosely integrated processes, with some patterned aspects, some persistences of form, but controlled by discrepant principles of action expressed in rules of custom that are often simultaneously incompatible with one another." (1986, 74). Elsewhere he uses the term 'field context', "a totality of coexisting social entities such as various kinds of groups, sub-groups, categories, or personalities, and also barriers between them, and modes of interconnection." (1968, 90–91). In some ways this is different from Bourdieu's notion of field, but this formulation obviously indicates a need to incorporate both objective (structural) and subjective factors, and the notion of struggle is clearly present. But Turner also uses the notion of field in a way that is very similar to Bourdieu's usage, for example in his discussion of the ritual field and its interaction with the field of power (Turner 1968). In his discussion of Mukanda (initiation ritual) this involves the pattern of inter- and intra-village relationships within the Ndembu 'vicanage', including the "contemporary interests, ambitions, desires, and goals" of the participants in Mukanda, as well as the historical factors shaping contemporary relationships which have an effect on "the purposive activities of individuals and groups, in pursuit of their contemporary and long term interests and aims." (ibid., 138). Much of Turner's early work is devoted to understanding how ritual performance is an outcome of history and the agents interacting within a field, that is, how the structural contradictions in Ndembu social life were expressed, worked out, sometimes ameliorated or given new meaning in ritual performances. In this the effect of colonisation on Ndembu social dynamics was an important element within the field context, and Turner himself characterized his analysis of Mukanda as concerned with power and the political field intersecting with the ritual field, which he described as "an overlapping of two force fields" (ibid., 143). His concern with change is also evident in his stress on the need to go into the history of the field context, to establish how it came to be what it is.

In addition to this, the characteristics of performance outlined above are suggestive as far as the question of how Bourdieu's notion of the habitus interacts with and adjusts to forces and developments within the field as he defines it. Turner and other performance theorists suggest a mechanism for change which is absent in Bourdieu's theory. Liminality and the reflexivity associated with it in performance allows people to take stock of and evaluate their social situation, suspend social reality, consider alternative modes of existence and act these out in a metalanguage (verbal or non-verbal, consciously or sub-consciously) within a frame, providing new ways of thinking and doing that are carried into the future. And it is in periods of "restlessness and uncertainty", Turner suggests, that reflexivity is provoked, and during which new performative genres may be generated, providing the ability to respond to change (Turner 1982, 23–28). A detailed example of how performance theory and practice theory converge in ritual and help to account for change is provided in chapter 7.

Other approaches to performance echo many of Turner's key points. To Richard Bauman (1992), for example, performance is "a mode of communicative behaviour and a type of communicative event", an aesthetically marked and heightened occurrence, framed, with an audience to whom the performer (oral poet, healer, priest, or whatever) is responsible for his/her acts. Bauman, Hymes and others within the field of 'the ethnography of communication' emphasize the action itself, as opposed to a script or text, not unlike Bourdieu's stress on practice and Turner's emphasis on performance as part of the social process. Performances are not scripts—their full meaning emerges only in their doing, as Turner put it, "from the union of script with actors and audience at a given moment in a group's ongoing social process." (Turner 1986, 24). The enactment within a social context is always more than the text: "All performance... is situated, enacted, and rendered meaningful within socially defined situational contexts." (Bauman 1992, 46). Neutral performance of a text is not possible—interpretation is always required, and performance is thus always 'emergent'—no two performances are exactly the same. Performance can never be text, because it disappears once it has accomplished something. This, too, illustrates the potential connection between performance and practice theory and the role of performance in social change. Performances "create their effects and then they are gone—leaving their reverberations (fresh insights, reconstituted selves, new statuses, altered realities) behind them." (Schieffelin 1998, 198).

One is reminded of Bourdieu here also in the sense of the habitus being synonymous with 'text', as Schieffelin (1998) has indicated. To Bourdieu, while habitus predisposes people to feel and act in certain ways, how they act is due to the interaction with others in a field, including the struggle for power and position, which requires improvisation and creativity. Practise always involves improvisation also "because situations and the people that participate in them are always only analogous to each other, they are never exactly the same." (ibid., 199). Similarly, the acting out (performance) of a ritual, for example, occurs within a field (in Turner's sense as well as in Bourdieu's) in which circumstances require improvisation and adjustment. Such improvisation "embodies the expressive dimension of the strategic articulation of practice" (ibid., 199). Schieffelin refers to this as a possible definition of 'performativity', "the way a practice is practiced", the way a particular exemplar of a practice is carried out, provided with meaning, interpreted, given significance and efficacy, not all of it consciously intended. In this sense, performance transforms habitus into action, always within a particular context. If performance is always emergent, unfolding, arising and being shaped in a particular context and therefore reflecting the creativity of agents, it is important to look at how this characteristic is acted out, to study the improvisations and the tactics involved, by relating the performance to its context. Viewing performance as praxis rather than as a fixed text means avoiding abstract models and too much concern with system and pattern (Drewal 1991).

What gives ritual the power to bring about transformation and change? To Turner the power of ritual to facilitate reflexivity and adjustment lay in the nature of the symbols that it deployed and in terms of which ritual was structured. Dominant symbols, in particular, have many meanings and refer to axiomatic social and moral values, values that are seen as basic to the social order (though they may be conflicting or contradictory). We know this by looking at how people use symbols in particular ritual contexts. Symbols are effective because of the property Turner calls "polarization of meaning" (1967, 28). By this he means that a dominant symbol brings together, in a single form, axiomatic values (at the 'ideological' pole) and gross physiological and emotional sensations (at the 'sensory' pole) which they arouse. In ritual these two meanings are fused or exchanged, imbuing axiomatic values with desirability and making the physiologically desirable morally good. This does not occur in a vacuum but in the context of specific rituals which have goals and where dominant symbols may be used instrumentally by agents to achieve these goals. Ritual symbols (like the rituals that they help to constitute) are involved in the social process, have to be analysed in relation to other events, and are "associated with human interests, purposes, ends, and means" (ibid., 20). It is in the role that ritual plays within the social process, in adjusting to conflict, realigning social relationships or facilitating adjustment to change, that ritual symbols effect transformations and give ritual a performative character.

Other anthropologists have answered the question of ritual's power to transform with reference to its illocutionary or performative force, a notion derived from the work of J. L. Austin and other speech act theorists. As is well known, Austin (1962) argued that there were certain kinds of verbal utterance that needed to be judged in terms of the effect they had rather than in terms of whether they were true or false. These were utterances that did things, that were 'speech acts', bringing about a certain state of affairs through their utterance. Some simple examples that he gave were naming a ship, pronouncing a verdict in a court case, or apologising. What the speech act did was referred to as its illocutionary force, and such an utterance, called a performative, changed something (e.g. it gave the ship a name, it made a person formally guilty or innocent). Such utterances also had 'perlocutionary' force, by which he meant some consequence of the act performed, such as people referring to the ship by its name, or sentencing a criminal to a term in jail. Some speech acts can be performed only by persons authorised to do so —a judge, a person appointed to name a ship, etc., and there has to be a conventional procedure followed, of which the act is part—a court case, a naming ceremony. In other words they are formalised and they are constitutive. In addition, the acts have to be 'felicitous' and can be invalidated if they are not. So the person who names the ship after her pet cat instead of pronouncing the name that the owners have agreed on would not thereby be naming the ship 'Bubbles'.

Speech act theory has been applied to ritual by anthropologists such as Rappaport (1999) and Tambiah (1985), both of whom add to our understanding of the nature of ritual as performance, though in different ways. Rappaport's posthumously published book, *Ritual and Religion in the Making of Humanity* (1999) is probably the most recent and extensive application of Austin's important insights. In it he suggests that ritual is a basic social act associated with the creation of obligation and the establishment of commitment, and that it thus has significant moral and social implications. This approach is one that is of some relevance to Xhosa beer drink rituals and will be referred to from time to time in the following chapters and returned to more fully in the conclusion. Here I wish simply to outline his performative approach in the context of the larger body of work on the anthropology of performance.

Not all rituals are clearly performative, directed at achieving conventional effects through conventional procedures. However, Rappaport argues that rituals are metaperformative and that the specific transformations that do take place through ritual are due partly to this 'higher order' of performativeness. Ritual is defined as "the performance of more or less invariant sequences of acts and utterances not entirely encoded by the performers" (1999, 24). This may be abbreviated to "the acting out of a liturgical order" which comes into being through its enactment. This is the 'higher order' performativity that is associated with ritual. In the process, the performers become part of and indistinguishable from the liturgical order that they are realizing through their acts and utterances. To perform an order is thus to conform to it, to accept it and be morally and socially bound to it (belief and sincerity are irrelevant). The liturgical order is associated with norms, values and beliefs and to perform it is to be obligated to abide by these and to encourage (but not to enforce or ensure) compliance with them. Performance thus forms the basis of social order. It is in ritual that obligations are created and commitment and trust are forged, and it is thus the basic social and human act. Ritual brings into being a moral state of affairs, establishes commitment to this state of affairs and to the social order of which ritual is a part. In this way ritual provides the basic conditions specified by Austin that make performatives possible, namely that there should be a conventional procedure with a conventional effect, with acceptance of the one implying acceptance of the other.

The establishment of convention is thus a metafunction of ritual which in its performance legitimises the conventions concerned and brings them into existence. Performing a ritual such as initiation does more than transform a boy into a man, it also establishes and legitimises the existence of a conventional procedure for transforming boys into men. Without the acceptance that participation signals the convention cannot exist as such.

The power of ritual to transform depends also on its ability to communicate meaning, in accordance with social conventions to which the participants subscribe. Given that ritual establishes convention and signals acceptance of this by the performers, the consequences for the specific messages that it conveys are significant. The formality of ritual establishes that these messages are serious and important, it signals acceptance of them and encourages compliance. Ritual's association with supernatural powers may enhance this. The form of the ritual is crucial and constitutes the metamessage concerning the status of what is performed and the relationship of the participant to the performance, but specific meanings are conveyed through the form which effect and constitute specific transformations. The meaning conveyed in ritual makes the performatives explicit and important, and spells out the implications or consequences, producing reflexivity on the part of the performers which translates into perlocutionary force.

As Rappaport's definition implies and his exposition makes clear, the form of ritual is all important, and his analysis is essentially a formal one. While highly suggestive in many respects, the concentration on the formal qualities of ritual means that he neglects questions of change as well as the relationship between ritual and everyday life, including politics and power. Thus Rappaport does not help us to refine Bourdieu's theory of change, unless it is further developed and extended (though it does help us to understand the link between habitus and performance). Some of the material on Xhosa beer drinking in subsequent chapters suggests how this might be done. In chapters six and seven, for example, the empirical material suggests that people can use a conventional ritual procedure to bring about conventional effects of a similar kind to those usually associated with the ritual but applied to a different, new field of activity in which the participants have become engaged as part of a process of change. Here a ritual to welcome a returning traveler or a warrior gets transformed into one to welcome back a migrant worker, on the basis of an analogy constructed between war, travel and migrant work. All involve danger, uncertainty and risk. Such analogical transfer allows people to be creative within the context of convention as part of a habitus responding to changes within a field (Bourdieu 1977). Similarly, a conventional effect can be brought about by using a different conventional procedure from what was used in the past due to the latter becoming redundant, inappropriate or in some way suspect. So, in chapter seven I show how the ritual killing of an animal for the ancestors to welcome home a returned migrant became transformed into a beer drink for the ancestors and the community. Here the analogical transfer is from one kind of conventional procedure to another, with the effect being similar. This suggests a matrix of procedures and effects which are interchangeable to some degree and which can be used innovatively to make new meanings under changed circumstances.

There are other possibilities. Rappaport defines the ritual form as 'more or less' invariant, allowing for changes in both procedure and effect, though he regards such change as infrequent, but he does not stipulate the characteristics of ritual (as Turner does) that enable such changes to take place. We also have to be careful to distinguish the appearance of convention or invariance with actual invariance, since even new rituals, with new meaning as far as the actors are concerned, can be constructed so as to appear to be following a 'traditional' form, as we shall see later. The conventional procedure may become elaborated or contracted or changed to enable it to deal with changed circumstances—yet remain 'conventional'. In this way, as suggested in chapter two, a variety of new kinds of beer drink rituals developed in the Transkei around the early part of the 20th century in response to a variety of changed social and economic factors. Or new procedures may be used or adapted to produce conventional effects and given the characteristics of the old—Tambiah (1985, 128) cites the case of cricket in the Trobriands, so well illustrated in the 1975 film by Gary Kildea and Jerry Leach, *Trobriand Cricket*, where the British game was transformed to produce the same kinds of effects as older kinds of *kayasa* display.

Tambiah (1985) is explicitly concerned with the apparently dual nature of ritual performance as both fixed and invariant in terms of its structure and meaning, and variable in the sense that no two performances of a ritual are the same, given that performance is always linked to a context in which power and interest have to be taken into account. This may further assist in the attempt to specify the mechanisms for change that Bourdieu neglects. In looking at the formal and universal aspects of ritual Tambiah (like Rappaport and others) points out that rituals are commonly structured in certain conventionalized ways and differentiated from 'everyday' activities, involve communal activity that is purposive, directed at a predictable outcome, and that this is activity of a 'heightened' or intensified kind (ibid., 126–29). But rituals are also grounded in culturally specific cosmological constructs (fundamental values and perceptions, or ultimate truths), and it is through the combination of these with the formal aspects of ritual that ritual action becomes performative in character. Ritual acts out beliefs, and beliefs come to life in ritual action. In analysing ritual we need to ask what it is that is being communicated, and why it is that the ritual form is chosen for such communication.

There are three ways in which ritual is 'performative', he claims—in the Austinian sense, in the sense of a multi-media, staged 'performance', and in the sense that it is linked to indexical values, which it invokes. In looking at the conventional or formal nature of ritual Tambiah makes use of Searle's contribution to speech act theory to argue that rituals as performatives are subject to two different kinds of rules—regulative and constitutive (ibid., 135). An example of regulative rules is table manners, which regulate the way in which food is eaten, but the eating of food is logically independent of the rules. Constitutive rules, on the other hand, constitute as well as regulate an activity that is brought into being through the application of the rules. A game of chess or a ritual like marriage would be an example of this. You can eat without table manners, you cannot get married without exchanging marriage vows or play chess independently of its rules. In both cases the establishment and/or constitution of the rules is performative in the first, Austinian sense. As indicated in the chapters that follow, beer rituals may be either regulative (e.g. in relation to co-operative work) or constitutive.

Another characteristic of ritual formality is 'distancing', in that spontaneity and intentionality are restricted. The values and beliefs that are enacted are in the public rather than the private domain, and ritual affirms a public morality and world view rather than allowing for the expression of individual inclinations or emotions. Linked to this is the question of repetition and redundancy in ritual communication, often in the form of 'canonical parallelism'—similarities in successive, symmetrical sequences of the ritual and its information content. This applies to both acts and utterances, basic patterns being repeated over and over again, both within and across rituals, though this does not imply absolute invariance or that context is irrelevant (ibid., 140–41). Together with features such as music and dance this produces a heightened and intense state among the participants, and an intense form of communication. This is the second sense in which ritual is performative, one that Tambiah refers to as 'ritual involution', "an overelaboration and overprolongation of ritual action woven out of a limited number of "technical" devices and stylistic complexes." (ibid., 153). This characteristic of beer rituals will be apparent in later chapters.

This formality cannot be analysed independently of the cosmological notions that it realises and of the social relations that exist between the ritual participants whose participation in the conventional acts and utterances of the ritual constitutes such realization. In asking why ritual has this characteristic we have to return to its semantic content: It is because it both represents the cosmos "and at the same time indexically legitimates social hierarchies" (ibid., 156) (I would prefer 'the structure of social relations' instead of 'social hierarchies' to allow for at least the theoretical possibility of egalitarianism being represented.) He elaborates on this through the notion of indexical symbol, a symbol that both represents an object and is existentially linked to the object that it represents. In ritual, symbols may both represent cosmological ideas and be existentially linked to the participants in the ritual "creating, affirming or legitimating their social positions and powers." (ibid., 156) Such symbols (or icons) are both cultural (representing basic values, norms and attitudes) and pragmatically related to what they represent. Indexicality, which seems to me to be an elaboration on what Turner called the 'polarization of meaning', is the third sense in which ritual can be performative.

In this discussion of indexicality, Tambiah also provides an example of how ritual change and social change are interrelated, consistent with Turner's views on the processual nature of ritual. Without repeating the ethnographic details that he cites, the claim is that under conditions of social change details of ritual form may be innovatively altered, added, omitted or magnified by agents such as ritual officiants, without changing the overall nature of the ritual but producing 'emergent' meanings which "ride on the already existing grids of symbolic and indexical meanings, while also displaying new resonances" (ibid., 161). Innovations do not appear to be riding roughshod over custom, but as the emergent meanings become conventional meanings and new emergent meanings arise over time, significant change can occur.

This seems to me to be another way of speaking of the interaction between Bourdieu's habitus and field, except that it specifies the agents of change more precisely and locates them within the framework of ritual as a performative event in a way similar to that described by Schieffelin (1998) as discussed above. However, it is 'multi-performative', combining all three of the ways in which ritual is performative. The indexical nature of changes made to the ritual form or its conventional procedure means that the performative nature of the form itself is altered to produce outcomes or transformations which are not quite the same as the conventional ones. One might argue, however, that the first two meanings of performative (the indexical and the formal) are in fact inseparable and that indexicality is merely an element of the formal nature of ritual through which it acquires its power. After all, if the formal aspects of ritual always incorporate cosmology then all rituals are indexically (existentially) related to the participants. Nevertheless Tambiah suggests a number of characteristics of ritual that help us to analyse beer drinking rituals in terms of performance, and I shall draw on his insights in following chapters.

Endnotes

1. I am indebted to Chris Houston of Macquarie University, Sydney, for his insightful comments on an earlier version of this chapter.

2. My approach takes up some of Bourdieu's key ideas as outlined below but not others. For example, I am not concerned with classificatory systems or with the logical properties or symbolic structure of rituals in an abstract sense.

3. Some areas, such as Pondoland, were not taken through war but simply annexed, and the amount of land lost by indigenous chiefdoms varied considerably.

4. *Amagqoboka* means 'people with a hole' and is said to refer to the 'hole' opened up in the Xhosa nation by those who adopted Christianity.

5. However, the analysis that I present is not simply a materialist or cultural materialist one since it is not only ecological and/or economic factors that are significant but rather the combination of factors of which these are simply part and in which they do not play a determining role.

6. For a recent collection of articles largely in this vein, see Bryceson (2002).

7. For a recent discussion of the general notion of performance as an approach in social science and the humanities see Brown (2003).

8. Such reviews may be found in Fabian (1990), Drewal (1991) and Bell (1992, 1997).

9. I do not necessarily accept the implications that, according to Bell (1992, 39) follow from this, namely that culture can be defined in terms of performances or that it is through performance that culture as an otherwise abstract notion takes on a concrete dimension. This would not be compatible with a practice approach.

10. In my opinion Brown's (2003) claim that Turner saw ritual performance as manifesting indeterminacy because of its liminal and anti-structural elements is not quite accurate since these elements, contrary to Brown's claim, are usually scripted, part of the ritual form. My interpretation of the problem of indeterminacy in Turner's writing on ritual thus differs from Brown's.

11. For examples of analyses of performance that illustrate this point see Schein (1999), Hoem (1998), Mach (1992) and Cohen (1993).

12. Drewal (1991, 16–18), for example, misunderstands and misrepresents Turner's approach as removing performance from the course of everyday life and presenting ritual as a closed system. Others (e.g. Bell 1992, 41) also mistake Turner's work on ritual and the social drama for a 'culturalist' approach akin to that of Geertz.

4 Characteristics of the Rural Field[1]

In this chapter the nature of Shixini and its people is described, particularly with regard to the contemporary manifestations of the series of historical changes outlined in chapters two and three. In this respect it is necessary to look at the social and economic characteristics of the area, especially labour migration, the nature of rural production, and the co-operative relationships between individual homesteads. I have written in detail about demographic, ecological, economic and social circumstances in Shixini in an earlier work (McAllister 2001), but need to sketch out some of the basic details here as an essential context for the beer drinking rituals with which I am primarily concerned, since these are but part of a rural social field that has been moulded by history and the objective realities of apartheid rule. It is therefore necessary to examine some of the broader characteristics of this field relevant to beer drinking rituals. Once this has been done I shall turn (in the next chapter) to a general discussion aimed at defining beer drinking rituals and then (in chapters six and seven) to one particular type of beer drink associated with labour migration, as a major aspect of historical and apartheid power relations affecting the rural field, to demonstrate the ritual portrayal and effect of these relations in the productive relations between homesteads in the present and how the rural field is intertwined with the wider one of power.

The approximately 5000 people who occupy Shixini and adjoining areas are historically part of the Gcaleka chiefdom, the senior branch of the Xhosa proper (Hammond-Tooke 1975). Shixini is one of the 39 Administrative Areas or wards that make up Gatyana district, also known as Willowvale, together with the town itself and its commonage. Shixini and an adjoining ward, Ntlahlane, make up Jingqi Tribal Authority (Map 3), and the chairman of this Tribal Authority is also Shixini's headman. During fieldwork this was Chief Mandlenkosi Dumalisile,[2] the genealogically senior living representative of the right hand house of Hintsa, who was paramount chief or king (*ukumkani*) of the Xhosa and head of the Gcaleka chiefdom in the early 19th century. The current Gcaleka chief or king, who is also paramount chief of the Xhosa people, lives at Nqadu, some 40 kilometers from Shixini in the same district.

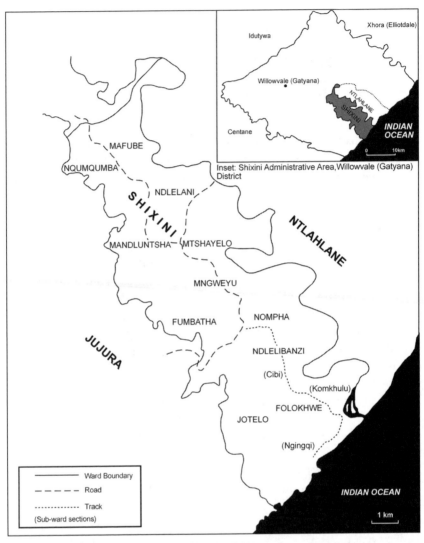

Map 3   Shixini sub-wards and Folokhwe sub-ward sections

Older people in Shixini are culturally conservative and readily identify themselves as Red, as described in the previous chapter (Illustration 1). However, the Red habitus as described earlier became more and more difficult to sustain in Shixini and elsewhere as the South African economy underwent structural changes from about 1960 onwards. Greater employment opportunities and the demand for better educated and skilled workers put a premium on education and regular wage employment. A sharp increase in wages in the mining industry in

1. Shixini women with pipes

the mid-1970s, and the growing demand for more skilled labour, combined with more stringent conditions of employment that prevented migrants from spending long periods at home if they wanted to be sure of obtaining a future contract, put the Red way of life under pressure. By the late 1970s the youth organizations were no longer operating in most Red areas. In Shixini, where not many men went to the mines, the youth organizations effectively ceased to function in about 1980. There were sporadic revivals over the next ten years but these were short lived, and by the mid-1990s were gone, it seemed, for good. However, the senior adult equivalent of the youth organizations called *amatshawuza*, was still in operation in 1998, illustrating the tenacity of Red values among older people.[3]

The economic boom of the 1970s also provided access to a greater variety of employers, while changes in accommodation policy on mines made it more difficult for Red migrants to be housed together. Under these circumstances of long periods in town and short periods at home, greater exposure to urban values and higher wages with which to enjoy what the cities offered, 'encapsulation'—being in but not of the town—and remaining 'country-rooted', became more difficult. Pressures also emanated from rural areas themselves. In Shixini, for example, the local authorities banned attendance at the boys' *umtshotsho* dances in the mid and late 1970s due to the occasional violence that erupted at stick-play, which led to serious injuries, and attempted to enforce school attendance through levying fines on the parents of non-attending pupils.

Gradually both Red and School world views lost their coherence, the latter more rapidly than the former, both giving way in most rural areas to a more secular, urban-influenced way of life. In some areas, however, mainly in coastal Transkei, and including Shixini, the Red world view has left a heritage that remains in evidence today. Although the ideal-type dichotomy between Red and School belongs to an earlier epoch, distinct elements of it remain pertinent and most Shixini people may still be classed as rural conservatives, not in the sense of being politically conservative, but concerned with 'conserving' their rural lifestyle, although education, the churches, consumerism and other forms of westernization have made inroads there as in all parts of the Transkei. Even now, however, most Shixini adults have only three or four years of formal education; many have none at all, and those employed as migrants are almost exclusively in unskilled jobs, primarily in the Western Cape farming sector and in the fishing industry on the west coast. They thus remain strongly oriented towards their rural homes and attached to an agrarian lifestyle.

In Shixini, the ancestor religion is strongly adhered to, and rituals directed at the ancestors are frequent. Christianity is represented primarily in the form of African Independent Churches of the 'Zionist' type, though churchgoers are a small minority, perhaps less than 10% of the population. Among younger people conservatism is not so apparent and some have opted for a life outside of the area at or near employment centres. However, many members of the younger generation value rural life and are committed to long-term involvement in it (McAllister 2001). Since the demise of apartheid in the early 1990s Shixini people have been free to urbanize, but many remain firmly committed to their rural homes and to agrarian life.

Physical features and settlement

Shixini is an area of approximately 80 square kilometers, located in the rugged coastal part of the district, on what tourists know as the Wild Coast. It is climatically and ecologically typical of the Transkei and Eastern Cape's coastal belt, situated in picturesque broken terrain with many steep hills and streams running down to the rivers on its north-eastern and south-western boundaries, rising from sea-level to an altitude of around 300m 15 kilometers inland. Annual rainfall is between 800 and 1000mm per annum, with 70% of this falling

in spring and summer between October and March (Andrew 1992). Poor
transport facilities help to make Shixini relatively remote from the main urban
centres. For most, unreliable and expensive private taxi services are the only
way of getting to and from Willowvale town and in summer the rains often
make the road between Shixini and town almost unusable. Like most other
parts of the Transkei, the area shows evidence of decades of neglect by previous administrations. Facilities of all kinds—educational, medical, etc.—are either absent or inadequate.[4] The first high school in Shixini was established in
2000, and its opening was described as follows in an educational publication:

> The construction of a R3,7-million high school, donated by Shell at
> the request of former president Nelson Mandela, in an area that could
> not even be reached by car this week—unless it's a 4x4—might seem
> a little odd. Indeed, the Shixini administrative area in the heart of
> Gcalekaland, the seat of Xhosa King Xolilizwe Sigcau, does not have
> telephones, nor electricity. The approximately 30 000 residents do not
> have access to clean water, nor is there a clinic in the area. This is
> about as remote as it gets in South Africa.[5]

A few small general stores in Shixini stock only basic necessities,[6] and there
are virtually no public amenities or services. Standards of health are low and
indicators such as infant mortality are high (Simon 1989). Water is collected
primarily from springs and streams, and some care is taken to ensure that toi-
let activities take place downstream from water collection points, though the
latter are frequently fouled by livestock. Fuel is locally gathered firewood and
dried cattle dung, or paraffin oil purchased from the local shops. Housing is
primarily of the mud-brick and thatch variety (Illustration 2), but in recent
years square houses with corrugated iron roofing have sprung up, and a small
proportion of wealthier people have large, western-style houses. Most of the
latter are in the area occupied by the chief in the upper-central part of Shixini.
     The territorial structure of Shixini is important for many reasons and forms
the main basis for the organization of beer drinking rituals. It is a system of
nesting units. There are ten sub-wards within the ward (there were eleven until
the mid-1980s when one was relocated and joined with another to make way
for a plantation), each under a sub-headman (*isibonda*) who acts as interme-
diary between chief and people. The chief is not often directly involved in sub-
ward affairs, though he remains the ultimate arbiter of local disputes and formally in charge of the land. In most of the ten sub-wards, homesteads are
widely scattered in the areas demarcated for residential use (Illustration 3).
Other areas within each sub-ward are set aside for fields and for grazing. Land

2. Homesteads

allocation and control of other natural resources is based on consensus at the level of the sub-ward moot, consisting of all senior males, presided over by the sub-headman, and ratified by the chief.

The sub-ward in which the chief and other members of the political elite live is densely populated and resembles a village, containing a number of shops, the tribal authority building, a building for a clinic (which is sometimes inoperative), a high school (since 2000) and half a dozen or so large, western-style houses. In the other nine of Shixini's ten sub-wards people live in scattered homesteads as they have done for generations rather than in village-type settlements. It is a pattern that makes ecological and economic sense in that it takes advantage of the topography and the distribution of natural resources, given the absence of infrastructure and facilities such as water and sanitation supply, and it provides a modicum of continuity with the pre-colonial situation (see chapter two). In many parts of Transkei (as in the rest of South Africa) rural areas were subjected, in the period 1950–1980, to agricultural 'Betterment' schemes. The deleterious effects of these schemes have been well documented (de Wet 1989; McAllister 1989) and need not be discussed in detail here. The basic idea was to relocate rural people into ordered residential areas, and to divide the land that remained into arable allotments and fenced grazing camps. A scheme of this kind for Shixini was approved by

3. Homestead with byres and gardens

the Transkei government in the early 1980s but was only partly implemented before being challenged and then aborted.

The suspension of the Betterment scheme means that for most of Shixini people the scattered settlement pattern has been retained. In certain parts of the ward, distinct clusters of homesteads in close proximity to each other on a ridge-top are often found, but this does not change the basic principles of land allocation and land use. Such a cluster is called *ummango*, 'a ridge' and it is often also a social unit. Sub-wards are divided into territorial sections or neighbourhood groups (*iilali, iziphaluka*) consisting of one or more *imimango* (ridges). These are informal groupings, which regulate their own affairs at the local level and are recognized by sub-ward residents and the sub-headmen. Many sub-ward sections are further sub-divided into sub-sections, usually consisting of an *ummango*, sometimes two. These territorial groups, especially the sub-ward sections and the sub-wards, play a vitally important role in social and economic life, and they are the primary basis on which both co-operative labour and beer drink rituals are organized and regulated.

Kinship, too, is important in Shixini. The effective kinship group on the ground is a small 'agnatic cluster' (Hammond-Tooke 1984), consisting of perhaps a group of brothers and their immediate families, or a father and two or three sons, each with their own homesteads. Xhosa speakers are pa-

trilineal, but members of the patronymic clan, lineage, and even lineage segment are widely scattered. It is usually only lineage segments that ever come
together as a group,[7] and then primarily in ritual contexts. Apart from this,
kin groups have no corporate existence and no corporate functions. Close
co-operative relations may exist between members of the agnatic cluster, as
it may between other categories of kin who live in a common sub-ward or
sub-ward section, but never to the exclusion of others (non-kin) from such
relationships. In other words, it is their presence as neighbours which is important, and which reinforces the kinship link. This is in accordance with
the way in which rural production changed in the early part of the twentieth century, as described in chapter two. It is against this background of interdependent homesteads located in nesting territorial groups, within which
a variety of kinship links are recognized, that beer consumption needs to be
understood.

Most of the fieldwork for this study was done in three of Shixini's sub-
wards, namely Nompha, Ndlelibanzi and Folokhwe (Map 3). In 1998 these
sub-wards had a total of 1220 people, living in 76, 41 and 77 homesteads respectively, an average of 6,3 per homestead.[8] In these three sub-wards, 54%
of homesteads are headed by men, 46% by women, usually widows. In addition to the substantial number of female household heads, women are in
charge of the daily running of the homestead in cases where a male head is
absent as a migrant worker (Heron and Cloete 1991). Significant for the maintenance of homestead agriculture is the fact that population numbers seem to
have remained fairly static in Shixini over the past two decades, at least (McAllister 2001; Andrew 1992; Heron 1990). This is due largely to permanent out-
migration, especially from the mid-1980s onwards, when the laws restricting
black urbanization were relaxed in some respects, and more recently as a result of the transition from apartheid to democracy.

A characteristic of these three sub-wards, and probably of most of Shixini,
is the relative stability of the population, not only in terms of size, as indicated above, but also in terms of mobility and the absence of immigrants. This
is of significance in understanding the nature of the relationships between
homesteads in Shixini, which are characterized by high levels of trust and reciprocity. The people who live in Shixini have, mostly, lived there for a long
time. In 1998, 70% of homesteads had been established more than 20 years
earlier, and only 19% of them in the previous ten years. Current residents were
the descendants of others who lived on the same site or nearby. Over 80% of
homestead heads' parents had lived on the same site or in the same sub-ward
as the current occupants and an additional 9% had lived close by elsewhere in
Shixini. All but one of the new homesteads built within the previous 10 years

had been established in the same sub-ward as their parents' homesteads, and women who leave to marry virilocally still go primarily to homesteads in the same or nearby wards and seldom marry into another district. This level of continuity and stability is important in understanding the social and economic characteristics of the area. It is probably unusual in the context of rural South Africa, many parts of which underwent extensive social disruption during the apartheid years.

Many of those who have chosen to leave Shixini for urban areas are young adults. Usually these are men or women in paid employment, who have chosen to live at or near their places of work on a permanent or semi-permanent basis, often with spouses and young children. However, a certain proportion of the youth who are away at work as migrant labourers return to Shixini after a number of years, usually once they have married and had their first children, to engage in agrarian activities, either by choice or because of sudden unemployment and/or disillusionment with urban areas. Given the growing problem of unemployment in South Africa (estimated at around 40% over the past ten years), it is possible that this trend will increase, though it is likely that a significant number will prefer to remain in urban areas whether they are able to find work there or not.

Migrant labour and agriculture

No Shixini homestead can survive without some form of cash income, and hardly anyone is able to secure access to significant amounts of cash by selling agricultural produce. Of the total of 194 homesteads in the three sub-wards surveyed in 1998, 80% had access to some cash income, usually in the form of migrant labour earnings and remittances, or social and disability state pensions.[9] The remaining 20% had no access to cash whatsoever, but some of these were able to acquire small amounts of money from time to time when necessary.[10] For Shixini as a whole, the official 1996 census results indicate that 27% of homesteads had no cash income.

Like other rural South Africans, Shixini people depend heavily on goods and services purchased with cash, but the importance of cash income relative to income in kind is not always easy to gauge. Agricultural produce is important for daily subsistence but the land provides, at best, all of a household's vegetable and grain requirements, possibly a small surplus for some, and a supply of meat and milk in a few cases where livestock numbers are adequate for this. The few who own livestock surplus to their needs are able to sell animals for cash on a regular basis, and some obtain a small cash income from the sale of animal products such as wool and meat. Most Shixini homesteads do not produce enough food for domestic consumption. All Shixini people need cash for a range of manufactured food products as well as many other manufactured goods such as clothes, footwear, cooking utensils and agricultural implements, and they need money to pay for transport, medical and school expenses, and so on.

Opportunities for local employment or self-employment are extremely limited, and although there is a wide variety of ways of obtaining some cash on an occasional basis, such income is not nearly sufficient for a household's subsistence needs (see McAllister 2001), except in the case of those who own large numbers of livestock (see below). One of the most common methods of raising money is the purchase and re-sale of alcoholic beverages, or the brewing and sale of a commercial alcoholic drink locally called *mangumba*, but this is used largely only as a way of making some money in an emergency. The costs are high (one has to travel to town to buy the liquor) and most people dislike the idea of their home being seen as a liquor outlet. Only two homesteads in the three sub-wards surveyed in 1998, one in Folokhwe and one in Nompha, sold liquor on a regular basis. Maize beer may also be made for sale, also on an irregular basis, but the only socially acceptable way in which it may be sold is through the convention of a beer drink known as *imbarha*, at which a good portion of the beer must be given out free of charge. It is regarded as a means of obtaining cash in an emergency, and not as something that should be done regularly.[11]

The primary source of cash in Shixini, apart from pension payments, is thus the remittances of migrant workers. Some 60% of homesteads had at least one migrant worker in employment in 1998, and an additional 20% had one or more members who wished to be employed as migrants, some of whom were away seeking work.[12] Most absentee migrants make regular visits home, some twice a year or more. The majority are men and boys and most of the married male migrants are not accompanied to work by their families. The pattern is thus still largely the one established under apartheid rule, namely that of unaccompanied, oscillating, male labour migration. However, many of the younger Shixini migrants have broken with this pattern in recent times and moved to town on a permanent or semi-permanent basis with their immediate families. There is also a growing minority of female migrants, which was unusual until about the late 1980s.

Attitudes towards labour migration, especially among the older generation, are encapsulated in the terms used to refer to the workplace. These have negative connotations and reflect the instrumental nature of migrancy. An absent migrant is said to be 'on an expedition' (*etorweni*), 'at war' (*emfazweni*), 'in service' (*enkonzweni*) or 'at the place of the white man' (*emlungwini*). The implication of such usages is that the workplace is foreign and dangerous, and that entry into it is undertaken only to serve the rural home. Associated with this particular attitude towards migrant labour, as indicated earlier, is a series of ritual actions performed by and for migrant workers on their departure for work and again on their return home. These are described in chapter six.

One of the consequences of this attitude towards migrancy was an attempt to limit involvement in it to what was absolutely necessary, and a characteristic of labour migration in Shixini was that migrants of all ages spent almost as much time at home as they did at work. As indicated earlier, this was a characteristic of the Red Xhosa habitus that developed in the context of colonialism from the late 1800s onwards. From the mid-1970s onwards, however, being Red became more difficult as conditions of service on the mines and in other industries changed, allowing men only short spells at home between contracts, and as jobs in general became scarce. This was not the case in the fishing and agricultural labour markets of the Western Cape, where many Shixini men work, and where relatively long spells at home of around two to three months between labour contracts still seem possible. There is always a proportion of men at home, made up of the chronically unemployed, the temporarily jobless, the retired, the few non-migrants, and those on leave.

Land and livestock

The Shixini landscape, together with observable everyday activities, suggests an agricultural lifestyle and gives the impression that residents practise mixed farming. Despite a heavy dependence on the cash earned as migrants, people place a high symbolic value on both the cultivation of maize and other vegetable crops and the husbanding of livestock. In their minds these activities both provide them with some of the necessities of life and help to define them as rural Xhosa, living the kind of lives that their ancestors lived in the past. Beer drinking rituals are an important component in maintaining this orientation.

Although the cash contributions from migrant workers and pensioners are crucial to sustaining livelihoods, this does not change the self-image of most Shixini residents; on the contrary, it sustains it. Many researchers in southern Africa have illustrated the interdependence between cash income and agricultural production (e.g. Spiegel 1980, Beinart 1992). The local view of migrant labour as a necessary evil justifies wage labour as a means to 'building' the rural homestead, where the term 'building' includes activities such as raising livestock and cultivating the soil. In addition, many migrants are still able to time visits home to co-incide with the period associated with ploughing, planting and the initial cultivation (November–January). The perception of migrant labour as the antithesis of an agrarian lifestyle is also blunted by employment of many migrants in fishing and agricultural enterprises. This places them at the bottom end of the migrant wage scale, with few prospects for improvement or occupational mobility, and it is not surprising that they look to their rural homes and communities for a sense of belonging and meaning.

All homesteads in Shixini have the right to gardens, which adjoin homesteads (see Illustration 3). Since most of the area escaped agricultural Betterment, gardens can be quite large (up to 2 hectares, sometimes larger),[13] their size being limited primarily by the amount of labour and other inputs that the homestead has, as well as by the location and rights of neighbours. Although the majority of homesteads can claim access to a field (usually located at some distance in river valleys), infertility and soil exhaustion means that most fields have to all intents and purposes been abandoned and replaced by gardens, an important adaptive response that has helped to maintain homestead production. The decline in field-use was at least partly compensated for by the higher fertility of gardens and the greater intensity of garden cultivation. Fields were used primarily for maize monoculture, at least in recent years as they became less fertile, whereas gardens are much more suited to intercropping. Since every homestead is entitled to a garden, very few have no arable land.[14] Eighty per cent of homesteads have a large garden adjoining the dwelling site, and a quarter of these have a second, smaller garden as well, sometimes used for early maize and other vegetables but primarily for tobacco. The large gardens are used regularly, primarily for the staple, maize, but a variety of other crops are also grown. Those without gardens, or with small gardens only, are relatively new homesteads which have not yet accumulated enough resources to establish one, but which intend to do so in the future.[15]

Rights of residence are automatically also rights to use the grazing and other resources of the sub-ward in which one lives. Most homesteads own livestock of some kind,[16] though a significant number (35%) do not have any at all. The average number of cattle per homestead in 1998 was 3.5 head, or 6.3 for those homesteads having cattle. This is slightly higher than for the coastal half of the adjoining district of Xorha/Elliotdale (ARDRI 1989) and for the Transkei as a whole, where the average cattle owner has six head (Porter and Phillips-Howard 1997). Sheep and goats are also not plentiful and, like cattle, they are unevenly distributed. The average number of goats and sheep per homestead was eight and six respectively. While Shixini people feel that they require more cattle, homesteads are now much smaller than they used to be and current

4. Storing maize

population levels in relation to available grazing would probably not permit a large increase in the number of livestock. Combining cattle for purposes such as ploughing and transport makes the best use of available cattle without putting undue pressure on other resources.[17] Cattle are the most commonly owned type of livestock; almost all ploughing is done by ox-draught and the most common means of local transport is by ox-drawn sled. In addition, oxen are killed in all major ancestral rituals, goats in more minor ones, providing occasional large supplies of high quality protein.

One crop of maize, the staple food, is produced annually during summer (Illustration 4). Few homesteads have the resources to plough and plant their gardens by themselves, and rely on their membership of co-operative work groups to get these tasks done (see below). Once the maize plants have developed to a height of about 10 cm., it is necessary to remove the weeds by hoe or, if planted in rows with a planter, by ox-drawn mechanical cultivator. A second hoeing is required about eight to ten weeks later, depending on rainfall. If there are two or three members of the household available to hoe, each period of hoeing may last for a number of weeks. Frequently, the homestead does a portion of the hoeing with its own labour and organises a work-party to complete the task. Subsidiary crops such as pumpkins, melons, calabashes, cowpeas, beans, sweet potatoes, and others are planted in the spaces between

5. Harvesting

the maize plants and in vacant parts of the garden, and also in the smaller garden. Maize and other vegetables are consumed directly from the fields as soon as they are ready, but the bulk of the maize crop is allowed to dry on the stalks before it is harvested in early winter (May–June) (Illustration 5).

The tempo and ethos of life in Shixini is primarily agricultural. In ploughing season attention is focused on the weather and crop prospects, on the amount of rain that has fallen or is expected, and much discussion revolves around this and other matters agricultural. Preparatory activities include the repair of fences, the readying of equipment and making arrangements for co-operative ploughing. Social activities at this time also revolve around cultivation. No beer drink or ritual may commence till mid-day, when those who labour in the land stop work, and many beer drinks that take place are held to reward agricultural 'companies' for assistance with ploughing and planting. During the growing season (December to March) most people are pre-occupied with their gardens, hoeing, planting subsidiary crops, thinning out maize plants, and setting their dogs on errant pigs. Livestock owners have to ensure that their animals are well tended and do not destroy crops, and many men and boys spend the days out in the grazing lands herding their animals, taking advantage of their proximity to forest and bush to cut poles or branches for building purposes, collect medicinal plants, and forage for edible wild-foods and other useful items.

The appearance and fertility of gardens evokes frequent comment and comparison. In May 1996, for example, people were excited about the large crops about to be harvested and many were busy constructing new granaries. Talk inevitably turned to those with very good harvests—the number of people required to help in the fields, the size of the granaries, the number of sleds of maize brought in from the garden, and the amount of beer that was going to be brewed later. Shortly after the harvest there is a flurry of beer drinking activity as people brew 'beer for the harvest', to give thanks to the ancestors for what they have received, and to publicly recognize the assistance of those who did the ploughing and harvesting. During the fallowing period, gardens are extended, fences repaired, and manure transported from the cattle byre to the garden and left there to be ploughed into the ground during the first turning of the soil in the new season. In the past this was also the time for building new huts, repairing or replacing livestock byres, and for rituals, including male circumcision. This is still partly the case but now many rituals are conducted around December-January, when migrants who work in town return for their annual holiday.

That agriculture is important to local subsistence is indicated by maize yields, which in good years are comparable with the average per hectare yields of dry-land commercial farmers in South Africa's 'maize triangle' and make a substantial contribution to the food requirements of at least some households (McAllister 2001). In addition to maize, there are many other crops grown which are used almost exclusively for household consumption.

Co-operative work

Homestead production is possible in Shixini largely because of the dense network of relationships between homesteads, involving collaboration and interaction in a variety of agricultural and other activities, including co-operative work groups. Labour co-operation takes place within the territorial framework outlined above, and is perceived by people as a manifestation of Xhosa custom and tradition, and as an aspect of their rural Xhosa identity. Individual homesteads put their animals together in joint herding arrangements; they organize work parties to overcome shortages of labour, implements and oxen, and they assist each other reciprocally in a variety of small but significant ways on a day-to-day basis. Labour combinations are also a means of re-distribution, and to some households providing labour for others is an important (though always partial) means of securing subsistence, as well as of ensuring reciprocal labour at some time in the future.

It is at the level of the sub-ward and its sections that virtually all everyday economic and political activity takes place. Control of land (homestead sites, grazing, arable allotments, etc.) is exercised at the section level, and decisions and allocations ratified by the sub-ward as a collectivity under the sub-headman, and then by the chief. Sections are also important in ritual and ceremonial matters and in law. Senior male members of the section constitute a court or moot for the purpose of resolving local disputes and hearing cases involving minor local misdemeanors, while more serious matters go to the sub-ward moot, from where they may be referred to the Tribal Authority. Sections are, in effect, closely knit neighbourhood groups, which play a vital role in many aspects of the social and economic life of any individual homestead. This structural relationship between individual homestead and wider territorial community is mirrored in beer drinking rituals, as we shall see. At the larger work parties in particular, it is at the beer drink that follows the work that participation is dramatized and the experience of labour placed within a wider social and ideological context.

The individual homestead is the basic unit of production, and productive activity is carried on by households for their own individual benefit, but with the help of extra-domestic labour provided by others. As indicated in chapter two, relations of production within the individual household, based on factors such as age and gender and shaped by social norms, rights and obligations, became inadequate to meet subsistence requirements as homesteads declined in size over time and their composition changed. Everyday tasks are performed largely by its resident members, but some of the chores associated with daily work may also be done collectively, either with the informal help of a small group of neighbours or through recruiting a larger and more formal work party. Those collectively performed tasks which involve female labour include cutting thatching grass, collecting firewood (especially if a large amount is required for a ritual), making mud-bricks and harvesting. Male labour is required for collectively cutting poles, constructing huts, byres or fences, and for ploughing and planting (which are usually done together) (Liebenberg 1997, Heron 1990). Work parties performing tasks such as hoeing commonly involve both male and female labour. Hoeing to clear weeds from a field or garden is in fact the most common form of collective labour in Shixini (Illustration 6), along with ploughing and planting, with harvesting, cutting poles and cutting thatching grass not far behind these in frequency.

6. Work party

To organize a small, co-operative, neighbourhood-based work group a homestead has to ask for assistance, and the resulting group is called an *isicelo* (a 'request'). To hold an *isicelo*, a homestead head goes herself/himself or sends someone else to ask neighbours to come and assist with a particular task, also notifying them of the nature of the reward. The latter may be a small amount of maize-beer, but more frequently it is *mangumba*, made overnight from shop-bought ingredients.[18] Or the reward may consist of some other commodity or combination of commodities such as paraffin oil, meat, or sugar, or non-alcoholic *marhewu*. The reward offered is not regarded as a payment, but as a necessary incentive, provided "so that they do not get hungry, since they have come to help".

Not every close neighbour is necessarily asked to participate. As in the Mpondo case (Kuckertz 1985), the head approaches people whom he/she is on good terms with and who will be expected to help. Failure to heed the request to assist without a very good reason would be a breach of friendship and neighbourliness. Such work has to be rewarded: "The person I hoed for will be expected to hoe for me, but this does not mean that she should be asked to hoe without reward!" In terms of the ideology of mutual helpfulness (*ukuncedana*) or neighbourliness (*ubumelwane*, which literally means 'supporting each other') assistance is given to people with whom one has some kind of actual relationship based on friendship, neighbourhood, kinship, or obligation.

A somewhat different way of securing labour through the provision of material goods is to make a commodity (such as meat) available, and to invite people of the neighbourhood to partake of it in return for labour, either immediately for a specific task, or at a later date. There are well-established conventions relating the amount of goods taken to the number of days of labour payment. The difference between this form of work and an *isicelo*, based on a request for help, is that no individual neighbour is personally asked to volunteer labour. Instead, an invitation is made; those who are approached or who hear of it indirectly and who feel like doing so will take it up. However, this is more than simply accepting a payment for labour service, it is also a friendly neighbourly act which people expect from those with whom they have a close relationship and which they regard as deserving of reciprocation at a later date. As with *isicelo*, the basis of the relationship is clearly more than simply material, but the material element is necessary for the transaction. Thus long-term reciprocity on the basis of neighbourhood, kinship or friendship co-exists with short-term reciprocity—the exchange of labour for goods. People who offer their labour under such circumstances are said to demonstrate *isintu* (human kindness) indicating the presence of a moral element; *isintu* also means human-ness in the sense of human custom or culture, and carries a connotation of moral rightness. It is similar to the well-known concept *ubuntu*, the abstract quality of humanity, of being a proper, upright human being.

On rare occasions, workers are employed for a cash wage, but this is well below the cash value of the goods offered in the exchanges of commodities for labour.[19] A cash transaction carries no further obligations on the part of either employer or worker, but as we have seen above, exchanges of goods for labour are governed by a moral norm which stresses obligation and reciprocity, on the one hand, and a material reward for labour, on the other. Both parties can assume that there will be a balancing out in the medium or long term, at least, and therefore it is more 'profitable' to offer a commodity such as paraffin in return for labour than it is to offer a cash wage.

The other disadvantage of engaging wage labour is that it signals that the transaction is a western-style, commercial one, not associated with reciprocity. In this it is contrary to the general ethic of mutual helpfulness. As in pre-industrial Britain, cash payments signify the absence of a moral relationship. To give cash in return for favours or assistance was insulting because "with beer one thanks, but with money one pays" (Harrison 1971, cited in Adler 1991,

389). In non-wage transactions in which labour is rewarded with some kind of commodity, Shixini people are at pains to stress that the reward is not a payment. This is symbolized at work parties for hoeing, as Heron has pointed out, when the workers deliberately leave a patch of the garden or field un-weeded for the homestead to do itself. If the beer or other reward provided was a payment, they say, the homestead head would be entitled to demand that they complete the job. Leaving a patch un-weeded symbolizes the fact that they are not hired labourers and that they were 'just helping' (Heron 1990, 108).

One of the more important forms of co-operative work in Shixini is what is colloquially known as the 'agricultural company' (*inkampani yokulima*). This consists of from four to twelve homesteads, which combine their labour, implements and draught cattle to perform agricultural tasks such as ploughing, planting and, to a lesser extent, harvesting. Most homesteads belong to one of these companies, though there are a few who do not, either because they do not cultivate, or because they prefer to work independently and are wealthy enough to do so. As with the request for help (*isicelo*), these groups operate on the basis of notions of reciprocity and co-operativeness. In one sense the reciprocal element is both short-term and quite strictly adhered to, in that work such as ploughing is done for each member in turn every season, and a member who fails to contribute as expected, for no good reason, can be expelled from the group. In another sense, however, reciprocity is longer-term, in that resource imbalances are recognized and may have to be tolerated within the company for many years. No beer is brewed when company members come together to work at the request of a member, though their contribution to the homestead is recognized when it brews 'beer for harvest' later in the season (see chapter 11). If they work on behalf of a non-member, however, the latter must brew for them.

Some of these companies seem to be based primarily on agnation, with the members of a local agnatic cluster belonging to a single company. Such companies may be conceived of in terms of kinship solidarity and the obligation of kin to help each other. Most companies, however, include members of a variety of agnatic clusters and clans within a common locality. The members of an agricultural company, whether they are agnates or not, are almost always drawn from a single sub-ward section or sub-section.[20] The effective basis of recruitment to companies is thus locality rather than agnation, since agnates within a common territory do not necessarily plough together, and agnates living in different areas cannot do so, for practical reasons. Other kin are also commonly members of a company, but since most residents of any one section can trace some kind of kinship connection with each other, this is not surprising. Long term imbalances in terms of the contribution made by members are found in many companies, with the non-contributing members being 'carried' by the others. Such members may or may not be agnatically related to the other members of the company, but they are always drawn from the same sub-ward or sub-ward section.

So perhaps these companies are best characterized as being of diverse composition; some consist only of kin, in which case membership and activities are characterized by a kinship ideology; in other cases they consist of members of a variety of agnatic groups and include non-kin. In this case, the ethic of mutual helpfulness need not rest on an idiom of kinship but is more general and based on reciprocity and good-neighbourliness. In both cases, membership is recruited from the immediate sub-ward, usually exclusively from the sub-ward section, and in this sense they are neighbourhood groups.

The companies are relatively enduring and their membership remains stable from year to year, though changes occur when companies split due to becoming too large or for some other reason such as conflict. Occasionally, new members are accepted into a company or an existing member leaves to join another. Not all companies have acknowledged leaders but are based instead on consensus among the majority of members, especially those who make significant inputs in terms of cattle and labour (which in many cases includes all the members). In other cases a prominent or wealthy man is seen as the leader of the company, and the company in a sense forms around him. It is in such companies that dependent members are most likely to be found; people who have little to contribute but their political loyalty to the head plus some labour in times of weeding and harvest. Members who make very little contribution to the company's resources usually have little choice about the timing of their cultivation, and must usually wait until the other members have done their own land.

So although recruitment takes place, in statistical terms, from within sub-wards and sections, the actual networks of co-operation in ploughing groups reflect a variety of other factors, based on mutual interest, individual resources, friendship, individual ability, past experience of working together, reputation, political allegiance, and so on (see Holy 1977). The moral norm that kin ought to plough together, for example, is modified in a variety of ways by practical and social considerations, such as the actual distribution of labour, oxen and implements, or by relationships of close friendship or antagonism between kin. Relationships within the group, for example, depend in part on the resource contributions they make rather than on their kinship relations, as some of Heron's case-studies show (Heron 1990). In entering into arrangements of this kind, individuals are not simply acting in terms of norms associated with kinship and neighbourhood, but also pursuing the practical strategy of developing their homesteads, a topic which is of crucial importance in understanding both work and the beer drinking associated with it.

The need for agricultural companies arises for a number of reasons, both ecological and material. The optimum time for ploughing and planting is limited to a few weeks at the beginning of each season. Heron (1990) has shown that once allowance is made for all the days on which this work is not possible due to weather and soil conditions, or not allowed by cultural ones, there remain relatively few days on which to get the ploughing and planting done in the three-month period from October to December when this work is normally done. Shortages of oxen, implements and labour make it necessary for people to pool their resources and to plough and plant each other's land in rotation if cultivation is to take place at all in most gardens. It is on this basis that the companies are formed, and on which they split, either because they grow too large to rotate the work effectively, or because of dissatisfaction or disagreement about the order of work in relation to the relative contributions made (ibid.). This is a crucial point in the agricultural season, and the importance of optimal ploughing and planting creates a certain amount of pressure and tension (ibid., Gulliver 1971).[21]

Herding groups are usually composed of neighbouring homesteads that also belong to the same agricultural company (in small companies the overlap with the herding group may be complete). These homesteads pool their livestock for herding purposes, and for dipping, in the case of cattle, thereby economizing on labour.[22] The animals leave their individual byres each day and are herded to the grazing areas, where the herdsman (often a young boy) keeps watch on them until it is time to return again in the afternoon. This is particularly important in the growing season, when a few cows astray in someone's garden can wreck the maize crop in a very short space of time, and cause serious conflict between neighbours.[23]

Agricultural companies or parts thereof may assist each other on an informal basis, and sometimes two companies which were once one have a standing agreement to call on each other in times of need. Alternatively, a homestead may brew beer and ask a number of companies to assist it with cultivation. This is called an *umgqibelo*[24] group, and it is usually composed of companies drawn from the same sub-ward section, almost invariably from within the sub-ward. The homestead head making the request may or may not be a member of one of the companies involved. Usually the task is to plough and plant the homestead's field or garden in one day of intensive work, thus enabling it to take advantage of favourable conditions. Between some small companies (usually only two) there is an agreement to form such a group on a reciprocal basis on behalf of any individual member of the companies involved. In such cases beer is not brewed. Should they require a third company, however, or be called by someone not a member of the companies,

or involve companies that do not have such an agreement, the person making the request must brew beer for the group. In some cases the beer drink
takes place immediately after the completion of the task; in others it takes
place some weeks later.

Agricultural companies and their combination into *umgqibelo* are specialized
work groups in that they involve the use of cattle for a limited number of tasks.
There are two other, non-specialized work-parties, involving generalized appeals
for assistance rather than requests to individuals, and of a larger scale than the
work arrangements discussed above. Both types involve *amandwandwa*, literally
'precious things' (Kropf 1915, 90), the term used to describe the workers, and
must be accompanied by maize beer. Other food is usually also provided. The
smaller of the two is called *indwandwa yekhaya* (home or section work group)
or, more commonly, a 'congress' (*ikongresi*, lit: 'a gathering').[25] It is recruited
from the local sub-ward section or from more than one section where such sections have an agreement to call on each other for work-party purposes. This is
the case of Ngingqi and Komkhulu sections of Folokhwe sub-ward, for example, and a Ngingqi man may ask part of Komkhulu as well as Ngingqi people to
join his 'congress'. The background to this is that Ngingqi is relatively small and
was once part of Komkhulu until it split off to form a separate section.

The larger type is called an *indwandwa yelali* (sub-ward work group) or
simply *indwandwa* (Heron 1990). In this case all sections of the sub-ward are
called on for help. The announcement that assistance will be required is made
at some public gathering such as a beer drink. The size of these groups (about
fifteen to twenty people for an *ikongresi*, thirty or more for an *indwandwa*) is
also related to the amount of beer provided. The smaller event requires around
sixty or seventy litres, the larger 120 litres or more. As with other beer drinks,
word soon gets around how much beer is being prepared, and larger quantities attract more workers as well as more non-workers to the subsequent beer
drink. These work parties may be called for tasks such as cutting thatching
grass, hoeing, fencing, harvesting, and so on, but the commonest is for weeding. As with ploughing groups, although the pool from which workers are recruited may be defined in formal terms, participation in a work group is related to the actual relationships between people, based on close friendship,
mutual interest and reciprocal obligation.

What becomes evident from the above is that labour in Shixini, most of
which is directed at agricultural tasks, is initiated by individual homesteads
but dependent on assistance from others, almost invariably neighbours (who
may include close kin) within the sub-ward or, more frequently, within the
sub-ward section. This is explicitly conceptualized in terms of *ukuvana*
(friendliness or mutual sympathy/ understanding), mutual helpfulness and

good neighbourliness, and is based on an exchange in which labour reciproc-ity features prominently. People who live together in the same local area help each other and share resources with each other on a reciprocal basis, to the benefit of each individual household.

To conclude, co-operative work and the morality on which it is based is an important aspect of the practice of Shixini people, based on a habitus that op-erates within the rural social field and in terms of which labour is associated with collective well-being as well as with the survival of individual homesteads. Beer drinking is a vital component of this, often directly linked to co-operative endeavors, as indicated above. But every beer drink, whether associated with co-operative work groups or not, is homologous with this pattern of labour co-operation, acts out important principles of reciprocity and mutual assistance, indicating and constituting an interdependence between homesteads without which few would survive. This theme is developed in detail in the chapters that follow.

Endnotes

1. This chapter is a highly condensed version of chapters 2–5 of McAllister (2001), to which readers are referred for greater detail on the social, economic, demographic, eco-logical and agricultural characteristics of Shixini, and on the organization of co-operative work groups.

2. Ntlahlane has its own headman.

3. *Amatshawuza* are senior men who hold regular dance meetings attended by their lovers and other adult, unattached women. Both men and women dress in traditionalist, Red-style finery, including elaborate beadwork, and spend a weekend dancing, beer drink-ing and discussing issues of mutual interest. The meeting also functions as a way of rais-ing money for the person who sponsors it.

4. Until 2000 there were three junior schools and one junior-secondary school in the ward, but no senior (high) school, to serve a population of some 4800 people. Medical fa-cilities were limited to two clinics staffed by nurses, with occasional visits by doctors from town, but these seem to have ceased operating by 2000. The nearest hospitals are two to three hours by motor vehicle from Shixini, in the adjoining districts of Centane, Elliotdale (Xorha) and Butterworth (Gcuwa).

5. *The Teacher*, 22 February, 2000. The figure of 30,000 population is grossly overesti-mated, and there are, in fact, a few telephones in the area, mainly at trading stores.

6. This includes products such as maize and maize products (samp, mealie meal), flour, sugar, tinned foods, patent medicines, household utensils, paraffin oil, some building ma-terials such as windows and doors, and clothing.

7. Except in the case of small and relatively localised lineages, where it is possible for all members to come together.

8. Figures such as these are approximate because the number of homesteads changes constantly and it is not always clear whether a homestead without occupants has died out or is still viable.

9. Old age pensions in 1998 were R520, approximately US$50 at the exchange rate at the time.

10. Through selling their labour locally, brewing beer for sale, or selling livestock.

11. Nevertheless, there are two or three female-headed households that seem to brew *imbarha* more frequently than others, but this frequency is too low (about twice a year) and the amounts of money made too small, around R100-R150 (US$10–15) each time, to be regarded as a significant means of obtaining cash income.

12. Many of these were people who had recently lost their jobs, with 37% of homesteads reporting members who had become unemployed due to retrenchment, dismissal, ill health or old age.

13. The average size of arable land holdings in the Transkei is 1.5 hectares (Porter and Phillips-Howard, 1997). Holdings in Shixini are much larger than 2 hectares if one includes fields, but since fields are hardly used this would be misleading.

14. In 1998, 8% of homesteads had no arable land, largely due to their positions at the beginning or towards the end of the household developmental cycle.

15. There are also a few homesteads that have undergone decline following the death of the male head and the emigration of younger members, leaving perhaps only an elderly woman in residence, which no longer cultivate and have abandoned their gardens. Some of them lack the labour and other resources to do so, and subsist primarily on old-age pensions; others do not rule out the possibility of creating gardens in the future.

16. Livestock ownership is erratic and fluctuating. Disease and the use of livestock in rituals and bridewealth payments are the main reasons for the absence of cattle, sheep and goats from the byres of some homesteads; others may receive numbers of livestock in the future through, for example, incoming bridewealth, or the cash income from a migrant worker.

17. Botanical surveys in Shixini by students and staff of the Department of Botany at Rhodes University have demonstrated that grasses are, in general, not seriously overgrazed (Burchmore 1988).

18. Strictly speaking, *mangumba* is not beer, which is brewed from maize and called *utywala* or *umqombothi*.

19. A day's work in 1998 was worth R5 (US$0.50) if paid for in cash, but R9 if paid in paraffin (5 bottles or 3,75 litres per day), R10 in tobacco (approx. 700 grams), R12 in dried beans (1 small tin-full—approx. 1 kg.), R12,50 in pork, R12,80 in maize (2 billy-cans full, or 4 kg.), and R17,35 in sugar (4 small tins-full or 5 kg.).

20. Occasionally they include a member from an adjoining sub-ward, but this is rare and usually due to the voluntary re-settlement of a member (or his son, since membership is partly hereditary).

21. Conflict and tension is perhaps more likely to occur where there is a lack of formal cultivating groups and homesteads have to compete with each other for labour, as among the hoe-cultivating Ndenduli (Gulliver 1971).

22. Five sub-wards in the lower half of Shixini share a single dipping tank, and cattle have to be driven to the dipping area and back on dipping days.

23. Many of these details on co-operative labour in Gatyana, collected between 1976 and 1998, are surprisingly like those recorded for the Mpondo by Hunter (1936), based on fieldwork in the 1930s, and for the Xhosa and Mfengu people who were the subject of the Keiskammahoek rural survey, fieldwork for which was conducted in the late 1940s (Wilson et al 1952). In both cases work parties were based primarily on locality, participation implied reciprocity of some kind, and reliance on them was extensive. Kin would be in-

vited to attend if they lived nearby, but the obligation to assist kin was no greater than that to assist neighbours. Rotational ploughing and planting among an enduring group of neighbouring households was common in both Keiskammahoek and Pondoland, and other work parties were organized for cutting grass, collecting firewood, and similar tasks. The reward was beer for the larger groups, in which non-workers shared, but meat or other food was sometimes provided for an ordinary work party (*ilima*), especially in Christian households where beer was prohibited.

24. The term is derived from *ukugqiba*, 'to complete' or 'to finish', and in non-work party contexts *umgqibelo* means Saturday, which ends the working week.

25. Other terms used to describe this group are *umtabata*, which Kropf (1915, 401) defines as "a number of people who club together to work in a garden", and *igxabaxu*.

5 Ritual Beer Drinking, Other Drinks and Other Rituals

Beer plays an extremely important part in Shixini life, as it does, or did, among other Bantu speakers in South Africa. Many of the characteristics of beer in Africa, sketched in chapter two, are found in Shixini today, but there are certain distinctive features that need to be mentioned. The political context within which beer drinking occurs is also, as indicated in chapter three, distinctive and important.

Most social events in Shixini, whether of an economic, ritual or festive nature, are marked by the brewing and consumption of beer. This does not mean, however, that beer has the same significance or plays the same role whenever it is drunk, or that all Shixini events at which there is beer should be called 'beer drinks' or 'beer rituals' (terms I use interchangeably). However, any one event at which beer is present must be understood in relation to the range of events at which beer is found, because each of these carries something of the meaning of the others. It is therefore important, if we are to consider beer drinks as a distinctive category, to indicate the key features of other rituals, because some of these features are invoked at beer drinks, creating metaphorical associations between them. Similarly, any one type of beer drink must be understood within the context of the general category 'beer drinks'. In addition to this, the 'meaning' of beer must be related to the everyday realities of those who participate in them, interpreted in terms of the particular social context in which it is used. This will become clear in later chapters. In this section, an attempt is made to outline Shixini people's attitudes towards beer, compare it with other alcoholic and non-alcoholic drinks, illustrate the range of situations in which beer is used, and define 'beer drinks' as a class of events distinguishable from the other social occasions at which beer is present. An outline of different kinds of beer drinks will also be provided.

After maize beer, the commonest alcoholic drinks in Shixini are *mangumba* and brandy. *Mangumba*, which in other parts of the Transkei is called *jabulani*, is easily made from processed, packaged ingredients bought from the local shop. It is ready to drink after about 24 hours, in contrast to maize beer, which takes from five to eight days to brew. Many people dislike it and say that it is highly intoxicating and leaves one with an unpleasant hangover. It is sometimes brewed by women to reward those who make up a small hoeing party or other kind of small work group, and informants often referred to *mangumba* as "merely something for hoeing". A few women, all widows or deserted by their husbands, make *mangumba* on a regular basis and sell it in their homes. It is bought and drunk without formality or ceremony, quite unlike the sale of beer, which is highly formalised. *Mangumba* "has no *umthetho*"—i.e. it is not drunk according to customary rules. *Mangumba* is not used in any ritual contexts, or for public events of any kind other than small, informal work parties.

Of the commercial alcoholic beverages, brandy is the most highly prized, although other spirits, fortified wines and bottled beer (*ibiya*) are also bought. Some of these, chiefly brandy and beer, are sold by local women, who obtain supplies from the bottle-store in Willowvale town. Brandy is purchased chiefly for occasions like the arrival and departure of important visitors, payments or gifts to some local official, or when one wants to reciprocate for a favour received. Brandy is also of some ritual significance and is used, for example, in bridewealth negotiations, male initiation ceremonies, and rituals associated with labour migration. When brandy is drunk, it is distributed tot by tot in a formal, ceremonial manner, modelled on the way in which beer is distributed. The first drops from a bottle are poured onto the hearth, or onto the floor of the cattle byre, in a manner similar to the offering of beer to the ancestors at certain rituals. Tots are distributed in order of seniority, and the last portion of the bottle is reserved for elders, as is the case with beer. Whenever one has brandy in the home, close neighbours are invited to come and partake of it. The difference between beer and brandy, however, is considerable. The one is *utywala besiXhosa* (Xhosa liquor), the other *utywala besilungu* (white people's liquor). Beer is cheap, regularly available in large quantities, with a low alcohol content and high food value. Brandy is expensive, therefore relatively scarce, and highly intoxicating. Beer is the only drink that is regarded as both alcoholic beverage and food. Although brandy has been incorporated into Xhosa life and values, and into certain rituals, it is beer that features most frequently in social and ritual contexts of all kinds.

People in Shixini love to drink maize beer, and do so frequently in large quantities (Illustration 7). The whereabouts of beer, its quality, quantity, or its scarcity, is a frequent topic of conversation. At festive events such as an *umgidi* (large feast) associated with male initiation, large amounts of beer are present and people may spend three or four days there, returning home only

7. Drinking beer

when the beer is finished. Because of its low alcoholic content it is possible to drink beer in large quantities, and one way of praising someone is to comment on his or her beer drinking ability. Yet the fact that it is alcoholic, while seldom producing intoxication, means that it is different from everyday food and drink and must be handled carefully. The many conventions governing its consumption testify to this.

Brewing beer 'for people' indicates one's humanity and generosity: "If you are a [proper] man you cannot say 'I have no maize' and drive people away from your homestead. Similarly, you cannot be stingy with beer. If it is there, it must be distributed." Furthermore, beer must be consumed in a socially approved manner. At a beer drink in Ndlelibanzi, the younger brother of the local shopkeeper came driving past in his truck, having been making deliveries in Folokhwe. Seeing men gathered together and drinking beer, the young man stopped the truck, jumped out, and went over to the nearest beaker, taking it from the man holding it and helping himself to a drink. The response was muted (due to his association with the shop) but revealing. There was much clicking of tongues and shaking of heads; some people called out comments like: 'Who do you think you are?' and 'You are at a beer drink now fellow!' Another called him an *irhumsha* (turncoat, traitor to the Xhosa lifestyle). He left. Clearly, this was not the way things were done. Beer is not something brewed 'just to drink', like *mangumba*, but something in which people have 'rights' and which must be drunk according to certain conventions or 'rules' (*imithetho*), in a very loose sense of the term.

Brewing beer is regarded as essential for the well-being and prosperity of the homestead and its inhabitants. In using the homestead as a unit of analysis I do not assume that its different members are in total or continuous harmony with each other or that individual members do not act out of self-interest. The interests of different members may be significant and differ along the lines of gender, age (seniority) and kinship affiliation (Holtzman 2001). Nevertheless, and one might even argue *because* of this, there is also a common interest in the homestead's prosperity, and much co-operation between homestead members in terms of daily labour, agricultural tasks, livestock husbandry, and so on. I therefore regard the homestead as a "collective subject" (Bourdieu 1998, 70), which is reinforced by its status as an important emic category, which men often refer to in their oratory at beer drinks: "There are two things that a homestead needs—blood [ritual killings] and maize, with which to brew beer. There is no third thing." Brewing indicates the homestead head's good character and spirit (*umphefumlo*), and that the homestead is part of the community. "A homestead without the smell of maize sediment is no good...".

As in other parts of Africa (see chapter two) there is a social and moral obligation on every Shixini homestead to brew beer at regular intervals, and often the sole reason given for brewing is: "We have not brewed for a long time". In brewing the homestead demonstrates its generosity, converting economic into symbolic capital, though self-interest is not consciously articulated. The ideology of brewing is probably a case of what Bourdieu calls 'misrecognition', since brewing beer is always thoroughly euphemised as "I felt in my heart that I should brew..." or some similar sentiment, and actors brew out of a sense of obligation in terms of what he calls the "sincere fiction of disinterested exchange" (1990, 112) or the logic of 'disinterest' (Swartz 1997, 90). As a rural Xhosa one is required to brew; it is part of the habitus and the actors are not conscious of any return in a material or non-material sense except in the case of beer for sale. I found no evidence that Shixini people felt that a beer drink brought a certain status to the holder, however temporary. Of course, as much of the argument in this book illustrates, it is in the political and economic interest of the host to brew because in brewing he/she shows acceptance of the importance of the community and of the reciprocal ties that bind people and through which economic life would not be possible.

The holding of beer drinks is thus said to 'build' the homestead (*ukwakh' umzi*), and 'building' has at least three meanings. Firstly, the homestead must be 'built' in a material sense, and the blessings of the shades, secured partly through beer drinks, are needed to ensure successful work-spells, good harvests, healthy herds, etc. 'Building' also has a social meaning, in that by brewing and providing beer for people, the homestead acknowledges its membership of a wider community and makes explicit the values of good neighbourliness and mutual co-operation and affirms its place within a social network upon which it depends for its social and economic existence. Thirdly, 'building' also has a religious meaning; a homestead is 'built' by doing whatever is necessary to en-sure ancestral favour, and this includes brewing beer for communal consump-tion. Beer is closely associated with the ancestors, who liked to drink it while they were alive and must therefore be offered it by the living. It is metaphori-cally spoken of as *ubulawu* (medicine of the home), a liquid with sacred prop-erties used at many ancestor rituals, and it may be used as a substitute for *ubu-lawu* in certain ritual contexts. All beer drinks are religious in the sense that the ancestors are thought to want their descendants to brew and to partake of beer 'in spirit'. Some, as we shall see, have more specifically religious motives.

Beer drinking rituals—a distinctive genre?

What makes it possible to speak of 'beer drinking' rituals, and to argue that events so named share common defining features? Since beer is a common feature of most rituals, this question is not easy to answer, and it is sometimes difficult to discern hard and fast boundaries between the different kinds of rit-uals involving beer in Shixini. Nevertheless, making the attempt helps to throw some light on the events that I am concerned with. A 'beer drink', as the term is used in this book, is *a public event, complete in itself, held in an individual homestead and for a particular purpose, at which beer is the central element and is distributed and consumed in a formally prescribed manner according to a set of social conventions.* In attempting to define beer drink rituals in this way as a particular category I attempt to discriminate between the different events as-sociated with beer and avoid referring to all of these as beer drink rituals, un-like, for example, Karp's discussion of Iteso 'beer parties' which include a wide variety of ritual and social events including various mortuary rituals, wed-dings, the celebration associated with the birth of twins, work parties, and so on (Karp 1980).

To elaborate, beer drinks are open to all adult members of the local com-munity as well as to visitors from more distant areas who happen to be pres-ent in the area. Children, youths, newly married women and young men who have not yet been admitted to beer drinks, may not attend, though they are present and involved during the preparation, and receive an allocation once the brewing is complete (see chapter eight). Being public, beer drinks attract relatively large numbers of people—never less than about 30, sometimes hundreds. Generally, no one is specifically invited to attend and everyone in the vicinity is free to do so; the long brewing process is advertisement enough, and people learn by word of mouth where beer is available and when it will be ready. Cook (1931, 27) comments that "the Bomvana simply feels the presence of beer".[1] A beer drink as defined here is not part of a series or cluster of ritual or ceremonial activities but an event that is complete in itself. It may be indirectly linked to other events of a ritual nature (e.g. the beer drink for releasing a widow from mourning can only take place a certain time after her husband's funeral) but it is not directly linked to or dependent on other ceremonials or rituals. This excludes certain phases of initiation rituals, for example, at which beer is available.

With one exception (*inkazathi* beer drinks held to collect money for a public fund) a beer drink is organized by an individual homestead and held in that homestead, but the men of the sub-ward section as a group are in control of the procedure, not the individual homestead head (see chapter eight). This is an important factor distinguishing beer drinks from other ancestor rituals, which may also be initiated by an individual homestead head, but where the senior male members of the agnatic kin group are in charge, and neighbours are secondary. The reasons for holding a beer drink may vary, but the purpose or goal is achieved through brewing beer, the attendance of people, the consumption of the beer by those who attend, and by the words spoken by the participants. Furthermore, it is only in this way, in practice, that the goal can be achieved—there are no alternative ways of achieving the same aim. The distribution and consumption of beer is of primary importance, and the main focus of attention. Beer is the only foodstuff provided, and it cannot be substituted with something else. The beer is given out and drunk in a particular, sanctioned way, according to flexible rules or conventions based on principles of territory, age and sex, and, to a lesser extent, individual kinship links and individual status. The proceedings take place inside a hut and/or outside next to the *inkundla* (courtyard—the area between huts and cattle byre), and never in the cattle byre itself, which is associated with animal sacrifice. Other social events at which beer is consumed may possess some of the characteristics that are attributed to beer drinks, but generally the distinction is clear. Shixini people themselves make a distinction between *iindywala* (beer drinks), *imigidi* (large, public feasts associated with certain rites of passage) and *izizathu* or *izisusa* (ancestor rituals). Although these terms are sometimes used fairly loosely in everyday speech, they generally mean very different things.

But what makes a beer drink a ritual? Anthropologists have recognized the difficulties inherent in the term 'ritual' and the great variety of ways in which it is applied, some would say to the extent that it has very little meaning and may not be very useful in delineating a particular class of events (Goody 1961; Humphrey and Laidlaw, 1994, 3 ff.). Humphrey and Laidlaw argue that ritual is a distinctive way in which an action is performed and that in studying ritual we therefore have to look at the particular quality that such action has. Drinking beer is, of course, an action related to everyday consumption, to assuaging the need for food and drink. However, unlike other food in Shixini, beer is not something for everyday, private consumption, but a drink to be shared with others with a degree of formality or ceremony. Even if only a small quantity is brewed, say four beakers (30 litres), for an honoured guest, or to welcome a son back from the mines, or for a small work group, close neighbours are always invited to the homestead to partake of it. The formalities on such occasions include at least a short explanation by the homestead head as to why people have been called, and a short formal reply from one of the visitors. The beakers are allocated to men and women separately, and people sit according to sex and age (see chapter eight). Although beer consumption is ritualised here, these small occasions, attended perhaps by a dozen people or less, twenty at the most, are not 'beer drinks' in the sense that I use the term, although their formal or structural elements occur in more elaborate form at beer drinks as well as other rituals. They are not fully public; other foodstuffs (bread, tea, samp, etc) and other liquor (e.g. brandy, *mangumba*) may be provided. Brewing beer is but one option among many on occasions like this. The guest can just as easily be honoured with the slaughter of a pig or sheep; workers with tea and food, and since the migrant's exact day of return is seldom known brewing beer for this purpose is the exception rather than the rule.

Including a religious element in the definition of ritual may help to refine the definition of beer drinks offered above. Although beer is always to some extent associated with ancestors, there are occasions when this element is not explicit and perhaps only minimally present. This would apply to the beer sometimes made in the past for the meetings of the youth organizations—the *umtshotsho* dances of boys and girls, and the *intlombe* dances of young men and older girls. It is also an important part of the *umtshawuzo* dances attended by senior men and *amankazana* (unattached women) who form a kind of voluntary association, members of which are collectively known as *amatshawuza*. *Umtshawuzo* dances still took place in the late 1990s, but they were of a secular nature. All three of these types of events, in any case, are not regarded here as 'beer drinks' because the main focus is on other matters such as dancing, display and courtship. The beer is a secondary though important element. *Umtshotsho* and *intlombe* were often held without it, though not *umtshawuzo*. Furthermore, none of these events were public in the sense that participation was not open to all. Attendance was restricted by criteria of age, marital status and subscription. Spectators could attend but participation was limited to those recognized as members.

The religious element associated with beer is more explicit at the large, elaborate ritual events which are part of male initiation, most stages of which are accompanied by beer drinking. The largest of these are the public feast which starts immediately after circumcision and entry into the seclusion hut, and a similar feast to mark the 'coming out' of the initiates and their entry into manhood. But although religious to some extent, I do not regard these as beer rituals because they are part of a long sequence of ritual activities, some of which include animal sacrifice, and at which the centre of attention is the successful transformation of the youths into men. Brandy and other food is also usually distributed, and the proceedings are directed by the senior kin of the initiates. Similar considerations lead me to exclude other important rites of passage such as marriage and *intonjane* (female initiation). These too proceed through a number of stages, some of which involve ritual killings and the consumption of beer.

Beer drinks, though rituals which are of religious significance, must also be distinguished from major ancestor rituals or ritual sacrifices, involving the killing of an ox or a goat, though at some of these beer may substitute for an animal killed. In Shixini, as in other Xhosa-speaking areas, beer is an important part of rituals such as *ukuguqula (ukubuyisa)*, to effect the 'turning back' of the spirit of a deceased man to his homestead; *ukupha* (to give), which involves the gift of an ox or a goat to a designated male or female ancestor; and *intambo*, which is a piacular ritual, or ritual of affliction, through which an appeal is made to the ancestors to cure the illness or misfortune affecting an individual. By all accounts other rituals involving animal sacrifice, such as that for remote ancestors or diviner ancestors, called *izilo* or *amarhamncwa*, that for 'making known a [new] homestead' (*ukwazisa umzi*), and *inkobe*, the killing of a goat for a deceased mother, also involve beer brewing. In the case of *inkobe*, however, beer may be brewed as an alternative to the sacrifice of a goat, and such an event conforms to the criteria set out above. The name means 'boiled maize' and metonymically evokes the image of a woman and mother, associated with the provision of basic foods. The killing of a goat to mark a new homestead has largely been replaced by a beer drink called *ntwana nje* (see chapter 13), and where it still occurs is not accompanied by beer. From my observations in Shixini, beer is not brewed for *ukukhup' umtana*, the killing of a goat to mark the end of the seclusion period for a new-born child and its mother (also called *ukusindela* or *ukubingelela*); it is not brewed as part of the burial rites, nor for the *ukuzila* (mourning) ritual, held some time after the burial.

In the case of some of these major religious rituals beer is an important element, but it is secondary to the animal killed and to achieving the aims of the ritual, that of communication and communion with the ancestors. One can 'bring back' a dead father, for example, with the animal alone, brewing beer at a later date when maize is available, but one cannot effect the return of the shade with beer, and follow this up with an ox at a later date. In such a situation one can but 'beg pardon' (*ukungxengxeza*) for the delay by brewing beer or killing a goat and assuring the ancestor that he has not been forgotten and that he will be brought home as soon as an ox is available. On all three days of a ritual like the 'bringing back' of an ancestral spirit, the feasting starts with the meat and is followed by beer. The secondary importance of beer is indicated also by the fact that some of it is distributed in the idiom of meat, which is never the case at a beer drink. For example, the beakers given out on the first day are called *imibengo* (lit: collops or strips of meat).

There are a number of important characteristics of ritual which mark such events as being major religious rituals designed to communicate and commune with the ancestor(s) and which distinguish them from beer drinks. The religious aspects of beer drinks are often displayed by making metaphoric connection between beer and these features of major ancestor rituals. These features include the manner in which the animal is killed in the cattle byre, using the 'spear of the home'. It is necessary for the animal to cry out, indicating its 'agreement' to mediate between man and ancestors and its acceptability to the latter, and special portions of meat are ritually tasted by the subject of the ritual (e.g. in the case of piacular rituals) and/or by members of the kin group. When meat and beer are available, the ritual tasting takes place first with meat, then with beer. At such events beer is used as a libation to the shades, being poured onto the manure at the entrance to the cattle byre after the meat and beer have been ritually tasted by the kin group. Medicine of the home is used at piacular rituals, where the afflicted person washes with it as part of the attempt to secure ancestral blessings and a cure. Actions such as these are designed to facilitate communication with the ancestors, and there is also usually a formal invocation to the ancestors (*unqulo*) by the chief officiant, and sometimes also by others, in which the purpose of the ritual and the response required from the ancestors is made explicit. At beer drinks the religious aspect is less explicit. No animal is killed, and no *materiae* as such are identifiable and ritually manipulated, except the beer itself. There are usually no specific actions which can be seen as set apart from others, the purpose of which is to invoke or commune with the shades, though there are a few exceptions to this, as we shall see. Most ancestor rituals are directed at a specific ancestor or are held for specific living people (e.g. a sick person, a mother and child, a kin group). Some beer drinks do mark changes in individual status, but except when held as a substitute for a sacrifice beer drinks are not held for a specific ancestor, and they are not held to cure illness.

Members of the agnatic group or 'clan-section' (see Kuckertz 1984, Hammond-Tooke 1984) and other kin are specifically called to attend major ancestor rituals and are required to stay at the homestead for the duration of the event, which may take three or four days. The religious corporateness of this group is expressed in a number of other ways too, such as the use of special dress and decorative items of ritual importance, and in the spatial symbolism involved. Male members of the kin group sit together in the senior position in the cattle byre, where most of the action takes place, irrespective of their territorial affiliation. They are allocated meat and beer as a group, and certain portions of the animal are reserved for them. Other men sit and are given food according to their territorial affiliation. Most of the ritual takes place in the cattle byre, in public, but there are aspects which are private and attended only by kin, marking the division between kin and non-kin, although the latter do play an important role in ritual, as neighbours, and have specific rights in meat and beer. However, the division between kin and non-kin and the exclusion of non-kin from participation in certain aspects of the proceedings, marks rituals as distinct from beer drinks as defined earlier.

While the importance of certain kinship ties is recognized at beer drinks, there is no suggestion of kin as a group sitting separately from the others, or receiving an allocation of beer as a group. Instead, the spatial and other symbolism emphasizes neighbourhood and territory, and it is this spatial principle that forms the basis for the allocation of both seating places and beer. Kin who live nearby (e.g. in the same sub-ward) are sometimes called to be present at some beer drinks, but the event can be held without them and they are not obliged to attend. Kin who live far away (e.g. in another ward) are not informed or called.

The contrast between major ancestor rituals and beer drink rituals helps to shed light on the nature of the latter. I have argued elsewhere that the messages conveyed in the symbolism of animal sacrifices are of a largely atemporal kind (McAllister 1997). The stress is on genealogical order and the unity of the kin group as a timeless entity. Actual events in the past are referred to occasionally but they are of a general, unspecified nature, and there is frequent reference to 'custom' as an unchanging, spiritually sanctioned practice handed down from the remote past. Time is collapsed as the world of the living is fused with the timeless world of the ancestors and the authority of the past is conferred on the present (Bloch 1975, Feuchtwang 1993). The world of dreams becomes fused with the conscious world and the ritual is presented as part of a fixed, unalterable cycle. These rituals may well reinforce the solidarity of the celebrating kin group, members of which come from far and wide to participate, and they are, of course, testimony to the importance of the ancestors, but they shed little light on the contemporary relationships relevant to everyday economic and political life. In this sense they contrast markedly with beer drinking rituals.

Types of beer drinks

A number of beer drink rituals are held for what seems, initially, to be no particular reason. Shixini people say that every homestead ought to brew beer once or twice a year. Such beer drinks are euphemistically, with characteristic understatement, referred to by descriptive terms such as *isichenene* (a little drop), *intselo* (a drink) or *intwana* (a small thing). Any of these may have *nje* ('merely' or 'just') appended; e.g. *intselo nje* (just a drink), but the amount of beer brewed can be considerable. When asked, people are often vague about why they decided to brew, or why they decided to do so at that particular time, saying simply that it has been some time since the household last brewed. The frequency of brewing probably depends on a combination of factors—the availability of money or maize, personal inclination, and circumstances affecting the homestead and its inhabitants. A person brews "when he has maize, and when he feels like doing so", or "when he feels in his heart that it should be done", or "when you realise that it has been a long time since brewing… [and] you have the means to do so…". What is important is that people enter the home, where they are given hospitality. Beer is brewed from time to time, said Ndlebezenja, in the course of a speech at one beer drink, "so that there should be a saddle seen by people passing by on the road [who will say], 'there is a horse over there, with its saddle on; let us call in there men, whoever's home it might be'. That is what brings good fortune".

Some people brew more frequently than others, but I came across no homesteads which did not brew at all, and informants in Folokhwe did not know of any. Even the few homesteads which contained members of an independent Christian church, who are not permitted to drink beer, fulfilled the moral obligation to brew 'for people' from time to time. Beer brewed for no explicit reason may also be referred to as *utywala besintu*, a term which reflects its essentially moral quality. *Isintu* means 'the human species' and also 'human-ness' in the sense of human action or custom, and carries a connotation of moral rightness. It is similar to the well-known concept *ubuntu*, the abstract quality of humanity, of being a good, upright human being, and it refers to the acting out of this quality. This event therefore conveys a quality of moral righteousness, as the proper thing to do as a person (*umntu*) and member of a community. At one beer drink held for no particular reason other than to provide beer for people, those who attended were told simply that "this beer does not proclaim anything. I have brewed simply so that there should be drinking in the neighbourhood."

In one sense then, beer drinks are held as part of a system of generalized beer exchange governed by reciprocity. However, unnamed beer drinks sometimes conceal a private and unannounced reason for brewing, such as the fact that the homestead has enjoyed a windfall of some kind that it does not wish to make public, or, on the contrary, that some misfortune has befallen it, attributed to ancestors desiring beer in 'their' home. Secondly, because of this, a homestead head sometimes decides to brew an unnamed beer drink as a prelude to the holding of some larger and important ritual. The beer drink focuses the attention of the shades on the homestead and ensures that they will respond favourably to the ritual that follows, when the achievement of something specific is sought. However, there is no *necessary* connection between the two events, and no requirement that the one should precede the other. Certain cases of *ntwana nje* have as their primary objective the introduction of a new homestead to the community and the shades, and are substitutes for the ritual of making known the homestead. Other cases are held prior to the departure of a migrant worker, with the covert objective of ensuring good fortune at work, but the reason for brewing is not made public for fear of evil-doers (see chapter six).

Other beer drinks are associated with more specific motives, often of an explicitly religious nature. At these events people speak of the beer as 'beer of the home' (*utywala bekhaya*), a term also used for beer brewed for major ancestor rituals as distinct from the 'beer just to drink' (*intselo nje*). One of the commonest beer drinks held in Shixini is 'beer for harvest' (*utywala bomvuno*) which is brewed some time after the harvest has been brought in from the field or garden and stored, in order to give thanks for what was obtained, and to ensure that the next year's harvest will be as good or better. This beer drink is also called *utywala benkabi* ('beer for the oxen') or *isabokhwe* (from the Afrikaans *sjambok*, a rawhide whip used to control oxen). In explaining the purpose of the beer drink speakers often pay public tribute to the oxen, which is simultaneously a thanksgiving to the ancestors for the harvest they have sent, saying that since the oxen were guided with a whip when working, the beer was brewed 'to soothe the weals' on their backs.

There are three other beer drinks where the religious component is quite explicit. Two of these, *inkobe* and certain instances of *ntwana nje*, are substitutes for ritual killings while one, *umsindleko*, was developed to take the place of a killing. *Umsindleko* is a beer drink held to welcome home a migrant worker which will be considered in detail in chapters six and seven. When *inkobe* is performed as a substitute for the killing of a goat in the prescribed ritual manner (for a deceased mother), it loses the characteristics of an animal sacrifice and takes on those of a beer drink, which become essential elements in ensuring its success. It is for this reason that I consider it to be a beer drink rather than simply an ancestor ritual performed with beer instead of a goat. The substitution of beer for the goat changes the character of the occasion, as will become evident when this process is discussed more fully below. The same applies to *ntwana nje*, which is a substitute for the sacrifice held to make known the homestead (*ukwazis' umzi*).

Both *umsindleko* and *ntwana nje* for a new homestead involve transition or change in status—in the one case from absent migrant worker to returned member of the community and resident of the homestead; in the other from non-homestead head to homestead head. There are a number of other beer drinks involving transitions but which are not, to the best of my knowledge, substitutes for ritual killings or developments from these. Two of these are associated with death and mourning. The first, termed *utywala bohambo* (beer of going about) or *ukukhulula usapho* (releasing the family) is held two or three months after the death of a senior family member to enable his/her immediate family to be freed from the restrictions of mourning and to allow them to participate in community life again. If it is a male homestead head who has died, his widow remains in mourning for an additional month or two and is only released from this status and incorporated back into society, in the new status of widow, through a beer drink referred to as *ukukhulula umhlolokazi* (releasing the widow). Another beer drink linked to women's status is *ukuqhutywa komfazi* (promoting the wife). Its object is to mark the change in status from the position of junior to senior wife, and to incorporate the person so promoted into the ranks of senior women.

Other beer drinks revolve around a service rendered or work done by other members of the community. For example, beer is brewed in conjunction with the allocation of a homestead site, and also when a field is allocated. An application for a site is made to the sub-ward moot (*ibandla*), consisting of all its senior men. The moot, in considering the application, concerns itself primarily with what those living in the vicinity of the proposed site feel. If the applicant's future neighbours are happy about the site being granted, the moot approves the application and sets a date for a visit to the site, so that its exact location can be verified. On the date set the men of the sub-ward go down to the site, and the applicant (or his/her father or other senior kinsman) makes available the beer brewed for the occasion. The beer drink then follows the inspection of the site and is referred to as *utywala benxiwa* (beer of the site). According to informants, the procedure is similar in the case of an application for a field, with the beer drink taking place after the location of the field and its boundaries have been confirmed.

There is some difficulty, this time at the secular end of the continuum, between beer drinks and other types of events, in relation to beer drinks associated with the work parties discussed in the previous chapter. In theory, beer may be brewed for a small group of two or three people in recognition of (or reward for) work done by them. In practise this seldom occurs. Since brewing beer entails considerable effort it is not practical to brew very small amounts. For slightly larger groups, say of eight or ten people, a woman will sometimes buy some beer from a nearby *imbarha* (beer for sale) or make *mangumba*. For other work parties, however, as indicated earlier, it is necessary to brew beer. One of the commonest of these beer drinks is the one for an *umgqibelo* work group made up of two or more agricultural companies. Although meant primarily for the workers, other people also come along to work party beer drinks in the knowledge that beer will be distributed after the work has been completed, and that all who are present will get something to drink. I regard such public events as beer drinks because it is only by brewing beer that a homestead head can achieve the result he desires (e.g. get the garden ploughed and planted), because it is primarily for beer that people assemble, the non-workers usually outnumbering those who laboured, and because the beer is distributed and consumed in a formal, prescribed manner.

There are other kinds of events involving beer drinking which I was told about but which have not taken place in Shixini for many years. These include beer to initiate a new cast-iron pot of the largest size, or to mark the purchase of a new plough; beer for a race horse (to help it win or to praise it for doing so) and beer brewed to mark the allocation of a new field (no new fields have been allocated in the southern part of Shixini since the early 1970s). Others which do take place, but which I have not witnessed, are the brewing of beer on instructions from a diviner, for example when lightning strikes a homestead. The beer drink is meant to reinstate the homestead's normal status after it has undergone rites to purify it, its occupants and close kin. Beer is also brewed when bees swarm into a hut or cattle byre. The bees are referred to as 'visitors' or *abahlekazi* (great chiefs) and are associated with founding clan ancestors. People also mentioned to me that misdemeanours could be punished by sentencing the offender to a fine of a certain quantity of beer, which was then consumed by the community, but only one such case occurred during fieldwork and the sentence was, in effect, suspended. I did attend one case of beer brewed for agnates when they met to arrange an ancestor ritual, as occurs also among the Ndlambe near East London (Bigalke 1969, 139), but I have excluded this here because it is not a public occasion and is directly linked to the ritual sacrifice it is held to plan. Excluded too are the informal Christmas and New Year's Day festivities, when beer, other liquor and food (mainly meat) are consumed. On these occasions, people who do not brew go from house to house to drink the beer brewed by others. Within a small locality such as a sub-ward section there are usually two or three small beer drinks on each of these days (six to ten in the sub-ward as a whole) attended mainly by the people from one's immediate neighbourhood.

Finally, there are beer drinks at which the bulk of the beer is sold. These are *imbarha*, which is brewed and sold by an individual homestead, and *inkazathi*, which is a communal effort, held in order to raise money for something (e.g. school funds). These beer drinks are not quite as formal and as highly structured as those at which beer is not sold, but they are more than just commercial events, as we shall see in chapter 11.

We have now laid the empirical, historical and theoretical groundwork for a more detailed consideration of some of the beer drinking rituals outlined above, and for placing particular beer drinks within the theoretical framework outlined in chapter three. We start this process in the next chapter with a consideration of *umsindleko*.

Endnotes

1. Bomvana are Xhosa speakers who are historically associated with the districts of Mqanduli and Xhora (Elliotdale), immediately adjacent to Willowvale.

6 Going to War: Rituals of Labour Migration[1]

Co-operative work in Shixini (as outlined in chapter four) provides part of the ethnographic evidence for the historical changes in the nature of rural production associated with labour migration and declining homestead size, and of the economic interdependence of individual homesteads. The beer drinks associated with co-operative work groups link the exchange of beer to the exchange of labour and assets in a direct, easily comprehensible way. But I have argued that beer drinking in general, whether associated with work parties or not, is based on the same principles as the exchange of agricultural and other forms of labour. This is because in holding a beer drink a homestead utilises its labour (and its maize, the product of communal labour) to benefit the community at large, in the expectation that other homesteads will themselves brew in due course as part of a system of generalized reciprocity. In doing so it draws on its close relationships with other nearby homesteads for assistance in the brewing process, and expects in turn to render assistance to those homesteads when asked to do so in the future.

As argued earlier, co-operative work drew homesteads into reciprocal labour arrangements with each other as a strategy to maintain rural production. The absence of males as labour migrants was one of the factors necessitating this, and we can find further evidence for the historical changes outlined in chapter two and the rural response to them, as well as for the general claims that I am making about beer drinks, by looking closely at those associated with labour migration. One of these, a beer ritual called *umsindleko*, will be examined in detail below, because it allows one to muster the contemporary symbolic evidence relating to the series of interconnected historical changes that continue to govern local economic activities. The logic of this is relatively simple—to survive as a rural entity, each individual homestead needs access to cash and also to make a contribution to the common good, and to draw on the assets (including labour, agricultural implements, oxen, etc.) available in other homesteads. Very few can muster enough money and enough labour to become self-sufficient agricultural producers, and in the quest for money through wage labour in mine or town potential labourers (and decision makers) are temporarily removed from the homestead. This places migratory labour at the centre of rural production, since it is through migration that the money required for agricultural inputs, including cattle and implements, is acquired. This is the general framework in terms of which *umsindleko* needs to be understood.

Theoretically this beer drink lies at the point where the rural social field intersects with the field of capitalist production, and where the competition for labour between dominant and dominated is thrown into relief. As such it represents aspects of practice linked to a habitus that is the outcome of the historical processes discussed in chapters two and three and it shows how those with the power to define the rural field attempt to maintain a particular set of dispositions and orientations towards migrant labour. *Umsindleko* demonstrates how senior male Red migrants and their contemporary successors in Shixini have attempted to control and define their labour power in the field of economic production thereby subverting (at least in part) the aims of the dominant forces in the field and asserting its relevance to the rural social order that they valued and sought to conserve. In addition, however, this ritual enables one to gain a perspective on beer drinks as performative events intimately related not only to everyday practice (such as labour migration) and its logic, but also to the particular realities affecting specific individuals. In other words an examination of *umsindleko* allows us to ask precisely what it is that is being transformed and established through the performance of the beer drink, and to relate this transformation to the individual concerned. In this way, performance emerges as a manifestation of practice in a particular social context.

Umsindleko is merely one part of what I have termed elsewhere 'rituals of labour migration', so it is first necessary to briefly outline the other parts of this complex to place it in perspective, and to indicate that it is but one aspect of a wider strategy through which the struggle over labour is pursued.

Departure and return

In preparing to leave for work a migrant is concerned to ensure that he will travel and work safely, and that he will return home with the fruits of his labour in the form of cash, to be invested in the rural homestead. One danger at this stage emanates from the possible action of witches and sorcerers using their occult powers to subvert the migrant's intentions, by causing misfortune on the journey and/or later, while at work.[2] As among other Xhosa speakers and Southern African peoples in general (Hammond-Tooke 1974), there is a lively belief in witchcraft in Shixini (see also chapter seven). To prevent sorcery or witchcraft from attacking him on the journey or spoiling his efforts at work the migrant may consult a herbalist, who is able to provide protective medicines, and he takes care to secure the blessings of the ancestral spirits. His homestead is also theirs, so he solicits and expects their support. Shortly before leaving he should, ideally, brew beer for a small beer drink. Those who attend are not told of his impending departure (for fear of witchcraft) but they will, as at any beer drink, 'give forth words' which, along with their physical presence, are thought to ensure that the migrant will be spiritually accompanied to work 'by many people', that his ancestors will become aware of his intention and be ready to accompany and protect him on his journey, and that they will assure good fortune and success at work. Right from the start then, the individual's work spell is rendered as something related to the wider *rural* community, something in which there is a collective interest.

On the day of his departure a migrant rises before sunrise and places his luggage next to the cattle byre. Here he washes with 'medicine of the home' which has been prepared the day before and left in the byre overnight to enhance its potency, the byre being closely linked to the ancestors.[3] The medicine of the home has sacred properties, and washing with it brings him into communion with his ancestors. He then invokes the ancestors, calling out the clan praises and asking for protection and success at work. In the case of young migrants, not yet men, this invocation is done on their behalf by their father or other senior male agnate. Prior to departure, young migrants are also instructed by their fathers on how to conduct themselves at work, reminded of their obligations to their rural homes and made aware of the dangers of absconding, which needs to be guarded against. Such admonitions do not, of course, always work, and many people in Shixini know of young men who went off to work and never came home again, leaving their parents, or sometimes a wife and young children, to struggle on without them. After the invocation and washing, the migrant picks up his luggage and takes to the road without entering his homestead again. Included in his luggage is *umphako* (food for a journey) provided by his wife or mother. It is spoken of as 'food of the home' and symbolizes the link between labour migration and rural home, expressed in terms of the need to 'build' the homestead and the importance of wage earnings in this regard. The food is eaten by the migrant on his journey and is thought to bring good fortune or blessings from the ancestors, both for the journey itself and the period spent at work. The performative force of these ritual and symbolic actions, very briefly sketched here and indexed later in *umsindleko*, serve to separate the migrant from his rural home and society and to effect his entry into the liminal, harsh and potentially dangerous world of migrant work and to stress that he is leaving in order to work for his homestead.

The worker's return home is an occasion for rejoicing, thanksgiving and worship. Before entering any hut the returnee invokes his ancestors at the gate of the cattle byre; he calls out their praises, informs them of his return, thanks them for their blessings and protection, and asks them to continue to look after him in the future. People soon hear of his arrival and gather at the homestead to bid him welcome (immediate neighbors are summoned to be present), and he then embarks on the formal and obligatory presentation of bottles of liquor (usually brandy and other spirits) and other gifts to specific groups and individuals. *Ihambidlane* ('the thing he has been eating on the way') is the first bottle given out, and this is followed by others termed *uswazi* (a switch)[4], for both neighbours and kinsmen, and finally, *ivanya* (literally 'beer from the second straining'). Individuals such as the migrant's father or senior kinsman, and his *usiphatheleni*, the caretaker who looks after the absent migrant's rural interests, are presented with bottles and/or other gifts, and gifts are also given to other kin, neighbours and friends.

The initial distribution of liquor takes place in the main hut, where the ancestors are thought to be ever-present, and the first few drops from the first bottle are gently poured onto the hearth in the centre of the floor. Informants speak of this as propitiation or appeasement and say that "there are others above us who must drink before we do". The presentation of liquor and gifts symbolizes success at work and the benefits of this to the homestead and community. In an extension of the meaning of the rituals associated with departure, the liquor and gifts also indicate the migrant's dependence on kin and neighbours and involvement in a community, his acceptance of the moral authority of the rural home and society, but also the social dependence of junior on senior (in the case of young migrants). The presentation of liquor to the senior men of the community by the younger both accords them respect and serves to indicate that the elders' authority is still accepted, at least symbolically. This, too, is an aspect of the struggle over labour, but in this case confined to the rural field, where elders seek to secure their authority over their juniors and, by extension, over the fruits of their labour. In *umsindleko*, the most elaborate of the rituals associated with migrant labour, this symbolism is present in more explicit form.

Newly returned migrants sometimes hold a small beer drink to mark their homecoming. This is similar to the complex of liquor and gift prestations in that it celebrates the migrant's safe return and his return to the community, and involves the community in welcoming him back through common participation in the beer. The recognition of people and groups and the respect accorded them is expressed in the distribution of beer and in gifts of beer to individuals. This beer drink is spoken of as 'beer for invocation': "When I come home I report to the ancestors with a beaker of beer…since I have worked well and there has been nothing bad…People must come here and say a few words."[5]

The *umsindleko* beer drink

Umsindleko (a provision) is a large beer drink sometimes held in conjunction with a migrant's return. An analysis of this event, and attention to the detail of the formal oratory that accompanies it, illuminates the rural Xhosa view of labour migration and the strategies that have been developed to deal with incorporation into a wider society and at the same time to resist it. It offers important insights into the contemporary nature of rural Xhosa society (but only in so far as Shixini is representative of this), its relationship with the wider political economy and the historical development of both migrant labour and beer drinking as a ritual form. In what follows, the general importance of brewing *umsindleko* is outlined and case studies are provided.

Literally, the word *umsindleko* means food prepared for a traveler by his wife to await his arrival (Kropf 1915, 391). As with other beer drinks, as we shall see, this name says something about gender relations and establishes a link with the food provided by the wife or mother on the migrant's departure, since *umsindleko* is often spoken of as being done for the migrant by kin. *Umsindleko* does not take place each time a migrant returns, however. When I inquired abut this in the field, most of those whom I asked said that it was held if the trip to town was successful. My initial understanding was that success was gauged by the migrant's safe return, not having experienced any misfortunes at work and, most importantly, by what he had to show for his efforts. On the other hand, during fieldwork not everybody who met this latter proviso had *umsindleko*. This puzzled me. I was told that circumstances at home were important and that other needs might preclude the brewing of the large quantity of beer required. Generally however, it was said that if a migrant has 'worked well'—i.e. earned a good amount and spent his money wisely (e.g. bought livestock)—*umsindleko* ought to be done for him by his close kin if the homestead had the means to brew. However, it was clear that this was not always done even in wealthy homesteads, and it seemed to me from the cases that I learnt about that *umsindleko* was done at fairly long (perhaps five or ten year) intervals in the migrant's career. Some migrants have never had it, others (aged sixty years or so) four or five times during their lives. Some men had *umsindleko* for the first time when they were already married, yet there were boys and unmarried men for whom it had been held two or three times. In some cases it seemed that it was held at the conclusion of a period of intensive oscillation, after a man had been out to work four or five times in close succession, achieved some goal and was preparing for a fairly long stay at home. Ndlebezenja, for example, had only had it once before, about twelve years previously, after which he stayed at home for about two years before going out to work again. At the *umsindleko* held for him during fieldwork, his younger brother, Nqakaba (referred to by Ndlebezendja as "the person whom I left behind to look after this home") explained to the people assembled that he had decided to brew for Ndlebezendja because:

...He often spends much time at work

This is the second time that he repeatedly goes to work

While I remain behind

During his absence it became clear that I should make a plan and brew *umsindleko* for him

I am providing for him in order to honour him

Because he often goes up [to work]

He comes back nicely without having been troubled by anything

He comes back with the things that he went to work for

Without being short of anything...

It is I who am junior to him

But it is he who always arrives back from contracts

Now then, it is I who decided that this thing should be done

He is not sick and there is nothing amiss

It is being held because he persistently comes back so nicely

We realized then that we should cook something for him...

In another case (that of Ndabanduna's *umsindleko*, discussed below), it appeared that the event was held because after an unsuccessful earlier spell at work Ndabanduna had slaughtered a goat to give thanks to his ancestors for a narrow escape from a dangerous situation. His next work contract was successfully completed and he returned home with a good deal to show for his efforts. This was attributed to the ritual that he had held earlier, and he had therefore indicated to kin that *umsindleko* would be an appropriate way to signal this and to acknowledge the role of the ancestors.

However, I was surprised and initially confused to find later that *umsindleko* was also sometimes associated with a *failure* to work well and to earn much money, whether due to a particular reason or misfortune (e.g. loss of money) or not. After attending two such events, however, I started to realise that there was nothing contradictory about this, and that the principles and beliefs underlying these beer rituals were similar to those held for successful migrants. In what follows, extracts from a number of cases of *umsindleko* are presented. Two of these were held for senior, highly respected men who had enjoyed some success at work, two for young men and one for an unsuccessful migrant.

Ndabanduna and Ndlebezendja[6]

Ndabanduna, who lives in the Chibi section of Folokhwe sub-ward, is a senior member of the local Ntshilibe clan. According to him the event was initiated by his wife, "because my mother is dead", who made the suggestion to Jija (his FBS), who agreed and assisted with the organization. In the first of the formal speeches made, Jija explained the purpose of the beer drink, and he was followed by a number of others:

> …This is what it is all about, people of my home!
>
> Here is the beer which the woman of this homestead has decided to provide for her husband!
>
> She said to me: 'Brother! I am going to brew some beer here at home for my husband's *umsindleko*'
>
> Chiefs! This is the same beer which you see here in this homestead
>
> The woman of this homestead has provided for her husband
>
> On all the other occasions [that he returned from work] she had nothing to complain about
>
> It is she who has been lazy [in not brewing]
>
> This time she decided to do something
>
> This is his *umsindleko*
>
> There in that cask is the man [beer for men]
>
> In that pot is the woman, [it is] five beakers

I have said it then.

Honono (Ndabanduna's BS) spoke next, drawing an analogy between a migrant worker and a hunting dog:

> ...It is the custom that when a dog goes out to hunt
>
> Not a person, a dog
>
> The first thing to be done is to cook for it here at home
>
> Then it is sent into the forest
>
> Similarly, when it returns from hunting a pot is put on the fire and food is cooked for it
>
> When this man went to work, when he took his contract and left
>
> He had food which he took with him
>
> Today he is back
>
> His wife is saying: 'I have a small thing which I have prepared for him
>
> On all the other occasions I made only bread
>
> This time I should make the food of the men of this home!'[7]
>
> We of the Ntshilibe clan are grateful for her change of heart
>
> She thought correctly, this woman
>
> A person's blood is appeased, because of his work, having been working with his hands
>
> If he is not appeased the body becomes lazy
>
> Because there is something that has not been recognised[8]
>
> There is a dog called Englishman[9]
>
> It is said that when it is indecisive, when its stomach is empty
>
> It chases and gets to its prey but does not bring it down
>
> I stop there my chiefs.

Modi (a Ntshilibe of a different lineage) stood up to thank Honono for these words, and with mock indignation asked why this *umsindleko* was being held. He maintained that it was done when a man had worked well, but that they had not been told what the results (in money or cattle) of Ndabanduna's spell at work were. Another speaker supported Modi,[10] drawing a parallel between the food provided by the wife when the migrant leaves for work and the *umsindleko* that she brews on his return, concluding that: "A person who has returned with nothing is not provided for; a dog will not chew bones unless something has been slaughtered." Modi's question is a rhetorical one which is usually asked at *umsindleko* and to which no reply is given or expected. A man does not tell the assembly how much money he has brought home, or what he has bought with his earnings. That is a private matter, not communal business. The question serves, however, as a statement emphasizing that the beer has been brewed to mark and to reinforce the ideal of a financially successful work spell.

As indicated here the role of the wife (or mother) is stressed at *umsindleko* beer drinks. The beer is a provision by her—she brews "food of the men of the home" on her husband's (or son's) return, as she earlier provided the food of the home on the migrant's departure. The success of the migrant's efforts depends also on her. Without the food that she provides for the journey he may fail to achieve his aim and if there is no recognition afterwards he may become discouraged. The analogy of the hunting dog also links past work spells with later ones, relates the fruits of his labour to the homestead and indicates that the migrant relies on others for good fortune at work. The dog must be fed by its owner in order to hunt well. If it fails to catch its prey it is brought home and slaughtered for, so that it will succeed the next day. An informant later elaborated on this, saying that slaughtering an animal for a hunting dog was equivalent to making a necklace called *intambo* for it. The migrant worker too was being symbolically provided with a necklace, "so that he should be humble and know that next time he goes to work he should do likewise [work well]". This necklace is made from the tail hairs of an ox or cow associated with the ancestors and is believed to ensure their protection and beneficence and to put right what is wrong (e.g. cure illness). By analogy, the migrant worker depends on the ancestors for a successful work spell, but at *umsindleko* it is 'made' by the presence and participation of the community, including kin.

The association between beer and the ancestors, and the sacred nature of the beer brewed for the migrant, was evident also at the *umsindleko* held for Ndlebezendja (Cirha clan) when he stated, in the course of his explanation to the gathering, that:

...It was realized that a small plan should be made

So that I should be washed with medicine of the home by my people, by the Cirha clan

In order that I will return in good health in future

Because I will be leaving again soon

This will enable me to find what I am searching for

I will find it if I am encouraged

I have been encouraged today, and I will find it when I go up [to work]…

Through *umsindleko*, the migrant is honoured, flattered or entreated (*ukubongoza*) and is given confidence, energy and courage (*ukukhalitshiswa*). He is symbolically washed with medicine of the home, by means of his clan ancestors, so that he will be encouraged and continue to work well. This is achieved through the participation of the community and parallels the process followed on departure, where the migrant washed with medicine of the home before leaving. Both washing with medicine of the home and having a necklace made occur at piacular rituals, which are indexed here.

As indicated here the returned migrant, if a senior man, is also expected to speak to the assembly and to explain the circumstances surrounding the decision to brew. In Ndabanduna's case, he referred to Modi's query about the proceeds of the work and reflected on the nature of migrant labour itself, making reference to the dangers of the work-place and the importance of the ancestors in ensuring a safe return and success at work:

…I am going to refer to Bhasimiti

I say, Bhasimiti

[When] I went up to Pretoria, apart from the time when the two of us went together

I traveled with the son of 'what's-his-name' from over there in Ngoloza

He said that there was work available at Spili mine

There he took us to a gate at which people were forbidden to enter

We were with the son of Mjelo

We were bitten by dogs

Have you ever seen a person reduced to rags by dogs?

Now then men, I will stop talking

This is not the time for talking

The one in charge of this occasion is Jija

But do you remember now Bhasimiti?

There was fighting there

I had just started working

A white man said: 'Come here you, you will be a cook'

There was fighting there and it was said

'It is you, it is Ntshilibe' [who is responsible]

Hence [on returning] I went over to Mpuncu's place, took a black castrated goat, and slaughtered it here

I was invoking because of my escape from danger

I did not slaughter it for my own use, I was invoking because I was safe

It was I who was singled out

It was said that I was responsible

I myself said, 'Wow, God makes an effort when he has done something like this'

I associate myself with Bhasimiti's word

If something has happened at your home and people associate you with that madness they will not succeed

Two people died

On my return I went to buy a goat at Mfunquli's and slaughtered it here

I was propitiating because I had escaped

The fault was not mine, as if Bhasimiti is accused of killing someone whereas he was over there pissing

Chiefs! Be careful of what people say

It might seem that a human being is a fool

A person is no fool; he has brains in the head

I arrived here at home, a ragged person without even a pair of trousers

In order to come back I had to use Malahle's money

I arrived and paid him here at home

Chiefs! I am thankful

I hand over to the assembly to speak.

Although this speech appears somewhat incoherent because Ndabanduna leaves much unexplained and speaks somewhat disjointedly, as a reflection on the nature of migrant labour it provides a picture of a violent, uncertain and unfriendly work place, where one is 'bitten by dogs', arbitrarily ordered about by whites and falsely accused. He is referring to a past work spell which, due to the circumstances he outlines, resulted in him returning home penniless. He says that he felt it necessary to propitiate and thank the ancestors (by slaughtering a goat) for ensuring that he had returned safely. The implication is also that his more recent success at work was due to the fact that he had done this, because he is referring to Modi's query as to why this *umsindleko* was being held. His reply, in effect, is that it is held to ensure a trouble free work spell and to give thanks for having been able to return safely, which in turn facilitated the success of the next spell at work. In drawing a picture of an immoral and dangerous work place Ndabanduna was clearly also expressing the moral paramountcy of the rural home and the absolute necessity of return to the home for ultimate security and peace of mind.

At Ndlebezendja's *umsindleko*, a speaker by the name of Njembeyiya, of the Qwathi clan from Jotelo, widely renowned as a forceful and amusing orator, asked the rhetorical question about the proceeds of the work and urged Ndlebezenja and Nqakama to make explicit what they meant by a 'plan':

Now then Mangono [Ndlebezenja]

Even though those here of the area have not yet stood up to speak

There is something disgraceful about you

I am referring to the practice of calling something a plan

This makes the people of your area become ignorant

Mangono, you worked [but then] we were apprehensive

You spent a long time here without going [back] to work

But you then worked for yourself until you had two wives

Do not be timid, Mangono, this is something you must avoid when you speak

Your courage should be evident, as when you fought as a boy and danced as a young man, it showed!

You will be teaching people who do not know any better

I do not want *umhlinzeko* to be held for one who goes to work

And returns with a guitar and a concertina

Arriving home with nothing to show for his efforts

Why does he not buy maize?

He does not buy anything to indicate [that he has] a home

You revere work and say it is a 'plan'

Do not say that it is a plan, you will make the people you live with stay ignorant

In brewing for you your younger brother is thinking to himself

'My elder brother has found something that resembles a kid'

The words I speak have never been answered before the end of the beer drink

Mangono, I identify with you because you are my equal, you were born shortly after me

I don't feel sorry for you, I merely feel shy when I see you, but I don't feel inferior

Because I was a senior boy, you acknowledged me immediately anywhere

You flew high then, you did, you were not taken by the *amatshawuza*, because you were not surpassed

Now that you move about with the *amatshawuza*, nobody surpasses you

No one at all!

There is an idea, Mangono, that he who goes about with the *amatshawuza* will be a failure

There is this thinking, Mangono, that he who makes love will go down, he who makes love to women

If you go to his home then, to the one who does not make love, you will find that he has pimples and a sweaty face

There is nothing really—I mean to say, stop this avoidance; where is the 'plan'?

You are having *umhlinzeko*, be aware of what you have done; you are having *umhlinzeko*.

I have stopped.

Njembeyiya's words were greeted with frequent interjections of approval and laughter by the audience. Using an alternative word, *umhlinzeko* (see chapter seven), he poses the same rhetorical question asked by Modi, and while his criticisms might seem to be serious the audience is aware that he is speaking tongue-in-cheek. Beneath the gloss of criticism there is a good deal of praise for a man who was highly regarded and widely admired. Ndlebezenja is said to have worked well, and to have done so in the past (enabling him to take a second wife). Njembeyiya refers to Ndlebezenja's prowess in fighting, as a boy, and in dancing, as a young man, evoking the youth organizations of Red people. He refers also to Ndlebenzenja's membership of the *amatshawuza*, and to the view that this will lead to failure in life, and indicates that this view is contradicted by the case of Ndlebezenja.

Umsindleko for young men and unsuccessful migrants

Umsindleko for a boy or young man is often spoken of as being done by his father or a father's representative such as a senior male agnate, and takes a slightly different form. The youth and his companions are allocated a large share of the beer and drink it in a separate hut.[11] The official proceedings are attended only by senior men and by younger men who have been admitted to beer drinks and thus attend such events on a regular basis. Women sit outside in the courtyard or nearby. After the preliminary beakers the youth is called into the men's hut and seated next to the beer at the back of the hut, a sacred place. The speakers then address him, after which he ritually tastes a little of the beer from the men's cask. He does not speak in reply, as more senior returned migrants do. He then rejoins his peers in the other hut.

Senior men consider that if the young migrant does not have *umsindleko* "the ancestors will no longer be with him. He needs to be praised." But there is another important element, that of reinforcing the father's authority. A father of three migrant sons put it this way:

> If my son has been to work, has been obedient and loyal to me and has worked well in that he has sent money home and asked me to buy cattle for him, and if he has brought money home when he returned, I will instruct his mother to brew beer for him.…At the beer drink the ancestors will be invoked. If there are people here drinking beer, then the ancestors will also be doing so.

The theme of obedience and loyalty to the father is also prominent in *umsindleko* oratory. The words addressed to the youth indicate that the elders are trying to ensure that he interprets his success at work correctly, that is, in the elders' terms, and that he continues to accept their authority. Thus while *umsindleko* in general addresses the question of the meaning of labour in the migrant labour context, when it is brewed for young men and boys it also concerns the struggle for meaning within the context of rural power relations. The economic success and independence of the youth is clearly a potential threat to the power of the elders, and this is countered by emphasizing the youth's social dependence on them, particularly on his father or the senior members of his lineage. This is simultaneously an aspect of social reproduction, an attempt to inculcate and reinforce a rural orientation or disposition.

The following are extracts from speeches made at an *umsindleko* for a young man, Mbuntshuntshu, son of Bokhwe of the Ntshilibe clan. His father being dead, the beer drink was organized by his FBS, Gamalakhe, who was the first to speak, soon after the youth had been called into the men's hut:…

> Now that you are all seated and listening
>
> As I have already said, this beer which has been brewed
>
> Has been brewed for this young man of Bokhwe's who is called Mbuntshuntshu
>
> It is his *umsindleko* because he has returned from work
>
> He has come back having done well at work
>
> Since at this home no cultivation took place
>
> Cultivating was done on him, on his shoulders
>
> With this beer with which we are doing *umhlinzeko* for him

We are flattering him, because we have ploughed on him, on his shoulders

Even tomorrow, let him have strength

A person who lives at a homestead provides for it...

[Addressing Mbuntshuntshu]

Let me say that you should not be foolish at work

And waste your money on prostitutes and coloured women

And not pay regard to your homestead

So that there is starvation here and people forsake it

A homestead never disappears when it has a [proper] man in it.

This event is being done in order to strengthen you

I stop at that point.

Ndabanduna, Mbuntshuntshu's FB in a different house, emphasized the young man's dependence on Gamalakhe and the other members of his agnatic lineage, whatever house they might belong to:

...Concerning what is said by your elder brother

Try to associate yourself with it

Why? It is not desirable for you to stand alone and not to look to Gamalakhe

Should that happen and you discard Gamalakhe

You will marry with difficulty

[You will say] 'My senior brother, I want to find a wife, I desire a woman'

And Gamalakhe will say: 'I too have no cattle, I am bankrupt'

No, as far as I can see this will confound me

'That young man', says Gamalakhe, 'he says he desires a woman, that son of Bokhwe'

Then we will know that so and so and so and so and so and so in these houses

Ought to do something [to provide bridewealth]

According to the custom of people who live together

This word that has been spoken by Gamalakhe here

Heed it; teach yourself to associate with it, as a human being...

A number of the other speakers also referred to Mbuntshuntshu's dependence on and respect due to his senior agnates. This must be seen against the economic independence of the young man, who has been responsible for supporting the homestead, implying the potential for individualism and independence.

At first glace *umsindleko* oratory appears to be dominated by kin. However, the spatial symbolism (see chapter nine) and the way in which the beer is distributed (chapter 10) indicate that these are community affairs and not rituals of kinship. The words addressed to the migrant come from his close agnatic kin as well as from other senior members of the sub-ward section, while spokesmen from each of the other sections and sub-wards present also address him. That his work is of concern to the wider community is indicated in a speech delivered by Shoti of the Ntlane clan from Jotelo sub-ward, addressing Mgilimbane, son of Giladile of the Qhinbe clan of Folokhwe. Mgilimbane had recently returned from work, where he had managed to save a good deal of money. Although this does not always occur, one of the conventions of beer drink oratory is that a speaker ought to be 'agreed with' (*ukuvumiswa*) from the floor, an action that marks the formality and conviviality of the occasion and punctuates the speaker's words. One of the men present performs this task with frequent short interjections. The *ukuvumisa* (refrain) is shown here in parentheses.

All right then, pardon chiefs

All right here is a point (Quiet! There is someone speaking here!)

The one who is speaking comes from over there at Jotelo

It is I of the Ntlane clan (Right!)

That young man of Giladile's is also of the Ntlane clan (Gosh!)

Because his father was born to the Ntlane clan (Gosh!)

All right, that's fine (Truly!)

It is good that a person does something to be seen by others (Truly!)

The reason we are here is because you have done something, so that we should see it

This young man knows his achievement

Seeing that he is doing something familiar to you all (Truly!)

It is not going to be unearthed by any of us

We can see that he is well established (Truly!)

We can see that he is stable, with our own eyes (Truly!)

We do not want to know what cannot be seen

We want a youth to make it clear

It is already clear now, we have seen him, he should not stop [his good work] (Truly!)

He should excel and not say he has done nothing for a particular period (Truly!)

We grew up with Giladile as boys, ploughing down there with two oxen (Truly!)

He would harvest more maize than people who used six oxen (Truly!) [Laughter]

Down there, with only two oxen man!

When the sod fell on its face he would stop his oxen, even if he was alone

And turn it so that it lay on its side (Truly!) [Laughter]

His plough was a wooden one, but he ploughed till the sun was high

Its handles were made of wood, not of steel

His maize was plentiful, and he would require big oxen to harvest

He did not use those [first] two oxen (Truly!)

They were overcome by the size of the load

Yet the ploughing was done by just the two of them (Truly!)

A person starts slowly (Wow!)

And does something, by himself

And now when that thing has to be brought home, it requires [many] people (Truly!)

It will be like that with him, seeing that he is alone

He will do something big and when it comes home he will require the community (Truly!)

That thing requires the community, because it will be greater than him now, even though he did it alone

Just like those two oxen which ploughed together down below there, and the maize required many oxen (Truly!)

I stop there.

In this revealing address Shoti first identifies himself as a spokesman for Jotelo ward and establishes a distant kinship connection with Mgilimbane (the latter's father was born of a Ntlane woman, making him a classificatory cousin to Shoti). He praises Mgilimbane for holding *umsindleko,* thereby publicising his success at work and his return to, and acceptance of, the community. He makes it clear that it is the public *recognition* of Mgilimbane's work effort that is important, and that without this the work would be meaningless.

Shoti then refers to Mgilimbane's father and uses an extended metaphor to make the point that individual efforts may start off small but have big results. Two oxen might plough but in the hands of a skilful and diligent worker, such as Giladile was, the harvest will be very big, requiring six oxen to bring it in from the fields. Without those six oxen the harvest will be of no use. Likewise, Mgilimbane's work effort must be recognized and made meaningful by the community for it to have results. His work has the potential to contribute significantly to the development of his homestead, but for this potential to be realized requires the acceptance, participation and sanction of the community. What the metaphor of the two oxen does is to objectify Mgilimbane's work experience in the form of the beer drink and its attendant community, which is what makes it a success, and to enable reflection on it. In addition, it invokes the sanction of Mgilimbane's dead father for the message being conveyed, and it interprets migrant labour in terms of the rural economy, likening it to cultivation. Shoti's speech can thus be seen as linked to and partly constitutive of the beer drink as a performative act which fuses individual and community and dramatizes the interdependence of homesteads through communal participation in the event, which requires such participation for it to succeed.

The pattern of speaking at *umsindleko* appears to be that men (often close kin) who live in the same sub-ward section speak first, after the announcement of the reason for brewing has been made. They are then followed by others. The role of agnatic kin in securing ancestral blessings is made clear, as indicated above, but so is the role of the section and sub-ward in this respect. Shoti's speech illustrates this, and other examples may be cited from other events. At Ntanyongo's *umsindleko*, discussed below, initial speeches were made by local agnatic kin of the same section, followed by an immediate, unrelated neighbour, Stokwana, who emphasized Ntanyongo's dependence on and recognition of the community, concluding by saying:

> …Mhlakaza, take heed of what I have to say
>
> If you are a person, here at Mhlakaza's homestead, you are not alone
>
> You have a section![12]
>
> You called the section to announce that you are here at Mhlakaza's
>
> You have made it known that you are present today
>
> Know that when you go to work, as it has been said anyway
>
> You will return with a lamb…

As indicated earlier, *umsindleko* beer rituals for unsuccessful migrants were initially hard to make sense of, but eventually I came to understand why they were held. Whether it is a result of having worked well or having worked badly, *umsindleko* is an invocation to the ancestors. It is spoken of as *ukuzinqulela*, 'to invoke for oneself'. This invocation has elements of thanks and elements of request in both cases. When the contract has been financially unsuccessful, the migrant nevertheless has something to be thankful for. He has returned safely in good health and has not absconded. After all, the word *umsindleko* is derived from *ukusinda*, "to escape narrowly from accident or peril" (Kropf 1915, 391). He is asking that this should continue in future, but also that he should be able to return with money next time. Even where it is clear that the migrant has been successful, these points are made. The importance of returning home with money is balanced by pointing out that return in itself is a moral good and that a migrant's first duty is to return home, even if he has nothing, and not abscond 'at the place of the white man', never to be seen again. Others depend on him and he may be more successful next time he goes to work. The struggle over the meaning of labour is thus extended to a struggle over the person, his membership of the community, and the potential for future labour. Often, memories of an earlier, more successful time are invoked in this respect. At Ntanyongo's *umsindleko*, held because he was persistently unsuccessful at work, the initial explanation was made by Dlathu (Ntanyongo's FBSS), and he indicated the purpose of the event:

...The point that he is trying to make...

Is that he was cooked for in the past by his fathers and mothers

He has been thinking about that, because he has been working for a long time

He comes back from work without having achieved anything

He is cooking for himself, then, in remembrance of what used to be done

By his fathers and mothers...

Another speaker, Songxodo, a spokesman for neighbouring Jotelo, referred to Ntanyongo as having "come back naked" but that this had not been so in the past:

...Now then, you say that...this is not the usual thing

[Not] the custom which occurred during the time of your mother and father

You said that after they had spoken on your behalf

You brought something [from work]

It is our wish today

That you should return with this thing

After this work spell for which you have cooked for yourself

You say you are going to work again, and you will be able to buy something

Even if it is a chicken

And not come back having achieved nothing...

Whether successful or not, the migrant needs to be 'flattered', 'coaxed' and 'pleaded with' by the community and his kin. They want him to continue to go to work and to return as he does, in the one case to keep up the success, in the other to try and improve it. If the hunting dog fails to catch its prey it is brought home and slaughtered for, so that it will succeed the next day. In both types of *umsindleko* the migrant appeals to the ancestors and to the community through brewing beer for them; he relies on both of them for the success of the beer drink and thus for success (or continued success) at work. As one man expressed it when I asked if *umsindleko* was for the ancestors or for the people: "I bind them both with one rope".

In having *umsindleko* the unsuccessful migrant is symbolically washed so that misfortune will be driven out and so that his future work spells will be fruitful, with the help of the community, his kin, and his ancestors. The successful worker, too, is 'washed', to ensure that his good fortune will not leave him. Both thus involve transformation through the performance of the beer drink. In both, people must come 'to speak words', which goes together with the washing, the appeal and the thanks, and gives substance and support to these. As explicitly stated at these events, it is by bringing people into the homestead, demonstrating that it is a homestead 'for people', and through the words spoken by those in attendance, that the migrant communicates with the ancestors, that the ritual is effective.

One of the clearest illustrations of the performative nature of *umsindleko* as an invocation to the ancestors came from Ntanyongo himself when he said a few words after the men inside the hut had had their say. Here Ntanyongo confirmed the role of the people who attended the beer drink and apologized to latecomers for the fact that there was little beer left, and he concluded with an invocation to his ancestors (the refrain is again shown in parentheses):

Pardon, my people (There is someone who is standing; attention chiefs!)

Here is the point (Thank you!)

According to what is said regarding Xhosa custom (Gosh!)

When people give forth words

They must be well appeased (*Ah!*)

You will take it in good spirit, my people (Gosh!)

This chief [referring to himself] did not take it [maize] from just anywhere (Gosh!)

Mmh, he took it from what he had bought at the shop (Wow!)

And brewed beer from it (*Ah!*)

I received nothing from the land because of the drought (Gosh!)

You will take it in good spirit my people

And all of you here in this hut

Regarding the words you have spoken here in this home (Hope is not dead!)

Do not worry, my people! (All right!)

Do pardon me! (Be appeased!)

One of these days things will improve (*Ah!*)

Mmh

I have stepped down. (He has stepped down, let another who wants to speak stand up!)

In referring to 'my people', speakers can mean the men gathered in the hut, kin who are present, or (more usually) both. How to interpret depends on the context. At major rituals where the key roles are played by close kin and neighbours are less directly involved, it refers to the kin group, living and dead, while in the invocation that is made at such events it is directed at the ancestors and refers to the ancestral group. When used at beer rituals the term usually implicitly includes the ancestors. In Ntanyongo's case he starts off by asking for attention in the conventional manner—"Pardon, my people"— signaling that he wishes to speak. The next time he uses the term it is clear that he is referring explicitly to both the living, those present in the hut, and the dead: "You will take it in good spirit, my people". Finally, he shifts the reference from the living to focus exclusively on the ancestors: "You will take it in good spirit my people, *and all of you here in this hut*". This is followed by words spoken emphatically and directly to the ancestors: "Do not worry, my people! Do pardon me! One of these days things will improve."

That he was addressing his ancestors was also the understanding of the men listening, for after each of these last sentences a number of them called out *Camagu!* (Be appeased). This is always done after the invocation at ritual killings and after the animal has cried out, having been stabbed with the spear of the home. It is an urgent cry to the ancestors of the celebrating kin group to hear the plea that has been made and to grant the wishes expressed. However, at this *um-*

sindleko the people in attendance, too, had to be appeased (with beer), because they had come 'to give words', the words that ensured the success of the beer drink. And the response of the people, *Camagu!* was both a call to the ancestors and an indication that they accepted what Ntanyongo had said.

Oratory and the performance of *umsindleko*

Beer drink oratory is different from ordinary, everyday speech. The delivery is of a heightened kind, the speaking is a mode of performance different from other types of oral performance (Illustration 8). The speeches are set apart from speech at other kinds of rituals, court proceedings, and other speech situations. They are recognizable as beer drink talk by the heightened mode of delivery in conjunction with features such as humour and mock criticism, the air of entertainment and enjoyment that both speakers and listeners display, the degree of audience participation through comments and the refrain that often accompanies them, and their content, directly related to the context in which they occur. This aids the listeners in the interpretation of what is said.

An important theme in the oratory is that of 'building the homestead', a moral duty and the end towards which labour migration is directed. Returnees are reminded that those at home depend on this, and that without the cash brought home the homestead would be abandoned and die. Reference is thus made to the kind of behaviour that is *not* expected of a labour migrant, behaviour that would spoil his efforts and have a negative effect on his homestead. He should not 'eat' (waste) his money with "prostitutes and coloured women",[13] purchase things that add nothing to his homestead ("a guitar and a concertina") and so on. The homestead is embedded within a wider community and this is performed through the beer drink and reinforced by the speakers. The migrant's economic capital is framed in terms of its contribution to the homestead and rural society and is thereby transformed into social and symbolic capital. It is the presence and the words of the men of the section and sub-ward that recognize the migrant's work, make it meaningful and secure the future blessings of the ancestors.

Communicative competence at *umsindleko* means being able to verbalise the ideas and values associated with this view of labour migration and is a form of symbolic power wielded by senior men. It is through them that the migrant is honoured and given future success, since it is the presence of people and the speaking of words that secures the attention of the ancestors. The structure and organization of the beer drink are also important, as we shall

8. Speaker at beer drink

see in the following chapters. What this makes clear is that the ritual itself is a community affair, under the control of the sub-ward section, within which the individual homestead is subsumed, and which is concerned, through the distribution of beer, to regulate its relationships with other sections and sub-wards from within the space associated with the individual homestead to which the migrant has returned. The formal procedure that characterizes the event, as at any other formal beer drink, enables the migrant to experience rural society and structure afresh, as it were, and to make him part of it. The community strives to ensure that the migrant accepts the moral authority of the rural home and by participating in the beer drink he actually does so, embodying his incorporation into rural society. This is another way in which this ritual is performative. In addition, the central general message of all beer drink rituals is one that stresses the interdependence of homesteads existing in reciprocal relationship with each other. As Douglas pointed out in her analysis of middle-class English meals, "each meal carries with it something of the meaning of the other meals; each meal is a structured social event which structures others in its own image" (1972, 260). This metacommunicative aspect of *umsindleko* is part of its wider context as one kind of beer drink in a corpus of such events, and the messages that this carries need to be added to those linked to the specific ritual as a particular 'speech situation' (Hymes, 1972).

Many of the characteristics of *umsindleko* oratory indicate the use of a restricted or formal code guiding the oratory (Bernstein 1964; 1972; Bloch 1975). These features include the relatively fixed order of the speeches, repetition and redundancy, the use of a common body of metaphors, formulae and expressions, and reference to custom and tradition. The speeches are not contentious, the statements not contradictable or subject to argument. Even where the speaker appears to challenge the migrant regarding the results of his work, the challenge is merely rhetorical. The use of imperatives is common, particularly in the case of young migrants. As Bernstein pointed out, a restricted code "signals the normative arrangements of a group" and refers "to broad classes of interests" (1964, 255). It is 'homiletic' speech (Firth 1975, 42–43) and refers to common knowledge, accepted values and behaviour patterns and shared ideals. The use of such a code makes for social solidarity and reinforcement of the status quo, resists change, does not tolerate ambiguity, and seeks to legitimise the existing authority structure. A speaker using a restricted code limits the possible responses to what he says, follows a predetermined line, and to some extent predicts the nature of the next speech event, if the next speaker uses the same code (Bloch 1975). However, within the broad restrictions imposed by the code the speaker can use various alternatives, choose among various appropriate figures of speech and imagery, adopt a style of speaking that appeals to him, and so on. He can put his own twist to the situation, innovate, and manipulate available linguistic resources to produce a rich, effective and appreciated speech.

The *umsindleko* oratory also includes elements of an 'elaborated' or 'evaluative' code (Comaroff 1975), with reference to actual events and persons. The migrant, his actions and the actions of those closely associated with him are judged against a normative background. For a speech to be effective in the *umsindleko* context, it should have both of these elements, because the event is held due to certain normative expectations having been (or having not been) fulfilled. Those making the evaluation are the senior and elder men of the community, who speak backed by the status and authority of their position which is sanctioned by the ancestors. One cannot easily make a distinction between who speaks and what is said.

If he has done well the returned migrant is held as an example for others to follow ("you will be teaching people who are ignorant"). His action in going out to work and returning with the fruits of his labour, expressed with characteristic understatement as a lamb, a kid or a chicken, is defined as morally right and proper. But the oratory also places the individual migrant and his action within a broader perspective, that of the overall relationship between labour migration and rural society. In speaking about migrant labour, the orators are also speaking about their relationship with it. In interpreting the actions of the individual migrant, they make migration meaningful to him, the listeners, and to the community. In speaking at *umsindleko* the seniors thus engage in a performance on behalf of the wider community. Bauman writes in this respect that "performance as a mode of spoken verbal communication consists in the assumption of responsibility to an audience for a display of communicative competence" (1975, 293).

In this sense *umsindleko* seeks, through its performance, to present an authoritative version of what it means to be a rural migrant and constitutes a form of social reproduction and social control. The power and authority of the elders and of the community in general is aimed at ensuring that labour migration continues but that it does not threaten their rural lifestyle, in terms of which they interpret and sanction it and make it meaningful. Although clearest in Mbuntshuntshu's case, the element of control occurs in all *umsindleko* beer drinks. The emphasis on return as a moral good in itself, for example, serves to highlight not only the danger of absconding but also the fact that the rural home is primary, to be served by means of occasional forays into the mining-industrial world. As "speech designed to persuade" or "to form attitudes or to induce actions in other human agents" (Burke 1969, 41, 49), *umsindleko* rhetoric is transformative, it seeks to incorporate the migrant back into society and the object is union or re-union. In doing so it must transform the migrant and his work, but in this is it can succeed only temporarily. Why should this be so?

Umsindleko attempts to bridge the gap between two states, that of work and home, but it is forced to unite as well as separate them. In making migrant labour meaningful to rural society it seeks to impose a particular interpretation, implicitly addressing the problem of having to leave the home in order to maintain and develop it, which involves encouraging men to leave again in the future to continue their wage-earning careers. The struggle is therefore a continuous one, one that cannot be won, one born out of the contradictions and the dialectics of labour migration itself as a bridge uniting two fields. This is an example of the kind of social indeterminacy that Turner (1986) spoke of, the kind that cannot be resolved, but which is addressed in ritual in an attempt to grapple with it. The best that can be hoped for is to stay on top of it temporarily, to continue to reinforce one interpretation over another, and to ameliorate it through adjusting to changes that threaten the structure of power relations at home and that can be controlled. The following chapter deals with how one such threat was overcome, at least for a period.

Although I have interpreted *umsindleko* as a form of performance at various points in the above discussion, and alluded to many of the features of performance outlined in chapter three, this has been more to keep this issue in mind than to present a full interpretation of *umsindleko* in theoretical terms. We are not yet at a stage where we can reflect adequately on *umsindleko* in terms of the theoretical overview presented earlier. For this it is necessary to bring together the historical changes affecting Xhosa speakers as outlined in the second part of chapter two with the development of the ritual that we have been examining here, since it is in the context of this evolution and its historical stimuli that the theoretical issues become most pertinent. This discussion is therefore continued in the next chapter, where *umsindleko* is examined in historical terms.

Endnotes

1. Sections of the material in this chapter are drawn from McAllister (1981).
2. The conventional distinction between witches, who are believed to have occult powers or to work through a variety of familiars, and sorcerers, who make use of potent substances to do evil, holds quite well among indigenous people in South Africa (Hammond-Tooke 1974), though it is at times confounded—for example, by people becoming 'witches' through the use of medicinal substances.
3. Some wash on the night before departure, not in the morning.

4. This symbolizes the cattle that will be bought with the money that the migrant has, ideally, brought home with him.

5. Similar rituals associated with the return of a migrant worker have been reported among the Thonga (Junod, 1927 II, 397–98) and the Zulu (Vilakazi 1962, 115).

6. All senior men have praise names such as these, often linked to some incident during their youth, some personal characteristic, or the name of a favourite ox. Such names can be either laudatory or deprecatory. Nadabanduna means "affairs of a chief's councillor", while Ndlebendja means "dog ears".

7. The speaker uses the plural for bread (*izonka*) but the context indicates that he is referring to food rather than to loaves.

8. The Xhosa word *ukungxengxeza* connotes recognition and supplication, gratitude and appeasement, as well as apology and asking for pardon. For example, if a major ritual for the ancestors that requires the killing of an ox cannot be performed, a smaller offering such as a goat or beer may be made as a holding measure, and is referred to as *ukungxengxeza*.

9. *Ingesi*, literally 'English'. It is a type of dog with greyhound ancestry.

10. This speaker addressed Ndabanduna as 'Botliva'. Both Bhasimiti and Botliva are names derived from the work-place. Botliva is from Botrivier, the name of a town in the Western Cape where Ndabanduna once worked as a labourer. Bhasimiti is derived from Bass (Boss) Smit, one of Modi's supervisors at work. Apparently this supervisor was prone to violence, and Modi's boyhood stick-fighting skills reminded his friends of Bass Smit.

11. Except for a young man who has been admitted to beer drinks by his seniors. In such a case the young man would spend the duration of the event in the main hut with the others, seated with other young men of his status.

12. Stokwana uses the term *ilali*, which translates as 'location', an old term for administrative area. In Shixini it is used to mean either or both the sub-ward and the sub-ward section, but the context indicates that it is the section that is being referred to.

13. In South Africa the term 'coloured' refers to people of mixed ancestry, not members of any particular indigenous Bantu-speaking group. In terms of earlier apartheid legislation the entire population was officially classified as White, Indian, Bantu (i.e. African) or Coloured.

7 Snakes, Blood, Money and Migration[1]

Gidli, a great-grandfather, whose son had lived in his umzi, said, 'Formerly an umzi was under the thumb of the father, now it is under the thumb of the son. Things are bad now.' Everywhere there is complaint of the growing disobedience of children.

(Hunter 1936, 60)

Prominent in the *umsindleko* speeches is reference to the past, tradition and custom. Going out to work for the homestead is seen as a thing of old. As one speaker put it: "It is an old custom of Hintsa's that you are following here." Ntanyongo was said to be "bringing to mind that he was cooked for by his mother and father"; Mbuntshuntshu was told that *umsindleko* had been done for him before while his father was still alive, and that his father, too, had *umsindleko* done for him. In fact, however, one of the most interesting things about *umsindleko* is that it is of relatively recent origin. Unraveling this provides us with a clear link to the historical development of beer drinks as a ritual form as well as to their role and significance in the context of the changing nature of rural production amongst Xhosa speakers, outlined in chapter two. It thus provides us with insights into the construction as well as the possible destabilization of an earlier Red Xhosa habitus.

An old custom of Hintsa's?

Among Xhosa speakers in general, from at least the 1930s onwards, the return of a migrant worker to his home and community was marked by the ritual sacrifice of an animal. Among the Mpondo this was called 'to give thanks' (*ukubulela*). Hunter stated that: "Persons having escaped from danger may kill in thanksgiving to their *amathongo* [ancestors]. Nowadays it is an *isiko* [custom] to kill when a man returns safely from the mines." (Hunter 1936, 251). Among the Bhaca a beast was slaughtered as 'a special thanksgiving' (*umbuliso*) when a young man returned from his first spell at work, "to thank the *amatshongo* for keeping him safe" (Hammond-Tooke 1962, 240).[2] In Keiskammahoek this ritual was known as 'to give thanks to the ancestors' (*ukubulela abadala*) (Wilson et al

1952). Similar killings among these groups, called by similar names, were associated with escape from danger and with safe return from war or a long journey.

In Shixini, too, the return of a migrant worker used to be marked by a killing, referred to simply as *umhlinzeko* (from *ukuhlinza*, to slaughter).[3] People said that the killing took place "because when you return home there should be the smell of meat, it should be clear to all that you have returned". This was regarded as an invocation and a thanksgiving to the ancestors, though there was considerable variation among informants regarding the procedure involved. Some said that it took place inside the cattle byre, that the spear of the home was used, that it was necessary for the goat or ox to cry out, and that the returned migrant ritually tasted a special portion of the meat. In addition, an invocation to the ancestors by the migrant's father was made. These features indicate an ancestor ritual killing in the full sense of the term, but it is clear that it was a small, domestic affair. Agnates and other close kin who lived nearby would attend, as would close neighbours, but it was not a public, community occasion. In this sense it was similar to lesser rituals which are still performed today such as *ukubingelela* (for a newborn child and its mother).

Others say that it did not matter what kind of animal was killed, that the animal was killed outside the cattle byre simply by having its throat cut and that there was no ritual tasting. It is possible that these variations were associated with different households or clans, but it is also possible that informants were referring to different time-periods. To the extent that *umhlinzeko* still occurs it is not of a religious character. A man simply kills a sheep, goat or pig for himself or for his son, usually next to the cattle byre, without any ceremony and without calling kin to be present. The meat is consumed largely by the family concerned, though portions may be sent to neighbours and nearby kin. The father addresses the son briefly, saying: "You have returned from work. I am doing this for you because of that, in order to encourage you" or something similar. There is no other formal speaking. In accounting for the change from the killing to the beer drink I shall also try to account for why the killing, when it still occurs, has lost its religious character.

All the older men who I spoke to about *umhlinzeko* said that as boys and young men they had been slaughtered for by their fathers when they returned from work. Nowadays, very few such killings occur, and the custom has to a large extent been replaced with *umsindleko*, often a relatively large affair attended by hundreds of people, who come from neighbouring sub-wards as well as the local sub-ward sections. The two terms are used interchangeably to refer to either a beer drink or a killing. This practice is probably facilitated by *umsindleko*'s more general meaning as food prepared for a traveler, and also by its etymology as a term derived from *ukusinda*, 'to have a narrow escape'.

My attention was drawn to *umsindleko*'s relatively recent origin after a speech by Dwetya, an elderly man, at Ndabanduna's *umsindleko*. His words included the following:

> ...Dombothi, when I grew up it was said that when one comes back from service a slaughtering takes place
>
> There was a change: It was said: 'What's this?!'
>
> This person has come home with a snake', and this custom was discarded
>
> I myself was slaughtered for by Tela
>
> He discarded that practice
>
> And you were slaughtered for by Poni
>
> You have returned from service, from the business of serving Poni's homestead
>
> In my case, I was building Tela's homestead
>
> It has been like that since I was born
>
> I am speaking to say we fell down [changed]
>
> It was said: 'Oh no! He has bought it!'
>
> We came to this Dombothi
>
> To this that has been done by your wife in cooking for you
>
> Child of my grand-mother, on your return from work
>
> This thing, Dombothi, that is being done by your wife
>
> I commend it, even though it was not so at the beginning
>
> It was a goat slaughtered by your father
>
> He would say: 'My child, I am slaughtering for you because you are from service'
>
> That was changed [because] people said: 'No! He has bought a snake'
>
> Child of my grandmother! Dombothi!
>
> I say engrave these words in your mind...

After recording this speech I asked a variety of people to explain what Dwetya had meant. One man put it this way: "This change came about because people used their money to buy wisdom. This wisdom lives on blood, and fathers, in slaughtering for their sons, did not know if they were providing blood for wisdom or not, since they did not know if their sons had bought it or not." Asked for clarification, he said that 'wisdom' was a snake:

> A son goes out to work and he buys a snake there. If you slaughter here for your son you are slaughtering for a snake that is going to ruin your homestead…They say that this snake is a medicine. You put it in your pocket and keep it there while you move around. At night it becomes a beautiful girl and the owner must sleep with her. There are seven vaginas and you have to use them all that night. The next thing people hear is that your son is a witch and that he kills people. They will then go and burn down your homestead.

It is obvious to anyone familiar with Xhosa speakers that this snake is *umamlambo*, a witch familiar widely associated with male witches,[4] which is capable of rapid changes of form (from a herbal substance to a shiny bangle to a beautiful girl, etc.) and which at times manifests itself in the form of a fabulous, large, multi-coloured serpent. As a snake it is sometimes thought to live in rivers (the name means 'mother of the river') and it is sometimes identified with another witch familiar called *icanti*, the water-sprite (Hunter 1936, Soga 1931).[5] Its ambiguous and rapidly changing form in some ways makes it an apt symbol for labour migrancy, which is itself ambiguous, both threatening to the rural society and potentially enriching (like the snake, which can supposedly bring great wealth, but at the expense of one's family members, whom it kills). It is thought that labour migrants are able to purchase *umamlambo* at work from herbalists or *amaIsilamisi* (Muslims). Once *umamlambo* has been purchased, it is said to be exceedingly difficult to get rid of it. The snake issues instructions to and has control over its owner. If he fails to comply with its demands for regular slaughtering he will become insane. It lives on blood and can 'eat' him just as it is able to eat (kill) others. Some men are believed to obtain it unwittingly, having bought what they thought were simply magical potions which would enable them to become wealthy, attract women, or whatever, only to discover later that they have become possessed by *umamlambo* (cf. Wilson et al 1952, 189; Hammond-Tooke 1962, 285–86). If the owner tries to throw the substance away, it miraculously re-appears. It is said that one has to call in a skilled herbalist to rid oneself of it, but that the herbalist has to take over ownership and cannot drive *umamlambo* away completely, though he has the means to control it.

The usual motivation attributed to those who are thought to buy the snake is a desire for wealth, and this is achieved through killing those who stand in one's way. Any man can, in theory, buy a snake, but it is usually sons who are thought to acquire it, in order to kill their fathers and inherit the father's status, authority and livestock. Since the father cannot know if the son has returned from work with a snake or not, he refrains from slaughtering for his son, because, as one informant put it, this would be "marrying the snake to the son". People maintain that it will be evident from the son's actions if he does indeed 'take up a snake': "We will see it from his behaviour. He will demand that there should be a killing. Then we will confront each other." Whether young or old, nowadays a man demonstrates that he does not have occult powers, that he does not have a snake, and that he is not a threat to his seniors, by not slaughtering on return from work and by brewing beer instead. The snake is in the back of people's minds at every *umsindleko*. It informs their participation in the event and the words they speak; it is part of the historical and moral context in terms of which the migrant is evaluated and re-incorporated.

Relations of production and ritual change

What are we to make of this? Ideally, any sociological account of the change from the sacrificial killing to the beer drink should include reference to all or most of the features of both these rituals. This leads away from simple but plausible explanations such as a decrease in stock holdings coupled with increased maize yields during the period when large-scale labour migrancy was becoming institutionalized. These may certainly have been important circumstances, but alone they are not a sufficient explanation. They indicate that the ritual change may have been economically induced, and one might expect some rationalization for the change in mystical terms. However, this does not tell us why the change was conceived of in terms of witch beliefs, why a small, fairly private ritual was replaced by a large, public one, or why the participants in the latter address formal speeches which often have the characteristics of admonitions to the returned migrant, a feature that did not occur in conjunction with the killing. These are crucial questions, and need to be answered in accounting for the ritual change.

As indicated earlier in chapter two, a number of historical developments during the period from about 1870 onwards led to a series of important changes in the nature of rural life in the Transkei. To summarise these here, homesteads became much smaller as polygyny and the extended family declined and as young men established their own homesteads at an earlier stage than before. There was a switch from sorghum to maize, and changes in relations of production which emphasized reciprocal labour co-operation between homesteads. Labour migration became institutionalized as a necessary means for homesteads to acquire the material resources needed for rural production and homestead survival more generally. Coinciding with the later period during which migrant labour became firmly embedded in rural society, from about 1900 onwards, there was an increase in the frequency of beer drinking and the development of new types of beer drinks.

I would suggest, given the nature of labour migration and the role it played in the new mode of rural production, that a sacrifice attended by a few agnatic kin became inappropriate as a vehicle for reincorporating returned migrants and for making statements about the relationship between migrant labour and rural society. A beer drink took its place because it was more appropriate for this purpose. In all likelihood this occurred as beer drinking was becoming more and more widespread in rural Transkei and as new kinds of beer drinks arose, as indicated in the historical record. What beer drinks do is emphasize territorial groups rather than kinship, the interdependence between neighbouring homesteads and the reciprocal relations between them. It is suggested, then, that the ritual change from *umhlinzeko* to *umsindleko* coincided with, reflected and provided normative or ideological support for the historical process of change outlined earlier. From a ritual which correlated return from work with the unity and independence of the lineage segment or extended family, a new ritual emerged, similar in some respects to the old, but with a new emphasis, namely one where the importance of the local group and of the role that migrant labour played within it was recognized.

But why was this change conceptualized and justified in terms of witchcraft? Peter Geschiere (1997) has shown that witchcraft in Africa is not simply some remnant of the past but is instead very much a part of the modernizing process, and that witch beliefs are transformed in contexts of change to deal with new social and political challenges. Other authors have made the same point in different ethnographic contexts (e.g. Niehaus 2001, van der Drift 2002). It is worth summarising the case described by van der Drift since it, too, deals with the consumption of alcoholic liquor in the context of changing relations of rural production. In this West African case Balanta elders retained their authority in a situation where the labour of juniors and women became more and more important in cashew production. Alcohol played an important role in this process, with cashew liquor (a by-product) used extensively in ritual and festivities, bartered for labour, and sold on markets. The power of the elders was expressed in ritual through their power to communicate with ancestral spirits, but as women and youth became important for cashew production their power gained expression through the idiom of witchcraft. Resentment and criticism of the elders was expressed through a new religious and anti-witchcraft movement that attracted women and young men, and that challenged the authority of both elders and ancestors. This movement, although not fully successful, had "a liberating effect, sparking group solidarity among women and youth, in an ongoing process of democratization." (ibid., 191). One result has been an increasingly prominent role played by youth and women in festivity and ritual, and greater freedom to determine their own norms (including increased alcohol consumption) in such contexts.

In the Xhosa case, I believe that the belief in the *umamlambo* familiar has been used to justify and make intellectual sense of the switch from a killing to a beer drink, a switch that occurred as a result of certain ambiguities and strains in social life not unlike those affecting the Balanta. Anthropologists have conventionally regarded witchcraft as a response to situations of stress and ambivalence, allowing people to express conflict that is not otherwise resolvable in a recognizable idiom. In this case, these sources of ambivalence, tension and conflict originated in the complex of historical developments outlined earlier. In this respect we need to bear in mind authority patterns, in particular the changing nature of the relationship between father and son, which was subjected to strain and underwent certain changes with the son's increased independence and access to wage-earnings, and as sons moved out of the father's homestead to establish their own homesteads at a much earlier stage than before.

Seniority, filial piety and the jural authority of fathers over sons were, and to a large extent still are, extremely important principles of Xhosa life. In the past this was expressed largely in control over marriage, as expressed so clearly in Ndabanduna's address to Mbuntshuntshu at the latter's *umsindleko* (see chapter six). Previously, to become independent a young man had first to marry, for which he required bridewealth. He obtained cattle for bridewealth from his father and/or other senior agnatic kin though it was also possible to obtain cattle through raids and labour service for a chief or wealthy person (Wilson 1981). Colonialism, land deprivation and the growth of a money economy changed this. Raiding was no longer possible, and cattle became scarce due to various diseases and growing impoverishment. Migrant labour became a means of obtaining cattle independently of the father and senior kin (ibid., 140–41). This process probably occurred much earlier among the Xhosa proper, whose cattle holdings took some time to recover fully from the cattle-killing of 1857 and among whom labour migration became institutionalized at an early stage, than it did elsewhere in the Eastern Cape. In Pondoland (not affected by the cattle-killing) in 1931–1932 only 17 per cent of men in 115 marriages examined by Hunter had provided all their own marriage cattle, but this was at a time when "almost every homestead owned cattle and was largely self-supporting in food." (*loc. cit.*). Later, in Pondoland as elsewhere, sons became relatively independent of their seniors as far as finding bridewealth was concerned, threatening the power of elders, as indicated in the epigram at the beginning of this chapter. This was not unusual in southern Africa, and the role of migrant labour in fostering conflict between elder and junior has been widely documented. Harries, for example, has shown how in late nineteenth century Mozambique, migrant labour offered juniors "new strategies for throwing off the dominance of the chiefs and *numzane* [powerful homestead heads]" (1982, 150). Here, elders made vigorous attempts to retain their control over bridewealth and to maintain their position of dominance over juniors, but they were ultimately unsuccessful. Juniors lost respect for their seniors, refused to perform labour tasks for them, and opposed them politically (ibid., 154–55).[6]

In the Transkei, to be sure, while still resident with his father the son's growing independence was tempered by the fact that cattle bought by him were regarded as belonging to the father, and he still depended on his father and other kin in the marriage process and in ritual. But his bargaining power was improved. From a position of total dependence, the son became someone upon whom the father depended for the cash inputs needed to enable his homestead to survive. This weakened the father's authority and the political and economic power of seniors in general. The ability of sons to found their own homesteads at an earlier stage exacerbated this, and potentially deprived the father's homestead of a wage-earner. Access to wealth that could be had without the agency of seniors was a threat which, it is suggested, was manifested in the belief that sons could become witches *at work*, where they could *buy* a snake with their earnings as labour migrants. The belief that the snake sometimes takes the form of a beautiful girl with whom the son has sexual relations also makes sense, in view of the threat to the seniors' role as provider of bridewealth. The snake provides illicit sexual satisfaction and simultaneously subverts paternal control.

It is suggested that the *umhlinzeko* killing was stopped partly as a result of the change in the father/son relationship, that its cessation was symbolic of the desire by fathers to retain control over their sons, and an attempt to guard against the possibility of witchcraft. The *umhlinzeko* killing emphasized the bond between father and son and the son's status within the local agnatic group. Father slaughtered for son, emphasizing the son's dependence on the father and on agnates. By brewing *umsindleko* beer, on the other hand, the father avoided the possibility of feeding the snake but still acknowledged the son's role in contributing to the homestead and, through this, to the community, since the father's homestead was dependent on the son's earnings in order to retain its place in the new organization of production. This applied even when sons founded their own homesteads, since they usually remained near to the father's place, retained close contact with their fathers, supported them (ideally), and co-operated with them in the process of rural production. As Heron (1990) has shown, many Shixini ploughing companies have an agnatic core, and have persisted through time. *Umsindleko* addressed the ambiguity that had come to characterize the relationship between fathers and sons, and between seniors and juniors more generally. It allowed for recognition of the juniors' important role as wage-earners but interpreted this in terms of the relationship between homesteads and sought to reinforce the principle of seniority through the role that seniors played in the beer drink.

Brewing beer for the community as a whole indicates that the father is still the head of the homestead, and that his homestead, through the efforts of the son, is being built up and is a good one to co-operate with. The power of the son is thereby channeled and made relevant to a wider principle, that of neighbourhood, rather than that of the jural relationship between father and son. The *umhlinzeko* killing involved the direct father/son relationship, *umsindleko* the relationship between homestead head and other homesteads, through the son's efforts. The son as independent wage-earner was essentially ambiguous and disorderly—a threat to structure. By relating his role as migrant more strongly to the emerging principle of community or neighbourhood (in *umsindleko*) a clearer definition of the son's role in the re-structured rural space developed, and his potential disorderliness was controlled (Douglas 1966).

Danger in the margins

One could view this more broadly also, in terms of questions of boundaries and dangers, as suggested by Mary Douglas. Having been to work the migrant has breached the physical and moral boundary of the rural community and may be seen as potentially polluting, one who has left structure and experienced a foreign, dangerous and threatening reality, but one that also contains the means for rural survival and growth. For the home community to maintain its integrity rural society must be kept separate from the work situation and not confused with it. The returning migrant represents a mixture of the two and this is essentially disorderly and potentially dangerous. The danger is removed by negating the elements of liminality that may threaten the home structure. In a sense the 'snake' is but one of these; others are explicitly addressed in the oratory. He must show that he has not been permanently affected by his experiences, that he rejects the urban lifestyle and accepts the basic norms, values and institutions of rural society. The home reality must be affirmed as paramount, not only to him, but to the community as a whole, many of whose members are migrants or ex-migrants, and which is engaged with and stands to gain (and to lose) from migratory labour. The potentially positive aspects of the immersion in the dangerous work environment need to be stressed. Disorder "has potentiality. It symbolizes both danger and power" (ibid., 114). This power is recognized in ritual, where it is harnessed, and the dangerous elements neutralized. The oratory of *umsindleko* indicates that the experience of migrant labour is ambiguous—both dangerous and supportive, it can undermine rural society by enticing the migrant away but it is necessary for the money on which rural people depend. This ambiguity is (temporarily) resolved in ritual performance by keeping home and work apart, by rejecting the negative aspects of work and emphasizing the positive. The positive elements are interpreted in terms of rural structure and migrant labour is controlled, by using it to focus on home reality. Migrant labour is thus interpreted in terms of the fixed, known and orderly.

With regard to the snake, in particular, the ambiguous social position of juniors and their threat to seniors was reflected in the belief that they had access to a form of mystical power that rivaled the power of the ancestors available to elders. Resolution of the ambiguity, of the conflict between senior and junior, and of the threat of the uncontrolled power of witchcraft was achieved through substituting beer for the killing of a beast or goat.[7] Controlling migrant labour and ensuring that it would be a force for good could not be achieved by the killing. The very blood being offered to the ancestors in the killing was feeding the snake, which symbolized the potential disorderliness and danger of the migrant. Blood itself thus became an ambiguous symbol, standing for both the snake and the disorderly forces of witchcraft, on the one hand, and for the orderliness of society, represented by the ancestors and their earthly representatives, the elders. Substitution of beer for blood resolved this. This is also the likely reason why, when killings for returned migrants do occur today, which is seldom, they do not involve an invocation to the ancestors. They are not religious, and are seen merely as providing meat to honour the returnee.

To put it more simply, the *umhlinzeko* killing, with its emphasis on agnation, became inappropriate in the context of migrant labour and the co-operation of neighbours, and it stated a principle that was being challenged and contradicted by the very subject of the ritual. The switch to a beer drink accommodated both these contradictions. It re-aligned the father/son relation-ship in terms of the nature of the relationship between homesteads, and it re-lated migrant labour to the changed organization of production. In this case, then, witchcraft is neither simply a weapon of the weak nor a way in which the powerful attempt to maintain their position, though the belief in umam-lambo may be interpreted as either—fathers trying to bolster their positions weakened by the power of the migrant sons, or sons flexing their economic muscle in the idiom of the occult. But one could also interpret it as a mech-anism through which migrants demonstrate their moral commitment to their rural home and kin and assure their seniors that they are not attempting to subvert the rural moral order.

Habitus, change and performance

To conclude this discussion of umsindleko, it might be appropriate to reflect on the theoretical perspective outlined in chapter three, where an attempt was made to integrate Bourdieu's practice theory with the anthropology of per-formance. Performance was defined as a form of practice with a number of characteristics, to which umsindleko (and its predecessor, umhlinzeko) corre-sponds in many respects. In this chapter we have seen that umsindleko emerged as a new form of practice, or developed from an earlier one, in a context of structural change in South Africa as a whole and in the rural areas in particu-lar. What is the 'logic of practice' here? To Bourdieu, practices are aspects of strategies associated with a particular habitus as it is enacted within a field of forces in which there is a contest over capital which is ultimately a struggle for power and the authority to define meaning. Groups occupying different sub-ject positions and interacting within the field have aspects of their habitus in common with each other but there are also important differences correspon-ding to their positions within the field, their access to capital, and their sub-jective constructions of meaning. Structural changes within or affecting posi-tions within the field require adjustments on the part of agents, leading to adjustments to the habitus.

This seems to apply quite well to the switch from the ritual killing to the beer drink in the light of the implications that migrant labour had for rural social relations, given the changes to the social organization of production. On the one hand, juniors and seniors may be seen as engaging in a new form of contest as the former gained access to cash and potential independence and the latter strove to retain their positions of authority over their juniors. On the other hand, as kinship became less important as the basis of rural production, homestead heads were required to adjust to the structural changes having an impact in the rural field by realigning themselves with each other on the basis of territorial contiguity rather than on the basis of kinship (though in practice there was an overlap between the two). This involved a form of contest as well as co-operation, because it was in the interest of each homestead to show that it was able to make a contribution to the collective good. The interest of agents changed as the nature of the rural field changed. The stronger the homestead's economic position the more desirable it became as a partner in arrangements such as agricultural companies and the more favourable its position in terms of bargaining power within such groups, which affected matters such as the order of ploughing (see chapter four).

To do this the economic capital that juniors had access to had to be converted both into forms of economic capital that constituted the homestead's assets, and which dovetailed with the new form of production (cattle, ploughs, etc.), and into symbolic capital (at the *umsindleko* beer drink). This symbolic capital was deployed in the relationship between junior and senior as well as in the relation between homestead heads jostling for position within the co-operative structure that developed. Migrant labour could no longer be construed only in terms of the benefits to the individual homestead and its inhabitants; it became something of communal concern. *Umsindleko* reproduced the structure of relations in the rural field in symbolic terms, converting the economic power of juniors into symbolic power wielded by their elders, on whom they were held to depend for ancestral favour as well as for the social approval of their efforts at work. This involved an adjustment to the Red Xhosa habitus in terms of which the contest over labour was engaged in, though there was also continuity in terms of resistance to fuller incorporation into the wider economy and in the sense that labour continued to be construed in terms of the general contribution that it made in the rural field. The boundary between rural home and urban work place so crucial to the Red orientation remained strong. The *umsindleko* ritual, in instituting a state of affairs, also creates boundaries by confirming and communicating a particular rural Xhosa identity linked to that state of affairs and excluding other possibilities which are antithetical to the rural habitus (Bourdieu 1991, 120–22.)

At an earlier phase of this process, the evidence for the transposability of the habitus lies in the analogical transfer of meaning from a ritual marking return from war or danger to one marking return from work, as the Red Xhosa habitus developed its distinctive characteristics linked to the struggle with capitalism and apartheid-style colonial rule. In another sense, beer rituals as an emerging genre and aspect of the Red Xhosa practice provided the basic principles of organization onto which the new meanings of migrant labour were grafted. A move from co-operation between kin to co-operation between neighbours indicates a further shift and adjustment. Changes to the habitus represented by the development of *umsindleko* can thus be seen to have involved new forms of struggle over power related to the changing structure of the rural field. Such changes thus emerged from the relationship between present and past, from the nature of the past manifestations of the habitus and the socio-economic and political conditions relevant then which led to contradictions and ambiguities as these 'objective conditions' changed.

This process was facilitated by the performative nature of ritual and through the role of ritual in the social process. As framed action in which people achieve a heightened sense of awareness and receptivity, *umsindleko* is an ideal medium through which to enable public reflexivity on the nature of labour migration. This much has been amply demonstrated in the previous chapter in the many examples of the oratory associated with this event. In this sense it is also a re-enactment of experience, bringing together the subjective experience of labour migration and the structural conditions under which it takes place, transforming the individual experience into a communal reality. Ndabanduna's account of previous migratory experience is a good example of this, but it applies also to all those present who have been migrants in the past.

In this ritual process the individual migrant is linked to a body of beliefs and ultimate values concerning labour migration and its role in the rural social order, transforming the nature of the individual's migrant work by placing it in a social and moral context that cannot be questioned. Ritual institutes and sanctions a particular state of affairs (Bourdieu 1991, 119); in the case of *umsindleko* (as well as other kinds of beer rituals) it does so partly by acting out this state of affairs that it sanctions. It does this by symbolically re-creating the rural social order in terms of its territorial, age, gender and kinship structure and divisions (this is discussed fully in chapters nine and 10), framing this and sanctifying it within a ritual context, and specifying the place of labour migration within it. As *umsindleko* developed out of an older form (*umhlinzeko*), the changed structure of rural relations was enacted and constructed, and the migrant's place in that order made clear, making migration meaningful in terms of the new order and imbuing this meaning with authority.

In the *umsindleko* ritual, both beer and the migrant are powerful, indexical symbols, closely related to each other. Beer is made from maize, the product of agricultural labour and thus of the new relations of production based on co-operative work. Without the migrant to supply the necessary cash inputs, such production would be well nigh impossible, so in one sense the migrant *is* the beer consumed at *umsindleko*. More generally, consuming the beer is to consume the combination and the product of both migrant work and communal effort. In this way, through performance, migrant work is transformed into something that is relevant to rural production. In this respect, beer acts also as a powerful, indexical and bi-polar symbol. On the one hand it is the product of labour, associated with the axiomatic values of building the homestead, the elders and the community. On the other, it is associated with the mild but satisfying physical sensation of intoxication and well-being brought about through the commensality of beer drinking and the enjoyment of the oratory and debate that accompanies it. Here there is great redundancy, as indicated in chapter 10, with successive rounds of drinking continuing for as many hours as the beer lasts.

As a performative event that creates a particular kind of relationship between migrant and home, the struggle between junior and elder is won in favour of the latter. The young migrant is shown to depend on both the mystical power of the ancestors (accessed via the elders) and on the participation of the community in securing these blessings through the beer drink, and in making his migrancy meaningful and valued. This is performed and made real through the conduct of the beer drink, again with much redundancy; the point is made over and over again in the oratory associated with *umsindleko*. Those who possess symbolic capital are those who have the power and authority to construct and represent the nature of the social world (via oratory). Here it is the power that is vested in senior men, who exercise it over their juniors (and over women, but with a different purpose and in a different way). The elders use the symbolic power of their oratory to secure their status in relation to their juniors and over their less communicatively competent peers. Subjecting themselves to the structure and proceedings of the beer drink, the listeners tacitly accept the power of the speaker/s and of the legitimacy of the social hierarchy of which they are part (Bourdieu 1991, 23), and they too, in turn, will become seniors as they mature over time, so they have something of a vested interest in the maintenance of the hierarchy. The practice of *ukuvumisa* (to cause to agree) signals assent and therefore authorization—the one who *vumisa*'s does so on behalf of the group which, through him, literally assents to the speakers every utterance.

So the performative nature of *umsindleko* operates at all three levels specified by Tambiah (1985)—in the Austinian sense, the formal and the indexical. It is in terms of its performative characteristics also, as outlined immediately above and more fully in chapter three, I would suggest, again following Tambiah on the nature of ritual change, that *umsindleko* was able to succeed as an innovative form, producing a transformation that was linked to, but significantly different from the transformation associated with its predecessor, the *umhlinzeko* killing. The adjustment to the Red Xhosa habitus that took place was facilitated by constructing the new, emergent meaning of migrant labour in a performative ritual context that provided continuity with past practice but which also allowed the new emphasis to emerge over time.

Endnotes

1. This chapter is partly a re-worked and updated version of McAllister (1985).

2. Xhosa in Willowvale recognise the word *amathongo* or its Bhaca equivalent, *amatshongo*, but prefer to use the word *izinyanya* to refer to their ancestral spirits.

3. The etymological similarity between this word and *umsindleko* is easily recognizable, though the position of the alveolar fricatives (s, z) and the lateral plosives (dl, hl) are reversed. If they were not, the two words would be virtually indistinguishable.

4. Soga (1931, 193), Hunter (1936, 286–87), Hammond-Tooke (1962, 285; 1970, 129) and Wilson et al. (1952, 190).

5. In recent news reports a 'half-fish, half-horse' monster that inhabits the Mzintlava river in Transkei's Mt Ayliff district, and which has reportedly killed seven people who were trying to cross the river, by sucking out their blood and brains, has been identified as *umamlambo* by some. To the police, the victims had simply drowned. See: http://www.ncf.carleton.ca/~bz050/mamlam.html

6. Similar trends are reported from other parts of Africa. In Kenya, youths returning with money posed a threat to the authority of the elders and of the elders' control over women and bridewealth, "the fundamental basis of their authority" (Ambler 1991, 175).

7. One outstanding characteristic of the 'snake' is its ability to change form (Soga 1931, 193). As a familiar with ambiguous boundaries it is also an apt symbol for the ambiguous nature of the relationship between father and son that developed over time and that made a killing inappropriate.

8 Brewing, Beer Talk, Preparations and Preliminaries

I tell you, they were really dressed up. They had cleaned themselves. They were filled with awe; they were profoundly reverential. They were proud of themselves; they were preparing the beer.

Xhosa story-teller Nongenile Masithathu Zenani (1992).

A number of references have been made in previous chapters to the significance of the manner in which a beer drink ritual is organized and held in arriving at an overall understanding of its performative nature and of its status as part of a rural Xhosa practice. This applies to the formal proceedings, in particular, but also to the way in which the brewing takes place and to the preparations made for the event. These topics are the subject of this and the following two chapters. We commence with the brewing before moving on to the more formal features, especially the spatial dimensions (considered in chapter nine) followed by the way in which the beer is distributed and consumed (chapter 10).

The brewing process starts to illuminate the communal dimension of beer drinking rituals, the nature of the social divisions which are relevant at them, and the way in which they construct a certain social reality. This is elaborated on and made explicit at the beer drink proper when people are allocated seating places, an extremely important ordering process linked to the order imposed on the beer itself as it is divided into portions in preparation for the event. The distribution of the beer and its consumption takes this process to its logical conclusion and reaffirms as well as breaks down the spatial order constructed at the earlier stage. Together, these three chapters provide an indication of the elaborate formal detail that is associated with formal beer drinking. However, attention will also be paid to how agency and interest are superimposed on this formal structure, modifying it or contradicting it in relation to everyday power relations, networks and activities.

A beer drinking register

Once s/he has decided to hold a beer drink a homestead head sets about preparing for that day, the senior adult woman of the home as the chief brewer, under the nominal charge of a male head of the homestead or his proxy.[1] They may need to purchase maize, ask neighbours and friends to help with the work, and borrow some of the utensils required. Because many men are away as migrant workers, beer drinks are frequently initiated by women.

Alcoholic drink is often specially marked socially because of the specialized preparation that it requires, and because fermentation is "a quasi-magical transformation of food into a substance that, in turn, transforms [or has the potential to transform] human consciousness" (Dietler 2001, 73). Associated with the brewing, distribution and consumption of beer in Shixini is a specialized set of words and terms that constitute a beer drinking register and that help to give beer a particular status as a valued commodity. Many of these are technical but others are everyday words used creatively to produce specific contextual meanings at beer drinks. These terms hold clues to the significance of some of the ways in which beer is distributed and consumed, and the relationships that this speaks to, either during the brewing process itself or later. Some of the terms associated with brewing are later also used for specific beer allocations, establishing interesting metaphoric connections between brewing, the people involved in it, and the consumption of the end product. In the process it becomes evident that the words themselves are part of an elaborate etiquette that is used to impart cultural significance to the action of drinking and the relationships involved in this.[2]

Naming, in other words, is of performative significance (DeBernardi 1994). To name something is to construct it in a particular way and to transform it. But it is performative in another sense also: Shixini people speak Xhosa in a way that is distinctive from the speech of educated, urban Xhosa, and this signals their parochial-ness. They have manners of expression and specific words and terms, such as forms of naming and greeting, that mark them as culturally conservative, rural people. Some of the beer drinking terms discussed below are highly localised and many of them are not found in other Xhosa-speaking areas, which may have different terms for similar processes and events. The beer drinking register indexes this local identity. Language (including the use of place names and proper names) thus links people to place and is an aspect of their rural orientation.

As argued earlier, a rural Xhosa habitus developed out of the conditions governing the incorporation of Xhosa into the wider political economy and has to be understood in terms of the struggle between groups within this field.

In this case I suggest that the elaboration of beer drinking and the development of new forms of beer drinking rituals is similar to the development of a new genre in the field of art of literature, and constituted a creative response to the position that rural Xhosa found themselves in within the newly emerging field of capitalist production. The development of a beer drinking lexicon can be viewed in a similar way to the development of a distinctive way of speaking about art or literature, as part of a strategy to accumulate cultural capital. However, this aspect of capital is confined to participants in the beer drinking circuit, since there is no communication at this level with the dominant group who have never heard of, let alone participated in, rural beer rituals. This emphasizes the fact that we are dealing with intersecting fields here, not with a single field. Nevertheless, the beer drinking register enables rural Xhosa to construct a sense of distinctiveness as part of a world that is beyond that of wage labour but nevertheless linked to it. It is part of the cultural capital that enables them to speak of themselves as 'we Xhosa' or 'we Red Xhosa' and adds to the symbolic power that they attempt to accumulate in relation to the dominant, since their self-identification as rural Xhosa (and thus as distinctive) is both a cultural and political act emerging out of a particular structure of power relations (as shown in chapter three).

Anthropologists interested in the social nature of the consumption of alcoholic beverages have noted the importance of 'drinking talk', the conversation that accompanies drinking and which provides vital clues to its significance (Frake 1972).[3] However, the language associated with the process of producing, distributing, and consuming the beverage itself is a neglected topic.[4] Much of the ethnography of drinking, concerned as it is with social messages or the relationship between drinking and other social phenomena, has ignored the indigenous terminology associated with the beverage consumed, failing to document it or explicitly recognise its role in the construction of the analysis.[5] In this and also in the next two chapters, therefore, attention is paid to the language associated with the production, allocation and consumption of beer, as a way of indicating its significance and as a way of privileging the emic voice. This concern also reflects one of my primary fieldwork methods, namely that of trying to understand beer rituals by paying as much attention as possible to what was said at them, and by seeking the meaning of the wide range of terms associated with beer and of the many things said at beer drinks. In this sense a key aspect of the ethnographic process is reflected in the ethnographic product.

The lexicon associated with beer provides a range of possibilities rather than a fixed structure. Which aspects of it become relevant and what they mean changes to some extent from event to event so that meaning has to be determined in the context of practice. Certainly, the meaning of these lexical items rests partly on a wider cultural understanding, a wider knowledge system into which they fit and in terms of which they make sense (Keesing 1979), but the particular social circumstances in which they are put into motion as units in a system of exchange is important. The names of various kinds of beer drinks, for example, detailed in chapter five, hint strongly at the nature of these events, at their overall function and at their general sociocultural significance. The way in which certain procedures followed at beer drinks are conceptualized, what they 'mean', is at least partly embedded in the terms used to describe these procedures. The names given to specific beakers of beer provide the ethnographer with vital information, but only as a starting point for further inquiry. Certain general social and moral principles are embedded in the lexicon, but these principles as acted out in beer drinks are shaped by local events and current relationships. So the lexicon provides only a general structure which has to be examined against practice and precedent.

Of course, aspects of the beer drinking register define and restrict meaning. For example, a term describing a specific type of beer drink signals what sort of event is to take place. However, as was indicated earlier, there is often some choice here. A homestead that decides to brew primarily out of the moral obligation to provide hospitality, for example, may lexically signal the event in a variety of ways. In other cases the obligation to brew arises out of particular social circumstances and the event is named accordingly (e.g. beer to mark the end of mourning). Whatever the case, the overall significance and meaning of the event has to be gauged in terms of the specific circumstances and actors involved rather than solely in terms of a specific type of named ritual.

Having named the event, however, the host homestead creates a set of expectations regarding how much beer will be available, how it will be divided, who will receive allocations, and so on, according to a complex set of local conventions. The lexicon associated with beer distribution allows these expectations to be expressed and negotiated in precise material terms. Again, however, although certain kinds of named allocations of beer convey particular symbolic messages, there is often choice concerning factors such as whether to make the allocation or not, who it should go to, what size it should be, and at what stage of the proceedings to make it. Meaning does not inhere so much in the name itself as in how agents apply it and negotiate it with others.

In general, what becomes clear from this attention to words is that beer is not a homogeneous thing, but a social commodity that is used to give symbolic substance to a wide variety of ideas about moral and social relationships. Beer's status is based on its exchangeability, and emerges in the nomenclature given to it and in the meaning and value attached to it in particular contexts. Expressed slightly differently, beer's social potential is fulfilled through the various naming and associated distribution (exchange) strategies applied to it, which always occur in relation to specific practical realities. Through differentiating beer in a variety of ways and by linking it to other forms of symbolization based on the spatial and temporal features of beer drinking encounters, the exchange and consumption of this alcoholic beverage is used by people to imaginatively construct their world. In this sense Xhosa beer drinking is generally similar to the ritualised consumption of food (through feasting and so on) in many parts of the world. As with feasting, or with other forms of ceremonial drinking such as *kava* in the Pacific, it facilitates the construction of social reality and the negotiation of socio-political relationships (LeCount 2001, Turner 1992, Brison 2001).

However, the common set of expectations linked to beer drinking, much of which is embedded in the nomenclature, and which can be viewed as an aspect of the rural habitus, limits the extent to which agents are free to innovate. One of the most important general restrictions, at every beer drink, is the fact that the individual brewer (i.e. the head of the homestead at which the event is held) is allowed to control only a small portion of the beer available. The bulk of it is controlled and allocated by the men of the territorial section in which the homestead falls, making every beer drink not only the affair of an individual or an individual homestead, but also of a community. This partly accounts for the fact that maize beer has not become a commercial commodity in Shixini as it has in many other parts of Africa (Holtzman, 2001, Bryceson 2002). It is sometimes sold, as we shall see, but this sale is severely curtailed by certain conventions which receive expression in a set of specialized terms relating to the distribution and consumption of beer for sale.

Brewing and preliminary beer distribution

Details of how maize beer is produced are provided in Appendix One, but there are a number of important social dimensions to this which I am concerned with here. Brewing is hard work, particular the grinding of the maize, which is done twice, and in Shixini the word for 'grinding' (*ukusila*) also serves as the word for 'brewing' (Illustration 9). An important point that emerges from this is that brewing is a communal process, involving co-operation between a number of households. As such, the production of beer is one exam-

9. Grinding maize for beer

ple of the kind of co-operation between neighbours that is essential for the well-being of each homestead, an acting out in practice of the important principle that all homesteads depend on the assistance of others.

   People from other homesteads, or from other parts of the sub-ward, call in while brewing is in progress, out of curiosity and for sociability. They often lend a hand for an hour or two, or just sit and encourage or chat to the brewers. Towards the end of the process they also visit in the hope that some beer brought to maturity in advance of the rest may be available to drink. There is lots of noisy conversation and banter; sometimes the brewers break into song or relieve the monotony of grinding with an impromptu dance. While straining the beer women frequently help themselves to a dishful, and pass this around to others. Boys and young men come to the homestead, attracted by the presence of both girls and beer, and there are invariably lots of children around, not to mention pigs, chickens and dogs hanging about in anticipation of a feed of the lees (maize sediment). Brewing, then, is not just a matter of co-operation between homesteads, but also a very sociable, community event.[6] The end product, too, of course, is viewed as something to be shared with others. The public nature of the brewing also, however, means that the beer drink is, right from the start, identified with a particular homestead, spatially located in a specific sub-ward section.

(i) *Umlumiso*

Most beer drinking rituals take place over a period of three days, though this may be expanded or contracted according to the amount of beer brewed. On the day or night before the beer drink proper, close neighbours and nearby kin are called to the homestead to partake of a special portion brought to maturity ahead of the rest, called the *igwele* or *umlumiso* ('the yeast') beer.[7] This group of neighbours corresponds to the homesteads of the sub-ward section or, in the case of larger sections, to the sub-section. This is the same group that is called to the homestead whenever there is a bottle of brandy to be consumed (e.g. on Christmas day, or when a migrant worker returns home) or when there is a sheep or pig to be eaten (e.g. if slaughtered for visitors). Other members of the sub-ward are not turned away, should they be present. However, it is recognized that *umlumiso* is relatively private.[8]

Umlumiso beer is also sometimes called *umvo*, the simplest translation of which is 'a taste', but which is derived from *ukuva*, which means to hear, perceive, understand, feel, smell, see, observe or taste. It is an important Xhosa word also meaning to make apparent, transparent or perceptible, which, in this case, implies all of these things. As indicated in chapter four, with the addition of a reciprocal suffix -*na* (*ukuvana*) it refers to the mutual understanding and sympathy that governs everyday relations. *Umlumiso* is given to neighbours and close kin not merely so that they should taste the beer, but also so that they should know about the beer drink, see how much beer has been brewed, and become aware of the reason for brewing. The people of the section are formally called to be present.[9] Once they have arrived, the homestead head or his representative explains why they have been called and proceeds to give out the beer—usually one beaker for men and one for women.

Despite the formality, *umlumiso* is consumed in a fairly relaxed atmosphere. Women and girls carry on with the preparation of the beer, babies and young children play around inside the hut. Boys and young men may be present and are sometimes given a sip from the men's beaker, especially if they have been helping with the brewing. Strictly speaking, they do not have a right to any beer at this time, but often they are included.[10]

(ii) *Intluzelo*

Intluzelo ('the straining') is a quantity of beer set aside with which to reward those who assisted with the work of brewing and straining—the girls and young women—who share it with boys and young men. If senior men happen to be present, they too may be given a beaker of *intluzelo*. If a large amount of beer is brewed it is possible, if the homestead head and his wife feel so inclined, to give out *umlumiso* two days before the day of the beer drink, and to follow this up with *intluzelo* on the day before, as the case below illustrates:

Two days before Nothimba's *umsindleko*, close neighbours were called to the homestead for *umlumiso* beer. One beaker was formally given to men, and one to women. On the next day, many people called at the homestead, including boys, girls and young men, wondering if there was any chance of getting *intluzelo*. By mid-morning the straining was complete and a number of boys, men and women were in the hut. The boys were given a dish of beer and told to leave, and a beaker designated as the 'inspection' was drawn and placed in front of Nothimba, the homestead head. Nothimba took the first sip, and passed it to Bonakele, a neighbour, without saying anything. Bonakele drank and exclaimed: "Hey, you brewers, always brew like this [i.e. perfectly]! Always brew like this, brewers!" All nine of the women present were offered sips from this beaker by Bonakele and Nothimba. This reflects on ideal gender relations—women do the work, after which they may formally drink; men appropriate, examine and approve the product, and share it with women.

In the next hour or so a number of other people arrived and the hut became full. They were all neighbours from Ndlelibanzi and Folokhwe subwards (Nothimba lives on the border between the two) and included some close kin—his FBS, BW, BS and the wives of a number of their agnates who were either away at work or dead. There were seven men, 10 women, three young men and seven boys (who had returned hoping for more beer) in the hut. Nothimba's FBS dished up five beakers of *intluzelo* beer, two for men, one for women and two for the boys. The latter were told to go and drink outside, and after they had left Nothimba explained to all that this was *intluzelo* beer, and that it was being given out because he was having *umsindleko* the next day. The women's 'sitting down' beaker was given out early the next day, and was consumed mainly by Nothimba's wife and two other senior women from adjoining homesteads. A pot-full of *intluzelo* was carried over to Notimba's elder brother's homestead next door, where it was given to the girls and young women who had laboured. Boys and young men called there in the course of the day, and were given a share. As indicated later, *intluzelo* beer may also be part of the formal distribution on the day of the beer drink proper.

This process of brewing and preparing for the beer drink reveals a number of things and introduces a number of themes which are more fully developed at the beer drink proper. First, it is clear that a beer drink cannot be an affair associated only with an individual person or homestead, but is always a communal matter, involving extensive co-operation between a group of neighbouring homesteads and the interest and ad hoc assistance of other members of the section and sub-ward. Part and parcel of this involvement is sociability and good fellowship, especially among the workers. Despite the hard work, it is also 'time out' in a sense, a change from the hum-drum of everyday labour, and a degree of 'communitas' is in evidence in the camaraderie of the brewers and helpers. Secondly, certain boundaries and hierarchies are acted out in the brewing and the initial consumption of beer, such as that between male and female, men and boys, neighbours and others. However, these are not as marked as at other times. Boys and girls are given beer, and no formal distinction is made between either men or women on the basis of kinship or territory, as at the beer drink itself.

The final stage in preparing for the beer drink is when the homestead head and his wife, as the chief brewer, take stock of how much beer she has produced. The wife is called upon to point out precisely which pots and casks are available, which are for the day after the beer drink, which are from the second straining (the *ivanya*), and so on. The beer then has to be divided into appropriate portions, depending partly on the kind of beer drink to be held (Illustration 10). Kin and neighbours help and give advice in this respect, because they are important decisions for which the individual homestead is responsible to the section. It is the men of the section who ultimately control most of the beer, and a selfish or irresponsible division will land the homestead head in trouble. During the beer drink that follows, the person in charge of the brewing is again called upon from time to time to point out various portions of the beer, or to explain which containers hold specific allocations. Men compliment her on the quality of the brew but this does not translate into a formal beer allocation. In keeping with the Xhosa patriarchal ethic, Shixini women formally receive far less beer on the day of the drinking than the men, though they partly make up for this during the brewing process and in the less formal drinking on the day before and the day after the event itself.

Let us assume that after the preliminary distribution before the beer drink, two large barrels of beer remain. One of these, containing approximately 200 litres, might be designated as the men's main portion (*intselo*). There are three different sizes of tin beakers or billycans with which communal drinking takes place (there is no individual drinking from cups or glasses, or their equivalent). The largest beaker, *iqhwina*, holds just under 10 litres; the medium-sized *inxithi* contains seven litres, and the smallest, *utshevulane*, five litres. Any of these may be referred to as *ibhekile* (a borrowed word derived from 'beaker' or its Afrikaans equivalent, *beker*) if it contains beer.[11] Shixini people think of barrels in terms of large-sized beakers, and of pots in terms of medium-sized beakers. A full cask or medium-sized plastic barrel is called an *ingcwele*, and

10. Division of beer into portions

it contains 20 *amaqhwina* (10-litre beakers). There is a nice irony in this name: To Christian Xhosa, some of whom are opposed to beer drinking, *ingcwele* is something holy or sacred, the conventional meaning of the root *-ngcwele* meaning pure, undefiled, clear or holy. The cask of beer called *ingcwele* carries this name because it is full to the brim and has a wholeness and symmetry about it; it is unblemished. People know exactly how many beakers it contains, how much maize, water and malt is required to make one, and exactly how much beer each section and sub-ward is entitled to from it, according to prevailing circumstances and relations between these territorial groups. It is a reference point, a standard against which judgements about beer allocations are made when there is more or less than an *ingcwele* to give out. Often, it is the beer allocation reserved for men, and this barrel is then spoken of, in a manner denoting respect for such a large and important portion of beer, as *ingcwele yamadoda* ('the men's full cask').[12]

Having decided on the amount of beer for the men's portion, an amount is set aside for women, often a medium-sized pot-full containing eight *amanxithi* (medium sized beakers), a total of 56 litres. If there is not enough for this, then the one container of *intselo* will have to do for both men and women. The homestead head must also put aside a pot of beer for preliminary drinking of what are called 'customs'. This is usually a smaller pot, containing six *amanxithi* (42 litres). He now has roughly 102 litres left. Of these he keeps a small pot (four *amanxithi* or 28 litres) aside as *imifihlo* ('hidden' beer). This is placed in a separate hut and kept in case of emergencies such as the unexpected arrival of an important guest, and so that he will have something for immediate neighbours once the beer is finished and most of the people have gone home. A homestead head would also need to put aside a number of beakers, perhaps eight *amanxithi* (56 litres), to present as gifts to individuals. He now has roughly 14 litres (two *amanxithi*) left. These come in handy for those who turn up early, to keep them happy while they wait for the others to arrive. In addition to these pots and casks, which are subject to variation according to the amount brewed and the nature of the beer drink, there is usually a pot of the watery *ivanya*, as well as the *isidudu* ('porridge') beer, the latter kept for the day after the event.

In summary, the beer is subjected to a strict ordering process in preparation for the ritual itself, being divided and structured according to the way in which it ought to be consumed at the beer drink. The divisions imposed on the beer correspond, as we shall see, with the social divisions relevant at the beer drink itself, to which we now turn.

Endnotes

1. A homestead whose male head is dead or away at work has a 'caretaker' (*usipatheleni*), often an agnate, who acts for him (Heron and Cloete 1991).

2. For a detailed analysis of the Xhosa beer drinking register, which I draw on in part here, see McAllister (2003a).

3. For recent examples of the significance of the talk that accompanies drinking see Moeran (1998) and Tomlinson (2004).

4. This is evident, for example, from Douglas' (1987) collection of papers on drinking behaviour and Heath's extensive reviews of work on the social use of alcohol (1987 and 1987a). Some have noted the existence of a beer lexicon in parts of Africa (Karp 1980) but no published documentation or analysis of such a lexicon has appeared, as far as I can determine.

5. One exception to this is Crowley (1995), who has shown that in urban contexts in Vanuatu a new terminology linked to *kava* drinking and the preparation of *kava* has developed, reflecting a post-independence upsurge of *kava* drinking in urban areas, which the author considers to be an expression of national identity expressed in the new national language, Bisala.

6. Hunter (1936, 103–4) provides a lively account of the sociable nature of the brewing process among Mpondo that differs little from the description given here.

7. See Appendix One.

8. Bigalke (1969, 104) recorded a case in Tshabo (near East London) where men from one section of a ward turned up at a homestead in another section, where *igwele* was being drunk on the day before the beer drink. They were not given beer but sent away and told to return the next day for the beer drink proper.

9. Soga writes of beer called *umtsho* which seems similar to *umlumiso*. It is given to the heads of neighbouring homesteads, who are in this way "treated as members of the host's family. They are in effect having a private meal before the feast becomes a public affair" (1931, 402). Kropf translates *umtsho* as the portion given to a chief or headman (1915, 427). It can also be translated as 'something fresh'. Shixini people sometimes use this term to refer to one of the preliminary beakers.

10. On one occasion when *umlumiso* was being consumed a young man at the back of the hut said: "Hey, you old men, why must the beaker stop there and go back [to the seniors]?" One of the old men responded: "What's this then? Are we friends? Don't you know [that] this beaker [is for men]?"

11. An empty can is called an *iphanga*, and if it is only partly full, an *isigananda*. These terms are onomatopoeic.

12. If the barrel is a large one (an *ixhiba*) this is described as *ingcwele yexhiba* (a full *ixhiba*).

9 Space and the Social Order

It is difficult to describe the atmosphere of a beer drink, partly because the mood varies according to the type of event, the stage of the proceedings, and other, less easily identifiable factors. Most of the action takes place indoors, in a poorly lit hut, ventilated only by the doorway and, sometimes, a small square window. The hut is packed with men wearing woollen hats, tattered overcoats, over-alls, and blankets, sitting shoulder to shoulder, smoking locally made pipes, with their sticks and tobacco bags on the floor beside them (Illustration 11). At some beer rituals there are also women in the hut (Illustration 12), but usually they sit outside. The air is filled with the acrid smell of home grown tobacco, overpowering the mellower aromas of fermented beer, wood-smoke, freshly cut thatching grass, and cow-dung. The men converse noisily, argue, laugh, smoke and spit on the floor. They shout out greetings to new arrivals, debate current events, admire each others pipes and sticks, tease and beg to-bacco from each other. People come and go, women bringing in pots and empty cans, the homestead head readying the beer. New arrivals come in and squint through the smoke to find a place to sit, guided by where the other members of their territorial groups are already seated.

Before rounds of beer are given out the beakers are placed in front of the doorway where everybody can see them, and the hut becomes quiet. The *in-joli* or 'master of ceremonies' stands next to the beer and speaks. Attention fo-cuses sharply on him and there is a strong feeling of anticipation. Once the beer has been given out the buzz of conversation starts up with renewed vigour, everyone seemingly talking at once, passing beakers to each other, call-ing friends from across the room for a drink, taking long draughts of beer and proclaiming its quality, sending messages to women outside to come in and drink and generally having a good time.

There is a great deal of informal, friendly conversation, in which virtually any kind of topic of local interest may be discussed. These include the latest local gossip, the state of livestock and crops, conditions at places of employ-ment, the price of tobacco and goats, and a hundred other topics. Sometimes such discussions fan out from their point of origin until all the men in the hut are involved, especially if it is a particularly interesting matter or if those dis-cussing it are particularly able and amusing. A large part of the pleasure of beer drinking is listening to and engaging with eloquent and entertaining

11. Men in hut

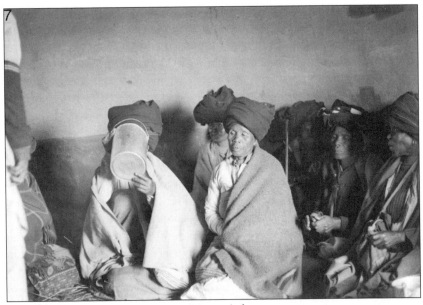

12. Women in hut

speakers. Beer drinks are an opportunity to discuss and debate a wide range of public issues, to canvass opinion, and to formulate 'public policy' (towards things like cattle dipping and inoculations, repair of the school buildings, etc). They allow the sub-headman to pass on information of importance to the sub-ward, and provide scope for ordinary people to request others to look out for lost livestock, to offer animals and other products for sale, or to indicate that they wish to buy something like a good horse.[1]

Beer allocations might be followed by long, sometimes heated discussions about whether a particular group has been given its rightful share or not. Controversies arise also about other issues, sometimes apparently trivial, and a debate may span hours and involve dozens of speakers, punctuated with periods of apparent chaos, four or five men on their feet gesticulating, with everyone shouting at once and nobody hearing what anyone else is trying to say. Many debates are relatively orderly though, with people listening intently to the speakers if they find the matter interesting, and telling them to sit down and be quiet if they don't. Seldom do arguments that arise at a beer drink lead to enduring bad feeling. People go to a beer drink to enjoy themselves, and practising one's skill in debate is part of that enjoyment. Behaviour may appear raucous at times, but it is strictly controlled, and men who threaten to get out of hand are censured or sent packing. The *injoli* and the host are kept very busy, making announcements about the beer, filling beakers, stirring the pots, distributing beer, collecting and rinsing out empty cans, and so on. They frequently consult each other and men of the host's section about the proceedings, trying to ensure that no mistakes are made, while the visitors look on expectantly, looking forward to their beer allocation but always ready to stand up and complain if they feel badly done by.

The mood of any beer drink can change from moment to moment. At *umsindleko* the mood ranges from one of seriousness and solemnity, when the returned migrant is addressed and admonished by the elders of the community, to the more usual light-heartedness and enjoyment, once these addresses are over. In general, the atmosphere is one of sociability and good-fellowship. Sometimes men burst into short snatches of song or give forth a short praise poem. Despite the noise, people sometimes doze off and it is not uncommon to see elders at the door fast asleep, heads against the wall. Drunkenness is rare, and is virtually always a result not of the beer consumed, but of what has been consumed earlier, on the way to the beer drink. The mood may also be altered by external events: The noisiest and most dispute-riddled beer drink attended during fieldwork changed dramatically about two thirds of the way through when a neighbour, Dhyubeni, arrived and announced that two people had been killed by lightning in a nearby ward. The dead were kin of his, and he was looking for advice on whether to go to the affected homestead or not. Suddenly the mood became solemn, the speeches orderly and uninterrupted, the listeners attentive, whereas before this a passer-by would have been certain that most of the men were quite drunk and the situation about to go out of control. After discussing and resolving the matter a number of speakers commended Dhyubeni for bringing this issue to the beer drink to discuss it 'amongst people' (*ebantwini*), saying that in doing so he was teaching them all 'Xhosa custom', especially the young and those who did not know about such things, whom he was 'enriching'.

In what follows, a generalized account of the proceedings followed at a typical beer drink is presented. In this respect there are three closely interrelated aspects of the proceedings that will be emphasized. These are, firstly, the spatial arrangements, the way in which the space in and around a homestead is used to organize and structure the proceedings. Secondly, there is the allocation and distribution of beer, dealt with in the following chapter, which is linked to space and follows a temporal sequence. Since the spatial allocation must be made before beer distribution can commence, I will start with and prioritise this. Thirdly, there is the verbal aspect of the proceedings. Here, what is said, how it is said, by whom and to whom are important, and will be discussed in chapter 12 as well as in subsequent chapters in relation to beer drinks associated with social transition. I will use the evidence of speech to strengthen this analysis as well as to make points that do not emerge from the spatial and temporal dimensions.

These elements—space, beer and talk—provide the basic general principles that need to be analysed to make sense of beer drink rituals. The beer has both a qualitative and a quantitative dimension—how much is given out and the temporal sequence of allocations. I would emphasize again, however, that any beer ritual occurs within a real-world context, which needs to be factored into the analysis. As an aspect of the rural Xhosa habitus, the conventions or 'rules' (*imithetho*) of beer drinking are basic guidelines only, which are implemented in practice in accordance with specific social realities. This is dealt with in detail in chapter 11, though the background for it is laid here and in the next chapter.

Structuralist approaches—a critique[2]

The spatial characteristics of beer drinks are, not surprisingly, closely related to the way in which Xhosa people design and use their homesteads, but this use of space and its meaning are also related to everyday social practice and the network of relations of which any individual homestead is part. Structuralist and structural-functionalist analyses of spatial symbolism are limited by their static and formal nature, and this becomes apparent in the case of Xhosa beer drink rituals once they are viewed as a form of practice rather than as a manifestation of a structural order. I address this issue in a general sense first before turning to beer drink rituals in Shixini.

The literature on the ritual use of domestic space in southern Africa is sparse, although there have been some prominent structuralist analyses of the spatial organization of southern Bantu homesteads, notably by Adam Kuper (1982, 1993). The Nguni residential unit occupied by a 'family', argues Kuper, is a basic economic, kinship, territorial and political unit, and its physical layout is not only closely related to the way in which the domestic group is organized, but is also "a symbolic representation of principles of the socio-cosmic system...[and] corresponds very generally with indigenous ideas about social organization." (Kuper 1993, 473). In Kuper's view, the organization of domestic space has been relatively constant for a thousand years and is based chiefly on a set of binary oppositions such as left and right, above and below, inside and outside, through which normative social principles based on agnation, genealogical seniority, gender, order of marriage and the ranking of wives are expressed and reinforced. The model is also a general one, extending beyond the domestic unit, encompassing "ideas about the organization of the world...[and] the organization of the state." (Kuper 1993, 472–73). So the social principles in terms of which domestic space is structured, such as the allocation of certain huts to wives in terms of their ranked order, are the same principles that govern the political structure (e.g. the ranking of territorial divisions of the chiefdom). Kuper's approach receives support from archaeologists such as Huffman (1982), who have identified a general southern Bantu 'culture system' expressed in settlement pattern.

While providing useful insights into Nguni social structural principles and the ways in which these are relevant in the political sphere, this kind of approach has been criticised for its limitations in analysing the everyday use and meaning of space (Schieffelin 1985; Moore 1986). A focus on an enduring structural and abstract order, or a set of organizing principles, would clearly not enable us to address the question of beer drinks within the context of the significant historical changes and developments outlined earlier. What is required is to supplement ideas about space with attention to the everyday social practices through which meaning emerges in the actual use of such space. Of course, key symbols reference basic values and principles, which may sometimes be gauged from their observable characteristics, but their meaning cannot be understood from this alone. Victor Turner pointed out long ago that the meaning of symbols needs to be assessed also from the ways in which they are used by actors in concrete social situations which are part of a social process and also from what people say about them (he called these the 'operational' and 'exegetical' meanings, respectively). He also noted that these various meanings can contradict each other (Turner 1967, 20–21) and called for an interpretation of symbols in terms of the social reality of the actors, as part of what he called the 'social drama', a series of interconnected events through which the meaning of symbols emerged. In other words, it is through viewing ritual as performance that spatial meaning emerges.

Davison (1988) provides a critique of structuralist analyses of domestic space in southern Africa along the lines indicated above, in an article on the spatial dimensions and use of space in Mpondo homesteads. Mpondo and Xhosa are very closely related culturally, live adjacent to each other and speak the same language. She bases her analysis largely on the ideas of Bourdieu, Giddens and Hodder, developing lines of argument provided by Moore (1986). Davison and Moore argue that one needs to look at specific social situations, at the ways in which space is actually used socially as part of everyday practice, for symbolic meaning to emerge. It is a question, not of the relationship between material culture and social organization, but of how "material culture takes on meaning in particular social and historical circumstances." (Davison 1988, 100). So, for example, the division of space within a hut into right and left, and the association of this opposition with that between male and female, constitutes a conceptual division, an aspect of a transposable habitus and an organizational principle that may, in practice, be manifested in various ways. It may be used to signal male dominance in the field of gender relations, but it may also be used in other situations (e.g. the field of kinship) to mark status distinctions of a different kind. Given that domestic space has a symbolic structure, the key task is to discover how this is strategically used to negotiate social relationships (ibid., 100). People participate in social situations in terms of specific organizational principles (often including a spatial structure) but these principles can be manipulated, adapted, selected from, ignored, reversed, etc., by the actors, to re-create and reinforce relationships or to signal changes in these, in terms of the interests and strategies of those involved in the context of particular fields of interaction and struggle.

Davison's examination of the use of space in Mpondo homesteads in the course of daily life shows how meaning emerges from the context of action and according to specific circumstances, by documenting a variety of ways in which practice is superimposed on the underlying spatial order, using, manipulating or subverting it to convey meaning. So while domestic space represents a conceptual order, meaning emerges, as Turner suggested, through the actions of agents engaged in the practice of daily life in which elements of the order are used and manipulated to convey specific meanings. Davison provides a number of examples involving everyday social practices by members of homesteads, all of which are linked to the relative power of men and women. None of her examples, however, involve ritual.

There is one other author who has written on both beer drinking rituals and domestic space in the South African context and who has grappled with the same kind of structural issues as Kuper, namely Heinz Kuckertz (1990; 1997). In the final chapter of his monograph on the Mpondo, Kuckertz (1990) presents the homestead as somewhat ambiguous; it is both highly individualistic, with all forms of social interaction originating from individual homesteads and serving the interests of homesteads, yet each homestead is embedded in sets of wider relations that transcend this individualism (e.g. a court system, a hospitality association, economic relations with others, an agnatic group). He then asks if there is "any observable social reality which unites these two opposing tendencies in a single pattern of interaction" and answers in the affirmative, that this unification is provided by the "art of ceremonial beer drinking" (ibid., 273). The individual homestead provides beer, which is consumed by the people of the locality who attend. Again, however, "individuality appears...in the very symbolizing of universality. How is this possible? The answer is that the homestead, as an ideal spatial organization, is a symbolic representation of the world and its order, in which the living and the dead, kinspeople (*sic*) and non-kinspeople, seniors and juniors, men and women, share." (ibid., 273). The homestead is a "symbol of the world", and beer drinking is "an enactment of the world as an ordered universe...[that] needs a given homestead in order to achieve a social reality; it depends on the spatial order defined by the main house (*indlu*) and the layout of the homestead...[which] becomes the lived social order as a ceremony proceeds." (ibid., 273).

This is an important insight with which I concur, but it is one that applies at an abstract level. Kuckertz is talking about an ideal, structural, cosmic order, not a lived social order, nor a specific social reality. He is concerned with social structure, rather than with actual behaviour (the latter glossed as 'social ambiguity'), a problem that he acknowledges in a postscript where he concludes that further study is required "on how [people] construct their social reality in the course of their interaction with one another." (ibid., 296). He therefore uses ceremonial beer drinking in the same way in which structural-functionalists used ritual, as an abstract model, sealed off from the ebb and flow of everyday social practice, through which to view the symbolic structure of the homestead and the value principles associated with this structure. Thus the spatial symbolism of the homestead's main house, in which beer

drinking takes place, is described in terms of "an oppositional relationship between male and female, agnate and non-agnate, senior and junior" (ibid.,
277). The result is an idealised description of a spatial order that expresses social norms (ibid., 278), though it reflects "in its active realization, the particular homestead in which the people have met" (ibid., 287).

This last observation becomes meaningful, however, only in a later article
in which Kuckertz analyses a *specific* incident at a *particular* beer drink (Kuckertz 1997). Here it becomes clear that the structural order represented by domestic space is merely a model against which actual beer drinks need to be examined, just as *ukuhlonipha* (prescribed avoidance behaviour or rules of
respect) acts as a model against which the morality of particular actions have
to be viewed. It is avoidance behaviour and morality, not the beer drink itself,
that is the subject of this article, but the conclusion applies as much to beer
drinks as it does to avoidance behaviour. Kuckertz presents a painstaking and
convincing analysis of the incident, which involved argument and moral reasoning around the question of the 'rules of beer drinking' and a breach of these
rules, which allows him to conclude that the incident and the reasoning that
accompanied it have to be understood within a complex of interrelated relationships and events, not in terms of some abstract scheme in which rules of
respect, seniority and kinship form elements of a structure, each performing
a function in relation to the others.

In the same way, I argue, any individual Xhosa beer drink is meaningful
in terms of the ongoing flow of social life and not primarily in terms of the
symbolic structure which forms the general basis for its organization. Yet
there are certain general notions of how a beer drink, thought of in the abstract, *ought* to be organized and conducted, and these notions involve clear
ideas about the spatial dimensions of beer drinking within a domestic, but
public, setting. These general notions concerning the conduct of beer drinks
may be seen as elements of the rural Xhosa habitus, generative models which
are manifested in particular objective, situationally relevant ways, acted on
in specific interactional situations. As general models, they are linked to and
interact with other ideas and norms concerning everyday social practice and
everyday morality relevant to these situations. A number of specific general
applications of the beer drinking habitus relates to how specific types of beer
drinks (e.g. beer for harvest, or beer for a work party), ought to be organized and conducted, with corresponding notions of how space ought to be
used at these. Some of these occur at regular intervals and are associated with
particular spheres of activity (fields) such as agriculture. As Bourdieu points
out, the habitus is "an acquired system of generative schemes objectively adjusted to the particular conditions in which it is constituted" and it has "an

endless capacity to engender products—thoughts, perceptions, expressions, actions—whose limits are set by the historically and socially situated conditions of its production…" (Bourdieu 1977, 95).

Yet to understand particular beer rituals we have to go a step further, as I indicate in subsequent chapters, by looking at how beer drinking conventions concerning the use of space are applied and sometimes manipulated or changed, according to specific circumstances affecting the homestead and its members, whatever the type of beer ritual involved. In this respect we move from the habitus as general model, or set of models, to beer drinking practice which occurs in terms of, and may thus be partly explained by, the habitus, but which always involves strategic action, selection from alternatives, or modification of the norms, and in which the meaning of spatial symbolism is not fixed but has to be assessed in the context of the specific event, and in relation to the ongoing process of everyday life. It is only later, in chapter 11, that this is discussed in greater detail.

Domestic space and territorial organization

The initial key to a general understanding of beer drinks in Shixini lies largely in the location of homesteads within a series of nesting territorial groups, as described in chapter four. As shown there, an important manifestation of these territorial groups lies in the organization of co-operative labour underpinned by an ethic of inter-household co-operation expressed in terms of the general moral principles of good neighbourhood and mutual help. Co-operative labour is a vital aspect of a general mutual interdependence of homesteads which is acted out at every beer drink, where the individual host homestead is constituted as an integral part of a wider set of relationships based primarily on territory, but also on kinship and friendship. How this is done has an important spatial dimension in which the puzzle outlined by Kuckertz (how to use the individual homestead to construct universal truths) is addressed. However, the question can be rephrased and simplified by asking: How is the individual homestead constituted as a social entity?

The homestead is constituted socially at beer drinks partly through the manipulation of its domestic space to model the co-operative relationships (based on the division of geographical space, as well as on kinship and friendship) in which it is involved. This allows participants at every beer drink to locate themselves socially in relation to the host homestead and to each other, and to interpret the significance of the event. The most important way in which domestic space is made meaningful at beer drinks is through the formal allocation of seating places to different territorial groups in an important process

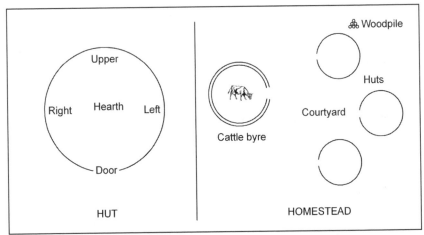

Figure 1   Spatial dimensions of a Xhosa homestead

known as 'the arranging of the hut' (*ukulungis' indlu*) a performative act which transforms the individual homestead into a universal model of hierarchy and unity based on the principles of territory, gender, kinship and age.

'Hut' here refers to the homestead's main hut, in which beer drinks are held, *and* its immediate surroundings, especially the courtyard (*inkundla*) between the main hut and the cattle byre, and an area known as *egoqweni* ('at the woodpile') well to one side of the courtyard near the cooking fire. At smaller beer drinks all activities and spatial referents may be confined to the hut alone, which stands metonymically for the homestead as a physical and social entity. At many beer drinks, however, the hut can only accommodate the men of the local sub-ward, so women, as well as men from other areas, have to sit out-side. The space inside the hut ranks higher than that outside it, and each of these spaces is further differentiated.

The main hut is divided, spatially, as illustrated in Figure 1. There are three interrelated dimensions—front and back, right and left, inner and outer. The front part of the hut, on both sides of the doorway, is referred to as *emnyango* (at the door). Opposite is the rear or upper part of the hut (*entla*), from the perspective of which the two sides, right (*icala lasekunene)* and left (*icala lasekhohlo)* are identified. The outer aspect is the circle against the wall (*edong-weni*), and the inner part is that nearer the central hearth (*ezikweni*).

The different elements of this spatial ordering inside the hut are ranked and associated with status differences. The right hand side is associated with men, the left with women. In everyday life men usually sit, eat and sleep on the right hand side, women on the left. The word for 'right' shares a common stem with words like *ubunene* (truth), *inene* (the truth) and *inene* (a respected person, a gentleman). So the right hand side, as Hertz (1960) pointed out in his classic essay on the subject, is also morally right and superior to the left. The word for left, *ikohlo*, has negative connotations, and is related to *ukukohla*, meaning to puzzle, to place in a difficulty, to confuse, disconcert or obstruct (Kropf 1915, 189). The front of the hut ranks higher than the back in terms of seating places. In both everyday life and at beer drinks, older people sit near the front, the eldest next to the door, while younger people sit towards the back, in the upper part (*entla*). Finally, the inner section ranks lower than the outer circle next to the wall. The highest ranked place within the hut, then, is against the wall on the right hand side next to the door. Although the inner part and the back are associated with juniority, the hearth and the back are also areas associated with the ancestors. It is at the back of the hut that the beer is kept (and meat, in the case of rituals involving animal sacrifice) and where the shades are thought to smell these. It is in the hearth that a sacred fire is made on such occasions. At these rituals the inner part of the hut is associated with ancestors and the kin group, and it ranks higher than the outer, which is where non-kin sit and observe the proceedings.[3] So the nature and ranking of domestic space is not entirely fixed but relative to ritual practice.

Within the outside space the area nearest the cattle byre ranks highest, the areas furthest from it in the vicinity of the household's outside cooking fire rank lowest. The courtyard itself, the area between the main hut and the gate of the cattle byre, is a sacred space but it is, strictly speaking, not used at beer drinks. Like the cattle byre it is associated with the ancestors and of major ritual importance, and it is kept free of people at beer drinks. If the wind is blowing hard, or if it is drizzling, men may sit up against the fence of the byre for shelter, but they do not go inside it.[4] Often, however, the outside space that is used practically verges very closely onto and may in fact overlap with a part of the courtyard.

Ideally, a beer drink is held inside the homestead's main hut, and not outside. In theory women and men sit inside the hut, but in practice women sit inside only at relatively small beer drinks and those that directly involve them (see chapter 14). In most cases women, and men from more distant areas, sit in a hierarchical arrangement outside the hut, which is occupied by men. If the homestead has only one hut, however, and the beer drink is fairly large, there is little alternative but for everyone to sit outside (Illustration 13). This involves a temporary re-organization of spatial values, and makes it difficult to dramatize the distinctions between groups and individuals, due to the removal of the inside/outside boundary and the boundaries and symmetry provided by the hut. For this reason, men feel uneasy about sitting outside, and attempt to avoid it.

One further aspect of the hut is used to determine the amount of space that a group may occupy, namely the rafters. The framework of the circular,

13. Drinking outside

thatched roof is made from eight main poles, which join at the apex of the cone, and these are used to divide the floor space into four or eight sections. People going to the places allocated to their group sometimes glance up at the rafters to take their bearings before sitting down. At one event in Chibi section a Ngingqi elder stood to complain about the amount of space available for his section. He said that when places were allocated Ngingqi was usually shown its place along with the other sections. He heartily approved of "this old Xhosa custom". What this meant, he argued, was that Ngingqi should not go beyond a certain pole, to which he pointed while speaking. Now, however, it seemed that Ngingqi's place was being determined by a different pole. He wanted to know why this was so, and when it had been decided on: "I want to know my rafter, so that when I am allocated beer, I should know my place."

In the 'arranging of the hut', carried out by the *injoli* in consultation with the other members of his section, men of the local sub-ward sections and adjoining sub-wards are allocated places. The host section occupies the highest ranked place, on the right next to the door, and allocates seats to other sections and sub-wards in terms of their relationship with the host section and its sub-ward. Relationships are often (but not necessarily) isomorphic with geographical proximity. The other (usually two) sections are ranked according to their relationship with the host section, one next to the host section, on the right towards the back (the most highly ranked place after the host section), the other on the left at the front. If the right hand side is full, the left hand side nearest the door is the next highest ranked place, followed by the

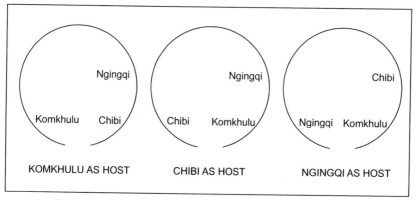

Figure 2   Allocation of seating places within Folokhwe sub-ward

area on the left towards the back of the hut. Since the beer pots, barrels, and beakers are kept at the back, this means that the section at the back (whether on the left or the right) has less space than the one next to the door. These places partly determine when and how people speak, how much beer they receive, and in what order.

The customs governing beer drinking thus emphasize the solidarity of neighbourhood groups, both sub-wards and sub-ward sections. The individual homestead is embedded in and identified with a larger social group, and the exchanges of beer brewed in individual homesteads are primarily exchanges between groups. As this and the other details concerning age and gender divisions indicates, the process is more than what I have translated simply as 'arranging', which is morally neutral; it is the construction of a spatial order in terms of specific social norms and values. The word *ukulungisa* (arranging) in fact also has a moral connotation, and can be translated as 'making good' or 'putting right' (Kropf 1915, 223).

In Folokhwe sub-ward, which has three sections, the seating convention is as illustrated in Figure 2. Note that Komkhulu ranks highest after the hosts in both Chibi and Ngingqi, while Ngingqi ranks lowest in both Komkhulu and Chibi. This is because Komkhulu is associated with the sub-headmanship, and because Ngingqi was the most recently formed section, which developed when Komkhulu fissioned some generations ago (see below). In Shixini, a sub-headman is, ideally, a member of the royal Tshawe clan. The homestead of any political authority figure is referred to as Komkhulu, meaning 'at the great place', and the section of the sub-ward within which the sub-headman lives is often called Mkhulu or, in the locative, Komkhulu.

The allocation of places and, later, of beer to territorial groups is known as *ukulawula*. This word means to govern or to order, as well as to allocate, and it indexes the political and territorial practices of the past. The founding of a political unit such as a sub-ward, ward or chiefdom is associated with the appointment of a sub-headman, headman, or chief. In the case of a sub-ward, when a sub-headman took up his position as representative of the headman of the ward in the past, he was accompanied by an ox, known as the *lawula* ox, 'the ox of authority' (Peires 1976, 41, 65; 1981, 27–28). Jingqi tribal authority, consisting of the wards Shixini and Ntlahlane, was founded when Hintsa, the Gcaleka paramount (1789–1835) sent his senior son in the right hand house, Ncaphayi, to rule over the area, which became a sub-chiefdom. Ncaphayi was accompanied by an ox called Jingqi, from which the area took its name. At large festive occasions in other wards, Shixini is allocated (*uku-lawula*) beer and meat as Jingqi. Jingqi is Shixini's *isitya* ('dish') or *inkabi* (lit. ox or 'beer name'; Cook 1931, 23).[5] Folokhwe, too, is the name of an ox, the ox that accompanied the first sub-headman, Maxego, grandson of Ncaphayi. The area in which Maxhego settled, and in which his successors (his younger brothers Xaketwana and Yohanisi) lived, and where Yohanisi's sons and grandsons still live, is the Komkhulu section of Folokhwe. Until about 1940, there was only one other section, called Chibi, after a small pond (*ichibi*) in that area. Ngingqi came into existence when Komkhulu became too large and a group of homesteads in a low lying area (an *ingingqi* is a hollow or low lying land) split off to form their own section, so that they would have their own 'dish' at beer drinks and rituals. The members of Komkhulu and Chibi, therefore, are seen as more established, ranking higher than Ngingqi in status. Ngingqi "is a person who has only recently arrived". This is dramatized in the allocation of seating places and beer, as is the historical connection between Ngingqi and Komkhulu. As we shall see below, there are also other historical processes which have contributed to the cultural logic of beer drinks, in that the meaning attached to the spatial organization is, at least in part, historically derived.

To conclude this section, the arranging of the hut allows a social group, the sub-ward section, constituting itself as the brewer, to manipulate the physical space in and around an individual homestead, using the values conventionally associated with that space to create a symbolic map of the social universe and the historical events and processes which give it shape. The territorial divisions in terms of which society is structured are drawn together into a single physical framework, that provided by the homestead and its environs, but within which the individual homestead is largely rendered structurally invisible. This is one of the performative effects of the formal aspects of beer drinking rituals, brought into being through the manipulation of homestead space, and reinforced through the formalities concerning the use of time and beer as well as by means of words.

Individual and community

Decisions about seating arrangements and beer distribution are made, not by the head of the host homestead, but by the senior men of the territorial section of which it forms part. They control the event and are responsible for following the correct procedure. It is the section that is regarded as the brewer, not the individual homestead that brewed and in speech it is personified and spoken of as such—e.g. "Komkhulu [section] is the brewer", or "Komkhulu is asking [for permission]". It is from the point of view of *umsili*, then, that the spatial organization of beer drinking needs to be viewed. Its solidarity and the subsuming of the individual homestead into the group are also brought into being and clearly indicated in the terms used to signify this group. The *umsili* is *mpi yakuthi* (our people), *mpi yakulo Komkhulu* (the Komkhulu group), *abantu basekhaya* (people of the home) and *amawethu* (our people).[6]

After allocating places to the other sections the hosts must consider the question of which of the neighbouring sub-wards to call into the hut, and where they should be placed. In this they consult with the other sections. Those that are asked to enter the hut are allocated places on the left hand side towards the back (if there is space left against the wall) or places in the inner circle. Visiting sub-wards represented by only one or two men are fully entitled to their own places (and beer) but are often, with their approval, placed with one of the host sections and not treated as separate groups after that. This eliminates them as distinctive sub-wards at the beer drink and simultaneously gives them the honour of being seated with the hosts, meaning that they will have access to the beer allocated to the host sections.

As with the allocation of space to sections, the way in which other sub-wards are incorporated, allocated space and offered beer embodies the way in which the members of the host sections and sub-ward relate to other sub-wards, and these relations change over time. Again, note that the individual homestead is irrelevant here, it is the relationship between groups that is being constituted through the allocation of space. At a beer drink in Chibi section of Folokhwe, for example, the highest ranking place after those of the Folokhwe sections goes to Ndlelibanzi sub-ward, followed by Jotelo sub-ward (see Map 3). In Komkhulu (and Ngingqi) sections, however, Jotelo gets a higher ranked place than Ndlelibanzi. The reason for this is that many Chibi people have close kinship and economic ties with Ndlelibanzi, but not with Jotelo. Ngingqi and Komkhulu, on the other hand, do not have especially close ties with either one of them. Jotelo, however, is directly adjacent to Ngingqi, while Ndlelibanzi is separated from Ngingqi and Komkhulu by Chibi. If there is still space in the hut after Jotelo and Ndlelibanzi are given their places, three other sub-wards, Fumbatha, Nompha and Mngwevu are allocated places, in that order.

In many cases a sub-ward called into the hut has hardly expressed its thanks for this when it asks for permission to go back outside, saying that the hut is too full. The hosts in fact expect this to happen and people say: "Let us call [so and so] into the hut so that they will see how full it is and go out" or words to that effect. Clearly, it is the gesture that is important. The invitation to come inside, and its acceptance, is a dramatization of what would happen if the hut was not so full, and thus of the relationship between the two areas. It is a public statement to the effect that the group called in has a closer relationship with the host sub-ward than those who are not. This is well illustrated in the following case:

At Thwalingubo's *ntwana nje* (see chapter 13), a large beer drink attended by a lot of people, Ndlelibanzi was the first to be asked into the hut, and placed next to Chibi, the host section. A group of sons-in-law was also invited to sit with Chibi, but they expressed their thanks and declined, saying that they would rather sit outside because the hut was full. Jotelo was then invited in, and it accepted. After Jotelo men had sat down, the nature of the beer drink was explained to all. Njembeyiya, spokesman for Jotelo, then stood to express his thanks for this explanation and to ask permission for Jotelo to go and sit outside. His clipped, rhythmic speech with the refrain 'Nkos! (Thank you!) from one of the audience in parenthesis, included the following:

> ...Don't let this disturb you, you people who are our neighbours ('Nkos!)
>
> We are people who become jealous of each other's [seating] places ('Nkos!)
>
> Someone may become jealous even though he has a place of his own ('Nkos!)
>
> [Saying] 'It is a good thing that they [Jotelo] go out, because they are thieves!' ('Nkos!) [Laughter and comments from the others]
>
> [Saying] 'It is right that Jotelo should go out ('Nkos!)
>
> So that there will be some space for the women to come in [for a drink]' ('Nkos!)
>
> It is a lovely day outside ('Nkos!)
>
> Jotelo would like to drink outside ('Nkos!)
>
> We have names ('Nkos!)

That we respond to very well ('*Nkos!*)

But really, dogs respond better than we humans ('*Nkos!*) [Laughter]

We are going out ('*Nkos!*)

Dogs are far superior to people ('*Nkos!*)

Take the cleaning of teeth for example ('*Nkos!*)

You never see a dog rinsing its mouth ('*Nkos!*)

Yet its teeth are white because it uses its tongue... ('*Nkos!*) [Laughter and comments]...

Gamalakhe, Chibi's *injoli*, responded:

...Allow me to say that you speak very well

Secondly, if you think that you will be comfortable outside

The Folokhwe group says 'thank you, you are free to go'

That's it

If you feel like sitting outside, that's all right....

Apart from illustrating the formality with which people address each other on these issues, this case shows that men are very conscious of the places allocated to them, as they are of the amount of beer they receive. It indicates also that calling groups into the hut is sometimes merely a formality or a convention, and that asking to go out is almost as much part of the convention as being called in. At all stages of these proceedings the *injoli* makes formal announcements, concerning which sub-wards have been asked to come into the hut, requests by a sub-ward to stay outside, or to leave the hut and return outside, and so on.

Seniority and gender are also relevant. Young men are given a separate place in the rear of the hut. Within each territorial group inside the hut, senior men sit closer to the door, less senior further from it. Usually, women are placed outside next to the *igoqo*, a large, neat pile of firewood near the main hut and outside cooking place. It is a space associated with them and a symbol of a woman's industriousness and housekeeping ability (wood from it is only used in emergencies or unusual circumstances) (Illustration 14). If the weather is bad they are allowed to sit in the lee of the cattle byre fence. If it is raining heavily, they may occupy one of the other huts, but if the homestead has only one hut and it is full of men, they must suffer the rain or go home.

Early on the day of the beer drink women may sit in the hut with the men who arrive early, remaining, perhaps, for the preliminary beakers. As more

14. Women outside near woodpile

men arrive and the hut becomes fuller, the women are told to leave, often with a curt: "Women, outside!" There are exceptions to this. When a family is released from mourning, women sit inside. The same applies when a widow is released from mourning, and women play an important role at this event (see chapter 14). Both of these, however, are small affairs, and do not attract large numbers of people. It is thus not difficult to accommodate them in the hut. I have also seen women remain in the hut at an *umsindleko* for a boy, and leave immediately after the men had admonished the boy, when the boy, too, leaves the men's hut.

Internal divisions among the women are modelled roughly on the spatial distribution of the men, but the way in which they sit also partly subverts the men's formal order. Much less fuss is made about who sits where and from a distance women often look as if they form a single undifferentiated group. Although women's groups are based on the same territorial divisions as that of the men, they are not as distinctly separate from each other as the men's groups are, and there is less concern with the 'proper order' of things. They do not have a formal allocation of seating places like the men do and insofar as they do form separate groups it seems to be due to the fact that groups from the different areas tend to arrive together as groups, and thus to sit together.[7] Junior married women, however, do form a separate group and sit well away from the other women on the very edge of homestead space. Like young men they are allowed to attend beer drinks only in the section in which they live.

To conclude this chapter, it seems that the allocation of space at Shixini beer rituals produces a concrete, embodied representation of a set of abstract social constructs which are used to order social life, relating to territory, age, gender and kinship. As a map of society, however, it remains devoid of some important detail which it acquires through the distribution of beer and through the oratory that is associated with this. Nevertheless, at this stage it is evident that it is more than just a 'representation'. As Lincoln remarks in his analysis of the seating arrangements for the feast of Tara in medieval Ireland, the implementation of a seating pattern based on status and hierarchy "actively constituted the differential ranks of the nobility, as it rendered the relative status of each rank visible...." (1989, 78). Constituting and making visible also, however, has another consequence, which is that it makes the social order open to contestation and negotiation. This may occur as a consequence of seating arrangements alone, but it is much more likely to take place in relation to the distribution of beer and after the hosts have an opportunity to address the gathering (which confirm the statuses associated with seating places). In mediaeval Ireland contestation became possible through the way in which the meat was carved at feasts "in such a way so as to re-distribute honour and thereby reconstruct the social order in rather pointed ways" (1989, 81) or to disrupt elements of the social order by stimulating competition and confrontation over the allocation of places and food, and thus of honour. As is indicated in the following chapter, how one gives out the beer is important. Even acts such as giving a visiting group a rusty beaker instead of a newer one, or making it wait longer than is normal for its share because a beaker is temporarily unavailable, can be construed as slights and provoke retaliation at a future event. Thus although the link between the use of space and historical or practical realities has been hinted at in the above, I have been concerned largely with the abstract notions associated with domestic space at beer drinking rituals. In subsequent chapters it is evident that spatial order by itself is often inadequate for discovering meaning —it is in the use of this space for the distribution and consumption of beer that meaning emerges.

Endnotes

1. Such announcements are received fairly stoically. No would-be buyers and sellers respond in public. If there are to be transactions, these occur privately, outside, or perhaps after the beer drink has ended. People also meet privately outside the hut to arrange participation in a ploughing company, or to discuss matters that do not involve the assembly as a whole.

2. This section is an abbreviated and adapted version of McAllister (2004).

3. For a description of the spatial arrangements at Mpondo beer drinks see Kuckertz (1984, 188–89). At these, usually relatively small events, everyone sits inside a hut in two circles, arranged according to sex, agnatic kinship, and age (seniority). Left and right as well as inner and outer are the reverse of the Xhosa case (ibid., 342). The inner circle has high status and is reserved for agnatic kin, the outer circle has lower status (ibid., 188–89). The symbolism of East and West, important to the Mpondo, is not relevant at Shixini beer drinks, perhaps because not all huts face the same direction.

4. Cook (1931) says that Bomvana beer drinks were sometimes held inside the byre, but this is not the case in Shixini, and it is possible that these were substitute rituals like *ukungxengxeza* (see chapter five).

5. Davies (1927) and Cook (1931, 18) say that *inkabi* was used to denote the name of a chief or headman and his followers, and applied also to the area (*umhlaba*) over which the chief/headman ruled, though the latter might sometimes have a different name. In many cases, however, the two names coincided. Among both Bomvana and Gcaleka local areas derive their names from the first chiefs living there (ibid., 24). A commoner homestead head could have his own *inkabi* if he so desired, and his homestead would then be known by that name, which was frequently the name of his lead ox (*loc. cit.*). Often the *inkabi* was the same as the clan name, among both chiefs and commoners. In asking for an *inkabi* or 'beer name' a man invited the chief to a beer drink at his *umzi* and said "I ask for a dish (*isitya*)" because "I am increased" (i.e. his family had grown). At future beer drinks he would be given beer (*ukulawula*) in the name of his *inkabi* or *isitya*.

6. They are also addressed as *iinkabi zalapha* (big men (lit: oxen) of the area), *izidwangube* (great councillors) *iindlezana* (most generous ones) and *iingwevu* (greybeards). Most of these terms are also used when referring to the sub-ward as a whole—e.g. *impi yakuthi yakuloFolokhwe* or *yakwaFolokhwe* (our people of Folokhwe), or *izidwangube zomhlaba* (great councillors of the area). Among other Cape Nguni some of these terms are reserved, it appears, for agnatically related kin and their ancestors (Hammond-Tooke 1984, Kuckertz 1983/4).

7. Women have different names for the sub-ward sections as part of the language of 'avoidance' that characterizes their speech. In Folokhwe, women use Dam instead of Chibi, Jiti for Ngingqi, and Sithi for Komkhulu. This is part of a wider pattern known as *ukuhlonipha* ('to respect') in terms of which women show respect to the senior kin of their husbands, e.g. by not mentioning their names or using words that sound like their names, and thus having to invent substitute words, by avoiding places associated with men such as the cattle byre or right hand side of the hut, especially while they are junior wives, newly arrived in the husband's homestead. These avoidances serve to mark women as subject to certain linguistic and behavioral restrictions and to define their status in relation to men. Men, too, are subject to certain avoidances, such as avoiding contact with a mother-in-law. Generally speaking, these are not as extensive or as restrictive as those affecting women.

10 Beer Distribution and Consumption

*From time to time beer is served out in large vessels; beer, having some relish of wine,
sparkling and palatable, and diffusing a joy of frankest character*

Delegorgue's Voyage Dans L'Afrique-Australe, 1847[1]

The distribution and consumption of beer is, of course, the heart and soul of
any beer ritual, superimposed on the spatial dimensions of the homestead outlined in the last chapter, both making space socially relevant and, almost simultaneously, somewhat confounding it. It is through the sequential distribution of
beer, its differentiation in terms of quantity, and its allocation in spatial terms,
that hierarchies, boundaries and social categories are constructed, and that many
of the dispositions that are part of the rural Xhosa habitus come into play. It is
through the consumption of the beer that groups are embodied and come into
being, but there are also certain practices that break down the boundaries constructed by space, time and beer. As Dietler has pointed out, "nearly all feasts
serve to mark, reify, and inculcate diacritical distinctions between social groups,
categories, and statuses while at the same time establishing relationships across
the boundaries that they define" (Dietler 2001, 88). In the process the performative and transformative nature of drinking becomes apparent.

Arriving at a beer drink people call out a greeting and sit roughly in the
place they expect will be allocated to them later.[2] The greeting is loudly declaimed in a manner known as *ukukhahlela*, a stylized form of announcing
one's arrival in which the host's clan name or praise name (*isikhahlelo*) is used,
prefaced with a short, sharp *Ah!* as in *Ah! Ndabanduna!* or *Ah! AmaNtshilibe!*
The name of the clan, sub-ward, its sub-headman, or of the chief of Shixini
may be used instead, or the greeting may incorporate reference to the others
already present, especially if the host's clan name is used.[3] To keep the early
arrivals happy, one or two preliminary beakers are given out 'just to drink' or
'to while away time with', and the host may give an informal preliminary indication of the amount of beer available and the nature of the event. Thus a
preliminary beaker may be called *ibhekile yokwazisa* (beakers for making
known). At Gulakulinywa's beer for harvest, for example, it was said that the
preliminary beaker was "a beaker for informing you: this beaker is to indicate

[the size of] that cask". He was saying, in other words, that there was plenty of beer to come.

Beer prestations (*iminono*)

Before the proceedings start in earnest the homestead head is able to give gifts of beer to individuals closely connected to the home. These are called *iminono* and they go primarily to certain categories of kin who live at some distance and to what might be called 'beer friends'. Such gifts, taken from a pot set aside for this purpose, may continue intermittently until near the end of the event. The head's wife, too, has a portion of beer that she uses in this way, independently of her husband. *Ukunona* means literally 'to be respected' and *umnono* (pl. *iminono*) can be translated as neatness or carefulness. This beer is also known as *umahluko* (difference or distinction) and as 'things with which to provide hospitality' (*ukonga*). Thus the etymology indicates that the receivers are singled out for special treatment, as people who have a particular status in relation to the giver. This is one way in which the space allocated to individuals as part of their territorial groups is *not* linked to the beer that they receive.

The main receivers of *iminono* are affines, especially sons-in-law, including SWH, BSWH, FBSSWH and wife's agnates (WF, WFB, etc), as indicated in Table 1, which summarises the destinations of 121 beakers of *iminono*. Of these, 52 (43%) went to affines and 18% to matrilateral kin (mainly MZS).[4] Other consanguines such as ZS, FZS and FZD (6%), patrilineal kin (4%) and clansmen (6%) were also sometimes recognized, but infrequently.[5] Given the overlap between section membership and agnation this is not surprising, since the host section receives plenty of beer. Only 21 *iminono* (17%) went to members of the same section—the majority went to people from other sections within the sub-ward (35%) and to people from other sub-wards (48%). Fifteen percent of *iminono* went to unrelated friends, and 7% to high status people such as sub-headmen from other sub-wards, men of the royal Tshawe clan, and people regarded as wealthy and influential. Friends included men who had undergone circumcision with the host, and some who worked with him in town. In many cases, the exchange of *iminono* is a relationship that is inherited, two homestead heads giving each other *iminono* because their fathers did so before them.

Table 1   Distribution of *iminono* gifts

By Kinship Category	%	By Territorial Affiliation	%
Affines	43	Same Sub-ward Section	17
Matrilateral Kin	18	Other Sections of the Sub-ward	35
Other Consanguines	6	Other Sub-wards of the Ward	48
Patrilineal Kin	4		
Clansmen (no genealogical link)	6		
Unrelated Friends	15		
Unrelated High Status People	7		
	100		100

In most cases these gifts form part of an ongoing exchange. Many pointed out that "one gives to the person whom one expects to receive beer from when he has an occasion" and men are able to name those that they used to give *iminono* to in the past, but no longer do so because of a failure to reciprocate, often attributed to poverty.[6] However, this is not always a clear-cut matter, and deciding who to give to and who to leave out is tricky. Invariably, the amount of beer set aside is inadequate to allow the head to give to as many he would like, and he offers an apology for this, asking those whom he has neglected to forgive him. If he fails to do this he runs the risk of someone who is expecting an *umnono* beaker standing up to complain. One way around this is to give *iminono* to the really important guests (e.g. wife's father) and to group the others together, two or three to a beaker. In this way, at a large event one might give out 12–15 beakers of *iminono* to thirty or more people.

The importance of *iminono* is illustrated by the public fanfare and formality with which it is distributed. Having consulted kin and members of the section, the host directs an assistant to draw a number of beakers (up to four or five at a time) and to place them in front of the door. He then calls for silence and tells the assistant where to place each beaker, calling out the name of the receiver, and often mentioning the specific relationship. Mgilimbane spoke as follows when giving out *iminono* at his *umsindleko*:

... Take this beaker, to Limangele and Helesi [pause]

For Helesi, umm, and Tandabantu — the three of them

Take another beaker, and put it here, for Canca, together with Ndaba...

Together with, with my brother in law, Skeyile — the three of them

Take another beaker, and put it here next to father [Mgilimbane's WFB]

Are they—are they finished now? Is there still one left?

Take another beaker, and put it there next to Pat

Yaaah! That's all right now

So, chiefs, this is what I have found, there is nothing else [to give out]

I thought that you should receive these spoons-full

The people that I did not get to, chiefs, should not complain

I had hoped to give them too

[Interjection: It is impossible to attend to everybody!]

As this indicates, as a visitor to Folokhwe I was sometimes given *iminono*, and by passing it around and calling people to drink from it found it a very useful way of publicly reciprocating favours received and acknowledging relationships that I had developed in the field. Perhaps this is why *iminono* are frequently referred to as 'feathers' or 'wings' with which to 'fly', as indicated in the following—spoken by Dwetya at the latter's *ntwana nje* (see chapter 13), when a kinsman from Velelo arrived quite late in the proceedings:

...The son of Wafunqula has just arrived, along with that woman

They have only just come

There are no more feathers my children

There are no more feathers left in this home with which we might fly to you

Be at peace, my children, and do not say that this is not a home today

It will be a home next time you come, if you arrive in good time

Please forgive me my children

Strictly speaking there should be something [for you], if this is indeed a home...

A similar reference was made when a specialist circumciser attended a beer drink in Folokhwe after having completed his work at an initiation ceremony nearby. Dlathu gave out the beaker saying that "the woman of this home says that she has not yet seen you chewing the corn of the home. She would like you to eat...".

So what *iminono* signals is that the individual homestead is able to provide for a wide range of people and to acknowledge reciprocal relationships with certain kin who live at some distance. In this way it demonstrates its moral quality, managerial ability and economic vitality. These qualities, and the relationships involved, are acted out or performed through the public way in which the beer is given, and embodied in the beer itself. Although a beer drink is largely the affair of the section as a group, with beer allocation signalling and indexing relationships between territorial groups, gender and age categories, *iminono* allows for individuality and the recognition of individual interest. The people who give each other *iminono* change over time as relationships and interests change, as old links fade and new ones are forged, and as new marriages are contracted and the range of affines changes. Similarly, practical circumstances (in the above case a circumcision ritual) affect the way in which this beer is distributed.

Individuality as expressed through kinship also leads to modification of the spatial order through the practice of inviting certain categories of kin to sit with the host section. In effect this is an alternative to giving them *iminono*, with similar performative effects, since the hosts always provide well for themselves and have lots of beer to share. Most prominent among such kin are sons-in-law, who should be given high status seating places. Other affines such as WB, WF, WFB, including classificatory affines,[7] and other categories of kin (but seldom agnates) are also afforded this honour, especially if they are from outside the sub-ward.

The *injoli*—master of ceremonies

After the distribution of the preliminary beakers and *iminono*, which are largely the responsibility of the individual host, the latter hands over the beer and control of the event to his sub-ward section, represented by the section's *injoli*. All sections of the sub-ward must be well represented at this point, unless the hosts are aware of what is delaying the others and know that they will arrive late. Once the *injoli* has taken charge, the host is required formally to explain what kind of beer drink it is, or what prompted him to brew. Spokesmen for the other groups respond, saying that they are grateful for the explanation and that they should now proceed. The explanation also specifies the amount of beer available for general distribution, and whether women have their own portion or not. Frequently, the beer is personified, e.g. "There in that full cask is the man [beer for men]...the woman is in the pot, [containing] four beakers." The host must also indicate, on behalf of his section, whether or not the various groups present can expect to be given the amount of beer that they are entitled to and, if not, point out that there is a shortage and ask permission to withhold certain beakers. There is often discussion or debate about this. The explanation of the event is also directed at the host's ancestors. Informants explained that if people do not know the reason for brewing they will be unable to talk about the event and to thank and praise the brewer. They must be allowed to do so because "they are the witnesses to what you have done, and the people below [ancestors] are also witnesses."

At this point the *injoli* announces that he is going 'to arrange the hut', having consulted with the senior men of his section about this. It is here that the topological features of the homestead outlined earlier become relevant. After asking other sub-wards to go outside, he allocates places to the host sections, young men and women. Then the question of which of the neighbouring sub-wards to call in, and where they should be placed, is dealt with. From this point onward things proceed cautiously. The event has been transformed by the explanation, the handing over to the *injoli* and the arranging of the hut, and is now framed and constituted as an affair involving groups. The host section as a collectivity makes decisions about allocations to other groups. Even if an important guest arrives he cannot be given *umnono* from the main beer, which belongs to the section, and he will have to go without unless there is something 'hidden'.

The *injoli* is also responsible for the beer. He supervises the drawing of all beakers for distribution, announces each one as it is given out, and is responsible for placing the beakers in front of the groups or individuals that they are destined for (Illustration 15). He must choose his words carefully to show that rights are being respected; for example: "This is your beaker, it is a full *iqhwina*, as it should be when there is a full cask for men." Such allocations are based on the reciprocal beer-exchange relationship between groups, but the *injoli* must be on the alert because this changes over time as the overall relationship between groups changes. In this sense the beaker allocated to any particular group (and also beakers given to individuals) has a 'biography' (Kopytoff 1986). As in the case of other commodity paths, precedent is not always followed and diversions are frequent as long as this is made known beforehand. Appadurai (1986, 17) points out that the flow of commodities is always "a shifting compromise between socially regulated paths and competitively inspired diversions."

The *injoli* liaises between the hosts and those outside of the hut, and conveys the thanks (or the complaints) of the visiting groups to the assembly as a whole. He is responsible, generally, for ensuring that the event proceeds smoothly and in an orderly fashion, and he helps to ensure that people abide

15. Distribution to men's groups

by the oratorical "rules for interaction" (Saville-Troike 1982, 147), such as those governing turn-taking and not interrupting speakers. If someone wants to speak, they ought to ask the *injoli* to call for silence. If they have a question or a request they channel it through him. He collects the money when beer is sold and sees to it that the beakers to be given out free of charge are made available, announces when the beer is all gone, and so on. He is, in effect, in charge of the beer drink on behalf of the section and he consults frequently and at length with other members of the section, including the individual host.

Customary allocations (*amasiko*)

The first few allocations of beer after the arranging of the hut are called *amasiko* (customs) beer. These consist of a number of named beakers, at least some of which must be given out at every beer drink. There are three other terms which are synonymous with *amasiko*. These are *amalungelo* (rights, privileges, claims, advantages), *iimfanelo* (property or, in the singular, suit-ableness, propriety, desert, duty) and *iziqhelo* (habits, expectations). These indicate that this beer is valued property allocated to particular groups by customary right, and such allocation demarcates a hierarchy of local groups as well as, in some case, divisions within them. It consists of a number of different, named beakers, as follows:

(i) *Iimvuko* (awakening)

The first and most important of the *amasiko* is called the *iimvuko* beer, allocated to the host section only. The amount varies. In Folokhwe, Ngingqi section gives out two *iimvuko* beakers, one each for men and women. Komkhulu gives out three, two for men and one for women, and the men's beakers are divided between the two sub-sections, Mbukhuba and Mtyibilizini. Ngingqi has no sub-sections. Chibi section gives out four *iimvuko*, three to men and one to women. The men's beakers are divided according to Chibi's sub-sections— Bamba, Ntshilibe and Ntlane. Women do not subdivide their *iimvuko* in any of the sections. The sections and sub-sections are similar to the hospitality groups (*izithebe*) among the Mpondomise (Hammond-Tooke 1963) and the mat-associations found among the Mpondo (Kuckertz 1984, 346).

Note that in Chibi the sub-sections have clan names (though their members are not exclusively members of these clans) and they are important divisions because they relate to genealogical history, the splitting of lineages and conflict between kin groups (see chapter 11). In Komkhulu the sub-sections have area names and are not associated with clans. Komkhulu men tend to play them down, saying that it is simply a convenient way of dividing *iimvuko* beer. They emphasize the unity of the section, where the Cirha clan[8] is dominant. In this case, the distribution of beer is linked directly to historical and everyday processes. It is only with regard to *iimvuko* that the sub-sections are recognized for beer distribution. All other allocations are on the basis of section or sub-ward.

Like other formal allocations, *iimvuko* is allocated in a stylized manner that publicises the fact that the host group is performatively constituting itself as a unit in relation to the others, but also as a unit with specific characteristics. These beakers are described as *iimfanelo zelali*, 'the sections privileges', or as 'the things for living together as neighbours in a section'. They are for 'the people I live with' and they indicate 'the way we look after each other'. As one man explained: "We do not drink beer with people from far away, it is living together that counts. *Iimvuko* has to do with our living together". Once, when my colleague Chris de Wet accompanied me to Shixini, he and I and a field assistant were recording a praise poem in our hut and were late in arriving in the hut next door (in the same homestead) where a beer drink had started. The *iimvuko* had already been distributed, and Dlathu, acting for the homestead head, Mzilikazi, who was at work, publicly chastised us for arriving late, saying that we were "the men I live with" and that we should have been present. He had been waiting for us for a long time, but we were busy "working in another hut", he said. So they had gone ahead and the *iimvuko* was already finished. It was a requirement of a custom, he said, that if one wanted it, one had to be there for it; one had "to work in the hut of the beer drink…There should be no working on one side, there should be working here."

The word *imvuko* itself means awakening, from *ukuvuka*, to wake up, and some people emphasize this derivation. *Iimvuko* is distributed "because we arrive early in the morning—we of the section bring out the *iimvuko* beakers"; "It is for waking up, because they wake up from their homes and come here to this home. [We say] I am waking you up with this beaker". One man commented that the people who lived together in an area ought to start off with their own beakers to "rid themselves of jealousy", that is, to indicate the harmony and good relations that exist between them by drinking together, as 'people of the home'. So, through *iimvuko* the host section is singled out, constituted as a corporate, exclusive group, which shares beer because the members live together and assist each other in daily life, and who do so on a reciprocal basis in terms of the morality of neighbourliness (*ubumelwane*) and mutual helpfulness (*ubuncedana*). Drinking *iimvuko* is thus the performance and embodiment of harmonious relations that transforms a network of potentially co-operating and sharing people into a group who actually share a special portion of beer.

The formal setting emphasizes this. *Iimvuko* is consumed right at the beginning of the formal procedure, once all the sections and sub-wards have been allocated their places and are waiting in anticipation, closely watching the *injoli* and the hosts to ensure that the correct procedure is followed. At no other stage of the beer drink is attention focused so sharply on what is happening. And what does happen is that the beer is given *only* to the members of the host section, men *and* women, before anyone else receives anything. The unity of the section is publicly and powerfully acted out, before proceeding to distributions that address their social ties with other sections and sub-wards.

While the *iimvuko* is being consumed other sections and sub-wards have to wait patiently. Sometimes one of their number tactfully suggests that it would be nice if they, too, were allocated beer. For example, Gavini once put it like this, addressing Bhadela, the *injoli*:

Hey Bhadela!

No there is no problem

There is nothing wrong Bhadela

It is a good thing that a person should brew

And [also] that he should open his eyes

Because these people here are hungry now

What has caused the hunger?

It is the home [section people being served first]

One gets jealous of these beakers which are given to people

While there is nothing that is given to oneself

That is the point

The home causes hunger; yes...

As with all beakers, however, the *iimvuko* are not consumed entirely by the section to which they are allocated. Members of the section call those from other sections and sub-wards to drink from these beakers. Although, as one man put it, "there can be no case against us if we do not", not to share this beer with others would be unthinkable. In this way, the formal boundaries between groups are broken down through informal sharing between individuals. This practice, called *ukurhabulisa*, is discussed in more detail below.

(ii) The sub-headman's beaker

This part of the *amasiko* (customs) is obligatory at all beer drinks at which the sub-headman or his delegated representative is present. The sub-headman invariably calls others to drink from it, or sends it across to other sub-headmen who may be present. This beaker embodies the role that the sub-headman plays in everyday life. As Jija put it: "The sub-headman attends to our affairs, represents us at the chief's great place, and reports our opinions to him. If there is a meeting there, he reports back to us on what was said. When one brews beer, it must be remembered that the sub-headman is the one who runs about for us." This beaker is also called *umpath' isibonda*, 'controller of the sub-headman'. In other words, it is a symbolic (and practical) means of ensuring reciprocal relationship with him, and a statement about the nature of that relationship. In addition to receiving a special beaker, the sub-headman is always asked to sit with the host section. The status of sub-headmen from other areas is also recognized, by being invited to sit with one or other of the local sections, inside the hut. The same applies to members of the royal

Tshawe clan, "because the *amaTshawe* are chiefs." Influential men from other areas, such as a chief's councillor, are treated similarly if they happen to be present.[9]

(iii) *Intluzelo* and *isikhonkwane*

While *iimvuko* indexes close harmonious relations within the section, including mutual assistance in work, other forms of the 'customs' beer address the ethic of mutual co-operation within the wider unit of the sub-ward more directly. At beer drinks associated with work parties there are specific 'customs' which must be given to the workers (see chapter 11) and at *umsindleko* for a returned migrant the *iimvuko* are replaced with beakers called *intluzelo* ('straining'),[10] given to all the sections of the sub-ward. I was unable to obtain explicit reasons for this difference, but suggest that it may be linked to the community-wide significance of migrant labour and the important aim of integrating the returnee back into the sub-ward. In addition, members of the sub-ward come to *umsindleko* to 'work' for the migrant's homestead to make the event successful. For the same reason, *intluzelo* also forms part of the free allocation of beer when it is sold at *imbarha*, given to the sub-ward men because they have come to 'work' for the homestead by buying the beer on offer. It is not one of the 'customs', however. At *imbarha* there is only one 'customs' beaker, called *isikhonkwane*, which will be discussed later in chapter 11.

(iv) *Umcakulo* (the first dip)

The distribution of *umcakulo* effects the orderly transition from one phase of the beer drink to another—from the distribution of 'customs' to the distribution of the main beer (the *intselo*). *Umcakulo* is itself a boundary in that it consists of the top, frothy part of the *intselo* cask,[11] though it is regarded as part of the customs. It is issued only when the men have a full cask and the women have a separate portion, and it is given only to men, one beaker for each of the sections.

Intselo—the main drink

(i) *Ukugabu* (to allocate by numbers)

At beer rituals where both the amount of beer and the number of people present are small, section and sub-ward membership may be ignored for the purpose of the allocation of space and beer. Men and women sit separately and are told that there are no sides (*amacala*), or that there are no seating places (*amabala*). Instead, they are divided into groups on the basis of numbers (*ukugabu* or *ukugabula*) and the beer is given out on this basis and known as *ugabu* beer. Distribution by *ukugabu* is disliked; it marks the beer drink as somehow different (e.g. as associated with mourning—see chapter 14) or as very small and insignificant.

(ii) *Ukulawula* (to allocate by social groups)

Ukulawula is by far the most preferred and most common form of allocation. *Umlawulo* beer is beer 'with places' (*bunobala)* in the sense that its distribution follows the allocation of space to various groups. The same term, *ukulawula*, is used to refer to the allocation of both places and beer, and one of its meanings, as we have seen, is to arrange or to give order to. It gives the host section scope to manipulate and control the event because it allows for ordering, discrimination, definition of boundaries, and differentiation between groups. As indicated previously, *ukulawula* also means to govern or to rule over, and this is exactly what the host section does—it presides, controls and defines the situation in its own terms, but recognizing the relative positions and rights of others: "When there is drinking it is done by rights, area by area. The [seating] places are as they are so that we drink by rights."[12]

The principles underlying the distribution of *umlawulo* are as follows:

1. The amount of beer given to sections and sub-wards is directly related to the places they are allocated when the hut is arranged. Those with higher ranked seating places receive more beer than those in low ranked positions, and they receive it before them.

2. The host section receives far more beer than other sections of the subward, the host sub-ward more than visiting sub-wards. The host sections receive beer individually, and well before visiting sub-wards get any.

3. Men receive more beer than women, and well before the woman receive theirs.

4. Strict reciprocity prevails between groups, and the amount of beer allocated to a group is determined (in theory) by the amount received from it at previous beer drinks. In practice the nature of the relationship, as defined in terms of the size of the beaker, is frequently negotiated and renegotiated.

5. Older people receive more beer than younger people, and well before the latter get anything.

Umlawulo may be given out in two or three rounds following a "logic of in-corporation" (Tambiah 1985, 151) that proceeds progressively in terms of ter-ritorial and social space, then gender and age, and that basically involves se-quencing rules which are repeated in cycles for the remainder of the event, making for considerable symbolic redundancy but progressively constructing a symbolic map of the social world. In the first round, the host section allo-cates two or three beakers to itself and one to each of its fellow sub-ward sec-tions. Half an hour or so later, the sub-wards with which the host sub-ward has the closest ties are given one beaker. After another delay of 30 to 60 min-utes, more *umlawulo* is given to the host sections, and to the more distant sub-wards which have not yet received any. Often, the more distant sub-wards re-ceive a smaller beaker than the closer ones. If it is not possible (due to a lack of beakers) to allocate to more than one sub-ward at a time, the one that is closest to the givers, in terms of geographical proximity and relationships, gets its beer first. Sub-wards which maintain a particularly close relationship with the host section are sometimes given an extra beaker of *umlawulo*, called *iz-ibuko* (a ford), "because they have come here from over there, across the river".[13]

When the host section receives more than one round of *umlawulo*, the first round (all two or three beakers) is given to the senior men, and the less sen-ior (those aged under 45 years or so) as well as the *abafana* (young men) are excluded. The less senior receive a beaker only in the next round, and this beaker may include the young men, or the young men may receive a separate *umlawulo* beaker even later. If there are two or three beakers in an allocation of *umlawulo* to a single group, the *injoli* indicates where each beaker should begin and end, pointing to the man who should start the drinking and the one who gets it last. In other words, there is a division (based on numbers, as in *ukugabu*) within the section receiving *umlawulo*.[14]

Visiting sub-wards are keenly aware of how much *umlawulo* they are en-titled to and if the brewers are not able to provide the right amount, calcu-lated in terms of number and size of beakers, they must explain why, express their regret, and ask permission to give less. If this is not done, the visitors will complain, a long argument may follow, and the hosts may have to give up some of their own beer or risk being treated in like fashion when the roles are reversed. In this way, relationships between groups are negotiated in terms of beer.[15] Strictly speaking, men from sub-wards from further away, which are not neighbouring sub-wards, are *abasarhi*, a term indicating that they do not have formal rights to beer, that they have come only in the hope of getting some (*ukusarha*). In practice it is difficult to apply categorically, since one part of a sub-ward may have a close relationship with another that is some distance away, while other parts do not, and this term is seldom used except at work-party beer drinks, where it is applied to the non-workers (see chapter 11).

Ukurhabulisa — informal sharing

In the midst of all this structure there is, as one might expect, some anti-structure, given that we are dealing with rituals (Turner 1969). Divided by the formal conventions (*imithetho*) of beer drinking, in another sense all present are united in a single homestead. A major manifestation of this is the way in which the beakers of beer are actually consumed, as opposed to the way in which they are formally allocated. No sooner has an allocation been announced, the beakers distributed and the *injoli* stood down, when the beer drink dissolves, as it were, into apparent disorder, and the assembly in the hut is transformed from a still, attentive, structured group into a noisy, moving, chaotic mass. Men take up the conversations and banter that they had left off earlier, start loudly discussing how the beakers should or should not circulate, resume calling out greetings and comments to friends across the room and to new arrivals, offer the beakers to each other, and shout messages to women outside to come and drink. People start moving in and out of the hut, and backwards and forwards within it; men go out to meet with friends or to urinate, and women enter in twos and threes, drink from the beakers offered them and leave. The host, the *injoli* and his assistants scurry about, searching for empty beakers and getting ready for the next allocation, when structure will be re-imposed before dissolving again, in a repetitive, cyclical process.[16]

Giving someone a drink from a beaker is called *ukurhabulisa* (lit: to cause to drink) and this practice evokes a line from a popular Xhosa song: "Move on beaker, don't linger in one place".[17] No beaker is consumed entirely by the group (or the individual) to which it is allocated, making one wonder why so much fuss is made about seating places, beer allocations, beaker sizes, and so on. Certainly, care is taken to ensure that each member of the group drinks from the beaker allocated to it, in turn, and that the beaker stays more or less within the control of the group. However, each person is permitted and is expected, when the beaker is passed to him (or her), to call someone else from another group to drink from it before s/he does (Illustration 16). And the person invited may choose to bring someone else along for a drink (see Hunter 1936, 360). Obviously, if each member of the group does this, the group's allocation is consumed mainly by others, and this is exactly what often occurs.

16. Calling others to drink

As each man receives the beaker, he may call others. At these times the air rings with shouts such as:

Nothusile! Nothusile! You are offered a drink here!

Come here Nogamile! Have a drink!

Modi, put down that pipe! [and come and drink]

Hey, Govuza! Stand up! [and have a drink here]

Bodli, you are being called!

You are being called to drink fellow, come here!

The receivers reply with thanks or acknowledgement: 'Right!', 'Wow!', or 'Thank you; do so again in future!'

This informal sharing is a practical manifestation of commensality, friendship and harmony, which mirrors the ethic of mutual help that informs so much of everyday life and work and proclaims a wider unity than the formal allocations do: "We call each other to drink to make each other happy at beer drinks, since we are people who live together in one place, who drink together happily, and who help each other. That is why one gives drinks to others." Those who call each other are frequently kin, close neighbours or good friends and the practice also signals continuity in a relationship through reciprocation: "I call those who give to me". There is no point in having beer if it cannot be given away to mark links with a wide range of others. Feasting practices in general, as Dietler has pointed out, mark boundaries but "simultaneously express relationships of mutual dependence across those boundaries that, in turn, represent and naturalize ideologies structuring larger societal relations of production and authority." (2001, 91). This does not mean, however, that conflicts, real or potential, and the disharmonious elements of social life, are not also present and expressed at beer rituals, as we shall see in later chapters.

It is because of the value and status attached to giving and to reciprocity that the *injoli* (even one who does not drink beer) is sometimes rewarded for his work with a beaker with which to call people, and that *iminono* gifts are given to people who do not drink beer. Similarly, a person who does not drink is called in the knowledge that he or she can bring along someone who does drink beer, and in turn become the giver. Even a woman who does not drink is called, said Dlathu, "because she brews beer for people at her homestead".

Giving beer away is also, however, associated with power differences between giver and receiver. In some cases this is linked to an enduring status distinction, such as that between men and women, elders and juniors, and sub-headman and others. The differing amounts of beer allocated to these people may be interpreted as a means to act out the status and power differences between them through the receivers being able to call those who formally get little. This is a general tendency, but there is nothing to stop a junior from giving a drink to a senior, a woman to a man, or a visitor from afar to a member of the host sub-ward or section. Because of the way in which the beer is divided, however, this does not happen frequently except in circumstances where women or young men receive a lot of the beer, or at phases of the beer drink when men and women receive similar amounts of beer such as during the drinking of *igwele* beer on the day before the beer drink proper.

Status differences are embodied in the way in which juniors offer drinks to seniors. The junior person cannot shout out in the manner illustrated above, but must respectfully take the beaker over to the senior, wait for it there, and then carry it back again. Alternatively the beaker may be sent over to the person being offered a drink with a third party. This latter method is also used when high status people call each other, thus avoiding both calling the one over to the other (signalling the higher status of the giver) and the giver taking the beaker to the receiver (signalling the higher status of the latter).

Within the framework of these general tendencies, the individuals most likely to be called to drink are as follows:

a. Affinal and matrilateral kin. Men call their wives and mothers and their agnate's wives and mothers, as well as other affines and matrilateral kin, especially those from other sub-wards.[18] Women tend to call their husbands and husband's agnates and clansmen.

b. People who are highly respected, wealthy or politically influential, such as sub-headmen, and the wives and mothers of sub-headmen.

c. Visitors to homesteads within the sub-ward, and who may be spending some weeks or months at those homesteads.

d. People who arrived late and who have not yet had anything to drink.

e. People from whom a favour has recently been received, or from whom a favour may be sought in the near future, as well as people who have ongoing mutually beneficial relationships with each other.

In practice, who calls who to drink also varies according to who happens to be present, the kind of beer drink, and other circumstances. At beer for a work party it is primarily workers who call non-workers. Being able to do this is regarded as part of the reward for working. This is also one of the few occasions when women may be allocated more beer than men, and thus are able to call men to drink. People are keenly aware of who is offering and being offered beer, and frequently voice comments in praise or criticism in this respect. It is considered bad form to call more than one person or to call the same person to whom others have just offered a drink. On one occasion in Jotelo, a Folokhwe man called three other people for a drink from the beaker allocated to Folokhwe, without other Folokhwe men noticing. When the others realized what was going on they commented adversely about this, asking the offender if he was "trying to put people in his pockets" (trying covertly to curry favour) by giving beer to so many without making other Folokhwe men aware of this. When Canca called a Tshawe who had just been called to drink by someone else, Bavumile criticised him, saying: "Why do you call someone who has his own beaker, when there are people without beakers?" On the other hand, a man who called a number of women whose husbands were at work was praised for doing so, because they would otherwise have got very little to drink. It is regarded as improper to call women to the exclusion of men, or to call people from only a particular section or ward. There is evidently a concern that all who are present should satisfy their thirst.

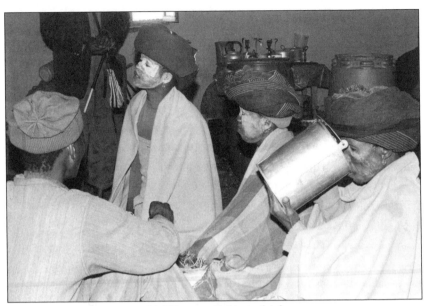

17. Women called in to drink

The entry of women into men's space to receive a drink dramatizes their formally inferior status but also the threat that they pose to the formal male order. When a woman is called from outside she is permitted to 'carry' (*beleka*) a friend with her (Illustration 17). The two women wrap their shawls tightly round their shoulders, and enter the hut, where they go down on their knees just inside the door (the only spot where there is any free space) and stretch forward to receive the beaker, not approaching the giver too closely. Sitting back on their heels they drink from it in turn and then the one who was called passes it back to the man who called her with appropriate expressions of thanks. Younger women, especially, do not initiate conversation and they keep their eyes downcast in an attitude of respect (*ukuhlonipha*). A senior or assertive woman may be confident enough to take two friends with her into the hut, and in the flurry of activity the beaker may also get passed to women called in by others, and before very long be almost emptied. So although the practice of calling women emphasizes patriarchy, senior women can use the moment to assert their status and subtly undermine male dominance, through making considerable inroads into the beakers that they are handed. There are frequent complaints from men against their fellows for 'allowing' women to drink too much. It is the male callers who get into trouble—no case can be brought against the women who drank the beer—illustrating the position of women as social minors.

Women's allocation

After *umlawulo* has been given to all the visiting sub-wards, the *injoli* announces that he is about to attend to the women, who are referred to in the same terms as the men's groups, as an *inkabi* (ox), *isipani* (span) or *umkhosi* (regiment)—e.g. *la mkhos' uphandle* (that regiment outside). They receive very little beer, a strategy designed to make them dependent on being called by men for sips from the men's beakers. Their subordinate status is also illustrated in their seating position outside next to the *igoqo* (woodpile) though as indicated in chapters 11 and 14 there are exceptions to this. The women's *umlawulo* is usually only about one quarter of the amount that men get, and they receive theirs much later than the men do. Women are often given the old, rusty beakers for this purpose, while the men have the newer ones. The gender distinction at beer drinks is thus marked spatially, temporally, qualitatively (poorer quality beakers), quantitatively (less beer) and behaviourally (being called by men to drink). The women's *injoli* divides their share, without fuss or formal announcements, according to sub-wards in a much more egalitarian fashion than men, taking care to give each group the same as the others. This egalitarianism is signalled also by the merging of young and older women at some beer drinks. Women do have rights at beer drinks, and can complain to the *injoli* if they feel that they have not been given their share. They also have rights to beer in relation to each other, as territorial groups, like the men do, but the reciprocal beer-exchange relations between women are independent of those of the men, and may follow a different pattern, depending on relationships between them.

That women do not necessarily conform to the structure imposed on drinking by men is indicated also by the way in which men rationalize the way in which women are treated at beer drinks. Stokwana, a senior man, claimed that women were irresponsible and that they had to sit outside because:

> ...they do not keep quiet and stop talking [when required to]. In the hut, one person speaks at a time; so we say 'Women! Be quiet!'. But women do not use their ears. We cannot drink with women at a beer drink because of the noise they make. They do not care what is being said in the home by the person who has brewed. [We say] 'Stop, women! Be quiet!' But these people cannot be controlled, they are troublesome...A woman has no respect....

In some situations, however, the role that women play is recognized in the division of beer. At work parties composed of men and women, the latter receive almost as much beer as the men. When the work party consists only of women, it is women who control the beer and allocate to men (see chapter 11). At *umsindleko*, the role of the wife in helping ensure the success of her husband's spell at work is recognized, and women get a larger share of the beer than usual. In Pondoland too, women depended on invitations to drink, but when beer was brewed for a mother some ten days after she had given birth, most of the beer was drunk by women (Hunter 1936, 155, 359).

Emptying the pot (*ukuqwela*)

After the *umlawulo*, a high point in the proceedings, there is a lull. Men leave the hut for some fresh air, to urinate, or to meet privately with someone to discuss a matter of mutual concern. Outside, they sit at random in small groups, seek out people they want to talk to, and converse quietly. After an hour or so, the *injoli* might indicate that the proceedings are about to start up again, and people drift back into the hut. If the pause is too long men get restless, especially if they know of other beer drinks in the vicinity. They ask the hosts 'to clean out the pots' so that the proceedings may be brought to a conclusion. The host section then asks the *injoli* to give out the last of the *intselo*, called the *iqwele* beer. The action of issuing this beer is known as *ukuqwela* (to empty the pot).

If there is sufficient beer *iqwele* is distributed to all the sections of the subward, and even to other sub-wards, but if the amount is small it is given only to the host section. *Iqwele* is always given to the older men, who circulate the beaker among themselves and call others over for sips, acting out the important principle of seniority in Xhosa life. The beaker starts with the elder next to the door, who asks a junior to take the first mouthful (*ukungcamla*). As the Mpondo put it, this is to symbolically 'remove the poison' (*ukukhupha ububi*) from the beer (Kuckertz 1984, 348) and is linked to the custom of a chief's retainer always tasting his food in case it is poisoned by his enemies. The other elders then drink in order of seniority until the last recognized elder is reached. Each of them calls one or two others to drink from it, before passing it on. The beaker then passes back up the line till it reaches the man next to the door again. Ideally, there should be about a cup-full left at this stage, which the senior elder at the door shows to the others, saying that 'it is finished' before draining the beaker. As with any other beaker, it is good manners to announce when it has 'fallen' (*iwile*), i.e. that it is empty.

Towards the end of the proceedings *ivanya*, made from re-straining the sediment of the proper beer, is distributed. People do not care for it very much and many may leave before it is given out. It is issued in much the same way as the main drink, but more equitably, other groups receiving the same amount as the hosts. In a reversal of the norm indicating its status as an inferior product, *ivanya* starts with the young men at the back, and an older man tastes the beaker before passing it down to the younger men. Women, too, receive *ivanya*, often only after the men's *ivanya* is finished and most of the men have left.

The principles of seniority and section solidarity are enacted again through one beaker of proper beer, taken from the 'hidden' portion, allocated to senior men of the host section at the same time as *ivanya*. It is called *ivanya enendevu* (bearded *ivanya*) or *ivanya yamadoda* (men's *ivanya*). As with all beakers it is announced by the *injoli*, e.g. "Here is the bearded beaker; the old men have been whingeing [about it] a lot". The elders control this beaker very carefully, passing it around among themselves and calling others to sip from it, but making sure that it returns to them every time. As with the *iqwele*, a dozen or more people drink from the beaker before it returns to the elder next to the door. At about this time, at large beer drinks, the women who ground the *imithombo* (malt) may also be given a beaker of the proper beer. *Ivanya* marks the end of the beer drink, and the completion of the *injoli*'s task. Any further beakers given out are the responsibility of the host, and are also taken from the 'hidden' beer. One such beaker is called *ibhekile yokubulela* (beaker for thanking) or *ibhekile yamazwi* (beaker for words). Before the men from other sections and sub-wards leave, they formally thank the homestead head for brewing, and speak about the reason for brewing. The beaker for words is given out in acknowledgement of these speeches. Another beaker that may be given out is called *ingxotha* (chasing away). It is to encourage the departure of those who are still there, "so that those who are still left should go home and sleep".[19]

With a bit of forethought, the homestead head will have preserved a beaker or two of beer from the original amount set aside as hidden, to give out to close kin and neighbours on the evening after the beer drink has ended. The event thus ends with a small group of neighbours gathered together for a little beer, in the same way that it started. On the day after many beer drinks, neighbours are again called to the homestead to partake of the *isidudu*—that small pot-full of beer kept one side during the brewing, the fermentation of which is delayed in order to bring it to maturity on this day. The atmosphere is relaxed and informal, members of the homestead going about their daily business while the beer is consumed.

Drinking and the social order

In Mary Douglas' British household, drinks ranked lower than food, were named more rarely, and were less structured. Drinks, unlike meals, were "not invested with any necessity in their ordering. Nor is the event called drinks internally structured into first, second, main, sweet...to count drinks at all is impolite" (Douglas 1972, 255). In her society, sharing drinks expressed "the detachment and impermanence of simpler and less intimate social bonds" (ibid., 258). This is clearly very different in the Xhosa case, where *not* to count the beakers of beer allocated, to order them and to invest them with meaning, would be not just impolite but unthinkable. Beer rituals, instead, are much more like the English meals that Douglas wrote about, where the different courses and the different kinds of food served enabled one to say something about the nature of social and cognitive categories. Beer, then, conforms to what Douglas said about food: "If food is treated as a code, the messages it encodes will be found in the pattern of social relationships being expressed. The message is about different degrees of hierarchy, inclusion and exclusion, boundaries and transactions across boundaries." (ibid., 249).

Following from this, we might use Douglas' structuralist notions about bodies and boundaries to make sense of much of the material presented in this and the previous chapter, where there is an obvious concern with the creation of order and structure. One could interpret this within the wider framework of the contrast that culturally conservative Xhosa make between their rural homes and the world of migrant labour, as illustrated in the discussion of the *umsindleko* beer drink in chapters five and six. As Douglas (1966) has shown, pollution is attached to things, actions and places associated with disorder and ambiguity, that threaten an accepted classificatory system or world view. Xhosa rural society has an established form, but beyond its boundaries there is formlessness, threat, danger and confusion. However, there is power in the formless and in the margins. This power both threatens and sustains established categories, and when the migrant returns he crosses a boundary and has to be redefined and reclassified and his power, the power of the marginal work place, harnessed to the good of rural life.

One could extend this from *umsindleko* to all beer rituals as manifestations of a rural Xhosa habitus within the field of capitalist production, as I have suggested earlier, within which there is a struggle for the power to define the nature of capital, particularly the nature and function of labour. Beer rituals in general may be viewed as concerned with this definition, which is in some ways synonymous with the construction of order. The arranging of the hut is an obvious example here, a cognitive separation of order from disorder. Order is structured and its elements ranked, with the senior men of the host sub-ward at the centre, or at the pinnacle, and the other elements structured analogously with the central structure. Thus a holistic scheme is produced, each element making sense only in relation to the whole (ibid., 260). And the entire system is re-constructed with a different territorial group at its centre at the succeeding events, which themselves need to be placed in the wider context of a system. Different kinds or classes of beer drinking rituals add another variable to the mix, providing a taxonomy which affects the structure in definable ways.

Why so much concern with order? Could it be that beer drinking rules function in a way similar to that which Douglas has suggested of the dietary prohibitions of the Israelites, that working for white employers and the place of the whites is polluting, 'matter out of place'? Red Xhosa in an apartheid state were anxious to keep themselves separate from the wider political and economic system which demanded their labour but denied them humanity. Their response to apartheid, as Mayer (1980) argued, was to turn their backs and reaffirm the moral superiority and integrity of the rural home and its agricultural base, however diminished the latter might have been. This demanded control and order at home to contrast with the disorder and lack of control outside it; this extended to the food, religion, education, aesthetics, clothes, and other material artefacts associated with the outside. As Douglas suggests, "whenever a people are aware of encroachment and danger dietary rules controlling what goes into the body would serve as a vivid analogy of the corpus of their cultural categories at risk." (1972, 272). Beer drinking rituals in this sense are manifestations of a focus on the integrity of the structure at home, on the integrity of the boundary. Every beer drink is in this sense a positive act of affirmation, a construction of a particular rural identity in contrast to the world outside.

As persuasive as such an argument might be, there has to be more to it. Red resistance could not have succeeded for as long as it did if constructed only at the level of thought or ideology. It had to have a practical component. This forces us to look beyond the structural dimensions of beer drinking rituals and to the way in which they link with everyday practice. Beer drinks are related to a variety of practical acts underlying the symbolic and that have to do with the maintenance of rural production. This is what the boundary encloses, not simply a particular world view, but also a structure of relations of production based on inter-household co-operation and interdependence.

In addition, beer drinks are directly linked to immediate social practices and contexts, to historical developments and to individual biographies. The next chapter takes this up in more detail.

Endnotes

1. Cited in Bird (1885 I, 477).

2. Unless there are women in the hut, in which case all men sit on the right, women on the left.

3. For example, *Ah! AmaBamba neenkosi!* (Bamba clansmen and others), *Ah! MaFolokhwe!* (Folokhwe people!). Another form of greeting used by men is *Eb'khosini!* (lit: At the chieftainship or place of authority).

4. Affines presented with *iminono* at the beer drinks for which I have data include SWH, WB, BWB, BSWH, WFB, SWFB, FBDH, WZH, SWF, ZBH, FZH, WMZDH, FZDHB, FFBSSWF and SWM. Other matrilateral kin given *iminono* were MZD, MZ, MMZD and MFMZS.

5. Classificatory kin were included in all of these categories.

6. Sometimes an *umnono* beaker is given to, say, a younger brother, in the name of his absent elder, being told that "this is the beaker for your elder brother." This can be taken a step further. If the homestead head's wife wishes to give a beaker to the wife of X, in recognition of the relationship between X and her husband, and X's wife is not present, she may give it to the wife of X's younger brother or other close agnate.

7. It is common for a homestead head to regard as his sons-in-law the husbands of daughters of a man of his own clan, but with whom he can trace no further connection.

8. Here and elsewhere the term clan is used to refer to a number of genealogically un-related people sharing a clan name and consisting of more than one agnatic group.

9. The allocation of space and beer to sub-headmen can also be used to make state-ments about the relationships between sub-wards. There were three sub-headmen present at Nontwaba's beer for harvest, in Komkhulu. All three sat with Komkhulu until the ar-ranging of the hut. At this point Ndlebezenja stood and addressed Chibi men, saying that it was customary "that when the chiefs are crowded together in one place, a request is made to that group [for them to be spread around]". One of the 'chiefs', he suggested, should sit with Chibi. It was not good for them to sit together, "beating each other with their shad-ows", i.e. pitting their statuses against each other. Ndlelibanzi's sub-headman was thus asked to sit with Chibi, while the other two remained with Komkhulu. This led to a sham argu-ment among some of the Komkhulu men. One said that the Ndlelibanzi sub-headman was the greater chief, and that he should stay with Komkhulu. Others pointed out that he was the sub-headman who knew the Chibi people best, while the other sub-headman (from Velelo) knew the Komkhulu people best, they said. Clearly, they were making a point about relationships, not only between individuals, but also between groups. Chibi and Ndlelibanzi people have a close relationship with each other, and the Ndlelibanzi sub-headman is affi-nally related to the dominant agnatic group in Chibi, of the Ntshilibe clan. Komkhulu and Velelo, too, have close ties with each other, and the Velelo sub-headman is of the same clan as the dominant Komkhulu clan, the Cirha clan. The placing of these two with the respec-tive sections thus served to recognize their status as political leaders, dramatize the rela-tionship between sections, and say something about the significance of clanship.

10. This is not to be confused with the *intluzelo* given to those who helped with the brewing and that given to neighbours on the day before the beer drink.

11. *Umcakulo* is another specialized and localised word which can be translated as 'sur-face beer', from *ukucakula*, "to dip from the surface of the water" (Kropf 1915, 54).

12. A group's *umlawulo* is given to it only at the place allocated to it when the hut is arranged. If the group moves to another spot, for example to try and get some shelter from wind or rain, its beer is placed on the spot originally allocated to it, even if there is no-one sitting there. Someone has then to get up and fetch it.

13. Velelo is given this beaker in Komkhulu section of Folokhwe; Jotelo receives it from Chibi and Ngingqi. When such a beaker is reciprocated, it is given to the whole of Folokhwe (i.e. at beer drinks in Velelo and Jotelo).

14. As mentioned earlier, however, the official sub-sections are not used as a basis for this division: "We of Komkhulu [section] are united [for *umlawulo*] and we give beer to Ngingqi, as well as to Chibi, that area up above there". This same informant spoke of Komkhulu as a neighbourhood group (literally our ridge—*ummango wethu*) in the context of *umlawulo*, although a minute earlier, when talking about *iimvuko*, he identified the sub-sections as distinct groups (*imimango*).

15. Similar data have been reported from other parts of Africa. For example, Mambila beer drinking is linked to the relationships between neighbouring territorial units though it takes place in the idiom of competitive beer exchange between individual beer partners. The beer exchange system maintains the status hierarchy as well as facilitating the development of village solidarity, since the village has to work together to provide the beer for large feasts (Rehfisch 1987).

16. Unlike Cowan's observations on dance in Northern Greece, where there is a gradual movement from structured hierarchy, order and difference towards egalitarianism, disorder and communitas (Cowan 1990).

17. *Hamba bhekile, suk' uhlala-hlala 'ndawo 'nye.*

18. Hunter (1936, 360) recorded that a homestead head was expected to call his wife, and that an *idikazi* (unattached woman) was called by her lover or admirers.

19. Bigalke (1969) mentions a beaker called *umpath'induku* (picking up sticks), given to close neighbours and friends who have remained at the homestead after the others have gone.

11 Modification and Improvisation

Up to this point we have been looking at the allocation of space and beer largely in terms of what Bourdieu calls the habitus—a set of ordering principles, dispositions and models in terms of which these rituals are held. In the previous two chapters some indication has been given that the formal features of beer rituals provide a general structural and organizational template, and that these are linked in a general way to social realities. The close relationships of an everyday economic and political nature that exist between the homesteads of a section and sub-ward are recognized in the way in which the 'customs' beer is allocated and in the names given to these beakers. Similarly, the everyday work of the sub-headman receives recognition through the beaker of beer reserved for him. Economic and kinship ties between sections and sub-wards are largely isomorphic with the way in which space and beer are allocated, and both may change over time.

It is now necessary to go beyond this set of orientations, and to look at how modifications to the order of seating and drinking may arise out of particular circumstances and contexts which have little to do with the structure of the specific beer drink being considered. The discussion of beer gifts (*iminono*), for example, demonstrated that the individual host chooses who to give beer to in terms of his personal kinship and friendship network, reciprocal obligations, and political interests. The distribution of some of the 'customs' beer, we noted, followed from the nature of contemporary and historical relationships within and between different sections of the sub-ward. Calling others for a drink (*ukurhabulisa*) is patterned not only in terms of the moral norm that all should get something to drink, but it is also often a means of expressing individual connection and interest. Similarly, the right to a specific allocation of a seating place and beer may or may not be acted out (though it will be acknowledged) if members of the territorial group involved are present in only small numbers, in which case their allocation is withheld and their rights recognized by placing them with another group in a higher ranking place than they would normally get. The relevance of practice in a general sense, and of the general mutual interdependence of homesteads, is thus unmistakeable.

Individual circumstances and life-trajectories are also important. In the case of *umsindleko* (chapter six) we saw that the event can only be fully understood in relation to the practice of labour migration and the relationship between labour migration and the rural society and economy, which has a historical dimension. However, any particular *umsindleko* beer drink needs to be understood also in terms of the individual which is the subject of the ritual, his relationship with others, his particular experiences, successes and failures, and migration history.

Major changes are also made at particular kinds of beer drinks, which require modification to the general spatial, material (amount of beer) and temporal (distribution sequence) dimensions. At the two beer drinks concerned with a woman's change in status, for example, women sit inside the hut along with men, occupying the left hand side, with the individual undergoing the change in their midst. These beer drinks are discussed in chapter 14.

Changes in the spatial order are noticeable also when a homestead brews 'beer for harvest'. At this event, which is an explicit thanksgiving to those who assisted with the homestead's agricultural endeavours, the organizing principles mirror the current network of reciprocal relations to which the homestead is indebted. Members of the group that own the cattle that ploughed and planted for the homestead sit with the host section irrespective of their actual section and sub-ward affiliation. Often they are members of the host section anyway, but this is not always the case, and they may include men from other sections and/or sub-wards. In some cases they sit with the host section for the entire event, in others they leave to sit with their usual sections or sub-wards once certain beakers of beer allocated to the ploughing team have been consumed. They control certain stages of the beer drink, which affects the amount of beer allocated and the order of drinking. The first to be given beer are the people (men and women, seniors and juniors) responsible for ploughing and harvesting. The young men who did the work are given a place (and beer) in a separate hut, from where they allocate a portion of their beer to the boys who assisted them. These boys are not present at the beer drink at all but receive their beer in a nearby homestead. The women who physically assisted with the harvest are given an extra allocation of beer, though their contribution is not recognized spatially.

Work party beer

As this indicates, the most dramatic modification of the spatial aspects of beer drinks often occurs at those associated with work parties. In one sense these events are directly tied to the economic practices in which people engage, but, like other beer drinks they are governed by general principles relating to their organization, including their spatial ordering. When the beer drink is immediately and directly linked to labour, it is the workers rather than the host section who control the beer and who allocate both places and beer to others.[1]

For example, when a number of ploughing companies is asked to come together to plough and plant a homestead's lands in one day of intensive work, the group is known as *umgqibelo*, and a beer drink of the same name is provided by the homestead concerned. At this event it is the senior members of the ploughing companies involved who occupy the most senior seating position and who control and allocate both places and beer to the local sections and visiting sub-wards. The host section occupies the next most senior seating place. Those in charge are entitled to allocate specific beakers of beer to themselves in recognition of their status as the men belonging to the ploughing groups that did the work. In addition, a portion of the beer is given to the young men who worked. If this group includes some who are not yet senior enough to attend beer drinks, they receive their beer in a separate hut, and they in turn allocate a small portion of it to the uncircumcised boys who helped them.[2]

The primary spatial distinction at work party beer drinks is between workers and the others who come to partake of the beer, who are allocated separate seating places, and who get much less beer than the workers even though they may far outnumber the latter. Non-workers who come along in the expectation of benefiting from the workers' generosity are called *abasarhi*, from *ukusarha*, 'to go about seeking beer or brandy' (Kropf 1915, 381), or porcupines (*iincanda*), after this animal's reputation for raiding gardens (eating food it has not worked for), and their initial allocation of beer is referred to as 'the porcupine beaker' (*ibhekile yobuncanda*). No matter how prominent their individual statuses may be in everyday life, this allocation signals their contextually inferior status as non-workers receiving beer by virtue of the generosity of those who laboured. The importance of the section in the organization of co-operative work, and the strength of the moral obligation to assist if possible, is signalled by the fact that members of the section who did not turn up to work dare not attend the subsequent beer drink as porcupines.

At some work party beer drinks the conventional allocation of places may be completely reversed. If the work group consists of both men and women, the places they are allocated are distinct from those lower ranked places given to men and women who did not work, but who nevertheless have a right to some of the beer as members of the sub-ward. If a beer drink is held to reward young men for a task such as cutting poles, it is they who are in charge of the beer distribution, allocating a portion to their elders. Where the work party consists only of women (e.g. to cut thatching grass), and includes senior women, it is they who occupy the hut and control the beer. They call into the hut women who did not work and the men, all of whom are classified as 'porcupines', have to sit outside. This means that men are subject to allocation (*ukulawula*) by women and the complexity of the term, as discussed in chapter 10, allows one to translate this as both 'given beer' and 'controlled', reversing the gender roles associated with most beer drinks. Since men receive very little beer in the formal allocation, they depend on being called into the hut for a drink by women. Needless to say, this reversal of the normal structure of dominance and control causes a good deal of leg-pulling and mirth among both men and women. This is another example of how practical matters associated with the kind of beer drink affect the conventions of allocating and drinking.

The nature of the 'customs' allocations also changes at work party beer drinks. With a hoeing party, early arrivals are rewarded with a couple of beakers called *emvikweni* ('on the verge [between fields]'), the strip of land that demarcates the field boundary to which the workers retire for rest and refreshment every now and then. Or they may simply sit down where they are working to drink this beer (Illustration 18). Later beakers are called *umnyenyetho*, defined by Kropf (1915, 306) as beer "given to workmen".[3] After the work has been done, the workers retire to the homestead to receive beer called *inkobe* (boiled maize). This alludes to the fact that workers are usually also given food other than beer, and it makes a metaphoric connection between the fruits of their labour, the maize produced in the field, and the beer that they get as a reward. The bulk of the beer is then handed over to the workers, who divide it among themselves, usually according to numbers (*ukugabu*). Beakers with these names are also given out at other types of work parties, such as those for cutting thatching grass. There are obvious parallels here with ordinary beer drinks, where it is the section that controls the beer, and its distribution symbolizes, among other things, the *general* nature of interdependence between territorial groups. Here, however, control of the event and the distribution of beer are linked to the specific work done and the individual workers involved.

18. Workers drinking in a field

Practice, interest and strategy

As the above indicates, at any beer drink the hosts draw on their practical knowledge of domestic spatial categories (what Moore (1986) refers to as the 'spatial text') in combination with the conventions of beer allocation, to create a pattern that reflects their practical knowledge but which also includes improvisation and innovation influenced by the particular social context, including current, and sometimes past, relationships, events and circumstances within the host homestead, section or sub-ward. Improvisation may be relatively straightforward. For example, in one case already alluded to in the previous chapter, a male circumcision ceremony had recently been held within the section, with sons of members of the host section being circumcised. The main officiant, who had come from afar but who was still in the area, and the man guarding the boys in the lodge, who was from another section of the sub-ward, were allocated high ranking places at a beer drink being held in a homestead within the section, and the circumciser given a beaker as a gift. This honour was accorded them because newly circumcised young men of the neighbourhood were temporarily in their care, but there is and could be no 'rule' that specifies this action. Rather, it was a spontaneous gesture based on a cultural competence expressed through the spatial logic of beer drinks to acknowledge the temporary high status and important social role of the officials concerned. In another, similar and equally revealing case, people from afar came to Jotelo sub-ward to prepare for a major ancestor ritual at the homestead of a kinsman, and at a beer drink in another, unrelated homestead nearby they were seated with the section of Jotelo to which the head of the homestead having the ritual belonged (the host section). This strategic improvisation, based on a 'feel for the game', on a practical mastery of beer drinking and on a general social principle that guests should be honoured, symbolically lent communal support to the homestead about to hold the important ritual, by publicly placing members of the kin group involved in a highly ranked place.

These kinds of examples illustrate the difficulty in talking about beer drinks as governed by 'rules', because this kind of action can not be formulated beforehand; the 'rules' become evident only in the action itself, through practice. Placing a visiting kin group or the circumciser with the hosts is based on certain general principles of social life and of beer drinking (on elements of the habitus) that the external observer can understand only once the action has been completed (Taylor 1999). It is not possible for someone to be aware of all the issues that affect the implementation of such practices, nor can we abstract from this a rule—just because a homestead offers a place of honour to a visiting circumciser does not mean that we have discovered a 'rule' of the society. It remains a practice that we observed. To abstract from it a rule both denies agency and obscures the circumstances in which the formulation or principle or disposition of honouring a guest is or is not implemented.

Rules can be transformed through practice (ibid., 41), just as they may be subverted or ignored in favour of alternative rules. The formula (prescription) exists only in the anthropologists analysis. In its operation, the rule exists in the practice it 'guides'. But the practice not only fulfils the rule, it also gives it shape in particular situations: "Practice is…a continual "interpretation" and reinterpretation of what the rule really means." (ibid., 41). So the rule exists only because of and in the practice, and the practice can modify the rule. Through the act of giving expression to meaning, the meaning comes to exist.

The choices that are made by the hosts can be affected by a large variety of factors—events at preceding beer drinks, the amount of beer available for distribution, the number of groups present, the presence or absence of individuals (e.g. certain affinal kin, the sub-headman) and so on. Decisions have to be made about whether the hut is full or not, the state of the weather outside, whether there are enough men from a visiting sub-ward for it to have its own place or few enough for it to be joined with another group. The importance of an affinal link in relation to other individuals present who might be given *iminono* gifts has to be assessed. Decisions have to be made about the amount of beer to set aside for gifts, how much to reserve as hidden beer, when to move on to the next beer allocation, and so on. These kinds of decisions are affected by who is present and who is not, recent changes in relationships between individuals and groups, the current interests of the hosts and the visitors, and historical events recalled through the presence of particular people.

The customs governing beer drinking, then, are not rules, not a set of hard and fast prescriptions, but a set of dispositions, strategies and principles, an 'organizing framework' (Jenkins 1992, 39) which is applied in a socially intelligent manner according to specific objective circumstances, and in which selection, discrimination and improvisation are not just possible but *necessary*. These principles operate largely outside explicitly formulated rules, and there are many regularities which cannot be linked to any explicit norms or rules— such as borrowing brewing utensils from neighbours (Bouveresse 1999). Bourdieu suggests that this is largely an unconscious process, though it has been suggested that there is considerable ambiguity in Bourdieu's writings on this (Jenkins 1992, 76–77). Certainly, beer drink procedure is subject to much explicit discussion and debate by the actors who can, and often have to, explain and justify their actions.

To return to the spatial dimensions of beer drinks, and to further illustrate the potential divergence between rule and meaning, the allocation of space to an individual or group at a beer drink does not, in itself, always or necessarily convey a specific meaning. It may do so, as in cases where an affine is placed with a high ranking group but is not given an individual beaker of *umnono* beer (because 'it is impossible to attend to everybody'). But it may not; spatial meaning has to be confirmed, acted out, as it were, by means of the allocation of beer to that place. And if the beer allocation pattern changes, due, for example, to changes in relationships, but the allocation of space does not, then clearly the meaning of the spatial order cannot be what it was before. It sometimes happens that a section or sub-ward that is allocated its rightful place does not receive part or all of the beer allocation that it is entitled to, perhaps due to miscalculation on the part of the hosts, perhaps for other reasons such as retaliation by the hosts for a slight suffered by them at a previous beer drink. But often it is the result simply of a certain amount of ambiguity inherent in a situation in which many variables come into play, which is why long discussions concerning the procedure often take place within the host section and sub-ward, and why the meaning of seating places is never completely fixed. In such cases argument and debate may be prolonged, and the matter resolved by 'finding' the missing beer from the portion that has been hidden, or by the offended party resolving to treat the miscreants in like manner at future beer drinks held in their own section. Which particular course of action follows the 'mistake' or oversight depends on actual relationships and interests, on who stands to lose what, and on how best to save face. The practice of beer drinking, then, can be seen as a game which people enter and attempt to master, implying an acceptance of the way in which the game is played and its overall objectives, but the 'rules of the game' are neither fully codified nor fixed, and the players have to negotiate, compromise and improvise.

It is also important to note that the allocation of a low ranking place does not necessarily mean that the individual or group given that place will have little or no say concerning the distribution of the beer or the amount of beer that they receive at that place. For example, at a beer drink to celebrate the harvest the young man who had been the leader (in his father's absence) of the ploughing company that did the homestead's agricultural work played a leading role in determining how the beer should be allocated, even though he did so from his low-ranking place with the other young men at the back of the hut, coming forward from time to time when necessary to discuss matters with the *injoli*.

What this indicates is that the allocation of places, in particular, is merely a formal model of hierarchical relationships at a beer drink, and a model of how things, ideally speaking, ought to be, which may not provide a complete or accurate picture of the state of current relationships, and which has to be supplemented with an analysis of other factors (primarily speech, the amount of beer allocated, and the order of its distribution) and placed within a historical context. One does not know, for example, from the formal model of spatial arrangements at beer for harvest, whether the homestead in question is satisfied with the ploughing arrangements of the previous season or not. In fact, this beer drink allows the homestead to take stock of its position within the cooperative work group to which it belongs, dramatize and reinforce changes in the composition of the group, and to express and publicly confirm strategic decisions made.

The allocation and manipulation of individual seating places, too, and disputes about these, can be revealing. Usually they have to be understood in terms of the particular individuals involved and relationships (past and present) between them and other individuals or groups. For example, Gavini was a senior man known to try and curry favour with people when he held beer drinks at his home by giving them senior seating places and more beer than they were normally entitled to, at the expense of members of his section and sub-ward. At a beer drink in his section he left his place on the right hand side near the door to go outside, and when he returned he found that his seat had been occupied by Mkeni, who was slightly less senior than Gavini, forcing him to find a place further from the door. After some minutes Gavini stood, called for silence, and asked why it was that he was sitting sixth from the door rather than third, his rightful place in terms of his seniority. "How" he asked, "am I going to get my *iqwele* [beer] if I am so far from the door?" He was supported by other elders, but some of the senior men provided somewhat tongue-in-cheek counter-arguments, and a spirited discussion followed which amused many. Someone asked Gavini why he had not simply spoken to Mkeni and told him to move down, but he replied that this was not how things are done (it would have been undignified); an old man ought not to have to demand his place, he said, he should be called to it by those already seated near the door. After a while all agreed that "we sit according to the spear (of circumcision)", i.e. according to seniority in terms of years of manhood, and that Gavini should resume his place. It was then vacated by Mkeni, who grinned mischievously as he admitted that he had no right to sit there, and re-occupied by Gavini. One of the others present commented that the reason Mkeni had done this was because Gavini tried to elevate his friends to senior positions when he had beer drinks at his home.

In another case where the beer was being distributed by a work group of men and women who had been tilling a field, one of the female workers sat in an ambiguous position between the men's group and the women's group. The senior male worker, an influential and respected man, suggested to her that she should go and sit with the other women, but she refused, saying that he had no right to tell her to move because he had arrived late, when she had already started working. The men started to poke fun at her, saying that they would give her a pair of trousers to wear (since she did not want to sit with the women), and criticising her for refusing to move, but she pointed at a young man sitting near the women, asking why he had not been told to move. The argument was defused by a senior woman quietly addressing her recalcitrant co-worker, asking her to come closer to the women's group, which she then did. The incident illustrates the high status of workers and the relative gender equality at this kind of event, where men and women work together. But it also has to be understood in terms of the close working relationship between the woman in question and the homestead, owned by a wealthy man who was, in a sense, her patron. She and her husband frequently participated in work groups at his homestead.

Local history, practice and the meaning of beer

As mentioned in the previous chapter, the recognition of distinct sub-sections through the division of 'awakenings' (*iimvuko*) can be used to make important statements about the nature of the historical and everyday relationships within the section, the relationship between the hosts and other sections, and changes in these. This is illustrated in the following case, where the link between local history, social practice and beer drinking practices is evident, and which again demonstrates that the 'rules' of beer drinking are flexible and modified in their application according to local events and relationships.

According to Folokhwe people, Chibi section of the sub-ward was, until three generations ago, divided into two sub-sections on an agnatic kinship basis with the sections named according to the clan affiliation of the majority of their residents. The members of the Bamba sub-section lived mainly in the north-western part of the Chibi section, while members of the Ntlane sub-section lived mainly in the south-east. Their members were drawn from the Bamba and Ntlane agnatic clusters respectively. People in Chibi who belonged to neither of these groups were affiliated to one or other of these sections. One day Poni, the son of a Bamba man, is said to have discovered that his genitor had been a man of the Ntshilibe clan, and he decided to switch clan affiliation. His sons followed suit, and a new agnatic cluster was born through fission. At first, they were part of the Bamba sub-section but as they grew they became large enough to form their own sub-section. A generation or so ago (so the story goes), at a beer drink in a Ntshilibe homestead, this sub-section was formalised when the hosts saw to it that three beakers of *iimvuko* were given out instead of the usual two—one each for the Bamba and Ntlane subsections, and one for themselves. In other words, it was through the performance of the ritual that the transformation took place and that the new sub-section was formally established.

Early in the 1970s the Ntshilibe and Ntlane sub-sections stopped giving each other *iimvuko* beer due to conflict between some of the members of the two groups. It seems that there was a fight between two men, one from each of the groups, and that the Ntshilibe man was injured. On his way to Willowvale town for medical treatment he met with an accident and was killed. The Ntshilibe group suspected witchcraft, and suspicion centred on the wife of one of the senior Ntlane men, but no action was taken against her. During this time of ill-feeling, Ntlane and Ntshilibe sections did not give each other *iimvuko*, and it was only in homesteads of the Bamba sub-section of Chibi that three *iimvuko* beakers were given out. Yet this did not affect the seating places that the sub-sections occupied at beer drinks in each other's areas, nor did it affect other beer allocations. By the 1980s the dispute between the two sub-sections had been at least partly resolved, and they started to give each other *iimvuko* again, though from time to time comments made at beer drinks referred to the fact that this had not been so for a while.

In addition to this, during the 1980s the Ntshilibe section formed a close relationship based on co-operative work with the Mkhulu section of the adjoining Ndlelebanzi sub-ward, and these two sections started to give each other *iimvuko* beer, though they occupied the seating places occupied by their sub-wards in the normal way. Although this was unusual, it was merely an innovative and strategic extension of the established principle that a section gives *iimvuko* to those with whom they have a close working relationship. I was told that the two groups had first met to discuss this, and had decided "to give each other *iimvuko*...because of their close neighbourly relations [*ngokumelana*]". The women of these areas followed suit, and the Ntshilibe women started to share their *iimvuko* beaker with the Mkhulu women, and vice versa. This required a degree of internal differentiation of section-based groups within the receiving sub-ward, though its different sections all occupied the one place allocated to the sub-ward as a whole. In another, similar case, the host section changed the order in which *umlawulo* beer was given to neighbouring sub-wards, but not the respective seating places allocated to these two sub-wards. What these improvisations illustrate again is that a knowledge of the social process is required for a proper understanding of beer drinks, and that the latter provide, initially, a formal means of recognizing and breaking off ties and, later, commentaries on and dramatizations of historical and contemporary realities.

As with *iimvuko*, the order and amount of *umlawulo* (the main allocation) given to other sub-wards is related to social realities in that it signals the nature of relationships between them and changes in these that have occurred or are in the process of taking place. Many beer drinks are marked by discussions about the amount of *umlawulo* allocated, as this has to do with the status of sections and sub-wards in relation to each other, which is subject to continual negotiation. For example, at Rhumese's *isichenene* in Ndlelibanzi, a Nompha man who had recently been to a beer drink in Mgwevu stood to speak to a small group of other Nompha men who had just arrived. It was about the fact that at Mgwevu sub-ward Nompha received its *umlawulo* beer after (instead of before) Fumbatha, a change that had started recently. He said that he was reporting this to them now, because they had not been there when it happened and he had said that he could not discuss the matter without other Nompha people being present. This was a matter that they needed to meet about at home. There were people who had a complaint against the group which had allowed Nompha to be subordinated to Fumbatha (or let Fumbatha be elevated over them). He did not want a reply from them, he said, he was merely reporting to them, that they should know about this complaint, and meet later to thrash it out (lit: 'chew it over'—*ukuhlafuna*).

An interesting example of how historical relationships between individuals affect beer drinking practices involves Ziwele, an elderly man of the Cirha clan, who had recently ended a long-standing ploughing arrangement with a neighbour and entered into a new ploughing company, all the members of whom were from within the same sub-ward section as himself. When Ziwele held the ritual known as 'beer for harvest' he explained the event to those in attendance, and made a number of references to the new ploughing arrangement, praising his new partners and expressing his dependence on "the goodwill of the Cirha clan". Although not all the members of the group were members of this clan, the head of the group was a Cirha, and the section as a whole is associated with this clan. With the approval of the section Ziwele did something quite unusual; he placed the head of the ploughing group in full charge of the beer drink, referring to him as the 'prime minister' of the event. He also referred, in veiled terms, to the fact that he had previously ploughed with his neighbour (who was of another clan), but that this had been unsatisfactory due to the neighbour's failure to reciprocate properly. While the neighbour was away at work, claimed Ziwele, he had always ensured that his fields had been ploughed and his family looked after, but now he had ended that arrangement and turned to the Cirha clan for help. In his speech, then, Ziwele was not only praising his new partners, but also saying that he was himself a good person to work with, aware of the need to do his bit. By innovatively placing the head of the new group in charge, he was giving the ploughing group an unusual honour and demonstrating both his gratitude to them and his awareness of his reciprocal obligations. He was able to do this without the section objecting because of the prominence of the Cirha clan (and of the leader of the ploughing group) in the section.

Spatial arrangements at this beer drink were also affected by the fact that Ziwele was not well, and the illness interpreted as *ukuthwasile*, i.e., a calling by the ancestors to become a diviner. Due to this the relative status of right and left hand sides of the hut were inverted and seating places were allocated accordingly. Diviners, as Berglund and others have pointed out, frequently reverse normal practices, including using the side of the hut usually reserved for the other sex (Berglund 1976, 371). Perhaps this ambiguity allowed Ziwele to make the other strategic improvisations that he did. Specific circumstances, history, social practice and interest are thus central to understanding any particular manifestation of 'beer for harvest'. In this particular case, the performance that Ziwele orchestrated fits Turner's model of the social drama rather well, manifesting a social process that involved conflict and its outcome in a realignment of social relations linked to agricultural work, with a ritual event facilitating and enabling reflection on this.

Beer for sale

In many parts of Africa indigenous beer is now commonly produced and sold for profit. In Shixini, although brewing for profit is not common, there are two types of beer drinks at which most of the beer is sold. The first, brewed by an individual homestead, is called *imbarha*, alternatively *ibhab-hazela*, which is derived from *ukubhabhazela*, to fly or to take off, which informants explained as a reference to the continually escalating price of beer at these events. The second is called *inkazathi*, a term commonly used in both town and countryside when people club together to buy something as a group. As a beer drink *inkazathi* retains this common meaning. It is organized by a group of people who club together to buy or provide the maize required for brewing, and to collectively undertake the preparation of beer for sale to raise money for communal purposes (e.g. the repair of school huts).

At both of these events, commoditisation (i.e. monetisation) of beer is restricted by a number of conventions, some of which are embedded in the lexicon associated with brewing for sale. The notion of flying associated with the term *ibhabhazela* also refers to the action of giving beer away as gifts, as described earlier. This dual meaning of the term applied to an event where the beer is sold thus refers both to the sale and to the compulsory free distribution of some of the brew. Shixini people do not approve of brewing maize beer for sale, and no self-respecting homestead head would like his/her homestead to be seen as a place where beer can be bought on a regular basis. This has to do with the status of maize beer as a highly prized commodity which ought to be made and distributed in a socially appropriate manner, and which always has religious associations. Brewing for sale in situations where a homestead 'has a problem' is acceptable, and allows for an exception to the general rule of not selling beer. This kind of brewing, which clearly ties brewing to an immediate matter of practical significance which can be solved only through raising money, is infrequent and is associated with homesteads that cannot find another means of solving the problem. These tend to be poor, female-headed households which engage in a variety of subsistence strategies, of which occasionally brewing for sale is one.[4]

A major constraint is that beer requires a lot of labour and spoils rapidly, so must be consumed within a day or two. In addition, *imbarha* beer, like any other, is subject to a set of conventions sanctioned by the local sub-ward community and thus subordinated to the general principles of mutual interdependence and co-operation that govern any beer drink. A large portion of the beer, perhaps a third, has to be given out free of charge. Thus commoditisation in the capitalist sense is restricted through linking it to indigenous forms of commoditisation (Appadurai 1986, 16). I would suggest that the free distribution of beer is necessary to maintain the important principle of generalized reciprocity that is so important to Shixini people, since the exchange of beer for a market based cash price is based on immediate, negative reciprocity. The use of cash to pay for field labour, similarly, transforms a long-term reciprocal relationship into an immediate one and is scarce in Shixini (McAllister 2001, 133–35).

The sale of beer is also restricted by the fact that it has a low alcohol content. There are alternatives, as we have seen, such as the sale of commercial liquor, more attractive to those motivated by a desire for alcohol, which can bring in larger amounts of money for less labour outlay. A variety of factors thus combine to restrict the sale of maize beer, and to limit its commercial potential. But the fact that its entry into the cash economy is limited does not mean that it has little economic significance. On the contrary, it is central to the local economy in the sense that it is through the (free) social distribution of beer that relationships of economic interdependence are reflexively constructed, perpetuated and manipulated.

At *imbarha* the main portion (after the free preliminaries) is divided into two casks or pots. Selling commences when the first beaker is bought by a friend or neighbour, to 'open the cask' (*ukuvul' ingcwele*). Anyone may then purchase beer, until the first cask is empty. The second cask is called *ummiso* (an ordinance) and is handled differently. *Ukumisa* means to set or fix (Kropf 1915, 227), and in this case what is fixed is the amount of beer that people are allowed to buy. The principle followed is that all the territorial groups present (i.e. the sub-wards and local sub-ward sections) must be given an opportunity to purchase from the *ummiso* cask, so that no one will leave complaining that they got nothing to drink.

The 'customs' when beer is sold consist of one beaker, called a 'peg' or 'nail' (*isikhonkwane*) This beaker is for the sub-ward as a whole and is also referred to as *umkhondo* (a spoor), or *ibhekili yomkhondo* (the beaker of the spoor). Shixini people are readily able to explain the symbolism: "It is the beaker for the spoor. If something is stolen from your home, you call together the men of the sub-ward to help you look for what has been stolen. This beaker is a reward for those who find [lost] things, so that they have something to drink." "It is the beaker for fire. If anything happens at this homestead I will shout, and people will come to put out the fire". In the sense that a peg or a nail is used for securing things, this beaker secures the assistance of the community. Its obligatory nature is indicated in the following remarks made to the gathering at Ndlebezenja's homestead by a spokesman for the homestead head, when an *isikhonkwane* was handed out:

> Excuse me, here is a word, people of Folokhwe
>
> As conveyed by the son of Mangono here at this home

He says that this beaker is the *isikhonkwane*

The beaker of the spoor

The *isikhonkwane* is something that we are very careful about

It is the beaker of the spoor

This is it here, being given out here at Mangono's home...

Certain other beakers also have to be given out free of charge. The main free distribution, to people of the local sub-ward sections, is called *intluzelo* ('the straining'). At most beer drinks, as indicated earlier, *intluzelo* is given to those who helped with the work of straining the beer, before the public beer-drink. Here too, however, a public distribution of beer with the same name alludes to the fact that people have come to 'work' for the homestead by purchasing beer, so that it will be able to solve its financial problem. Similarly, at every *imbarha* the host has to provide the sub-headman's beaker, an acknowledgement of the fact that the sub-headman's permission is sought before brewing for sale, and of the more general practice of giving gifts of liquor to the sub-headman in exchange for his services. Similar distributions are made at *inkazathi*.

Brewing beer for sale is also restricted by the convention that if a homestead has not brewed for the community for some time, it should do so before it brews beer for sale. This, like many other beer drinks where the beer is simply for hospitality, is known as *isichenene* (a small drop), and it 'clears the way' (*ukutshayelela*) for brewing beer for sale through making it known publicly that this is what is intended. Obviously, an *isichenene* of this kind is intimately linked to the homestead's interests and the strategy that it has adopted in pursuing its economic goals. In his explanation at one of these events the homestead head made it clear that the *isichenene* was being held to ensure that many people would attend to buy beer when he brewed for sale in the near future. Close attention to the spatial and other symbolic aspects of the *isichenene* was required to ensure that people were satisfied and would be happy to spend their money at his homestead next time he brewed. Here too then, as in many of the previous examples, practice has a distinctly temporal dimension. But this convention, like most of the others restricting beer for sale, throws into relief the principles underlying other beer drinks, or beer drinking in general. The restrictions clearly seek to emphasize the instrumental and unusual nature of brewing for sale, and to counter the elements that suggest instrumental relationships with those that stress moral ones.

Endnotes

1. In cases where boys or girls perform the work beer may be brewed as reward, but it is controlled by their elders, who give them a major share. Frequently, however, such work groups are rewarded with other kinds of food and drink, and no beer drink as such takes place.

2. In some cases (but not always) the boys drink their beer outside the homestead—either at some distance from the courtyard on the very edge of homestead space, or in a neighbouring homestead.

3 After *ukunyenyetha*, "to give a small quantity of beer to one's workers, shortly after they begin working."

4. The amount of money raised is small—around R150 (approx. US$15) in 1998.

12 Speech, Practice and Performance

Given the existence of a Xhosa beer drinking habitus, we need to ask how agency is exercised and how meaning emerges from the context of action. In previous chapters I have indicated that one has to look at beer drinks as a form of practice, rather than simply as a manifestation of structural rules, at how they are used strategically in the interests of individuals and groups to convey particular messages, negotiate social relationships, reflect on and influence social life, and to create meaning. But how is it possible that principles or dispositions concerning beer drinking practices involving the use of space, beer and time are applied, manipulated or changed, according to specific circumstances affecting the homestead and its members? What is it that allows for the possibility of strategic action and selection from alternatives? How do the actors implement and justify a particular reading of how these principles should be used, inverted or changed? Why do others accept it? At least part of the answer to such questions is already clear from the foregoing chapters. It lies in the verbal components of beer drinking, both the formal oratory and the other dimensions of speaking, which now need to be examined in more detail in relation to practice and performance.

Speech has at times been ignored in studies of ritual performance (Drewal 1991), and at other times rendered as highly stylized and predictable and thus as carrying no real propositional content (Bloch 1974; 1975). It has been argued that this is because of a visualist bias in Western epistemology which privileges space, the material and the text, which leads to a neglect, among other things, of ritual speech. It is this, Drewal suggests, that feeds structuralist, intellectualist and symbolist accounts of ritual, renders them static, and reifies performance "as a spatialized representation for mental cognition alone, as if detached from the human bodies that practice it". (Drewal 1991, 15). This may be overstating the case. Certainly, anthropologists working in the field of performance in Africa, such as Erlmann (who Drewal sees as an exception), Coplan and James, and also elsewhere (e.g. Cowan 1990) pay full attention to verbal dimensions. Ethnographers of communication are also usually specialists in performance, and practice approaches have recognized the central importance of speech or orality, as De Certeau et al (1998) call it, in both ritual and the general flow of everyday life.

Since beer drinks are conducted in a context sensitive manner, the non-verbal symbolism cannot be taken for granted or 'read' as a text, even though it contains certain shared and implicit meanings. As we have seen, it is always performatively vested with specific meaning in terms of the particularities of the event and the participants. Here, speech plays a key role, since speech does not simply reveal social reality but is crucial for its construction (DeBernardi 1994). Thus one has to explore the interaction between symbolic structure (the meanings encoded in space, time and beer) and the practical use of these elements in particular real life contexts (ibid., 862), as I have tried to indicate in previous chapters. In this respect, language use is related to practice, not to the structural code, even though language is itself a code, because it is through speech that the particular meaning imposed on the structure by human agents becomes possible and apparent.

Like others, including those working in the field of the ethnography of communication, Bourdieu regards Chomsky's notion of linguistic competence, the capacity of a speaker to produce an unlimited number of grammatically correct sentences, as too abstract and insufficient. It is necessary to look at language use. What actual speakers do is produce sentences that are appropriate to given objective circumstances (an existing social situation or set of social relationships) according to a practical competence which cannot be reduced to linguistic potential (Thompson 1991, 7–8). Speakers cannot state the 'rules' by which such judgements are made; it is a practical mastery. There are good examples of this in previous chapters, for example, in the oratory associated with *umsindleko* for a returned migrant, and in the case of Ziwele's beer for harvest (chapter 11), and further detailed examples are provided in chapters 13 and 14. In these cases, speech as a form of practice both indexes a number of shared dispositions as an aspect of a rural habitus, and is sensitive to context, with specific utterances being consistent with the origins of the habitus but linked to the social realities informing the event.

This approach adds to our view of beer drinks as performances that have illocutionary force. It calls for a further examination of what speech *does* at beer drinks, at the kinds of acts being performed through speaking. Here one has to look at both specific speech acts (explaining, invoking, thanking, etc.) and more general ones that emerge from verbal exchanges and speaking in general, as part of the continual construction and manifestation of a rural Xhosa habitus. This is in keeping with Bourdieu's view of habitus as both structuring and continually being constructed through practice. It has been demonstrated that language does not merely convey emotion and affect but also creates it (DeBernardi 1994, 869). Put slightly differently, speech is possible because of, and is a manifestation of, language as a generative scheme, but language exists because of speech which brings it into being (Taylor 1999, 42). If we want to know how rural Xhosa feel about migrant labour, for example, we can listen to what they say about it, and what they say about it in artful and creative beer drink oratory produces particular ways of feeling and thinking about migrant labour.[1]

To Bourdieu, speech acts are social acts which derive their power from the social situation in which they occur, and in which the speaker is embedded. It is this that provides him/her with the status and authority to carry out the act which his/her speech carries. The speaker must be authorised, linguistically *and* socially competent, so a speech act can only occur in terms of a set of social relations. Like Bloch (1974, 1975), Bourdieu regards speech as a manifestation of symbolic power and an instrument of domination, whether these are performative utterances (of the type described as 'declarations' by Searle) or descriptive ones subject only to truth conditions (Snook 1990, 172).[2] Both rest for their acceptance and effectiveness on the authority of the speaker. As we have seen, at beer drinks this is usually the authority of senior men, who exercise power over their juniors and over women. Austin did not fully appreciate this, claims Bourdieu. So the power of language to perform acts is external to the linguistic act itself. It is a social power that is expressed or conveyed by speech but not created by it (Bourdieu 1991, 69–70). The power of words does not lie in the words themselves but "is nothing more than the *delegated power* of the spokesperson, and his speech…is no more than a testimony…of the *guarantee of delegation* which is vested in him."(ibid., 107, emphasis in the original). Speech thus contains "the accumulated symbolic capital of the group" (ibid., 111) which has authorised the speaker who, through speaking competently, also gains symbolic capital.

Bourdieu's criticism of speech act theorists is, however, unwarranted. Snook (1990, 171) points out that Bourdieu was "careless in suggesting that Austin and his followers locate 'illocutionary force' and 'perlocutionary force' solely in language. They take pains to argue that the social situation is crucial in determining the 'meaning' of utterances." They recognized that part of the social situation, in the case of many speech acts, is the authorization given to the office of the speaker to perform such acts (the priest who forgives sins, the judge who pronounces verdicts, etc.). It is also possible that Bourdieu's criticism relies too much on speech acts which are part of a complex of ritual actions such as a marriage, as distinct from everyday interaction where acts such as 'apologising' or 'thanking' occur (Thompson 1991, 10). Here there is no conventional procedure except for the uttering of the words themselves, and no conventional outcome apart from the act having been performed and accepted. Nor is there any authorization involved—anyone can apologise or thank, given the appropriateness of such in the social situation in which it occurs. The power of words is, therefore, more than just a reflection of the authority vested in the speaker.

However, Bourdieu acknowledges that speech has power also because it is part of a conventional situation defined partly in terms of speech—the act cannot exist "independently of the institution which gives it its raison d'etre" (Bourdieu 1991, 74). Bourdieu extends the same argument to the form of the ritual, seen as performative in itself by Tambiah and Rappaport, among others. The form of the ritual—the prescribed acts, the etiquette, the redundancy and so on—is important but it is only one element in making it effective; without the delegation of authority by a group to those acting on its behalf it cannot be performative.

Explanation and consensus

It is easy to find support for the above in the conduct of beer drinking rituals, where the homestead head *qua* homestead head, and the men who speak on behalf of the sub-ward section, carry the kind of authority that Bourdieu is referring to. The fact that they are speaking on behalf of a group is particularly evident in the case of the section and sub-ward, where the spokesman has continually to ensure that there is consensus within the group before he speaks. Although the homestead head or the person speaking on his/her behalf is the one who explains the nature of the event, he has a responsibility both to the section and to his kin to ensure that the explanation is adequate and clear. If it is not, he may be criticised. Thus when Dlathu publicly explained that Ntanyongo's beer drink was an *umsindleko*, and did so in ambiguous and roundabout terms, he was criticised by members of the section (who were also kin to Ntanyongo) and forced to elaborate to make it clear what the nature of the event was. If they are happy with the explanation members of the section hosting the beer drink ought not to comment, but simply confirm it with phrases such as *Litsho!* ('The word is spoken') or *Nalo ke!* ('That's it!'), indicating their approval and that the matter is being referred to the other sections.

Beer that is not properly explained, said Jija, was not beer but *marhewu*: "There cannot be eating in a home without an explanation to people; it is the discourse of men (*umbuzo wamadoda*)...everything edible has its name...". Such explanation, he said, "creates unity (*isibamba*)". Clearly, an adequate ex-

19. Listening to an announcement

planation is essential for the construction of meaning, and it creates a common social consciousness in terms of which people can take part in and evaluate the events to follow. Once the nature of the beer drink has been explained
and the amount of beer indicated, spokesmen for the various sections and
sub-wards present know how to respond, thereby confirming that they understand the explanation. They are also able to assess whether their rights to
beer are being acknowledged (Illustration 19).

For these reasons people often speak about the importance of speaking at
beer drinks, providing metalinguistic evidence for the reflexive nature of these
events. After a disagreement about beer allocation at Ndlebezendja's homestead had been settled Modi commented: "…It is correct that you speak in
this manner; it is pleasant that you speak about something before doing it,
and not just do it without speaking…". At Ntanyongo's *umsindleko*, a visiting
sub headman praised him for explaining well: "If you have not said it with the
mouth you cause disagreements amongst people". At an *umsindleko* in Jotelo
one of the speakers said: "The thing about a beer drink is that we should speak
nicely and understand each other well (*ukuvisisana*)." Failure to explain things
properly causes confusion and disorder *(ingxaki-ngxaki)*. As Sonkebese put it,
without speaking at beer drinks "there would be chaos in Xhosa life". At
Mbuntshuntshu's *umsindleko* there was a complaint about someone who did

not produce *intluzelo* beer when he brewed at his home. As Gamalakhe saw it, the problem was that this man failed "to work with the mouth". There would be no difficulty, he suggested, if only things were properly explained: "It is speaking that counts! The important thing is the mouth!".

What this indicates so far is that we may extend Bourdieu's view on speech acts. It is possible to analytically identify 'explanation' as the primary speech act performed here, an act performed by an authorised person in a conventional situation. But this co-exists with another kind of performative, that of constructing consensus and harmony within a group through verbal exchange. This is a different kind of discursive process and does not rest on the authority of a spokesman. This point can be extended to the beer drink as a whole. As indicated in earlier chapters, speech is required at every stage, from the arrival of the first visitors, through the 'arranging of the hut', right to the final beakers allocated. All the participants must be fully informed at all times about what is happening, through announcements by those officiating, so that they can make sense of the allocation of space and beer and question them if needs be, as they often do. Space, time and beer serve as a general way through which to conceptualise the territorial, gender, kinship and age relationships, but these metaphorical constructions have to be rendered verbally to be accurately apprehended, related to the particular type of beer drink, and to actual relations within and across spatial boundaries. The formal aspects of the ritual have to be explained, discussed, negotiated and agreed on for them to have performative force. In the process, the conventional procedure is realized through bringing into being a state of informed consensus without which the beer drink can not be successful.

Establishing a sense of harmony and consensus involves not so much utterances by a communicatively competent speaker backed by the authority of a group but also a continuous repetition and exchange of information concerning the conduct of the event. This applies within sections, between them, and between sub-wards. Even though outside sub-wards have no say in whether to proceed or not, they too may respond to the initial explanation, usually rather more politely than local sections. At Thwalingubo's *ntwana nje*, a spokesman for Jotelo sub ward, which had been called into the hut prior to the explanation of the beer, responded as follows: "Chiefs, we too like to hear [what is said], which is why we came inside. No matter how crowded it is inside the hut, one ought to go in and hear what the homestead's occasion is. Otherwise we would all go about telling lies, saying that a certain thing had been brewed over at so and so's...Now we understand, because we have heard."

The initial explanation of the beer may be repeated a number of times in the course of the beer drink as groups of latecomers arrive. For example at

Mzilikazi's beer for his maternal ancestor, he and members of the section re-peated the initial explanation at regular intervals, e.g. "There are men who have just arrived. Chiefs, beer has been brewed here. Eeeh, anyone who has not received a beaker [an *umnono* gift] from me should not complain, because he has arrived when there is not much beer left. Now, chiefs, the person I am honouring is the old woman who is my mother. I have brewed this beer for her…". Similar, though shorter explanations occur within a section or sub ward to people who arrive late, or who happened to be outside when a par-ticular announcement was made or a beaker issued, e.g. "We have been given *umlawulo* beer here, with this beaker". When Canca arrived late at Nasonti's small beer drink, held to 'prepare the way' for an *imbarha* (see chapter five), Dlathu explained to him what had happened, in a low voice: "No, Cirha, Na-sonti has said that this is beer for clearing the way today. Yes, beer for clear-ing the way, so that when a person strains the beer for that *bhabhazela* [*im-barha*] that he is going to have, there should be an *isichenene* like this. He has excused himself because he has no beaker, no beaker to start with".

Constructing harmony

The explanations, verbal exchanges, discussions and debates that charac-terize beer drink rituals not only dramatize the unity and interdependence of groups, but are the performance (acting out) of the principle of co-operation and neighbourliness that governs everyday practice. The insistence that all the sections are represented, that they know what is happening, and that they agree with the way things are proceeding, gives a certain unity of purpose, bringing people together in a common task, creating harmony and order, and to some extent countering inequalities in seating positions and beer alloca-tions among men.

The relationship between speaking, on the one hand, and the achievement of consensus of meaning, order, and unity, on the other, is illustrated also in the interaction between speakers and audience through the rules governing speaking. People make it clear how they feel about what is being said, whether they want a would-be speaker to talk or not, whether a particular subject should be pursued or abandoned, and so on. Speaking involves the group, ac-tively, rather than just individuals. Speaker and audience together construct meaning, in a two way process. From the moment he stands up to speak a man enters into an interaction with the listeners. The latter indicate their will-ingness to listen to him with stock phrases such as 'Enter!', 'Let the words flow! or 'Go ahead!'. If there is too much noise they ask for quiet, with a comment like 'There is something being said here!', or 'Sssshhhh! Leave him, let him give forth!'. A speaker who is interrupted may be assisted by others, who appeal to the group to hear him out, or they may confirm that he should stop so that someone else can speak, calling on him to sit down. Comments made in the course of a speech indicate agreement with or confirmation of what is being said, people calling out phrases such as 'That is the custom!', 'Quite so!', or 'That is the Xhosa way!' If there is a disagreement with the speaker (usually it is because he is raising something controversial or sensitive) the audience may comment adversely or force him to stop with a mass of interjections, whistles and offers from other would be speakers. Of course, one could painstakingly identify all the individual speech acts involved in this process. What I am suggesting is that the whole is greater than the sum of its parts.

Audience participation is sometimes formalised, as we have seen, in the practice of the refrain, *ukuvumisa* (literally 'to cause to agree'). Formal, non-contentious speeches, such as those explaining the purpose of the beer drink, or those delivered by visitors when they thank the host for holding the event, are punctuated at the end of each phrase or sentence with a short refrain from a member of the audience (usually a young man), who performs this duty in a manner of apparent indifference but sometimes with great skill. The refrain may be a simple 'All right', 'Thank you!' or 'Mmmh mmh!'; it may be a clan name or praise name, or it may be a short phrase such as 'He says so!', 'Thus speaks the chief!' or 'Gosh father!'. Sometimes the phrase varies from line to line through the speech. The one who performs this function may also call for quiet if there are noisy interjections, fill in with additional phrases if the speaker pauses for too long, and call for further speakers as a previous speaker sits down. The effect of all this is to formalise and give rhythm to the speeches, which are often delivered in a manner similar in certain respects to that of a praise poem (Opland 1998). The speaker frequently ends with a closing formula, such as 'I have stopped' or 'I stop at that point'. The man providing the refrain then comments: 'He says he has put it to you! He says he has let it all out!', or 'He has stepped down! Let he who wants to rise, rise!'. Others may greet the end of the speech with comments such as '*Litsho!*' (Lit: It (the word) says so!), 'He says he has stopped', or something more idiomatic, such as 'He says he has fallen', 'The spade is broken' or 'The paraffin is finished here'. Positive comments praising the speaker's skill are also made.

Men say that the refrain "is just a custom to show that we are not quarreling", and that it takes place to show that the beer drink is "a place of happiness" (*ekonwabeni*). It is clearly a dramatic technique for bringing the speaker into close relationship with the audience and for regulating the interaction between them. It is also regarded as a way of encouraging a speaker, who "suddenly finds himself saying all kinds of things". No refrain occurs in situations where the talk is more serious or contentious, such as at meetings of the sub-ward moot, when cases are discussed, or when men engage in serious debates at beer drinks. It is done "when you want nice speaking in someone's homestead…so that person should be joyful and give his beer out nicely and not hide it and give it to women. Yes, we speak pleasantly at beer drinks, we do not do *ukuvumisa* at the moot, because [court] cases are discussed there". Cases are divisive, at least until resolved, while beer drinks are, ideally, unifying.[3]

Other "rules for interaction"(Saville Troike 1982, 147–48), based on the "shared values of the speech community", are also linked to the question of order, and to the aim of achieving harmony and agreement between the various groups represented. Every announcement of a beer allocation by the *injoli* must be referred to the other sections for their attention. Once this is done a reaction is awaited, other members of the host group remaining quiet until a spokesman for the other sections has had a chance to respond. Similarly, a member of a visiting sub-ward must not speak on matters that do not concern him, and must wait patiently for his beer allocation no matter how long the hosts take to decide how to proceed. At a beer drink in Jotelo, Bodli (Folokhwe sub-ward) became impatient while Jotelo were giving out beakers to themselves and commented: "We too want to drink, man!" Other Folokhwe men immediately turned on him and berated him for his bad manners and breach of etiquette.

In this sense the verbal rules for interaction act as yet another way to define boundaries and the composition of groups, helping to objectify groups and relationships, and to define significant social categories. It is senior men and elders who speak, not young men and women. It is those of the host section who speak most, who give the explanations and the excuses, who talk about the beer allocation and related issues. Members of visiting groups speak least. They complain if they feel badly done by, they praise the host for holding the event, and they ask for permission to leave, but they do not enter into many of the main discussions and debates about the allocation of beer and seats, unless it directly affects them. Yet other rules of speaking, as we have seen, such as the necessity to explain and to receive the go ahead from others, involve interactive communication across these boundaries and proclaim a certain unity.

Argument and dispute—negotiating meaning

This is also true of the vigorous debates that occur. Many of these are conducted in a good natured, tongue in cheek manner, the participants clearly enjoying the opportunity to practise their rhetorical skills, making points and accepting defeat with grace and good humour. Others are much more serious and intense, and may develop into heated arguments. It is not always easy, however, to tell the one type from the other. Either may go on for an hour or more, and involve a dozen or more speakers. In both types the *injoli* and others not involved in the debate may have their work cut out trying to keep it orderly, to prevent people from speaking out of turn and shouting each other down, and to give all who wish to a chance to speak. The result is frequently very noisy—people shouting at people shouting, a number of speakers on their feet at once, gesticulating wildly and trying in vain to make themselves heard. In the process, the disharmonious aspects of social life such as tensions between senior and junior, between and within territorial groups, or between men and women, are voiced and debated. The stress on harmony outlined above refers to an ideal, one that is often but by no means always fully achieved.

It happens, very occasionally, that men lose control of themselves and that a fight threatens, but this is always quickly snuffed out by the majority. Three such occasions were recorded during fieldwork. In one case an intoxicated senior man became troublesome, refusing to stop interrupting others. He was made to sit at the back of the hut with his juniors, shaming and silencing him. In another, a man threatened to attack his oratorically more skilled opponent with his stick and was expelled from the beer drink. Shixini people say that boys settle things through violence, men with words, and that someone who gets aggressive or abusive at a beer drink is sent home, because "he makes us anxious [*uyasixhalisa*]". As once expressed after a dispute about beer: "You see, Rasi, here is the point I commend; that of accepting defeat. It is not by physical power [*izigalo*, lit: brawny arms], but by spoken argument [*kukuthethwa*]".

Most of the debates concern the allocation of beer or seats, and the circulation of the beakers, once allocated. Their objective is to clarify matters that are not understood or that seem anomalous, and to achieve agreement between all parties concerned. Such agreement often leads to changes in beer allocations and thus affects the form of the ritual. The participants in such debates are structurally determined. Something like the failure of a homestead head to give out the *isikhonkwane* (peg) when beer is sold involves the sub-ward, but not members of other sub wards. It is different with other beakers: A complaint about *umlawulo* (the main distribution) involves the group giving and receiving it, i.e. two sub-wards, and any argument about it is confined to them. As is evident in earlier chapters, there is much potential for making mistakes in the complicated distribution of beer and seats, and with the way in which a beaker is circulated. The amount of beer allocated and the rights of groups to an allocation or the order in which they receive it, are probably the most commonly debated issues, and the ones that have the most relevance for the relative statuses of different groups. How the beaker moves within a group (where it starts), how much is being lost by offering it to others, and how much old or young men may drink from it, are other issues that are frequently disputed.

The following cases illustrate some of these concerns:

(i) At an *umsindleko* beer drink in the Elwandle section of Jotelo sub ward, there were five Folokhwe men present. They were given one beaker (*inxithi* size) as *umlawulo*, and considered this to be inadequate. They consulted among themselves before Dlathu got up to complain, asking if this was all that Folokhwe would be getting. The Elwandle group then discussed the issue softly among themselves. The reply was then communicated publicly to Folokhwe. The Elwandle group held that this was an *umsindleko* beer drink, and that no agreement had ever been reached between the two sub-wards concerning the amount of *umlawulo* to give each other at *umsindleko*: "We simply feed each other with something that has never been confirmed." Before responding, Dlathu referred the response to the other Folokhwe men, and they discussed it. Bodli indicated that he did not care one way or the other, saying that the matter was 'rubbish', but the others disagreed sharply with him, clearly regarding this as a highly irresponsible attitude. They indicated to him that they were not acting for themselves, in order to get more beer, but for Folokhwe as a sub-ward, and that this was a serious matter.

Dlathu then responded to Elwandle, saying that the nature of the beer drink was of secondary importance. What counted was that a certain amount of beer was available for the men's *umlawulo*, with the women having been given a separate pot. In such circumstances, Folokhwe was entitled to a beaker of the *iqhwina* size, irrespective of the kind of beer drink. A lot of discussion followed, with other Folokhwe and Elwandle men voicing their opinions. One Elwandle man pointed out that men of both Komkhulu and Chibi sections of Folokhwe were present, and that Folokhwe was thus well represented. Elwandle then decided to change Folokhwe's allocation to an *iqhwina*. This was first explained to the other Jotelo sections, and then to Folokhwe. Dlathu turned to his companions with a satisfied: "There you have it, gentlemen", and that was the end of the matter. A great buzz of conversation enveloped the hut as all those who had been sitting quietly up to this point discussed the issue and its outcome, until the next allocation of beer was announced.

(ii) At Ndlebezenja's *imbarha* there was an argument about the *isikhonkwane* beaker. Some men had not heard it being announced and thought that it was being consumed without any announcement. Others complained that it was being monopolised by Komkhulu (the host section) though it was meant for the sub ward as a whole. Part of the discussion went as follows:

> *Gavini*: (Chibi section): You say the *isikhonkwane* has been given out here at Mangono's?

> *Thekwane* (Komkhulu): This is it here.

> *Gavini*: Where exactly is the *isikhonkwane*, seeing that you are telling the location [Folokhwe] about it?

> *Stokwana* (Komkhulu): You inform your people while the beaker is being eaten.

> Do you understand Ntlane [Thekwane]?

> You are telling them while it is already being eaten.

> *Canca* (Komkhulu) claimed that the beaker had been announced, and that this had been acknowledged by others. Only then was it passed to a Komkhulu elder, to start the drinking. Another said that what was confusing him was that he thought that the *isikhonkwane* beaker was for Folokhwe, but it seemed to be staying with Komkhulu.

> *Thekwane* then spoke again, trying to ensure that a serious argument did not develop:

> No, chiefs, here is a point

> Give me ears, chiefs, stop, stop

> Do not get annoyed at a beer drink

> You will not help us at all if you get annoyed like this

> While speaking about the laws of beer drinking (Comment: Apart from sinking us)

> Exactly, you are going to sink us, exactly!

Here is the point chiefs

The ears did not listen because there was noise

That is why it is said that when a person asks for silence you should listen

Because he is going to help those of you in the hut

That is the truth

Now we are cross examining each other here

Even though the issue has been dealt with

Because we did not attend with our ears

Because we kept talking when someone called for attention

It is all right now, the matter is finished.

(iii) At an *imbarha* at Gulakulinywa's homestead Bodli laid a complaint against some men of Ngingqi section (including Molusweni and Ntlekiso), accusing them of misusing the *umlawulo* beaker allocated to Folokhwe at a beer drink in Jotelo two days earlier. The Ngingqi group was sitting slightly apart from other Folokhwe men, and the *umlawulo* beaker had been placed in front of them. Bodli said that they did not inform the rest that they had been allocated beer, and that when the beaker was passed over to them it was nearly empty. Dlathu had thus sent it back, saying that "we do not know this beaker".

Molusweni was asked to explain what had happened, as the men assembled in the hut turned, in effect, into the sub-ward moot. He said that he had not seen the other Folokhwe men until after the beaker had been issued. He then went over to inform them of the beaker, and that Ngingqi would drink from it first. Ntlekiso called a Ngingqi woman for a drink, and she brought a number of other women with her. Before they knew it the beaker was almost empty. Molusweni said that he had told the Ngingqi men that they would have to answer for this. He sent the beaker over to Dlathu but it was returned. Ntlekiso was also asked to give an account, and he confirmed what Molusweni had said, but blamed the women. Discussion then turned to why Folokhwe men were not all sitting together, and to why Bodli had said that he had not been informed of the beaker. He now admitted that he had been informed. Ntlekiso admitted that he was responsible for misusing the beaker, and asked for pardon.

The other men then decided that Bodli, Molusweni and Ntlekiso should leave the hut while the case was discussed. It was decided that both Molusweni and Ntlekiso were responsible and that they be fined an *inxithi* of beer. Bodli had not given a completely truthful account and it was suggested that he, too, be fined. However, after some further discussion it was decided that since these men were 'first offenders' they should have their sentences suspended. As Thekwane put it: "They have no records, they must be warned. There should be no friction among Folokhwe people. This is the first time they have offended us". The Ngingqi women, too, were to be called together and admonished. The three men were called back into the hut, and stood facing the others, caps in hand. Gavini, a Chibi elder, addressed them with the verdict, saying: "Here are the findings of the moot". He admonished Bodli for not giving an accurate report of what had happened, and told him to be careful of this in the future. Bodli sat down. Gavini then addressed the other two, reminding them that they had all grown up together in the area, and that they should act in concert with other people of Folokhwe. He told them that the moot had decided to be lenient, and to suspend their sentences, urged them to mend their ways, and warned them to be very careful with the *umlawulo* beaker. Other senior members of the gathering also spoke to the offenders, reminding them of the need to ensure that Folokhwe be respected at beer drinks, and asking them to exercise control over the younger Ngingqi men.

(iv) It is not only matters involving beer and beer drinking that are debated. Sometimes arguments rage about matters quite unrelated to the beer drink, over issues such as the procedure followed at a previous circumcision ritual, the raising of money for sheep dip or for repairs to the dipping tank, etc. In the following case a long and noisy debate raged over an apparently trivial issue, the definition of a word:

At Mamgwevu's *isichenene*, Modi, who loved nothing better than to stir up a good argument, stopped on his way out of the hut and asked me if I was an *iduna* (a male, but often used in the sense of 'a real man'). I replied in the affirmative. "How do you know?" he asked. "Because I am sitting here drinking beer", I replied. "No", he said, walking out, "you know that you are an *iduna* if you have a good brain". Others then started discussing his statement, some saying that an *iduna* was a man "with balls and a penis" and had nothing to do with intellect, only biology. Some said that an *iduna* was defined as the head of the homestead. So the discussion went on, and soon everybody was talking at once. Gavini claimed that Dyakalashe, some years his junior, would not give him a chance to speak and kept interrupting. Eventually Gavini was able to say something, and merely asked what it was they were arguing about. He was told. People were keen for him to give his opinion on the matter because he was an amusing and eloquent speaker, and they expected a definitive statement from him. However, he disappointed them. An *iduna*, he said, was "a man at his home". Dyakalashe asked if such a man was still an *iduna* if he wasted money, and so the debate continued until it died down as people lost interest.

The performative character of verbal exchanges such as these cannot be gauged through identifying the constituent speech acts (at least not without laborious detail, and it would be rather pointless to do so). It seems instead that it is the exchange as such that is performative, in that it is a reflexive engagement with a cultural notion, allowing people to formulate, express, question and reformulate their views on the matter.

What emerges from these examples of the discussions and debates that occur at beer drinks? How are they related to the view of beer drinks as dramatic performances? As far as the non-contentious discussions are concerned, about things like cattle inoculations and the local school, beer drinks involve the community acting as community. Such discussions are not just dramatizations of the community, they are the community in action, talking about things that concern it, and defining itself and its internal boundaries in the process. These discussions function to disseminate information, to allow decisions to be made, and to inculcate or reinforce norms and values. In the case of serious arguments about matters such as beer allocation, these are almost always ultimately resolved and the threat to harmony dissipated, though as indicated in chapter 11 there are cases where they are not and continue from one beer drink to another.

In cases such as the death of Dhyubeni's kin by lightning (chapter nine), and in the apparently silly controversy about the definition of *iduna*, the beer drink functions as a forum for the discussion and resolution of problems of a 'cultural' nature on a group basis, for the establishment of procedures and norms, or for calling these into question. A debate brings people into interaction with each other and creates a group. It is thus transformative. In this respect beer drinks are the equivalent, at a more senior level, of the meetings of the youth organizations of old where much debating and hearing of 'cases' took place. In talking about death by lightning or the concept of *iduna* people are collectively constructing meaning and establishing models for the interpretation of future experience. At the same time, beer drinks provide men with a forum at which to exercise and display their oratorical skills, on which political standing in the community partly depends.

In pointing out procedural mistakes and arguing about things like beer allocation, the participants at a beer drink are actively involved in the construction of its meaning. In so far as there may be different perceptions of that order, competing definitions of what ought to be, leading to debates about matters like beer allocations and seats, order and meaning are established through a process of negotiation and compromise. This enhances reflexivity, in that it involves discussion of conflicting viewpoints and alternative ways of doing things. In the end a result emerges which is (usually) to everybody's satisfaction. As a speaker put it in the course of one of the debates recorded during fieldwork: "Let us give each other law, let us give each other good spirit, so that no ill-feeling enters our hearts". As this indicates, there is an overriding concern to ensure that there is agreement and unity among those present, and especially within the section and the sub-ward. In certain cases, as illustrated above, men who threaten harmony by breaking the rules governing sharing and reciprocity, or who transgress the etiquette of speaking and circulating beer, have action taken against them. They threaten the establishment of a mutually agreed upon order and are therefore sanctioned, the emphasis being reintegration rather than punishment.

The disputes also point to the value of speaking out, of expressing one's complaints, objections or ill feelings. The link between beer drinking and reconciliation between quarrelling or disputing parties is widespread in Africa. Drinking from the same vessel among the Lovedu was symbolic of reconciliation (Krige 1936, 59), and among the Tsonga a 'beer offering' (actually grain representing beer) to effect reconciliation between quarrelling kin was called 'the beer of noise', "on account of the noise made by those who quarrelled"(Junod 1927 II, 399, 340). At Zulu beer drinks and at ritual killings the speaking out of ill feeling might be simply a complaint about the quantity and quality of beer, but it was held to be important because "there must be harmony before there can be a sharing of food"(Berglund 1976, 321). Berglund also notes that there was a close association "between the ritual of purification from anger and the common participation in beer (and sometimes meat)"(ibid., 325). The implication is that the disputes and arguments at beer drinks are a symbolic speaking out and dissolution of anger. Beer drinks are also, as noted earlier, associated with the symbolism of spitting, which is closely linked, all over Bantu-speaking Africa, with the expulsion of ill feeling.

Oratory and transformation

In some cases, such as *umsindleko*, beer drink oratory is linked to the transformation being undergone by an individual person (though as with rites of passage in general, close kin and associates are also affected). In this respect formal oratory outlines the nature of the transition, perhaps the background to it, and its anticipated effect (its perlocutionary consequences), which are specified in conventional form. But the words alone are not sufficient, and must be combined with a variety of other ritual acts—e.g. in the case of the young migrant worker having *umsindleko*, sitting next to the beer at the back of the hut and ritually drinking from a special beaker offered to him by his close agnatic kin. In other words, the transition effected by the ritual and the construction of the habitus are performed and embodied, by "the anchoring of certain values and dispositions in and through the body" (Strathern and Stewart 1998, 237). The examples of beer drinks associated with life passages provided in the following two chapters will provide ample additional evidence of this to add to what we have already noted in the discussion of *umsindleko* for a returned migrant.

Why is speech not sufficient in such cases? Possibly because, as Rappaport (1999) suggests, words are ambiguous and could be interpreted as mere formality, whereas actions 'speak' more unambiguously. At *umsindleko* the young migrant is seated among other men drinking beer, in this sense a special object and both the substance and ultimate symbol of sociability. The beer drink constitutes the social condition to which he has returned, a community of closely co-operating homestead heads. Drinking with the others embodies and constitutes his belonging and his membership, and his acceptance of the values and life-ways of the rural home. Perhaps it cannot be 'read' in any other way. The physical display has greater performative force than the utterance.

However, physical metaphors for sociality such as sitting with men in a hut drinking beer are also liable to misinterpretation, perhaps, at least as far as those *not* undergoing the transition are concerned. The distinction between embodiment and communication in ritual becomes relevant here (Strathern and Stewart 1998). To stay with the example of *umsindleko*, it is clear what the returned migrant is doing and what is being said metaphorically. He has re-assumed certain qualities, that of a social human being present in the rural home and part of a close-knit rural community, represented by beer drinking, that are *not* the qualities associated with a man at work. But what does this mean? He has been away up to this point. Does he really accept the moral authority of the home? How de we know that the performance is felicitous? Speech is required to specify and authorise the context, and to make explicit the nature of the transition in terms of which the qualities of the home are being re-assumed and the ambiguity of migrant labour addressed. Fernandez has pointed out that performance as a "figurative argument" employs the use of tropes to enable people to express and act out realities that are not fully conscious or fully grasped, the 'inchoate' (Fernandez 1986, cited in Drewal 1991, 9). To make them intelligible and real, at Xhosa beer drinks as elsewhere, such realities are communicated via the mobilisation of different media operating in parallel, at mutually reinforcing levels—here the allocation of places, the temporal allocation of beer, the way in which the beer is consumed, and the various types of speech events mutually reinforce each other. Furthermore, even within each of these media there is much redundancy, the same message being conveyed over and over in slightly different ways. So in speech we get a variety of metaphors, proverbs, and figures of speech designed to ensure that the basic message gets across.

The words spoken at beer rituals of this kind do not conform to the stereotypical notion of ritual speech, as characterized by Rappaport, and earlier on by Bloch. Rappaport (1999, 151) states that: "It is virtually definitive of ritual speech that it is stereotyped and stylized, composed of specified sequences of words that are often archaic...and great stress is often laid upon its precise enunciation." Even more problematic is his view that because of the fixity and inflexibility of ritual speech, "ritual cannot exercise language's ability to express gradation, qualification and the uniqueness of the here and now" (ibid., 151). This precludes a consideration of the particularities of ritual as a form of practice and the role of ritual in social change, and also somewhat contradicts his emphasis on the performative nature of ritual, given the growing emphasis on the relationship between performance and practice in anthropology. Ritual transformations are rendered purely formal if one takes this view.

In my opinion this characterization of ritual speech applies only to some rituals, particularly if one takes a narrow view that only part of the talk that occurs at ritual is 'ritual speech', but it does not apply at others. It is certainly not true of Xhosa beer drinks, where speech constantly refers to the social context in which the ritual occurs, to specific preceding events, and to the particular characteristics of individual ritual subjects. Beer drink speech is not 'ordinary', certainly, but nor is it lacking in subtlety, creativity and propositional content. One might argue against this by saying that it is possible to identify certain key utterances which effect the performance of ritual, and which are surrounded by other aspects of speech that are mere flourishes, inconsequential for the effectiveness of the rite. It is sometimes possible to identify such key utterances at Xhosa beer drinks, but not often, and the conventional procedure associated with beer drinks always includes more speaking that just these key utterances. At most of them, it is speaking in general that is explicitly thought to be effective in making the event successful, creating harmony among the living and securing the attention and the blessings of the ancestors. There are no specific 'ritual' words, for example, at the beer drink ritual to mark the development of a new homestead (chapter 13), or at the one to welcome back a returned migrant (chapter six). The words that effect the transitions involved are those spoken by people in the formal oratory and other forms of speech that characterizes beer drinks and which ensure ancestral favour. Shixini people say that the ancestors are attracted to their descendant's home because of the beer brewed there, the presence of people, and the 'noise' that they make (in rowdy debates and discussions). The performative making of noise among the living, *ukungxola*, becomes synonymous with successful invocation to the spirits of the deceased.

Some of these questions are illustrated in more detail and discussed more fully in the following two chapters where individual transitions are dealt with. The first of these is the establishment and 'making known' of a new homestead. The second is the beer drink held to 'release' a widow from mourning.

Endnotes

1. This is also what Geertz (1966) meant by religion and ritual acting as both a 'model' of and a 'model for'.

2. Declarations "bring about some alteration in the status or condition of the referred to object or objects solely in virtue of the fact that the declaration has been successfully performed." (Searle 1979, 17). Mere statements of fact are also, of course, speech acts (ibid., 1979).

3. At ritual killings, where people are concerned with the very serious business of ensuring successful communication with the shades, *ukuvumisa* is usually limited to phrases such as '*Camagu!*' ('Be appeased!') and the use of a clan praise name (e.g. 'Ncibana!').

13 Beer Drink Oratory and Social Reproduction

Given the centrality of the homestead in social life and the interdependence of homesteads in Shixini, the establishment of a new homestead is an important step for both individuals and the wider community (McAllister 1993a). An analysis of the way in which this event is performed allows for a further development of the themes and arguments presented so far. In particular, it illustrates one way in which the rural habitus is continually constructed through performance, and thus the important role that the practice of beer drinking plays as an aspect of this habitus. At the same time, it indicates the way in which power differences within the rural community are exercised towards this end, with power emanating from both senior kin of the new homestead head and senior men of the community in general.

Beer for a new homestead

For both the new homestead head and his wife there is a significant change in status. For the wife it means independence from her mother-in-law, her own home to run, and a fuller claim to her husband's migrant labour earnings. For the husband it means greater independence from his father or elder brother and an important step towards full manhood and seniority. It also involves a measure of religious independence, in that the head can now initiate and hold rituals at his own home. Economically, a new homestead confers the right to a garden and a field. From the point of view of the section and sub-ward, it provides a new potential co-operative participant in the sphere of rural production, so its economic significance extends to the wider community.

Shixini men tend to try and set up independent homesteads fairly soon after marriage and they justify this in terms of Xhosa tradition. Yet this tendency is in fact an innovation, as demonstrated in chapter two. In the late nineteenth century and earlier, married sons and their wives and children remained in the large, extended family homesteads of their parents until they were relatively senior. Nowadays, homesteads are frequently inhabited by only a nuclear family and the average number of huts per homestead is between two and three. As we have already seen, there is a strong set of values and beliefs which provide an ideological basis for the interdependence of homesteads that arose through the historical processes outlined earlier. This ideology recognizes the independence of each homestead but stresses the need for each also to be fully social, and to be part of a co-operative network within which people support and assist each other. This is acted out at every beer ritual, and the one at which a new homestead is constituted as independent also stresses its nature as a social entity, through both the ritual form and the public oratory associated with it.

The importance of establishing, maintaining and working for one's homestead is stressed in a variety of public, ritual situations, including male initiation, the rites associated with migrant labour and a variety of beer drinks. These ritual traditions have, as we have seen, as an integral part of each, an oral tradition through which the subject of the ritual (initiate, migrant, etc) is addressed in a manner appropriate to the occasion (i.e. admonished, instructed, praised, etc.). As shown in chapter 12, it is largely in this oratory and its associated ethnography (Saville-Troike 1982) that the meaning of the event is made explicit to the listeners. This chapter deals with these issues in relation to the beer drink associated with the establishment of a new homestead, recorded at three examples of a beer drink held for this purpose. In addition to contributing to the wider argument being presented, it is an exercise in the ethnography of communication, providing case studies illustrating the significance of beer drink oratory discussed in the previous chapter. Before turning directly to this, however, another innovation has to be mentioned.

The change in status that building an independent homestead entails is sometimes formalised in Shixini, as in other Xhosa-speaking areas, by the ritual killing of a goat together with consumption of beer. This is known as 'starting the homestead' *(ukuvula umzi)* (Bigalke 1969, 106) or in Shixini, 'making known the homestead' *(ukwazisa umzi)*. In practice this is not the only option open to Shixini people. They may kill the goat and leave out the beer, and brew at a later stage. Or they may decide not to kill at all and to hold a beer drink instead. The latter option, commonly simply termed *ntwana nje* (just a small thing), has now become the most common form of formalising a new homestead. It is not a promise of a killing to come, but a full substitute for 'making known the homestead', though it is not called by this name. It is complete in itself, and is a rather different kind of event from the killing, just as *umsindleko* for a migrant worker is very different from its predecessor, the *umhlinzeko* killing . As we saw in that case of change, the symbolism of animal sacrifice stresses kinship, and becomes inappropriate in a situation where territorial links have replaced kinship as the basis of local agrarian activities. A beer drink is particularly well suited to the construction and representation of relationships based on neighbourhood and territory, and has gradually come to replace the killing celebrating the establishment of a new homestead.

Thwalingubo's *ntwana nje* beer drink

Thwalingubo, a young man of the Bamba clan living in the Chibi section of Folokhwe sub-ward decided to brew *ntwana nje* because he had recently established his own homestead on a site next door to his late father's homestead, now occupied by his elder brother, Keneti. When I asked why he had decided to brew, Thwalingubo answered in this way:

> I decided to have this beer drink because everybody knew that I was living at my elder brother's place, at Balile's homestead, the son of Tela. People were looking at me thinking that I had no wife and no homestead. Some heard that I had a wife, some saw her. My father and Keneti decided that I should have my own homestead and this is the site that I got. Any person coming from Jotelo or Velelo [adjoining sub-wards] or wherever did not know where my home was. It was only neighbours who knew that this was a homestead of the son of Balile's. In March this year I collected all the people of the neighbourhood [Chibi section] and slaughtered a goat to announce to all that I was here now. The goat was used by Chibi people only. After that, other people were passing by on the path and not coming into this homestead. This beer was brewed so that everybody, even passers-by, should come into this homestead. This is the custom, everybody does this.

As Thwalingubo indicated, the earlier slaughter of a goat had served to notify only a limited group of people that he now had an independent homestead; primarily his male agnates and other close kin, all of whom lived in the Chibi section of Folokhwe sub-ward.[1] In other words, the killing of the goat was not a public occasion but restricted to only one section of the sub-ward and emphasized his kinship connections within that section.

At the beer drink, which was attended by a large number of people from all parts of Folokhwe and beyond, Thwalingubo's father's brother, Dwetya, called for attention and explained why Thwalingubo had brewed. He commenced with a short praise poem,[2] delivered in the highly charged manner of an *imbongi* (praise poet), before pausing and switching to an oratorical style. The refrain is a short, clipped 'Thank you!' (*'Nkos!'*)

Here's the point! (*'Nkos!'*)

[Comments from others trying to get the men to be quiet]

Here's the point!

Chiefs of the Bomvana

Of the pawing buffalo

5   Of those who squat in East London ('*Nkos!*')

Which are well known ('*Nkos!*')

Go out and spread the word

Chiefs who I see here ('*Nkos!*')

Those who should be drinking together

10   According to custom ('*Nkos!*')

[pause]

All right, this person here is my child ('*Nkos!*')

He was sent [to live] here by his father ('*Nkos!*')

To build a home, a homestead of his people

Of his mother and father, behind the homestead [of his father] ('*Nkos!*')

15   Balile said: 'Thwalingubo, build here' ('*Nkos!*')

Balile being alive then!

He said: 'Govuza, build there!' ('*Nkos!*')

Balile being alive!

I want to make it clear, my child is saying

20   That ever since he established this home

No one has entered this hut of his ('*Nkos!*')

So that his fathers should know that he lives here ('*Nkos!*')

Balile too should respond to him now ('*Nkos!*')

He who was taken by God, in his own way ('*Nkos!*')

25   His grandfathers do not know that he has taken this site ('*Nkos!*')

I want to say, my chiefs

This child of mine declares that this is why he has called you ('*Nkos!*')

To this home

His plea is simply that 'I want to be known by my people

30   That I live here

I have left my elder brother's place' ('*Nkos!*')

He is brewing for that reason

He is indicating that there is this cask here ('*Nkos!*')

Do you see it!?

35   It is exclusively for men ('*Nkos!*')

Here is a second cask! For the mothers! ('*Nkos!*')

There are four *amaqhwina*! ('*Nkos!*')

In this cask ('*Nkos!*')

For his mothers ('*Nkos!*')

40   So that there be spitting in the homestead of Fule![3]

This is what is intended by this child ('*Nkos!*')

That he should be known, by his fathers and grandfathers

All the people of Fu-u-u-le! ('*Nkos!*')

That he is living here now (He says he is independent!)

45   They should fill him with health (They should do so!)

Because he has left his elder brother (They say so)

Because Balile applied for this site (They say that)

I stop now, I am going to sit down (He says he is sitting down)

Having called for attention (l. 1–2) Dwetya starts off in the manner of an oral poet to preface his explanation of the nature of the beer drink. In the praises he implies that those present come from far and wide, exaggerated as an area bounded by the Bashee river in the north-east (the boundary with the next district, Xhora/Elliotdale, associated with Bomvana people) and East London in the south-west. He wants everyone to hear what he has to say (l.

9–10). He then switches to oratory, but still speaking rapidly in a style reminiscent of *ukubonga* (praising), using short, rhythmic sentences. However, his delivery is not as fast or as loud as in the first ten lines, and the meaning of what he says is not as obscure. Dwetya recounts the circumstances leading up to Thwalingubo's establishment of his homestead, indicating his dependence on Balile, his father, in this respect. Thwalingubo's younger brother, Govuza, is also referred to. Since this time, he says, Thwalingubo has not held any public events at his home to enable it to become known by people (l. 20–21) and in this way to let it be known to his ancestors that this is where he lives (l. 23, 25, 29–31). It is through the attendance of people and their participation in the beer drink, as expressed in the image of them spitting on the floor (l. 40)[4] that the ancestors will become aware of where he is (l. 42) and give him health (l. 45). Through brewing people are brought into the homestead, and in this way he hopes he will become known to and blessed by "all the people [descendants] of Fule", a lineage ancestor five generations removed, Tela's FFF (l. 43). Dwetya also indicates the amount of beer available (l. 33–39), in the usual, highly stylized way, emphasizing that men and women have their own respective portions of considerable size.

This opening speech can thus be divided into five distinct stages: poetry (l. 1–10), which may also be construed as a welcome and an introduction; history or biography (l. 11–18); the purpose of the event (l. 19–33); indication of the amount of beer available (l. 33– 30); and repetition of the second and third sections, with which it concludes.

Thwalingubo himself then spoke, deferring immediately to the authority of Dwetya, and going on to repeat some of the themes introduced by the latter:

This [Dwetya] is my father's younger brother (*'Nkos!*)

Who is speaking (*'Nkos!*)

He speaks here as the head of the home (*'Nkos!*)

[The head] of all the homesteads of his elder brother (*'Nkos!*)

5   It is he who instructs us to brew here

He is the person who teaches us everything (*'Nkos!*)

The reason for this [event] chiefs, is that I suddenly realized

That I often see people passing here behind the hut

Going to drink beer over there, going to drink all over the place (*'Nkos!*)

10 No one has ever been here, to this homestead

Some do not even know whose homestead this is (*'Nkos!*)

But today even a stranger passing by will know

That he has come across a homestead of the Bamba clan (*'Nkos!*)

[This is] the reason, chiefs, for making that beer over there (*'Nkos!*)

15 I made it because I have not brewed since I came here (*'Nkos!*)

I should say that it is not for anything in particular (*'Nkos!*)

[Comments: *Ntwana nje! Yaaaahh!*]

It is just something for my being here in this place

I have not yet brewed…I am still going to brew for the things [rituals] I think of

In my own time (*'Nkos!*) (*Ntwana nje!*)

20 Today I have not brewed for anyone in particular, but for any passer-by (*'Nkos!*)

That he should come in (*'Nkos!*)

Go out and piss (*'Nkos!*)

Fill his pipe, smoke, spit (*'Nkos!*)

And not say there is no spitting in this hut (*'Nkos!*) (*Ah!*)

25 I want to say chiefs, as my junior father has indicated (*'Nkos!*)

He speaks the truth, it is that cask! (*'Nkos!*)

And it is [also] that cask on one side (*'Nkos!*)

[And] that pot that mothers cook with (*'Nkos!*)

Yes, it is separate, it is four *amaqhwina* (*'Nkos!*)

30 The men's full cask is on one side for all to see (*'Nkos!*)

That's it then chiefs (*'Nkos!*)

(*Ah!*) (He says he has put it!) (*Ah!*)

After acknowledging the seniority and authority of Dwetya over himself and the other members of the Bamba agnatic group in the Chibi area (l. 1–6),

Thwalingubo repeats some of the earlier themes and indicates that this beer drink is a necessary preliminary to holding other important ancestor rituals (l. 18). In making his homestead known to the community and the ancestors, he is preparing the way for these events. This is also an assertion of the homestead's (and Thwalingubo's) independence, of his right to make important decisions about his homestead and its future.

Ndlebezenja, Cirha clan, a matrilateral kinsman to Thwalingubo and spokesman for Komkhulu section, then spoke. He praised Dwetya for initiating the event and said that Dwetya would find it easy to teach Balile's children because they had already been well instructed by their father, who had been responsible for their circumcision and initiation into manhood. He then recalled that he and Balile had been friends, going to beer drinks together:

> …I am going to make a small point, Bamba (*'Nkos!*)
>
> I used to associate with the old man Balile
>
> We attended beer drinks together (*'Nkos!*)
>
> With Nombayiso (*'Nkos!*)
>
> 5   Men who would have said that this beer brewed by Thwalingubo (*'Nkos!*)
>
> Is beer being given to all the dead people (*'Nkos!*)
>
> Because this beer being brewed by Thwalingubo
>
> Today, it is *ntwana nje!* (*'Nkos!*)
>
> One brews *ntwana nje* (*'Nkos!*)
>
> 10   So that people should enter the home (*'Nkos!*)
>
> To spit, to drive out misfortune (*'Nkos!*)
>
> To bring back good fortune (*'Nkos!*)
>
> You see, I used to go about with old people
>
> Nombayiso and Balile, people of experience who spoke the truth (*'Nkos!*)
>
> 15   Because nowadays we go about telling lies (*Ah!*)
>
> …

Ndlebezenja concluded by urging Thwalingubo and Govuza to heed their elder brother, Keneti, who would consult Dwetya in all matters regarding the agnatic group.

What is clear from these speeches is that this *ntwana nje* was brewed for the dual purpose of introducing the homestead to the ancestors and making it known to the community. It is clear also that it is through the fulfilment of the second aim that the first is achieved. The effect of *ntwana nje* includes securing the blessings of the spirits and good fortune for the homestead and its inhabitants, and the homestead's incorporation into the wider community. Having drunk their fill, people leave the homestead formally knowing who lives there and that it is a homestead that 'provides for people'. The new homestead has thus become a community entity and entered into a reciprocal relationship with others through the medium of the beer drink.

The beer drink thus has illocutionary force, a performative and transformative effect, in that it establishes the homestead as an independent social entity, as part of a wider community of people within which members interact on a reciprocal basis. At the same time the acceptance of Dwetya's authority signals continued loyalty to the agnatic kin group and to the principle of seniority within it. The homestead's newly constituted independence is tempered, through the oratory and the formal aspects of beer drinking, by its performative location within a wider group consisting of community and kin, to which it has obligations and from which it derives its social legitimacy.

Here again we can see the significance of Kuckertz's insight into beer drinks as uniting the two opposing tendencies of individualism and universalism, enacting in their symbolism the order of the world and uniting individual, subgroup and collectivity "in a single pattern of interaction" (Kuckertz 1990, 273). At beer drinks of a general nature, held 'for no particular reason', the particular subjective experience of mutual assistance and good neighbourliness, of the universal principles of the rural habitus, become objectified in the allocation of places and beer to groups, or particularized in the gifts of beer to individuals, as well as in the general sharing that occurs between individuals after each formal allocation. Being a member of a territorial group such as a sub-ward has a multitude of dimensions, but at a beer drink it is condensed to a space occupied, a beaker of beer received, and a period of time spent waiting for the allocation. Every person's experience of the principles that govern social life is different, but at beer drinks it is condensed to and expressed as a common membership of a particular group of people dependent on a particular host group for beer to drink.

At the beer drinks that involve the transformation of individuals the subjective experience of migrant labour, becoming a new homestead head, or of becoming a newly independent widow (see chapter 14) are again expressed in terms of the general principles of the habitus. As ritual performances, then, beer drinks bring together the individual and society, particular and universal, framing the subjective in terms of a habitus and thereby linking it with structure (Kapferer 1986).

Public reflexivity and the rural Xhosa habitus

Two other aspects of this particular beer drink need to be discussed in relation to the above. One is the extraordinary amount of controversy and argument that marked it, and the other, sometimes related to the first, was the making explicit of what at other beer drinks remained largely implicit and understood. Since this was also a feature of one of the other *ntwana nje* rituals held for a new homestead, this does not seem to be co-incidental. Both constitute, in my view, forms of public reflexivity, in Turner's sense, linked to the social reproduction of a rural habitus. Again, performance and practice are intimately related.

Thwalingubo's *ntwana nje* was well organized, run by people regarded as knowledgeable and experienced in these matters. No mistakes were made in the proceedings, despite the large number of people present and a lot of beer, making for complicated distribution. However, there was a great deal of discussion and argument, often over trivial points or issues that did not merit debate at other beer drinks. For example, there was a long argument about whether *iminono* (gifts of beer to individuals) should be given out before or after the 'customs' were given to local sub-ward sections. This discussion included frequent mention of the significance of each of these types of distributions, something that all men are well aware of anyway. There was no doubt in anybody's mind that the 'customs' would be forthcoming, and the controversy seemed unnecessary or exaggerated. At other beer drinks the beer gifts to individuals were always the first beakers given out, preceding the customs, and no similar arguments were recorded even though it sometimes happened that gifts were still being presented long after the customs had been consumed.

In giving out the various beakers as gifts, Dwetya elaborated on each of the relationships involved in some detail, something that is not usually done. For example, a beaker for an affine was announced with the words: "This beaker is for [so and so], you must receive this beaker here, because you are at your wife's home; there is nowhere else where you will receive such a beaker." One of the gifts was given to my assistant and I, and Modi shouted from across the hut, asking pointedly whether we would ever reciprocate, or whether Thwalingubo was "throwing away beer." Mzilikazi (at whose homestead we lived) stood to say that he would be the one who reciprocated on our behalf, since we were members of his homestead. We had been given such beakers at many other beer drinks without this question being asked.

Towards the end of the beer drink a visitor from another sub-ward stood to say that he was leaving, and mentioned that he was not a (classificatory) son-in-law to Thwalingubo, as some people thought, but that his mother was Thwalingubo's mother's sister. Dwetya then expanded on this, pointing out various other kinship links between this man and Thwalingubo. Ndlebezenja also contributed, confirming what Dwetya had said, and pointing out yet more connections between the visitor, Thwalingubo, and himself. Others referred to Thwalingubo's ancestry, the association between the Bamba agnatic group and the Chibi area, where they were original settlers, and made it clear to Thwalingubo that in calling them to be present at a beer drink he had certain obligations towards them as well as to the dead. In this respect there were discussions about whether people had been allocated their correct places, where exactly each section was entitled to sit, and about where sons-in-law should sit. Before the beer was explained there was discussion about the nature and range of the duties of the *injoli* (master of ceremonies) and about whether the men sitting outside should be called in. When some of the groups did come inside, there was further discussion about why this should have been done. In the course of all this there was frequent reference to Xhosa custom, the nature and customs of beer drinking, and the right way to handle beer.

Some of the debates that occurred referred back to what Dwetya and Ndlebezenja had said in their speeches. For example, a controversy arose in connection with the *ivanya* made from the second straining. When it was distributed older men asked if there was no 'beaker for words' (a beaker of proper beer given to seniors at this time). They were opposed by younger men who claimed that it was not right for them to ask for more beer and that Thwalingubo had provided enough for everyone to drink their fill. Skilled in debate, the seniors said that they were not asking for more beer, merely inquiring whether such a beaker was present, and accused the younger men of saying that it was not right for their elders to be given beer. One of the seniors put it like this: "According to Xhosa [custom] one does not ask for anything; it is the homestead head who gives on his own accord." Turning to Thwalingubo, he added: "All the speakers talked about you. You were circumcised by your father, and you have never had to ask for anything from anyone. You have your own home now, so you must call people to it; that is the custom. Your father used to drink beer even before you were born, so do not be stingy."

Discussions such as these, it seems, served to turn attention to the nature of the beer drink, the significance of having an independent homestead, and the ideal nature of the relationship between homesteads within the community. While it is fairly normal for some issues of this kind to be discussed and commented on at beer drinks, the number of matters raised, their apparent triviality (in some cases), and the intensity of the discussions leads to the conclusion that they were raised *because* this was a beer drink for a new homestead. The message being emphasized, largely through the symbolism of beer distribution and the accompanying oratory, was that the homestead was part of an interdependent community and that an orderly and mutually beneficial relationship between it and others was of the utmost importance. These features also indicate that this event was an occasion at which to socialise or re-socialise Thwalingubo into a rural habitus which was compatible with the Red Xhosa past. This is evident from the emphasis on Xhosa custom and on the past, invoked through recalling events associated with Thwalingubo's immediate ancestors, on the importance of kin as well as on the location of the homestead within a wider community within which it had certain duties and obligations, and on the importance of seniority and the ancestor rituals that would follow. To some degree this is a feature of all beer drink rituals in Shixini, but they were stressed here, I believe, because of the fact that this event was to establish a new homestead and to formally draw it into relationship with others. And the long discussions about beer drink etiquette reveal the important role that beer drinks as a performance genre play in this, in linking the individual homestead to the wider community and establishing an interdependence between them, allowing for reflection on this through its re-enactment in the idiom of beer. ·

Similar conclusions can be drawn from the large amount of apparently trivial argument at another of the *ntwana nje* beer drinks attended during fieldwork, held to mark the establishment of Honono's homestead. Here too the debates were about the way in which the beer ought to be distributed, and the relative rights to beer of young men and seniors. While in some ways such discussions are purely formal, in other ways they reveal real tensions in social life, such as that between junior and senior. Beer drinks provide an opportunity to inculcate aspects of the rural habitus, such as the principle of seniority, but also an opportunity for juniors to question and challenge this, and yet at the same time to accept it through this engagement, by insisting on their right to a specific beaker for young men, and to a particular seating place. At Honono's *ntwana nje* a young man stood to ask why there was no beaker for the young men present, and he was told that this was because the beer was being divided according to numbers and not according to territorial groups, which meant that the young men were simply regarded as part of the men's group in general. This led to an hour-long discussion concerning the difference between *umlawulo* and *ugabu* beer, between a pot full and a cask full and what young men were entitled to from each of these, the procedures involved, what kind of explanations were required prior to distribution, whether the young men should receive an apology for not being informed that they were not going to be recognized as a group with their own entitlement to beer, and so on. Eventually the discussion turned to the question of the entry of young men into beer drinks, which was a point of tension and dissent, largely because people disagreed on the proper way to manage this process.[5]

These beer drinks, then, can be viewed as dramatic performances in which men talk to themselves about themselves, dramatize their social arrangements, and manage the transformation being undergone, at the same time infusing everyday life with meaning in terms of the dispositions and orientations of the rural habitus. It appears that in talking to themselves about themselves at *ntwana nje*, men, particularly the seniors, attempt to inculcate certain principles and values in the new homestead head. Through exaggeration of the formalities of the beer drink, contrived complaints, exaggerated and in other circumstances highly redundant discussions about things like beer gifts, the procedure followed for the 'customs', the difference between a cask and a pot, and so on, seniors try consciously or unconsciously (or both) to facilitate reflexive engagement with what it means to be a homestead head, and how to conduct oneself in relation to other homesteads, using the idiom of reciprocal beer drinking.

This applies also at other beer drinks associated with passages or transitions, where the performative nature of these rituals is discussed more fully. In the case of one held to release a widow from a state of mourning (chapter 14) the community, through the oratory, attempts to provide the newly widowed woman with a perspective on what it means to be the female head of a homestead, and on how to relate to other homesteads as part of a community. The beer drinks and other rituals associated with labour migration (chapter six) are largely an attempt by the migrant's kin and neighbours to control his economic independence, transform the nature of his work, and keep him tied to the community, socially, morally, and economically. In the case of *ntwana nje*, the oratory represents an attempt to control the manner in which the establishment of a new homestead should be construed. This is done using the structure and symbols of beer drinking by dramatizing the nature of the relationship between the host and his homestead and the other members of the community. The homestead's independence is recognized through the idiom of beer brewing, and the nature of its relationship with others is specified in the same terms, thus controlling its independence and the potential threat of individualism. The power of senior men, exercised through their oratory in conjunction with the other symbols, asserts that there is a correct order that must be conformed to, and that it is an agreed upon, social order. The homestead's independence is recognized through the beer drink which, for its success, depends on consensus among members of the community. As illustrated in chapter 10, the homestead head does not have any say in how the bulk of his beer should be distributed. Instead, he must hand it over to the senior men of his locality. And the homestead space becomes one that is colonised by territorial, gender and age groups, representing the communal order. The community appropriates both the homestead and its beer, and thus controls the meaning of the event.

Not all of the preceding interpretation applies to a third *ntwana nje* recorded in the field, which took place under rather different circumstances, leading to a beer drink with rather different characteristics from those held by Honono and Thwalingubo. This case serves to confirm some of the interpretation of the other two, but also to demonstrate once more that beer drinks are conducted in a manner that is highly sensitive to the individual circumstances of the homestead involved.

Nontwaba (Tshezi clan) brewed *ntwana nje* beer on behalf of his younger brother, Rhwatiti, who was away at work. The fact that Rhwatiti was absent may be one reason accounting for the difference between this beer drink and those held by Thwalingubo and Honono, but there were also others. The homestead had been established for several years, but had lain unoccupied for about a year because Rhwatiti was away and his wife was living elsewhere. Furthermore, Rhwatiti and his wife were already relatively senior people and their eldest son was about eighteen years old. The beer drink was prompted by the return of Rhwatiti's wife to the homestead, and was as much an occasion to mark its reoccupation as its establishment. Rhwatiti had never held the ritual of making known the homestead, and this was the first beer drink ever held in it.

The tenor of the speeches at the beer drink was conciliatory and appeasing. The speakers praised Rhwatiti's wife and Nontwaba for holding the event, and gave the impression of welcoming back into their midst someone who had been absent, someone whom they were concerned about, and whom they wished well. It was as if this was a member of the community and a homestead that they had thought they might lose, and they were taking an opportunity to make sure that things would go well and that the homestead would not disappear. Of the various speakers, Thekwane was the most explicit and revealing. He spoke as follows:

...There is this thing called *ntwana nje*

It is something rare, chiefs

It is rare because before someone does it he must think in his heart

[Saying] 'since I live here at this home

5   I should sometimes make *ntwana nje*'

Yes, he soothes his home

Chiefs, a home is not soothed [only] by large rituals

It is soothed by means of *ntwana nje*

So that there will be no starvation in the home

10 When one brews *ntwana nje*, one is preventing famine

Eeee, so that anyone who enters the home may eat his fill

Even if it is a stranger who arrives

There should be something to eat in the home

You are securing blessings for that purpose

[pause]

15 Well, we are thankful Tshezi

That you should have this occasion

Having realized that you should prepare a small drink

So that there should be spitting

Right here in the hut

20 To drive out rats

So that they are not inside

Being suffocated by the spittle from pipes

Let it be clear then, Thsezi

That we are grateful for what you have done

25 You have done something beautiful

Chiefs, we are no longer grateful only for large occasions

Because this *ntwana nje*, it soothes, it is second [only] to those
large occasions

It is similar to them, because it soothes the home

It removes the dew from the home

30   So that life at home becomes good

Let it be like that Tshezi, we too say thank you

Yes, let it be good here at home, so that we drink beer here a
lot...

Others also made it quite explicit what they reckoned the effect of *ntwana nje* to be. Mzilikazi said that in doing *ntwana nje* Nontwaba was working for the security and uprightness (*inyaniso*) of the home, and Tshakmane said that the beer drink would make the home fertile and prosperous.

The oratory and ethnography presented above lend further evidence to the view that Xhosa beer drinks are dramatic cultural performances in which people talk to themselves about themselves; i.e. in which they dramatize and reflect on important aspects of their social lives, interpret their social practice, and provide themselves with models for future action. As Turner (1990) points out, every society needs some sort of "cultural-aesthetic mirror", through which to achieve self-reflexivity. In non-industrial societies this is often ritual and such ritual is sensitive to context, rather than concerned with macro-processes or abstract, generalized concerns, which is often the case with theatre in industrial society.

At the same time, beer drinks such as *ntwana nje* for a new homestead are means through which a rural habitus is inculcated and a particular kind of relationship with the wider world constructed, one that proclaims the primacy of rural home and society and links this to a Xhosa past. The oratory, in particular, indicates that this is a self-conscious, discursive process. The speakers consciously reflect on things like the significance of a new homestead and the relations between homesteads in everyday life. Moreover, they can explain why they say what they do. They are also able to explain why a beer ritual is an appropriate way to 'make known the homestead', as indicated in Thwalingubo's explanation of why he decided to brew. But why it should be a beer ritual rather than some other form of public gathering is another matter. It is here that people are operating on the level of habitus or practical consciousness

(Bourdieu 1977, Giddens 1984). A beer drink is simply a known, practical, habituated, established way of getting members of the community together, one that is flexible enough to allow for numerous applications and to be applied to new situations as and when they arise.

Endnotes

1. These included a large group of people of a local Ntshilibe lineage, matrilateral kin to Thwalingubo, who once viewed themselves as members of the Bamba clan rather than as members of the Ntshilibe clan (see chapter 11).

2. As Opland (1998) has shown, Xhosa praise poetry is usually composed as it is declaimed, often using well known formulas.

3. Fule is a clan ancestor.

4. Spitting on the floor is commonly invoked as indicative of the commensality and sociability associated with beer drinking. Since spitting is widely associated with purging oneself of any grievance or ill-feeling towards another, this stresses the communal harmony that ideally characterizes beer drink rituals.

5. In the past seniors used to visit the young men's *intlombe* meetings and announce which young men were now permitted to attend beer drinks, but this is no longer done, and there was uncertainty about what procedure to follow. Some seniors had taken to introducing young men to beer drinks on an individual basis, and there was disagreement about the validity of this.

14 Power and Gender[1]

In the previous chapter it is evident that the social recognition of a new homestead through ritual is accompanied by attempts to reinforce the power of seniors who, by means of oratory and debate, construct the establishment of a new homestead in a specific way. Similarly, at *umsindleko* it is senior males who attempt to dictate the terms under which male labour migrants (who are usually young adults) construct their experience of work and use the money that they earn. At beer drinks in general (with the exception of work party beer drinks involving female workers or young male workers) it is the senior men who control the allocation of space and the distribution of beer, and young men and women who are dependent on them for something to drink. The exercise of power over women is explicitly manifest at two beer drinks that are directly related to a woman's status. One involves the promotion of a wife to senior status. The other, which is dealt with in detail here, is for a widow.

Patriarchy and the widow's fate

In Shixini some beer drinks are held in association with the end of the mourning period after the death of a homestead head or other senior person. In addition, there is the beer drink held to 'release' (*ukukhulula*) a widow (*umhlolokazi*) from mourning the death of her husband. At such events the widow is addressed by senior members of the community with *iziyalo* (instructions or admonitions) in skilful oratory, and this will be examined here with a view to further illuminating the role of oratory at beer drinks, developing the notion of beer drinks as performative and transformative events affecting individual social status. At the same time, they are important as a manifestation of a rural Xhosa habitus through which the individual and society are brought together within a single performative frame. In this respect, aspects of structure, including the important principles of seniority and patriarchy, are made relevant to the subjective transformation being undertaken. In this case it will be necessary also to examine the mourning procedure and what it is that the widow is being released from. In other words the beer drink must be viewed as part of a broader social and cultural context.

Mourning and widowhood may be viewed as a number of interlinked stages which conform to the classic structure of rites of passage. There are two stages of mourning, which constitute the first stage of widowhood. The first stage of mourning is from the husband's death until special mourning clothes are put on a few days later, after the burial. The second stage of mourning then begins, and lasts until the beer drink at which the widow is released and at which she again changes her style of dress. This marks entry into the second stage of widowhood. On hearing of her husband's death a woman immediately goes into the first stage of mourning. The most obvious signs of this are the cessation of all social and other normal daily activity on her part, her confinement to her hut, and the adjustment made to her head-dress, which is worn low over her eyes. During the first few days she sits quietly on the women's side of the hut, eyes downcast, often weeping, with hardly a word or a gesture to those around her.

During this confinement, the widow sews herself a new set of clothes, called *impahla yokuzila* (mourning dress), assisted by those who keep her company. These take about two days to complete, and they are donned a day or two after the burial, without ceremony or formality. These clothes are made from the usual off-white calico sheeting that women ochre and dress in, but they are left un-ochred.[2] The old clothes that she was wearing when her husband died are discarded, given away or swapped for another set with another widow. Clothes so acquired may be washed and re-ochred in preparation for her releasing, when the white clothes are, in turn, discarded. Donning the white clothes signals entry into the second stage of mourning, during which the restrictions on the widow are less severe. She is now no longer confined to the hut, but may go out to collect firewood and water, and go about her daily business in and about the homestead. She may not stray too far from the homestead, however, attend beer drinks or other public occasions, join a work party, and so on. Her manner remains restrained and meek and her head-dress is still worn in the lowered position.

Obviously, mourning involves entry into a transitional state. In Van Gennep's (1960) terms, the first stage of mourning is a rite of separation, in which the widow is separated from the rest of society, her previous status symbolically cast off, and that of transitional or liminal being assumed. Her seclusion, her personal demeanour, and her social inactivity symbolically proclaim her to be a non-person. From this a new social identity must be crafted in classic rite-of-passage style. This begins with the putting on of the white clothes and the easing of the restrictions of the first stage. Others are involved in this process, especially her husband's close kin, who are concerned to ensure that the transition occurs smoothly. As far as the community is concerned, the widow is potentially dangerous and threatening and her intimate association with the dead man makes her polluting. The restrictions of the mourning pe-

riod allow the community to avoid the contamination of death and to neu-
tralize its threat, by safely transforming the wife into another kind of social
persona. This implies that the period of mourning, too, must be ended, for
only then is the process satisfactorily completed. So death is a communal affair, as is the need for the widow to successfully complete her period of
mourning and be absorbed back into the community once again. Thus the
formal release of the widow from the second phase of mourning involves the
community, and is not a private matter.

Approximately four weeks after the husband's burial, beer is brewed at the
homestead 'to release the family' (*ukukhulula usapho*) from mourning. Like
the widow, members of the homestead and other close kin must mourn the
death of the husband and homestead head. These people shave their heads as
a sign of mourning, and are not allowed to attend public or social occasions
until they have formally been released. This is a small event, attended by adult
kin of the deceased, and also by neighbours and members of the immediate
community (the sub-ward). The widow, who may assist with the brewing,
does not normally attend this beer drink, though there are exceptions to this.
She stays officially in mourning until about three or four months after her husband's death, when a second beer drink is held to mark her re-entry into normal life.

When the family is released the beer is consumed with little ceremony; a
close kinsman of the deceased (e.g. a full brother) acts as the host, and he explains to those assembled that the beer has been brewed to release the family
from mourning or, to put it in the local idiom, 'to allow them to go amongst
people'. Spokesmen from other parts of the sub-ward stand to thank the host
and to say that they understand what he has said. These speeches are very
short and to the point. There is no attempt at eloquent speech or oratory, and
there are no *iziyalo* (admonitions, instructions) addressed to the family. In
contrast, the beer drink held to release the widow from mourning is a somewhat more elaborate affair: More people attend, more beer is brewed, and formal admonitions are addressed to the widow. This occasion marks the end of
the second phase of the mourning period and the final stage in her transition
from married woman to widow and independent woman.

On the day before the beer drink at which she is to be released the widow
rises early and goes down to the nearest stream or river to wash, accompanied,
perhaps, by her young children or by a husband's sister. Later in the morning,
if she has not already done so well beforehand, she washes, ochres and dries a
set of clothes to be worn the following day. These are not necessarily new clothes,
but perhaps a spare set (perhaps her 'best') that had been in her possession since
before her husband's death, or perhaps a set obtained in exchange from another

widow. She spends the rest of the day completing the preparations for the next day's beer drink, straining the beer, getting the hut ready, and so on.

Early on the day of the beer drink, the widow is taken into her hut by her husband's female kin, accompanied by neighbouring women. Women from further afield sit outside, and men who are present stay in another hut in which the beer has been placed. In the women's hut, the widow goes to the women's side (the right hand side on entering) and takes off her mourning clothes. These are given away to a friend or relative, usually someone who is herself a widow (to give these clothes to a woman with a husband would be to portend his death, say women, and the gift would not be accepted). She then smears her whole body with red ochre, and puts on the newly ochred clothes and new head-dress. Red symbolizes (re)birth and a new social identity, as it does in other rites of passage such as marriage, birth, and male initiation. The new head-dress is worn well off the eyes in the style of a married woman, but her manner is still restrained, her eyes still downcast. Informants say that on the day of her releasing a widow is 'like a bride'. She is then admonished by the other women present. Not being able to attend these proceedings, I have no record of exactly what is said to the widow in these admonitions, but informants (men and women) say that they are similar to those given later when both men and women are present, and which are discussed in detail below.

During these proceedings a beaker of beer is brought in and passed around. Some informants say that the widow is the first to taste of this beaker, and that this tasting is similar to ritual tasting on other occasions, but others deny this, saying that the beaker moves in no particular order and that there is no ritual tasting: "It is just given to them so that they will do their work well." In the meantime, people assemble in the other hut and await the entry of the widow and those with her. While waiting, a beaker or two of beer may be passed around, but the main distribution of beer takes place only later, once the widow has arrived and the admonitions delivered. While these admonitions contain many standard elements, they vary considerably according to factors such as the time since her husband's death, the particular economic, personal and other social circumstances affecting the widow and her kin, the status of her late husband, and the personalities or inclinations of the speakers.

Nowinile and Nosajini

(i) Nowinile

Walata Mhlakaza (Cirha clan) was a well respected man who worked in East London for many years, returning home at regular intervals. After his death in East London his body was brought home and buried in the courtyard of his homestead. The burial was a large, well attended one. In East London he had joined a Christian burial society (though he was not a convert to the church) and it was the members of this society that brought him home. They provided Walata with a Christian-style burial, accompanied by elaborate singing, praying and preaching.

Nowinile, Walatha's widow, was released from mourning with a beer drink held four months later. The main officiant was Ndlebezenja Mangono, Walata's FFBSS and lineage head. By 10.30 a.m. 35 men and women had gathered in the hut where the beer drink was to take place. Nowinile arrived from the hut where she had changed into her newly ochred clothes and splendid new head-dress, along with the women who had been with her there, and sat amongst the other women in the hut. Preliminary comments and discussion among the men indicated that all sections of the sub-ward were present, and that the time was right to start the proceedings, because this was an occasion that had to be performed in the morning. Two beakers of beer were dished out. One was allocated to men and the other to women. Ndlebezenja announced this without ceremony, saying that "these are the beakers we are going to start with…lets drink then and get on with it." Once these two beakers were empty Ndlebezenja stood to formally announce the purpose of the gathering and to say that Mbambaza (Ngqunu clan), would be the one to provide the main admonition:

Gentlemen and ladies

Here is the point then, chiefs, the thing that has caused us to be here

We are going to receive that wife of Zwelibangile's[3], Nowinile

So that she will know that she should go amongst people

Yes, when we leave here we will be taking her with us

Now then, the person who is going to give forth words is this one of Sunduza's[4], chiefs

Eeeeh, the reason I called for attention is because he is going to give forth words

That's it then Ngqunu.

Mbambaza was a highly respected senior man, regarded as one who spoke skillfully and honestly. He therefore had the required "linguistic capital" (Bourdieu 1991, 18), for an occasion like this.[5] He was also a matrilateral kinsman to Ndelbezenja and an affine to Nowinile. His address to Nowinile included the following (the full text may be found in Appendix Two):

All right, my sister-in-law

It is said that I should produce a few small words here for you…

Here it is then sister-in-law

Today these Gcaleka here say they have come to fetch you

Seeing that you have been living like this, living abnormally

The time has come now for you to go amongst people again

When a person is to go amongst people she is given words of admonition

So that she should not do [bad] things, having been warned

So that it should not be said that that person was never admonished

But simply went out to beer drinks

And that she behaves as she does because of that

[Pause]

Now then, sister-in-law, we are here so that you should be taken out

Because of the departure of the great man of this home, your husband

I have every hope, sister-in-law, that you will conduct yourself correctly, nicely, as your husband did

Your husband [Walata's body] arrived here with strangers from across the Kei…

Although Walata was not born among them, they spoke about how good his character was

They asked that we too should talk about his life, about the way he lived here

We agreed with what they said, because the fellow [who spoke] said that Walata had a fine disposition while alive…

The thing that you must guard against sister-in-law is this

Avoid the madness of beer drinks

[Avoid] a person who drinks and then becomes aggressive

Until finally it appears that you [too] are a troublesome person who wants to speak in a disreputable way

It will be said: 'We saw Walata's wife fighting

Oh! How soon she fights with people!

Since when does she fight with others?!'

Whereas it was not your will

It was that you were influenced by those who stir up trouble

Wanting you to tear holes in the admonitions you were given and to ignore them

There is only one way to look after yourself; through respect

It is to oppose any person who comes to you full of evil, wanting to turn your mind

[If not] it will seem that you are a person who has not been admonished

Today then, going out to attend beer drinks does not mean that you will not come back home

Because you [women] tend to say: 'As for me, I ate [killed] my husband'…

'There is no one who is going to drive me by the small of my back if I do not want to go home yet'

There is that tendency then with you [women]

As a person, the way to conduct yourself is to say

'There is the sun [it is late]

I must go now and kindle a fire in the hut for the children of the deceased'

The way to conduct yourself is [to ensure] that the people who were the people of this homestead in the past should be such even today...

Let me say that it will not seem to be a homestead without its head if the wife is upright

It will become apparent if you divorce yourself from people

You will see the paths that lead here disappearing...

One will pass behind the homestead

One will lead below the garden

There will be no path leading here

This will stigmatise you as a person who is no good amongst people...

You [will] have a homestead that is no longer visited by many people

Whereas it used to be a homestead for people, this one of Mhlakaza's

It was loved when Walata was not present

When you were here in the hut doing things for people that used to be done by Walata...

Today, you are being allowed to go to beer drinks

It is not being said that you should wander about with people

It is not being said that you should go and sleep at beer drinks

And that there should be no smoke-spiral at this homestead of Mhlakaza's

There are many orphaned children here

Who have been left behind by Walata and who need to be raised...

That is what you have on your shoulders...

Ziwele, an old man of Komkhulu section, then spoke, saying that Mbambaza had "finished all the words" and that there was nothing to add. Bodli (Chibi section) also spoke, repeating some of Mbambaza's sentiments. Later, after the beer distribution, two of the neighbouring women also addressed Nowinile, repeating the themes that characterized Mbambaza's admonitions, but in a more conciliatory tone. This is one of the few beer rituals where women are expected to make formal speeches as part of the proceedings.

(ii) Nosajini

Nosajini's husband, Johannes Dumalisile (Tshawe clan), was Folokwe's sub-headman until he became ill, left the area in search of a cure, and eventually died. For one reason or another Nosajini's releasing was delayed for about six months, a delay that was regarded rather inauspiciously. At the time of her releasing, her two sons were away at work, and none of Johannes' agnates lived in or near Folokhwe. The caretaker at this homestead was Mbambaza who, like his father before him, had been chief councillor to Johannes. Therefore, it was Mbambaza who officiated at the beer drink. He also delivered the main speech of admonition.

Nosajini's daughter-in-law who lived in the same homestead had lost a newborn baby some weeks previously, and she was released from the mourning of her child at the same time. The event started unusually early, at 8 a.m., when there were 42 men and women present in the hut. Soon after 8 a.m. Mbambaza sent someone to call Nosajini from the other hut. Once she and her companions had arrived and seated themselves, Mbambaza addressed her, repeating some of the things he had said to Nowinile a few months earlier. He started by reflecting on the fact that this kind of event was frequent. He expressed mild surprise that it was not something that was done for a man after his wife's death, but this was how things were. He said to Nosajini that she was being released "to go amongst people" and that this should have been done sooner. He implied that her son's illness was in all likelihood related to this neglect.[6] As a released widow Nosajini should think for herself, he urged, so that nothing bad would come her way. The admonitions would be of no use otherwise. In particular, she should avoid overindulgence in beer because beer "wipes out the admonitions". There were people around, people who were "like Satan", who could cause her to ignore the admonitions and behave badly. As a mature woman she had to be careful of what people said to her and not be influenced by others. He then explained that Gidimisana's wife, Nosajini's daughter-in-law, was also being released from mourning her baby, though she had not smeared with ochre but that she would do so the next day. The full text of his speech is provided in Appendix Two.

Gqwetha of Komkhulu, an old man of the Ntlane clan, also spoke briefly, repeating some of the sentiments expressed by Mbambaza. There were no other speakers after him.

Four beakers of beer were served, two for men and two for women. A
beaker was also given to a number of young men who were waiting outside
the hut, in recognition of the fact that the graves had been dug by them.

Performance, power and the homestead

There are a number of reversals that characterize beer for releasing a widow
and mark it as an occasion associated with death. It should be held in the
morning and be over by mid-day, whereas other beer drinks can extend well
into the night. Another difference is that the beer is not distributed according
to territorial groups (*ukulawula*) but in terms of numbers present (*ukugabu*).
This is the case with other beer drinks if the amount of beer is small, but at
beer for releasing a widow there is never *ukulawula*, no matter what the quantity of beer is. As Ndlebezenja put it at Nowinile's : "It is not *umlawuo*, Chiefs.
It is simply to be dished out; it is not *umlawulo*—so and so's beaker and so
and so's beaker, a beaker for women, oh no–it will be dished up this side
[men's side]–finished–it is dished up that side [women's side]–finished. That's
it." Bhayisikile commented in reply that "the law of this beer is like that".

It is also noticeable that the division of beer between men and women is
more or less equal, unlike most other beer drinks. This, in conjunction with
the fact that the women sit inside the hut, with the men, and that they are expected to admonish the widow, indicates that this is an occasion on which
women participate on a more or less equal footing to men. Releasing the
widow is, in one sense, women's affair. It is a woman who is the subject of the
ritual, and who is being reintegrated into the ranks of the other women. It is
the widow's female affines (and others) who help her change her clothes and
who are the first to admonish her. Their participation is as important as that
of the men. Beer for releasing a widow is also different in that there are no
'customs' beakers, no gifts of beer to individuals and no 'hidden' beer put
aside. The reasons for these omissions, and for the other reversals, is that beer
for releasing a widow is an occasion associated with death: "It is not the kind
of beer to be given out by *ukulawula*, it is bad beer, beer for a funeral." Some
compared it with the mourning beast, killed (ideally) a year after the burial,
in a ritual that lasts for only one day, during which all the meat is consumed
(other rituals involving sacrifice are spread over three days).

As a beer drink this event has a specific aim—to effect and make public
the woman's status as widow and to incorporate her into society as such.
Brewing beer ensures the public nature of the event, and all sections of the
community should be present before the proceedings start. Community in-

volvement, however, is present from the moment that the woman hears of her husband's death, which is made tolerable by the continual presence and support of others. The restrictions of the mourning period are defined largely in social terms—the widow is not allowed to attend beer drinks, to join work parties, to socialise—and so is the removal of those restrictions. She dons her new clothes in the company of other women; it is the community as a whole that attends the beer drink, that has come to take, fetch or receive her, so that she should 'go amongst people' again.

The admonitions addressed to the woman outline the behaviour expected of her in her new role and the responsibilities associated with it. These norms are expressed partly in general rather than specific terms, but the individual characteristics of the particular widow involved inform what is said. When I asked Mbambaza about how he composed his speeches at such events, he said that in both cases he took individual personalities into account. As he put it: "I speak about someone whom I live with here in the sub-ward, whose character I know, whose lifestyle I know, and whose manner of behaving towards others I know." Even if speakers are only intermediaries, as Bourdieu would have it, they attempt to demonstrate their practical mastery of the situation and to enhance their reputations as eloquent speakers. In speaking they have to make an assessment of the 'market conditions' which will affect the reception of what they have to say and to deploy their linguistic capital so as to generate a social 'profit' (Bourdieu 1991). In this case the 'market conditions' include the nature of the individual person being released in the context of social relations in the community and the conventional nature of the beer drink both in general terms and in terms of its specific objective. Nowinile is known as a strong, competent and respected person, but she is one of the few people in Folokhwe who belongs to an independent Zionist church and who therefore prefers to associate with other church members, though she keeps on good terms with her neighbours. The emphasis on ensuring that her homestead remains a homestead 'for people' should be understood in this light. Nosajini, on the other hand, was a humble and mild-mannered person, possibly easily influenced, and the emphasis in the admonitions was thus on avoiding people who could influence her negatively.

However, if even 'a thousand mouths' will not change the way in which the widow is likely to behave, what is the point of all this talk? It is evident that it is the beer drink itself that effects the transition i.e. that it is the mechanism through which the status change is realized, and that the experience of bereavement and its outcome is construed and resolved in social terms. We need to consider this and the role of the oratory more closely, and to extend the arguments made about speech in chapter 12. As I have suggested earlier, it is useful to consider the beer drink as a 'cultural performance', along the lines originally suggested by Singer (1972) and developed further by Turner, Schechner, and others (e.g. MacAloon 1984). In this case it may also be viewed as the culmination of a 'social drama' that commenced with the husband's death (Turner 1974). As a cultural performance this beer drink provides a focused and ordered series of actions and a frame within which to handle the changing status of a widow. As part of the re-integrative phase of a social drama the beer drink performance has a conventional effect; it changes the widow's status, and it can be seen as an illocutionary act, which does something in the process of being enacted (Austin 1962, Searle 1979, Rappaport 1999). How does it do this? The answers to this question apply, in general terms, also to the other beer drinks associated with change in status considered in chapters six and 13.

Like any cultural performance this beer drink involves a conventional procedure, including the uttering of words of an appropriate kind by an appropriate (formally appointed) person. Ndlebezenja said as much when he introduced Mbambaza as "the person who is going to give forth words". It is a procedure which takes place according to agreed upon rules and conventions, and which serves to effect and constitute a transition between two states, which are also conventionally defined. By this I mean that the procedure in itself is both the means and the result of the transformation between the two conventionally defined states. A performance of this kind dramatizes or enacts something, and in the dramatization it is something. Transformation is thus inseparable from the dramatization itself. What the beer drink does through its enactment is to release the widow, to 'take her out' of the state of widow-in-mourning and transform her into a state of independent and socially recognizable widowhood. In Handelman's (1990, 28) terms this beer ritual is teleological, it is an event that models a particular outcome and effects this outcome through its enactment. This is explicit in Mbambaza's oratory. He says that people have come together to 'take' or 'receive' the widow into their midst, and this is what they actually do through their participation in the event. In the performance of the beer drink she is transformed, released from the restrictions of mourning and reincorporated into society. The beer drink is the means by which she is transformed and it is also the end product, the outcome of her having been released in the sense that it constitutes the state of affairs into which she is being released. It is more than just a symbol and a means. She is not just being told that she may 'go amongst people'; she is doing so at the time by being seated with other women at a beer drink.

Some qualification is obviously needed here. In constituting the end state the beer drink is selective, and it is finite. It is a partial experience of being a released widow and it is not the only experience of such. A social drama does not dramatize the whole of society, but selects and emphasizes certain themes (Douglas 1966, 64). What is being dramatized in the beer drink and spoken of in the oratory are certain key elements of the widow's new status, such as her incorporation into the company of senior women, which is enacted and constituted by her being present at and participating in the beer drink as part of the body of senior women.

As a ritual drama the reflexivity associated with this beer drink reveals to the widow, and to the other participants, in condensed but tangible form, basic truths about the status of released widow and female homestead head, about attending public events such as beer drinks and how to behave at such events, her relationship with other women of the community, the value of commensality and sharing, the importance of providing beer for people, the relationship between individual homestead and community and the importance of building the homestead. The ritual reveals these truths by acting them out and through the oratory, sometimes in exaggerated form such as in the subdued behaviour of the widow, which is a dramatic overstatement of how a widow ought to conduct herself at beer drinks. In this way the beer drink objectifies and naturalizes a number of values and ideals. It makes concrete what is otherwise abstract, and in so doing provides the widow and the community with a powerful demonstration of the meaning of being a released widow and of being a homestead head.

In this the oratory plays a vital part. What the speakers say defines and articulates the experience being undergone and the nature of the transition. In this sense the oratory helps to establish the frame and makes explicit what is being 'made visible' (Turner 1967) by the non-verbal actions. One of the oratorical devices that Mbambaza uses in this regard is contrast, through which he creates images of acceptable and unacceptable behaviour, moral and immoral persons and acts, socially acceptable and unacceptable homesteads. How to behave at a beer drink is contrasted with its opposite; getting home in good time as opposed to spending the night away. The well-behaved widow is contrasted with the one who causes tongues to wag; one who follows the admonitions is compared with one who ignores them. One who minds her own business is contrasted with one who is always slandering others. To make such contrasts effective Mbambaza uses frequent repetition, and devices such as reported speech, putting the widow into the picture that he draws, as it were.

The strategy of contrast is facilitated by the fact that beer itself is morally ambiguous, potentially both good and bad. On the one hand it is associated with the ancestors, sociability and the building of the homestead; on the other with the effects of drunkenness, which are disorderly and destructive. Beer

can be a force for good or for evil, depending on how it is used. It has the potential for either, and it must be controlled. This ambiguity surfaces in the
contrasts that Mbambaza makes: The widow must do things (i.e. brew beer)
for people, but she must not get carried away at beer drinks. Beer is personified as a devil who will lead one astray, in making the contrast between a
woman who cares for her home and children, and one who stays late at beer
drinks, so that she can meet with her lover.

However, Mbambaza's oratory does more than just support the message
conveyed by the beer drink itself, in that he is able to expand on the latter and
thereby broaden the meaning of the event. For example, the image of the foot-
paths leading to a homestead is used to emphasize the need for the widow to
work for and look after her homestead and to use it to help others in the
course of everyday life. Wealth (such as livestock) is of use only insofar as it
enables one to assist others. Such a homestead will continually have people
walking to and from it, not only when it brews beer. If one does not do things
for people, on the other hand, the paths will disappear, because "paths are created by people". In this way he explicitly extends the meaning of the beer drink
into a number of other aspects of everyday life.

The oratory is of importance also because it enables reflection. Public dramas are occasions for plural reflexivity (MacAloon 1984; Turner 1982), times
when members of society are provided with a chance to reflect on themselves
and their society. Mbambaza's metalinguistic commentary makes the reflexive nature of the beer drink quite explicit. In both speeches he was concerned,
firstly, with establishing the status of what he is about to say by defining the
ritual frame. Thus he says that giving admonitions is the usual thing in such
situations and that attendance and speaking at events such as these, is frequent. The reflexive nature of the beer drink as a whole is suggested also by
Mbambaza's style of speaking, including his use of pauses, and of repetition,
manifested in the use of the intransitive *qho* (often) and by instances of initial and final linking, sometimes in conjunction with *qho*, to produce an impression of reflective meditation (see Appendix Two). In both of his speeches
he indicates that admonishing the widow is an important custom, even
though it does not necessarily influence the widow's subsequent behaviour.
He indicates that the admonitions are necessary for the effective performance
of the ritual, in case wrong behaviour on her part is later attributed to the fact
that she was not properly released. An interesting aspect of his opening words
at Nosajini's releasing is his metalinguistic and metacommunicative reflection
on the fact that this event is never held in connection with the death of a
woman, to enable the husband to be released. Here he is clearly talking about
the event, about what he is going to say, and why he is saying it. In this re-

gard Mbambaza shows a fine awareness of the fact that this specific ritual context constitutes what Hymes calls a speech situation, which calls for a speech
event (the admonitions) of a particular kind, a kind appropriate to the situation (Hymes 1972). In this respect Mbambaza uses a number of terms that
are appropriate to the context, including performatives such as 'fetching' or
'receiving' the widow, 'releasing' her, and allowing her 'to go amongst people'.

This brings us to the question of the effect of the words on the listeners and
on the widow being released, to what Austin called the perlocutionary consequences of performative acts, the persuasive effects of what is done. One
might suggest here that by providing meaning and by affirming ultimate truths
and values, the event evokes feelings and sentiments and in so doing provides
a model for the future. In this particular case ideals such as providing for people and ideas about proper behaviour at a beer drink are not only verbalised
but acted out in what is a beer drink. Bringing these together—norms of behaviour and the acting out of these in the consumption of beer may be seen
as having a powerful persuasive effect. It is another example of what Turner
(1967, 30) referred to as the fusing of ideological and orectic properties in a
single symbol (beer, in this case), combining the physiologically satisfying experience of consuming beer with the social norms surrounding such consumption, making the experience normative, and the norms obligatory as well
as desirable.

The ritual and its oratory are also perlocutionary in that they are linked to
the maintenance of a rural habitus that places the homestead at the centre of
concern and that stresses the interdependence of homesteads in reciprocal relation with each other, to enable the survival of each. Mbambaza is at pains
to point out Nowinile's responsibilities to her homestead and children. She
takes her late husband's place as homestead head and to this end he talks about
Walata's good character and urges Nowinile to emulate him. He points out
that a homestead which is controlled by a woman of good character will not
appear to be one that has lost its male head. The widow is regarded as being
responsible for the good name of the homestead and for its maintenance, and
she is responsible for its inhabitants—in Nowinile's case these are her minor
children. Nowinile is also enjoined to ensure that her homestead remains a
social entity, part of the community, as it was before Walata's death. A key aspect of this, implicit in notions such as 'working for people', is that she should
hold beer drinks, ensuring that the homestead remains a homestead for people, and that the paths leading to it do not disappear. As indicated many times
already in previous chapters, each homestead is dependent, for its social and
economic well-being on being part of a network of relationships, on which it
relies and to which it contributes in a wide range of ways. Every homestead

that dies out and any homestead that does not conform to these general principles is a direct threat to the well-being of the rest.

In attempting to construct a particular model of how a widow should behave the beer drink is also an attempt to order or manage her change in status and reinforce the power relations associated with patriarchy. Here, the beer drink is again a frame that constructs an ideal or 'play' form of gender relations, providing a visual image of their ideal nature. This is characteristic of social dramas or ritual performances. For example, in Cowan's work on the dance in northern Greece she shows how dance embodies ideal gender relations in movement, gesture and posture, in spatial positions and in dance signs (Cowan 1990, 89). These "recall the taken for granted bodily "dispositions" that constitute the habitus; they reiterate culturally constituted meanings about male and female bodies in the everyday world." (ibid., 90). Here the subdued behaviour of the widow and her female companions, their occupation of the left hand side of the hut, and the other conventions of beer drinking (control of the beer by men, etc.) embody and emphasize their junior position and dependence on men.

Given that a beer drink embodies the ideal nature of gender relations, it is not surprising that Mbambaza's oratory uses beer drinking to reinforce it. Proper behaviour at beer drinks is discussed in specific terms and is a way of talking about gender relations, an 'externalization' of a status quo that men would like to maintain (Bourdieu 2001). In both cases the widow is warned to be careful at beer drinks and to avoid people who, under the influence of too much beer, might lead her astray. Nosajini is told that the one thing that might push her beyond the point of no return is beer. The widow should ensure that she does not neglect her homestead by spending too much time at beer drinks, and she should not spend the night at beer drinks. This is a veiled warning against over-involvement with lovers and neglecting homestead and children as a result. Perhaps this is why the beer is personified by Mbambaza as 'that man'. As widows no longer in mourning, Nowinile and Nosajini are free to have lovers or to renew relationships with former lovers (as long as these are not made public), relationships which, according to informants, are suspended for the period of mourning.

Controlling the future behaviour of the widow is seen also in the images of the homestead, such as in the hearth fire and the smoke spiral, and in that of watching the sun and getting home in good time to attend to the homestead. What is important here is the fact that although the status of the widow has changed, she is still a woman resident in her husband's homestead. From the point of view of her husband's agnates the basis on which she was first accepted into the home has not changed. She remains a wife and mother of the home. The homestead will always be formally known as her husband's, not as hers, and the alliance between the two kin groups, created by the marriage, remains in force. For this reason, the widow is often exhorted to respect and obey her husband's brothers, and to consult them in all matters. It is partly for this reason, perhaps, that many widows ultimately leave their husband's homesteads and return to their natal homes, establishing new homesteads there or living with kin.

Similarly, control is implied in specifying the kind of behaviour that will characterize someone who has not listened to the admonitions, someone whose heart is 'impoverished' and 'full of weeds' and who allows 'holes' to be torn in the warnings she receives. Such a person is one who goes around saying that she has 'eaten' her husband (that is, killed him through witchcraft) and that she will not be controlled by anyone, and who does the things she has been warned against. Relevant here also is the fact that Mbambaza mentions the sanctions for such behaviour—gossip and ostracism (the disappearance of the paths)— an image he repeats in various forms eight times. Good behaviour, on the other hand, will bring favourable comment from people.

In some cases it is the husband's brothers who give the speeches at these events and they make explicit their desire to exercise control over the widow. In the case of Nowinile and Nosajini this would have been inappropriate. There were no members of Nosajini's husband's lineage living in the area (ex-cept for her sons, in the same homestead) and Nosajini was known as a re-spectful person, who liked attending beer drinks but who always conducted herself well. In Nowinile's case, she was a strong, independent-minded and respected woman, and to advise her to submit to the control of her husband's agnates would have been fruitless and inappropriate. Instead, Mbambaza cast his admonition in the idiom of the way in which Walatha had been known to conduct himself, urging Nowinile to follow suit, and implying that this was the way Walata (and his agnates) would want it.

Endnotes

1. This chapter is partly a revised and updated version of McAllister (1986).
2. Missionized people use a black, shop bought dress, a practice that is becoming com-mon even among people who do not profess Christianity.
3. Walatha's praise name, 'Claimer-of-the-world'.
4. Sunduza was Mbambaza's father.
5. In Hymes' terms, he was known to be highly communicatively competent.
6. One of her sons had taken ill at work and had returned to seek the help of a healer in another part of the district.

15 Conclusion

Parsimony is a supreme value for those who already know; ethnographers...are destined to tell baroque and tortuous tales.

(Fabian 1990, 15)

Fabian identifies two potential shortcomings in a performance approach—"positivity and political naiveté" (1990, 16). The first has its roots in Durkheim's approach to ritual (and reaches its full expression in Radcliffe-Brown's) and arises because performance may tend to address social values and norms and ignore or neglect the negative, deviant or contradictory aspects of social life. A focus on beer drink rituals as partial manifestations of a rural Xhosa habitus could, I admit, suffer from this shortcoming, at least up to a point. However, as long as practice is considered—real beer drink rituals within their socio-economic and political contexts—a performance approach does also throw into relief some of the contradictions and negativities of social life.

There are two ways in which this has been discussed. In the first place, I have argued that beer rituals emerged out of the historical development of neighbourhood as the major and regular basis for economic co-operation. This contrasted with the former, kinship-based production process (with occasional inputs of collective labour) and the continuing composition of homesteads as kinship units. Ritual beer drinking as a burgeoning social phenomenon (including its substitution for certain animal sacrifices) facilitated the social transformation involved, as suggested by Turnerian theory. Performing the neighbourhood principle allowed for reflection on experience and cemented this ontological shift as the primary productive principle. It transformed the relative economic importance of kinship and neighbourhood. Ritual performance, with its characteristics of liminality and anti-structure, is here viewed as 'the drawing board' on which actors were able to formulate and confirm emerging forms of social practice (Turner 1986, 24).

There is, secondly, the question of contemporary 'contradictions and negativities'. Here too, I hope to have demonstrated that a performance approach is illuminating rather than obscuring. We have seen this in *umsindleko*, for example, where the problem of migrant labour, conflict between junior and senior, the potential dangers of migration for rural society, and the impossibility of resolving its contradictory aspects, are evident. It is in this vein that the negative aspects of migration, manifested in the belief in the witch familiar *umam-lambo*, become an essential part of *umsindleko* performance, even if they are not always explicitly addressed. Similarly, negativity is addressed in the ritual for releasing the widow, highlighted in the oratory as a potential for disorder and conflict that needs the prophylactic of the admonitions. Here too, beer drinks as such are portrayed as morally ambiguous, both desirable and dangerous. In the *ntwana nje* for a new homestead, too, there is evidence of a contest between senior and junior, of a need for inculcation of the habitus in the face of potential disunity and conflict. And at some of the other events described in preceding chapters, conflict and disunity are topics spoken about, acted out and partly resolved through beer drinks, such as Ziwele's falling out with his neighbour and the development of his new work arrangements, or built into the form itself, as in the dispute between Ntshilibe and Ntlane agnatic groups (both of these examples are discussed in chapter 11).

At the same time it is evident that beer rituals do address and highlight norms and values such as mutual harmony, co-operation between neighbours and aspects of kinship loyalty. What these rituals frequently do, then, is to juxtapose two, sometimes contradictory realities—the ideal and the real—from the point of view of the household and/or its section. As Mary Douglas has put it, drinking allows people to construct the world as it is, and also to construct an ideal world (Douglas 1987, 11–12). To express this somewhat differently, beer drinking provides, firstly, a general model of the groups and categories on which social life is based, and the moral norms associated with this. In this respect Fabian's reservation is well taken. At the same time, however, they are also a practical manifestation of these norms in actual relationships, imperfect though they may be, honoured or not, in which power, transaction and interest are important elements. Beer drinks thus expose and address difference and conflict while striving towards consensus and harmony. They also always index the immediate past, since the establishment of spatial patterns and meanings in the formal proceedings involves either a confirmation of or a change from those previously enacted, and they provide a template for the future in terms of meanings currently invoked. The general principles embodied in their spatial and other symbolism do not simply reference practice, but also act as a basis for the ongoing construction of a habitus, the conceptual scheme in terms of which activities are organized as well as being an expression of how these principles are adjusted and manifested in practice.

At first glance it would seem that the second charge, that of political naiveté, is more easily refuted, at least in this particular case of the performance of Xhosa beer rituals. I have stressed the development of a rural habitus as a vital attempt to regulate relations both within the rural field and with the dominant sector of society in the struggle over labour, an attempt to manage the nature of the engagement with the wider world, and to maintain a rural agrarian orientation and identity. Performance is always historically rooted, and I have shown that beer drink rituals emerged in the context of domination and labour exploitation, closely related to the development of co-operative labour and an ethic of mutual assistance as a way of maintaining homestead production. In Shixini, beer drinks are not only linked to the rural mode of production; they are also linked to the capitalist mode of production through migrant labour which has to be continuously engaged with, its benefits accepted, but also subverted and challenged. And they are related to the wider society more broadly in the sense that they represent historical dimensions of a choice to limit involvement in it and to conserve a rural Xhosa way of life. In this sense it is partly in beer drinks that we find the 'hidden transcript' (Scott 1990) of a particular group of rural Xhosa, where their response to domination is unconsciously performed and constructed as part of an agrarian habitus. Thus, I have considered the performance of beer drinking in its socio-economic and political setting and linked it to a particular way of reacting to domination.

A historical approach is necessary for analysing specific types of beer drinks as well as for an understanding of the emergence of beer drinking as a distinctive ritual form. As indicated in a number of earlier chapters, the habitus as described above is not a static phenomenon, but arose out of changes affecting the process of everyday life, giving rise to practices and circumstances requiring improvisation and innovation, and in which interest and strategy are key components. The habitus which provides the basis of Xhosa beer drinking in Shixini today, then, is a product of a collective history, but it is not a static product. New dispositions came into play as the old habitus was destabilised as a result of changed economic, political and social circumstances which generated new forms of practice. They were not completely new, in the sense of previously unknown. Rather, they were the result of a new emphasis on certain things at the expense of others, created by 'objective' forces beyond the control of the actors. Beer had long been an item in the Xhosa diet, but it became much more important from the early 1900s onwards; it had long been consumed in Xhosa ritual, but beer drinking came to be substituted for certain types of animal sacrifice, and new kinds of beer rituals were developed. Rural Xhosa people are not necessarily conscious of this history, of why beer drinks are such a prominent part of life, simply regarding beer drinks as part of Xhosa custom or 'the way we do things', a doxic acceptance that displays "genesis amnesia" (Bourdieu 1977, 79). Once adopted as a way in which to achieve a variety of objectives, new kinds of beer drinks arose to cater for new situations and contingencies, since the habitus enables actors "to cope with unforseen and ever-changing situations" (Bourdieu 1977, 72). The habitus, as "a matrix of perceptions, appreciations and actions" allows for "the achievement of infinitely diversified tasks, thanks to analogical transfers of schemes permitting the solution of similarly shaped problems…" (Bourdieu 1977, 83). Such analogical transfer, I have attempted to show, takes place performatively.

The general messages concerning the importance of mutual assistance and good neighbourliness which are embodied in every beer drink, and which co-exist with practical objectives and/or interests at each beer drink, are thus linked to the objective historical conditions in which beer drinks emerged as a dominant form of ritual and which are still relevant today, providing a de-gree of continuity between past and present without precluding change through innovation and improvisation. Again, Bourdieu's approach accom-modates this: "The habitus, the durably installed generative principle of reg-ulated improvisations, produces practices which tend to reproduce the regu-larities immanent in the objective conditions of the production of their generative principle, while adjusting to the demands inscribed as objective po-tentialities in the situation, as defined by the cognitive and motivating struc-tures making up the habitus." (Bourdieu 1977, 78).

The fact that beer drinks developed in this way *may* be somewhat arbitrary, in accordance with Bourdieu's (and conventional anthropology's) view of the arbitrariness of symbols (1990, 17), though this may equally not be the case here. It might potentially have been one of the other communal institutional forms instead—meetings of the local moot or sub-headman's court, ritual sacrifices, or rites of passage. But perhaps beer drinks were the only or at least the most appropriate form, pre-disposed to such development by their asso-ciation with co-operative work, as is/was the case elsewhere in Southern and sub-Saharan Africa, and by the fact that their development co-incided with and was made possible by increases in grain production. Besides, headmen and sub-headmen were being used by local magistrates and had become as-sociated with colonial rule, major rites of passage were large and relatively in-frequent affairs, and ancestral rituals associated with a non-territorial kinship group and the extremely serious matters of life and death, illness and misfor-tune, involving the relationship between living and dead. Beer drinks were an appropriate vehicle for representing the experience of community that emerged from the changed conditions of production that led to reliance of co-operative work groups and the rise of the neighbourhood principle, and for transforming and regularising this experience in normative terms, because a beer drink is the epitome of relaxed sociability in which people are, ideally, in harmony with each other. But as we shall see below, they were also appropriate because they were rituals, a form of communication using beer as a meta-language, the best way with which to speak about the interdependence of households and the importance of co-operation between them.

The problem of 'misrecognition'

The problem of political naiveté must also be addressed from another angle, in terms of what Bourdieu calls the question of misrecognition. In Bourdieu's writings this refers to a kind of collective self-deception (1998, 95) established through the maintenance of a habitus in terms of the objective conditions of existence, whereby both dominant and the dominated perceive the world in terms imposed by the relationship of domination which is in the interests of the dominant, but neither is fully conscious of this. In the case of the rural Xhosa habitus we are addressing a dominated segment of society who have re-acted to domination by the development of a system of dispositions and strategies in response to their socially subordinate position but which implicitly deny such subordination and establish a form of cognition that enables them to assert a reality of another kind. Is this also a form of 'misrecognition'? On the one hand the answer might be yes, since the objective conditions (colonialism followed by apartheid followed, perhaps, after the demise of apartheid, by continued marginalization and neglect) that maintain the dominant/dominated relationship have not changed significantly in the last hundred years. On the other hand, the development of cognitive structures and associated practices with which to provide a meaningful existence within a given structure of domination reflects an accurate perception of these structures even if the habitus is not fully consciously constructed and maintained.

Nevertheless we have to ask to what extent the existence of a rural Xhosa (agrarian) habitus has served the interests of the dominant as well as of the dominated. The beer rituals we have discussed are not perceived by the actors as linked to economic self-interest, but rather in terms of an ethic of good neighbourliness and mutual assistance. The maintenance of a rural homestead and agrarian lifestyle are (or were) not consciously perceived as acts of resistance to domination, but rural Xhosa were as aware as anyone else of the inequities of the apartheid system and of the fact that they were both sheltered from this, up to a point, and continually subject to it, in the rural areas. However, the real product of migrant labour was and is seen as the contribution that it makes to agrarian production in the countryside, to some extent hiding the relationship of exploitation between urban employer and migrant worker. So the question arises—have rural Xhosa such as the population of

Shixini contributed to their own domination? After all, it was usually in the interests of capitalist development (at least until the 1970s) and of successive governments in South Africa for rural people not to urbanize, not to aspire to becoming proletarians and to give up their rural homes. Various apartheid laws were designed to keep rural black people rural, to institutionalize oscillating labour migration, and to prevent their incorporation into the wider society as full citizens. This was, broadly speaking, the purpose of the reserves (later 'homelands'). And here we have people who apparently did not want it otherwise, who wanted to remain rural in orientation, though the law gave them little option. Today, conditions in urban areas such as lack of housing, high crime rates and high unemployment continue to act as a disincentive to turn one's back on the agrarian life and rural home.

The question can be asked directly: Do beer drink rituals obscure the real nature of relations between rural and urban, between dominant and dominated in Shixini? Or are they part of a realistic response to the 'objective conditions' that were imposed on rural Xhosa? The creation of rural reserves in which Xhosa had access to land was part of these conditions. This enabled some Xhosa, as Beinart and Bundy (1987, 12) point out, "to fend off the full demands being made by capital and the colonial state." The maintenance of a rural orientation in Shixini depends heavily on access to at least some rural resources (primarily land and livestock) as well as on a particular social organization through which the exploitation of local resources is effected. Through a strong community organization that manifests itself in real economic endeavours, as well as in other aspects of social life, the illusion of rural independence can be maintained and perpetuated, despite a heavy dependence on cash wages. Of particular significance here is the network of economic relationships within which individual homesteads are embedded. As we have seen, such relationships are based on the principles of kinship and of neighbourhood or territory, both of which are interpreted as elements of traditional social life.

Beer drinks can be seen as a means to perpetuate this, a means by which homesteads exercise a subtle kind of power over others and attempt to ensure compliance with the ethic of mutual helpfulness on which rural life depends. The obligation to both receive and brew beer creates a network of mutual indebtedness that reinforces and facilitates a general morality of reciprocity and mutual support. In this way, material capital is converted into symbolic capital which can again be converted into material capital. As far as relations between homesteads are concerned, this does not involve relations of domination and submission, as is the case in the field of power or the field of migrant labour, but relations of relative equality and the inculcation and re-inculcation of a particular habitus associated with the rural field. This does not make it any less 'political'. It is in the nature of beer drinking for symbolic power to be widely distributed across territorial and kinship groups and to prevent the emergence of a dominant faction and thus of inequality and exploitation. Thus while there is clearly an exercise of symbolic power, symbolic domination is contextual and related to age and gender hierarchies, construed as being in the collective interest.

The question of misrecognition also demands some attention to the nature of the 'interest' involved in hosting and attending beer drink rituals, and to my largely unqualified use of this term up to this point. Bourdieu's practice theory is not simply an 'interest theory' as characterized by Ortner (1984, 151), but his discussion of interest is sometimes ambiguous. On the one hand he rejects the notion of 'economic man' and rational choice theory, on the other he does give some priority to the material aspect of life. In one sense interest and strategy refer to motives and actions that may be unconscious and which arise from the nature of the habitus (Bourdieu 1998, 76–77), in another it has to do with individual gain. Individuals attempt to maximize 'profit', defined broadly to include material as well as non-material things, and it is largely in this dual sense that I have used the word. If people were motivated primarily by material interest it would be difficult to explain the rural agrarian habitus in Shixini, since they would potentially gain materially from a greater involvement in the wider economy and society.

Following the practices inculcated by the agrarian habitus is 'interested' in both economic and symbolic ways in that it is through the realization of the dispositions of the habitus—such as the development of a rural homestead and minimizing involvement in the industrial economy—that actors achieve their individual social as well as their economic goals, and the two cannot really be separated. To Bourdieu, humans are not merely utilitarian beings, but seek to maximize the satisfaction of living a socially meaningful life. Interest is thus socially constituted. In rural Xhosa society beer drink rituals offer one means of achieving this, a way of acting out the rural Xhosa habitus in concrete, everyday social situations, since it is through recognizing and acting out the social codes of rural Xhosa life in the game of ritual beer drinking that people unconsciously confirm their adherence to it and seek to achieve a meaningful life (Bourdieu 1990a, 109–10; 195–96). But perhaps one of the functions of beer rituals, as an aspect of the habitus stressing mutual interdependence and generalized reciprocity, is to hide the individual utilitarian or economic element. Beer drinks reproduce general relations of social and economic interdependence and express these through the idiom of beer exchange, elaborately and repetitively structured so as to disguise individual material interest, which is nevertheless necessary for the maintenance of these exchanges and which in one sense, according to Bourdieu's notions on gift exchange, lies at the heart of them. This conforms to his view that "the labour required to conceal the function of these exchanges is as important as the labour needed to perform this function." (1990, 112).

The morality of beer drinking

As performances, beer rituals both reflect and continuously create collective identity through communication, embodiment and communal participation that does not extinguish individual agency and interest, nor eliminate boundaries and hierarchies, but in fact facilitates and is articulated in terms of these. They therefore play a vital role in the construction and maintenance of the social arrangements on which the practice of local economic activity depends. As performances they provide a 'frame' within which members of society are able to portray, reflect upon and reaffirm their ways of thinking and acting. So beer drinks are a kind of metaexperience, an experience of experience, a realistic portrayal of reality which help to continuously reconstruct social relations. They make the principles that operate in everyday life tangible and invest them with value, thereby reinforcing and recreating them.

How Shixini people 'eat' their beer is who they are. Beer is made from maize, the staple food, symbol and substance of their rural orientation and lifestyle. Drinking it in a highly structured way ties individuals to each other and to the land, to their rural place, expressed in the territorial divisions of society. Thus to simply drink beer without order would be 'destroying the nation'. One could argue then, that far from obscuring the world of power and production, Xhosa beer drinks represent a reflexive engagement with it, enabling people to know their social reality by making abstract principles concrete and applying them to real-life situations, at the same time providing a template for future action and interaction.

Rappaport's views on ritual, outlined earlier in chapter three, are instructive here and allow us to take this a step or two further by examining the metaperformative and metacommunicative aspects of ritual more fully. We have to bear in mind Fabian's reservation about the positivity of performance approaches, however, as we do so. To Rappaport (1999), ritual is *the* basic social and human act because of its ethical and moral implications. It is in ritual that obligations are created and commitment and trust are forged. This is because of its performative and transformative nature. Ritual is self-fulfilling and teleological, enacting a state of affairs that it thus brings about, and (sometimes) vesting this state of affairs with supernatural sanction. This is where the power of ritual lies. It establishes commitment to this state of affairs among the participants and to the social order of which the ritual is a part. In the case of Xhosa ritual beer drinks, what they bring into being is a state of mutual co-operation and interdependence, establishing the morality of such co-operation and inculcating acceptance of it.

The performance of any beer drink in Shixini, I have argued, can be seen as the performance of mutual interdependence between homesteads, acting out in the idiom of beer the practice of co-operation in everyday life, casting individual experience in social and normative terms. In Rappaport's terms, this is the performance of a liturgical order, which is brought into being and made real by being performed. Performance is not just the expression of a liturgical order but is itself a crucial aspect of that order and its messages. A liturgical order as "a sequence of formal acts and utterances" (ibid., 118) becomes real only when it is performed, and the performer becomes part of the liturgical order in the process. To perform an order is thus to conform to it, making the performers indistinguishable from the liturgical order, which they are obliged to accept and cannot reject. Here we see again the close relationship between performance and the establishment and continuous maintenance of an embodied habitus.

The order that is performed in Shixini beer rituals, and accepted by being performed, is a public order. The obligation to live by that order is a social and moral obligation. To Rappaport, participation in ritual is thus not simply the expression of certain norms, rules, conventions and values relating to mutual co-operation and interdependence, but the very establishment of these and of an obligation to live by them—in this sense ritual is metaperformative as well as performative. But to turn again to the problem of positivity, Rappaport points out that ritual does not establish *compliance*—violations of the norms are possible, but this does not nullify them; their importance remains unchallenged and protected by the formality of ritual. Mbambaza recognized this when addressing the widows being released (chapter 14). So "the existence, acceptance, and morality of conventions are joined together indissolubly in rituals; they are, in fact, virtually one and the same" (ibid., 137). This is also the answer to the question: Why ritual? One cannot say the same of daily practice, or of legislation or decrees. It is the form of the ritual that is crucial in this respect, the fact that it is "the performance of more or less invariant sequences of formal acts and utterances not entirely encoded by the performers" (ibid., 24). It is this that constitutes the metamessage concerning the status of what is performed and the relationship of the participant to the performance. It is the form that makes ritual "without communication equivalents and thus, possibly, without functional or metafunctional equivalents" (ibid., 137–38).

So beer drinks, as ritual performances, establish the morality of the practices and the values related to inter-homestead relations, as being an aspect of 'proper Xhosa.' They establish the moral authority of the habitus as rituals which bring important aspects of the habitus into being.

A long period of stagnation at the hands of successive racist regimes in South Africa came to an end in 1994 with the election of the country's first democratic government. The neglect and marginalization of areas like Shixini, the rural Xhosa response to apartheid that was maintained there into the 1990s, and the resulting lack of modernization and development may well be coming to an end. In 1998, however, there were few signs of this happening, and more recent evidence from other, similar parts of coastal Transkei (Palmer et al, 2002), as well as from the Eastern Cape Province in general (Ainslie 2005, Bank 2005) indicate that it may be some time before it does. The signs that are there—new hospitals and schools, improved social welfare benefits, new tourism ventures, and so on—indicate a similar kind of process to that outlined by Counihan (1997). In such circumstances it is possible that beer drinking rituals of the kind described in this book will not remain a prominent feature of life, but who knows? It is just as possible that they will be adapted to deal with whatever changes modernization, if it ever makes a significant impact on the welfare of Shixini people, brings with it.

Appendix 1

Brewing Beer (Ukusila)

The manufacture of beer in Transkei has not changed much from the way in which it was made in ancient times (Katz 2003, 172), and the brewing process is similar throughout southern and other parts of Africa, though there are variations in details (see Soga 1931, 399–401; Broster 1976, 81–82; Krige 1936, 58; Bryant 1949, 274–77; Gelfand 1962, 45; O'Laughlin 1973, 101–3). The ingredients are simple, consisting of maize and water, but the process itself requires skill and experience. Initially, some of the maize (between one quarter and one third) must be turned into malt (*imithombo, inkoduso*) by steeping it in water for three days and then putting it out in the sun in hessian bags for a similar period. *Imithombo* is a Zulu word for sprouted grain (Doke and Vilakazi 1948, 800), but it is commonly used in Shixini. Once it germinates it is removed from the bags and sun-dried. It can be kept like this for some time or ground and used almost immediately. The equipment needed includes grinding stones, cast-iron cooking pots, plastic barrels, woven beer-strainers, and an assortment of buckets, dishes, tin-cans, grass mats, hessian bags, and so on. A good supply of fuel (wood and manure) is needed and also some food and drink for the brewers.

To brew fine beer one needs to use good quality maize, plenty of *imithombo* (skimping on this is easily noticed), maintain a relatively high standard of hygiene and have time available. From one 80 kilogram bag of maize it is possible to make 400 litres of beer and about 60 litres of *ivanya* (watery 'beer' from the second straining). Labour is the key factor. A woman and her teenage daughter are able to brew a small quantity of beer (say 40 litres) by themselves, but for a medium-sized beer drink one needs 200 to 400 litres. At one of the *umsindleko* beer drinks that I attended there were over 1200 litres of beer to dispose of, enough even for a good-sized *umgidi* (feast) such as the one associated with male initiation ceremonies. It is partly because brewing is a labour intensive business that beer drinks are commoner during the winter months after the harvest than during the ploughing and cultivating period (November to March) when labour is needed in the fields and gardens and the opportunity cost of brewing is high.

Usually it is the young women and teenage girls in the immediate neighbourhood, some of whom may also be kin, who are called upon to help with the brewing. For example, those who helped MamSiya, Nothimba's wife, when she brewed for Nothimba's *umsindleko*, were her adult, unmarried daughter, her HBW and HBSW from an adjoining homestead, together with four teenage girls and four women from nearby homesteads, none of whom were close kin to Nothimba or MamSiya. Not all of these worked for the entire brewing period, or at the same time. The utensils that MamSiya needed were borrowed from an almost entirely different set of neighbours from those which supplied labour. The helpers came from seven homesteads (some supplying both a woman and a girl), and the utensils were borrowed from eight homesteads, only one of which also supplied a helper. Right from the start, then, brewing is a co-operative process that involves a number of neighbouring homesteads (fourteen in MamSiya's case) during the five to eight days that it takes to prepare the beer; the exact time period depends on factors like the amount brewed, individual preference and the weather.

Assuming that the *imithombo* has been prepared and ground, the brewing (for an amount of about 300 litres) proceeds as follows: On the first day the maize is placed in pots and barrels and covered with water, so that it becomes soft, preparatory to grinding. It is left in the water for two days. On the second day the other utensils required for brewing are assembled, firewood and manure gathered, and water drawn. Such activities are repeated as and when required. On the third day the (now soft) maize is ground. The maize is placed on a large flat or slightly concave stone (*ilitye* or *ilitye lokusila*) and ground with a smaller, smooth round stone (*imbokodo*). For a large beer drink this may take the entire day, with five or six sets of grinding stones (some borrowed from neighbours) operating at once. The ground maize is pushed or allowed to fall onto a hessian bag or grass mat (*isithebe*) under and in front of the stone. Occasionally the workers replenish their dishes of soaked maize from the pots or have a rest, their places being taken for a short while by a passer-by or visitor. While grinding, their hands get caked with maize, which they wash off in a small basin next to the grindstones. This water is carefully collected together and later added to the pots. When all the maize has been ground it is returned to the pots and barrels and covered with fresh water. The old water is thrown out, because it is dirty and sour.

On the fourth day the ground maize (*intlama*) is taken out of the containers and ground a second time. The first grinding is called *ukuxhifa*, the second *ukurwexa*. Both of these are uncommon Xhosa words. In Zulu, *xhifi* is ideophonic for "crushing something soft" (Doke and Vilakazi 1948, 863) and *ukurwexa* in Xhosa means "to rub soft" (Kropf 1915, 377).The *imithombo*, too, may be ground on this day if it has not been done previously. While the second grinding is in progress, the floor at the back of the hut is swept and covered with a layer of dry, crumbled manure. The barrels are then placed on this layer. When the second grinding has been completed, each barrel is filled to about one third of its capacity with the *intlama*, now in the form of a coarse wet paste. Meanwhile, water is heated outside in large pots. Most of the water added after the first grinding is absorbed by the ground grain overnight, but that which is left is added to the pots of hot water, along with the water used by the workers to wash their hands, giving it the creamy colour of weak beer. The hot water is brought inside and added to the barrels of *intlama* along with the *imithombo*; the two are mixed together (*ukudidiyela*) with a hoe handle, and left overnight. Fermentation occurs spontaneously, though sometimes a starter is used (e.g. residue from the pots used in a previous beer drink). For smaller beer drinks the mixture is allowed to stand for a while and then cooked, but when the amount is large the cooking has to wait until the following day. Adding the *imithombo* is known as *ukufaka*, literally 'to put in'. When people want to know when beer will be ready for drinking they ask "when was it [the *imithombo*] put in?" They can then make the necessary calculation as to when it will be ready to drink.

On the fifth day the mixture is cooked outside in large cast-iron pots. The pots are filled with water and the rougher part of the beer mixture from the top of the barrels is added. The pots are brought to the boil before the rest of the *intlama*, the finer portion from the bottom of the pots, goes in. Once the pots come to the boil again they are removed from the fire and the liquid is taken out and cooled. Knowing when to remove the pots from the fire requires good judgement, based on the drop in the level in the pot (due to evaporation) and on the consistency of the liquid. Water may have to be added if it is too thick. After being boiled the mixture is called *isidudu* (wort, thin porridge) and it is porridge-like in consistency and aroma. Some of the *isidudu* is cooled by placing it in other, smaller pots, but with a large quantity of beer (or in case of a shortage of containers) the bulk of it is sometimes cooled in the following manner: The hut floor is swept clean and a small wall, about five or six inches high, is built from fresh cow-dung, to form a semi-circle from one point of the circular hut wall to another point on the same side, perhaps some three metres away from the first, thus 'damming' a part of the hut floor. The *isidudu* is then poured onto the floor, where it spreads out and quickly cools, but is contained by the manure wall. The dung wall is called *umyalo* in some parts of the Transkei (Broster 1976, 82).

By the next morning the *isidudu* is completely cool and is returned to the barrels, together with more water. The rest of the *imithombo* is added and the mixture is well stirred. The little dung wall is removed and the floor is cleaned. One small cask or pot is not stirred and the *imithombo* added to it simply remains on top of the thick mixture, to be stirred in at a later stage, so that its maturation is delayed by a day. This is the beer that will be consumed on the day after the beer drink, called *isidudu* beer. On this (the sixth) day the *igwele* (yeast or leavan) beer is strained and consumed by members of the homestead and neighbours. This is a small pot-full brought to maturity in advance of the rest (it is the first pot cooked and extra *imithombo* is added as soon as it is cooled). Some of the *igwele* is added to the main portion of beer to assist with fermentation, and some is added to the *isidudu* beer. The remainder is drunk. *Igwele* is also called *umlumiso*, from *ukulumisa*, 'to cause to bite'. The main portion of the beer remains in the pots and barrels while fermentation takes place. As the beer ferments the level of liquid rises and large frothy bubbles form and break on the surface. It has to be carefully watched to ensure that it does not spill over the sides in quantity.

The next day (day seven) the beer is strained. This may take the whole morning, four or five women straining at the same time. Ideally young men help, but I only once saw a young man do so in Shixini and in practice this work is usually left to the women. With a long cylindrical strainer (*intluzo*) in one hand held over a pot, a dish of beer is scooped up from the barrel with the other, and poured into the strainer. The strainer is shaken while the liquid pours through it into the pot, and then wrung vigorously in both hands to get as much liquid as possible out of the sediment. The sediment (*intsipho*) is then emptied onto a hessian bag lying on the floor, or into another pot, if there is one available. The *intsipho* constitutes roughly one quarter of the volume of the unstrained casks. It is kept for the making of *ivanya* and then fed to pigs and poultry. *Ivanya* is made some time later by pouring cold water onto the *intsipho* and leaving it overnight before straining again. The result is a rather insipid tasting liquid which is kept quite separate from the beer proper and never referred to as *utywala* or *umqombothi*, the proper words for beer, but always as *ivanya*, *ufaxo* (from *ukufaxa*—'to wring out') or sometimes somewhat disparagingly as 'water' (*amanzi*). At beer drinks the *ivanya* is not highly valued, as is indicated by the fact that it is allocated right at the end and mainly to young men, in contrast to the beer, which always goes primarily to seniors.

After straining, the beer proper is re-strained, to remove as much of the sediment as possible. When the straining is complete one beaker is drawn for the homestead head and other men to taste the beer, and one for women. The men's beer is called *umviwo*, an inspection, so that they may formally taste the beer and judge its quality. The women's beer is called *umhlalaphantsi* (a sitting down). Neighbouring women are called to be present for this beaker, so that they can tell the brewers how it tastes. Women also receive a beaker called *umcephe* (a spoon), sometimes in place of *umhlalaphantsi*, sometimes in addition to it. This name alludes to the frequent small dishes of beer that the women help themselves to during the straining, and it is used by both men and women in a sarcastic or tongue-in-cheek manner to indicate the surreptitious nature in which women drink while brewing which the men would like to (but cannot) control. In some cases, a quantity of beer called *intluzelo* is also given out on this day.

When the straining has been done and the *umhlalaphantsi* beaker consumed, the pots are washed, the hut tidied, and spilt beer mopped up with absorbent dry manure. When there is a lot of beer, however, the beer drink proper only starts the next day. The strained beer is kept in iron pots to keep it cool and prevent it from going sour, and is poured back into the plastic barrels before the beer drink commences. To prepare the main hut for the beer drink everything except the beer is taken out and placed in one of the other huts, unless the quantity brewed is very small and not many people are expected to attend. The mud floor is swept and may be given a fresh application of fresh cow-dung. Thatching grass (*Cympopogum Validus*) is cut and spread out over the floor, in addition to sleeping mats (*amakhuko*) for the guests to sit on. Neighbours may also assist with these tasks.

Appendix 2

Mbambaza's Addresses to Nowinile and Nosajini

To Nowinile:

All right, my sister-in-law

It is said that I should produce a few small words here for you

It is the usual thing to present words to a person who has been bereaved and is being received by other people

This thing is referred to as admonishing

Even though admonishing means nothing to people nowadays

A person [nowadays] simply ignores the admonitions and does what she likes

Here it is then sister-in-law

Today these Gcaleka here say they have come to fetch you

Seeing that you have been living like this, living abnormally

The time has come now for you to go amongst people again

When a person is to go amongst people she is given words of admonition

So that she should not do [bad] things, having been warned

So that it should not be said that that person was never admonished

But simply went out to beer drinks

And that she behaves as she does because of that

[Pause]

Now then, sister-in-law, we are here so that you should be taken out

Because of the departure of the great man of this home, your husband

I have every hope, sister-in-law, that you will conduct yourself correctly, nicely, as your husband did

Your husband [Walata's body] arrived here with strangers from across the Kei

People with whom he had lived and worked

There was no one who did not hear when they were speaking about this great man

Whom they had more knowledge of than we did

We too, however, knew him to be a person who was not evil

He was not a person who liked to quarrel with others

The only thing that Walatha opposed was something that was bad

I think that even your own ears were filled

When the visitors from across the Kei were talking

Although Walata was not born among them, they spoke about how good his character was

They asked that we too should talk about his life, about the way he lived here

We agreed with what they said, because the fellow [who spoke] said that Walata had a fine disposition while alive

It does not help to say 'I am rich in many things' if one's heart is impoverished

[If] the heart is not rich but impoverished, overgrown with weeds

Many livestock are of no use

Because a person cannot take them with him when he goes

The thing that you must guard against sister-in-law is this

Avoid the madness of beer drinks

[Avoid] a person who drinks and then becomes aggressive

Until finally it appears that you [too] are a troublesome person who wants to speak in a disreputable way

It will be said: 'We saw Walata's wife fighting

Oh! How soon she fights with people!

Since when does she fight with others?!'

Whereas it was not your will

It was that you were influenced by those who stir up trouble

Wanting you to tear holes in the admonitions you were given and to ignore them

There is only one way to look after yourself; through respect

It is to oppose any person who comes to you full of evil, wanting to turn your mind

[If not] it will seem that you are a person who has not been admonished

Today then, going out to attend beer drinks does not mean that you will not come back home

Because you [women] tend to say: 'As for me, I ate [killed] my husband'

A person even accuses herself and says:

'I ate my husband, I gave him poison to eat, I have no husband

There is no one who is going to drive me by the small of my back if I do not want to go home yet'

There is that tendency then with you [women]

As a person, the way to conduct yourself is to say

'There is the sun [it is late]

I must go now and kindle a fire in the hut for the children of the deceased'

The way to conduct yourself is [to ensure] that the people who were the people of this homestead in the past should be such even today

You see, daughter of Kedeni, it is like this

When it seems that this homestead is not seen [does not finish the sentence]

Let me say that it will not seem to be a homestead without its head if the wife is upright

It will become apparent if you divorce yourself from people

You will see the paths that lead here disappearing

They will disappear

One will pass behind the homestead

One will lead below the garden

There will be no path leading here

This will stigmatise you as a person who is no good amongst people

And it will be clear that a certain person [Walata] is not here

This is what is not wanted, sister-in-law

Avoid it, child of the Ngqosini clan

That behaviour that makes it clear that a certain person is not here

That will not make you a good person

You [will] have a homestead that is ho longer visited by many people

Whereas it used to be a homestead for people, this one of Mhlakaza's

It was loved when Walata was not present

When you were here in the hut doing things for people that used to be done by Walata

Do not stop doing such things

For if you do the paths that lead to this home will become scarce

Because paths are created by people

If the person inside the hut does not work for people

You will notice by the disappearance of the path

It will be said: 'So you think it is still as it was when so and so was still here, eh?

No, go away, there is nothing left!'

On the other hand if you remain as you are, as your husband used to be, no paths are going to disappear

Secondly, you will be well spoken of by people

It will be said: 'We know her, that Nowinile

She has never done anything disgraceful

It is so and so who has done something bad

Due to your knowledge of how to conduct yourself

Today, you are being allowed to go to beer drinks

It is not being said that you should wander about with people

It is not being said that you should go and sleep at beer drinks

And that there should be no smoke-spiral at this homestead of Mhlakaza's

There are many orphaned children here

Who have been left behind by Walata and who need to be raised

Some who are still small and some who are not yet completely grown up

That is what you have on your shoulders

The one plan then is to know how to conduct yourself in order to have strength

And to look after the things of this home properly

I have stopped now men.

To Nosajini:

...Referring to you Nosajini, the surprising thing is this

This [event] is a sad business

It is sad because it is sometimes said that when a person is being admonished...[interruption from others in the hut]

No men, no no no!

When a person is admonished it should not look as if the person who is speaking is talking nonsense

I do not talk nonsense

Allow me to say what I can, because of this beer here

Because we are frequently here against the wall of a hut

Standing in support of beer brewed for a person who is dead, often, often, often

Standing in support of beer for a man who is dead, often, often

Day after day we stand against the wall of a hut…[inaudible]

Speaking about this situation

We come to the wall of the hut

We speak about the beer for a man who is not here

Often!

What is surprising is that no man goes to the wall of a hut

To speak about a woman who is said to be absent and is being brewed for

[About] a woman who has died, to enable her husband to move about

I am standing so that I should start with this word

So that I can speak to the point!

In fact I will repeat it

We come to the wall of a hut

We come for a man who has died and been brewed for

Often

No woman has ever been brewed for

Let me leave that there[Pause]

You see then Nosajini, we are here now

We are here to take you out

So that you should go about amongst people

You have been here [secluded] for a long time

And now something else has happened[1]

It is not good for a person to stay [in mourning] for a long time

Because God will again knock and enter

Again do what he did before

While the person is still waiting

This will destroy a person's mind

You see Nosajini, the thing that preserves one is to think for oneself

What preserves one is thinking for oneself

You start by thinking, regardless of what happens

As soon as you think for yourself

Anyone who does anything to you will be shamed

If you do not first think for yourself, having been admonished

Bad things will come your way

If it is seen that you do not think for yourself

That you do not respect yourself

As someone who has been spoken to with words

By means of this very event

If you have thought for yourself you have looked after yourself

Because even if a person has been admonished by a thousand mouths

Much of that does not come to mind

And she does what she was warned against

That is exactly what she does

You see then, here is something that makes a fool out of people

This thing that we have come here for

That one, do you see it? [pointing at the beer pots]

It is no lie when it is said that that one is a devil

That man there at the back of the hut wipes out the admonitions

The admonitions do not work for a person who drinks beer

It is said now: 'Oh, what can be done, when someone carries on like this?'

When a person has passed Phungela's stone [i.e. gone beyond the point of no return]

She has overlooked the warnings that she was given

It is said that she has passed Phungela's stone[2]

Because she has passed by the admonitions of her father

The perversity of people

There are people who are like that

Who set out to destroy the admonitions

To make a person disregard them

Who will trouble you when they are drunk

Then you are seen talking, talking, talking

Provoking you, so that it be said that you have ignored your admonitions

With a person like you Nosajini, it is not necessary that we talk at length

You see I am thinking for you now, as I am standing here

If you cannot think for yourself and you cannot think carefully you will find out for yourself

You are a mature woman now

You already have daughters-in-law, so you need to be able to think for yourself

You are a solitary tree, you are a tree that stands by itself

Do not associate yourself with things said by people

You will be provoked in order to disregard these admonitions

Because there are annoying people who tend to negate [the admonitions]

It is continually being written and rubbed out

It is written and rubbed out

They are like Satan

God puts a person here and Satan takes him and puts him there

There are people who are like that

Think for yourself

Here then chiefs and also you women

This beer has been made to enable this woman to go about

And for this young wife of Gidimisana [Nosajini's son]

The reason why Gidimisana's wife has not smeared herself [with red ochre] is that she is not this woman's husband's sister

So they have not both smeared

She too is being released today, she is, and she will ochre herself tomorrow

She is released today but they have not both smeared because her husband is not departed

She still has a husband

The words from my mouth are finished now

Perhaps some other man wants to say something.

Endnotes

1. This was a reference, not to the death of Nosajini's grandchild, but to the fact that one of her Sons had taken ill at work and had returned to seek the help of a healer in another part of the district.

2. 'Phungela's stone' is a well known figure of speech. It refers to a (presumably imaginary) person by the name of Phungela who lived near the Kei river and helped people to cross it. It was safe to cross when a stone in the water was exposed, dangerous when the stone was submerged. The proverb *ukutsiba ilitye likaPhungela* ("to go beyond Phungela's stone") means to have reached the point of no return, to have become incorrigible and beyond help. "A person who goes beyond Phungela's stone is one who is mad, one who enters danger" (Mesatywa 1971, 153).

References

Adler, Marianna. 1991. From symbolic exchange to commodity consumption: anthropological notes on drinking as a symbolic practice. In *Drinking: Behavior and belief in modern history*, edited by Susanna Barrows and Robin Room, 376–98. Berkeley: University of California Press.

Ainslie, Andrew. 2005. Farming cattle, cultivating relationships: Cattle ownership and cultural politics in Peddie district, Eastern Cape. Social Dynamics 31(1) (in press).

Alberti, Ludwig. 1969. *Ludwig Alberti's account of the tribal life and customs of the Xhosa in 1807.* Trans. William Fehr. Cape Town: Balkema.

Ambler, Charles. 1987. *Alcohol and disorder in precolonial Africa.* Working Papers in African Studies No 126. Boston: African Studies Center, Boston University.

———. 1991. Drunks, brewers, and chiefs: Alcohol regulation in colonial Kenya. In *Drinking: Behavior and belief in modern history*, edited by Susanna Barrows and Robin Room, 165–83. Berkeley: University of California Press.

Andrew, Maura. 1992. A geographical study of agricultural change since the 1930s in Shixini location, Gatyana district, Transkei. M. A. Thesis. Grahamstown: Rhodes University.

Appadurai, Arjun. 1986. Introduction: Commodities and the politics of value. In *The social life of things: Commodities in cultural perspective*, edited by Arjun Appadurai, 3–63. Cambridge: Cambridge University Press.

ARDRI. 1989. Lima development report. Alice: Agriculture and Rural Development Research Institute, University of Fort Hare.

Ashton, Hugh. 1952. *The Basuto.* London: Oxford: Oxford University Press.

Austin, John L. 1962. *How to do things with words.* Oxford: Clarendon Press.

Bank, Leslie J. 2005. Of family farms and commodity groups: Rural livelihoods, households and development policy in the Eastern Cape. Social Dynamics 31(1) (in press).

Bateson, Gregory. 1973. *Steps to an ecology of mind.* St Albans, Herts.: Granada.

Bauman, Richard. 1975. Verbal art as performance. American Anthropologist 77 (2): 290–311.

_____ 1992. Performance. In *Folklore, cultural performances, and popular entertainments: A communications - centered handbook*, edited by Richard Bauman, 41–49. New York: Oxford University Press.

Beinart, William. 1982. *The political economy of Pondoland 1860 to 1930.* Cambridge: Cambridge University Press.

_____ 1992. Transkeian smallholders and agrarian reform. Journal of Contemporary African Studies 11 (2): 178–99.

_____ and Bundy, Colin. 1980. State intervention in rural resistance: The Transkei 1900-1965. In *Peasants in Africa: historical and contemporary perspectives*, edited by M. A. Klein, 271–316. Beverly Hills: Sage Publications.

_____ and Bundy, Colin. 1987. *Hidden struggles in rural South Africa.* London: James Currey.

Bell, Catherine. 1992. *Ritual theory, ritual practice.* New York/Oxford: Oxford University Press.

_____ 1997. *Ritual: perspectives and dimensions.* New York/Oxford: Oxford University Press.

_____ 1998. Performance. In *Critical terms for religious studies*, edited by M. C. Taylor, 205–24. Chicago and London: University of Chicago Press.

Benyon, J. A. 1974. The process of political incorporation. In *The Bantu-speaking peoples of southern Africa*, edited by W. David Hammond-Tooke, 367–96. London: Routledge and Kegan Paul.

Berglund, Axel-Ivar. 1976. *Zulu thought-patterns and symbolism.* London: Hurst.

Bernstein, Basil. 1964. Aspects of language and learning in the genesis of the social process. In *Language in culture and society*, edited by Dell Hymes, 251–63. New York: Harper International.

_____ 1972. A sociolinguistic approach to socialization, with some reference to educability. In *Directions in sociolinguistics: The ethnography of communication*, edited by John J. Gumperz and Dell Hymes, 465–97. New York: Holt.

Bigalke, Eric H. 1969. The religious systems of the Ndlambe of East London district. M.A. Thesis. Rhodes University: Grahamstown.

Bird, John. 1885. *The annals of Natal 1495–1845.* Vol. I and II. Cape Town: Maskew Miller.

Bloch, Maurice. 1974. Symbols, song, dance and features of articulation: Is religion an extreme form of traditional authority? European Journal of Sociology XV: 55–79.

_____ 1975. Introduction. *Political language and oratory in traditional societies*, edited by Maurice Bloch, 1-28. London: Academic Press.

Bosko, Dan. 1981. Why Basotho wear blankets. African Studies 40.

Bourdieu, Pierre. 1977. *Outline of a theory of practice*. Trans. Richard Nice. Cambridge: Cambridge University Press.

_____ 1979. *Algeria 1960*. Trans. Richard Nice. Cambridge: Cambridge University Press.

_____ 1990. *The logic of practice*. Trans. Richard Nice. Stanford: Stanford University Press.

_____ 1990a. *In other words: Essays towards a reflexive sociology*. Trans. Matthew Adamson. Stanford, California: Stanford University Press.

_____ 1991. *Language and symbolic power*. Trans. Gino Raymond and Matthew Adamson. Cambridge: Harvard University Press.

_____ 1998. *Practical reason: On the theory of action*. Stanford: Stanford University Press.

_____ 2001. *Masculine domination*. Trans. Richard Nice. Stanford: Stanford University Press.

_____ 2002. Habitus. In *Habitus: A sense of place*, edited by Jean Hillier and Emma Rooksby, 27-34. Aldershot: Ashgate.

Bourdillon, Michael F. 1978. Knowing the world or hiding it: a response to Maurice Bloch. Man (n.s.) 13. 591–99.

Bouveresse, Jaques. 1999. Rules, dispositions and the habitus. In *Bourdieu: A critical reader*, edited by Richard Shusterman, 45–63. Oxford: Blackwell.

Brison, Karen. 2001. Constructing identity through ceremonial language in rural Fiji. Ethnology 40 (4): 309–27.

Broster, Joan. 1976. *The Thembu: their beadwork, songs and dances*. Cape Town: Purnell.

Brown, Gavin. 2003. Theorizing ritual as performance: explorations of ritual indeterminacy. Journal of Ritual Studies, 17 (1): 3–18.

Brownlee, John. 1827. Account of the Amakosae, or southern Caffers. In *Travels and adventures in southern Africa*, 2 vols, by G. Thompson, 191–219. London: Henry Colburn.

Bruner, Edward M. 1986. Experience and its expressions. In *The anthropology of experience*, edited by Victor W. Turner and Edward M. Bruner, 3–32. Urbana and Chicago: University of Illinois Press.

Bryant, A. T. 1949. *The Zulu people as they were before the white man came.* Pietermaritzburg: Shuter and Shooter.

Bryceson, Deborah, ed. 2002. *Alcohol in Africa.* Portsmouth NH: Heinemann.

Bud-Mbelle, I. 1926. Transvaal liquor laws. Mr Yeast, Mrs Sikokiaan and co. South African Outlook, LVI, No 661.

Burchmore, Angela. 1988. The soils and vegetation of Shixini administrative area: toward a land use plan. B. A. Hons. thesis. Grahamstown: Rhodes University.

Burke, Kenneth. 1969. *A rhetoric of motives.* Berkeley and Los Angeles: University of California Press.

Cape of Good Hope. 1883. Report and proceedings with appendices of the Government commission on native laws and customs. Vol I and II. Cape of Good Hope: Blue Book, No G4.

Cohen, Abner 1993. *Masquerade politics: explorations in the structure of urban cultural movements.* Berkeley/Los Angeles: University of California Press.

Colson, Elizabeth and Scudder, Thayer. 1988. *For prayer and profit: The ritual, economic, and social importance of beer in Gwembe district, Zambia, 1950–1982.* Stanford: Stanford University Press.

Comaroff, John L. 1975. Talking politics: oratory and authority in a Tswana chiefdom. In *Political language and oratory in traditional societies*, edited by Maurice Bloch, 141–61. London: Academic Press.

Cook, P. A. W. 1931. *Social organisation and ceremonial institutions of the Bomvana.* Cape Town: Juta and Co.

Counihan, Carole. 1997. Bread as world: Food habits and social relations in modernizing Sardinia. In *Food and culture: A reader*, edited by Carole Counihan and Penny van Esterik, 283–95. New York and London: Routledge.

Cowan, Jane. 1990. *Dance and the body politic in northern Greece.* Princeton, N.J. : Princeton University Press.

Crais, Clifton. 1985. Wool, war and workers: Gentry and the oppressed in three districts 1820-1868. Unpublished mimeo. Grahamstown: Institute of Social and Economic Research, Rhodes University.

Crowley, Terry. 1995. The national drink and the national language in Vanuatu. Journal of the Polynesian Society 104 (1): 7–22.

(DNA) Department of Native Affairs, Blue Book on Native Affairs: 1883, 1884, 1886, 1887, 1904.

Davies, C. S. 1927. Customs governing beer drinking among the Ama-Bomvana. South African Journal of Science 24: 521–24.

Davison, Patricia. 1988. The social use of space in a Mpondo homestead. South African Archaeological Bulletin 43: 100–8.

DeBernardi, Jean. 1994. Social aspects of language use. In *Companion encyclopaedia of anthropology*, edited by Tim Ingold, 861-890. London: Routledge.

De Certeau, Michel, Girard, Luce and Mayal, Pierre. 1998. *The practice of everyday life*. Minneapolis/London: University of Minnesota Press.

De Haas, Mary. 1986. Sorghum beer in southern Africa: Continuity and change. Unpublished mimeo. Tetra Pak: Durban.

De Wet, Christopher J. 1989. Betterment planning in a rural village in Keiskammahoek. Journal of Southern African Studies 15 (2): 326–45.

Dietler, Michael. 2001. Theorising the feast: Rituals of consumption, commensal politics and power in African contexts. In *Feasts: Archaeological and ethnographic perspectives*, edited by Michael Dietler and Brian Hayden, 65–114. Washington and London: Smithsonian Institution Press.

Doke, Clement M. 1931. *The Lambas of Northern Rhodesia*. London: George Harrap.

Doke, Celement M., and Vilakazi, B. W. 1948. *Zulu-English dictionary*. (2nd edition 1972). Johannesburg: Witwatersrand University Press.

Donham, Don L. 1985. *Work and power in Maale, Ethiopia*. Ann Arbor: UMI Research Press.

Douglas, Mary. 1966. *Purity and danger*. London, Routledge and Kegan Paul.

_____ 1972. Deciphering a meal. In *Implicit meanings* by Mary Douglas, 249–75. Routledge and Kegan Paul.

_____ 1987. A distinctive anthropological approach. In *Constructive drinking: Perspectives on drink from anthropology*, edited by Mary Douglas, 3-15. Cambridge: Cambridge University Press.

Drewal, Margaret. 1991. The state of research on performance in Africa. African Studies Review 34 (3): 1–64.

Erlmann, Veit. 1992. The past is far and the future is far: Power and performance among Zulu migrant workers. American Ethnologist 19 (4): 688–709.

Evans-Pritchard, E. E. 1956. *Nuer religion*. Oxford: Clarendon Press.

Fabian, Johannes. 1990. *Power and performance*. Madison: University of Wisconsin Press.

Ferguson, James. 1999. *Expectations of modernity*. University of California Press.

Fernandez, James. 1986. *Persuasions and performances: The play of tropes in culture*. Bloomington: Indian University Press.

Feuchtwang, Stephan.1993. Historical metaphor: A study of religious representation and the recognition of authority. Man 28 (1): 35–49.

Firth, Raymond. 1975. Speech making and authority in Tikopia. In *Political language and oratory in traditional society*, edited by Maurice Bloch, 29–43. London: Academic Press.

Fox, F. W. 1938. Preparation, composition and nutritional value of certain Kafir beers. Journal of the South African Chemical Institute 21.

Frake, Charles. O. 1972. How to ask for a drink in Subanum. In *Language and social context*, edited. by P. Giglioli, 87-94. London: Penguin.

Gardiner, A. F. 1836. *Narrative of a journey to the Zooloo country in South Africa*. London: Crofts.

Geertz, Clifford. 1966. Religion as a cultural system. In *Anthropological approaches to the study of religion*, edited by Michael Banton, 1-46. London: Tavistock.

Gelfand, Michael. 1959. *Shona ritual*. Cape Town: Juta.

Gellner, David N. 1999. Religion, politics and ritual: remarks on Geertz and Bloch. Social Anthropology, 7 (2): 135–53.

Geschiere, Peter. 1995. Working groups or wage labor? Cash-crops, reciprocity and money among the Maka of southeastern Cameroon. Development and Change 26: 503–23.

_____ 1997. *The modernity of witchcraft: Politics and the occult in postcolonial Africa*. Charlottesville and London: University Press of Virginia.

Giddens, Anthony. 1984. *The constitution of society*. Cambridge: Cambridge University Press.

Goody, Jack. 1961. Religion and ritual: the definitional problem. British Journal of Sociology 12: 142–64.

Goody, Jack. 1982. *Cooking, cuisine and class: A study in comparative sociology*. Cambridge: Cambridge University Press.

Gulliver, Philip. 1971. *Neighbours and networks*. University of California Press.

Hagaman, Barbara L. 1980. Food for thought: Beer in a social and ritual context in a West African society. Journal of Drug Issues 10: 203–14.

Hammond-Tooke, W. David. 1962. *Bhaca society*. Cape Town: Oxford University Press.

_____ 1963. Kinship, neighbourhood and association: hospitality groups among the Cape Nguni. Ethnology 2 (3): 302–19.

_____ 1970. The Cape Nguni witch familiar as a mediatory construct. Man 9 (1): 128–36.

_____ 1974. World view 1: a system of beliefs. In *The Bantu-speaking peoples of southern Africa*, edited by W. David Hammond-Tooke, 318–43. London: Routledge and Kegan Paul.

_____ 1975. *Command or consensus*. Cape Town: David Philip.

_____ 1981. *Boundaries and belief: The structure of a Sotho world view*. Johannesburg: Witwatersrand University Press.

_____ 1984. In search of the lineage: the Cape Nguni case. Man 19(1): 77–93.

Handelman, Don. 1990. *Models and mirrors: towards an anthropology of public events*. Cambridge University Press.

Harries, Patrick. 1982. Kinship, ideology and the nature of pre-colonial labour migration. In *Industrialization and social change in South Africa*, edited by Shula Marks and R. Rathbone, 142–66. London: Longman.

Harrison, B. 1971. *Drink and the Victorians*, University of Pittsburgh Press.

Heath, Dwight B. 1987. A decade of development in the anthropological study of alcohol use: 1970-1980. In *Constructive drinking: perspectives on drink from anthropology*, edited by Mary Douglas, 16–69. Cambridge: Cambridge University Press.

_____ 1987a. Anthropology and alcohol studies: current issues. Annual Review of Anthropology 27: 99–120.

_____ 2000. *Drinking occasions: Comparative perspectives on alcohol and culture*. Philadelphia : Brunner/Mazel.

Hellman, Ellen. 1934. The importance of beer-brewing in an urban native yard. Bantu Studies 8: 39–60.

Heron, Gavin. 1990. Household, production and the organization of co-operative labour in Shixini, Transkei. M. A. thesis. Grahamstown: Rhodes University.

Heron, Gavin and Cloete, Laura. 1991. *Household survival strategies in Shixini,Transkei*. Pretoria: HSRC.

Hertz, Robert. 1960. *Death and the right hand*. Trans. Rodney and Claudia Needham. London: Cohen and West.

Hoem, Ingrid. 1998. Clowns, dignity and desire: On the relationship between performance, identity and reflexivity. In *Recasting ritual: Performance, media, identity*, edited by F. Hughes-Freeland and M. Crain, 21–43. London: Routledge.

Holtzman, Jon. 2001. The food of elders, the 'ration' of women: Brewing, gender and domestic processes among the Samburu of northern Kenya. American Anthropologist 103 (4): 1041–58.

Holy, Ladislav. 1977. Toka ploughing teams: towards a decision model of social recruitment. In *Goals and behaviour*, edited by M. Stuchlik. The Queens University papers in social anthropology, 2. Belfast: Queens University.

Huffman, Thomas N. 1982. Archaeology and ethnohistory of the African iron age. Annual Review of Anthropology 11: 280–98.

Humphrey, Caroline and Laidlaw, James. 1994. *The archetypal actions of ritual*. Oxford: Clarendon Press/New York: Oxford University Press.

Hunter, Monica. 1936. *Reaction to conquest*. London: Oxford University Press.

Hymes, Dell. 1962. The ethnography of speaking. In *Anthropology and human behaviour*, edited by T. Gladwin and W. C. Sturtevant, 13–52. Washington: The Anthropological Society of Washington.

_____ 1972. Models of the interaction of language and social life. In *Directions in sociolinguistics: The ethnography* of *communication*, edited by John J. Gumperz and Dell Hymes, 35–71. New York: Holt.

James, Wendy R. 1972. Beer, morality, and social relations among the Uduk. Sudan Society 5.

Jenkins, Robert. 1992. *Pierre Bourdieu*. London and New York: Routledge.

Junod, Henri A. 1927. *The life of a South African tribe*. (2nd. edn). Vols I and II. London: Macmillan.

Junod, Henri P. and Jaques, Alexandre A. 1957. *The wisdom of the Tsonga Shangana people*. Johannesburg: The Swiss Mission in South Africa.

Kapferer, Bruce. 1986. Performance and the structuring of meaning and experience. In *The anthropology of experience*, edited by Victor W. Turner and Edward M. Bruner, 188–203. Urbana and Chicago: University of Illinois Press.

―――― 1996. Preface to the 1996 edition. In Victor W. Turner, *Schism and continuity in an African society*, pp. vii–xix. Oxford ; Washington, D.C.: Berg.

Karp, Ivan. 1980. Beer drinking and social experience in an African society. In *Explorations in African systems of thought*, edited by Ivan Karp and Charles S. Bird, 83-119. Indiana: Indiana University Press.

Katz Solomon H., ed. 2003. *Encyclopedia of food and culture*. Vol 1. New York: Charles Scribner's Sons.

Kay, Stephen. 1833. *Travels and researches in Caffraria*. London: John Mason.

Kelly, John D., and Kaplan, Martha. 1990. History, structure and ritual. Annual Review of Anthropology 19: 119–50.

Keesing, Roger M. 1979. Linguistic knowledge and cultural knowledge: Some doubts and speculations. American Anthropologist 81 (1): 14–36.

Kopytoff, I. 1986. The cultural biography of things: Commoditization as process. In *The social life of things: Commodities in cultural perspective*, edited by A. Appadurai, 64–91.Cambridge: Cambridge University Press.

Krige, Eileen J. 1932. The social significance of beer among the baLobedu. Bantu Studies, 6: 343–57.

―――― 1936. *The social system of the Zulus*. London: Longmans.

―――― and Krige, Jack D. 1943. *The realm of a rain-queen*. London: International African Institute.

Kropf, Albert. 1915. *A Kafir-English dictionary*, 2 edition, edited by Robert Godfrey. Alice, Cape Province: Lovedale Press.

Kuckertz, Heinz. 1983–1984. Symbol and authority in Mpondo ancestor religion. African Studies, 42 (2): 113–33 and 43 (1): 1–17.

―――― 1984. Authority structure and homestead in a Mpondo village. PhD Thesis. Johannesburg: University of the Witwatersrand.

―――― 1985. Organizing labor forces in Pondoland: A new perspective on work-parties. Africa 55: 115–31.

―――― 1990. *Creating order: The image of the homestead in Mpondo social life*. Johannesburg: Witwatersrand University Press.

_____ 1997. Ukuhlonipha as an idiom of moral reasoning in Mpondo. In *Culture and the commonplace*, edited by Patrick McAllister, 311–48. Johannesburg: Witwatersrand University Press.

Kuper, Adam. 1982. *Wives for cattle: bridewealth and marriage in southern Africa*. London: Routledge and Kegan Paul.

_____ 1993. The 'house' and Zulu political structure in the nineteenth century. Journal of African History 34 (3): 469–87.

Kuper, Hilda. 1947. *An African aristocracy*. London: Oxford University Press.

LeCount, Lisa J. 2001. Like water for chocolate: feasting and political ritual among the late classic Maya at Xunatunich, Belize. American Anthropologist 103 (4): 935–53.

Lentz, Carola. 1999. Introduction - Changing food habits. In *Changing food habits: case studies from Africa, South America and Europe*, edited by Carola Lentz, 1–25. Amsterdam: Harwood Academic Publishers.

Lewis, Jack. 1985. Rural contradictions and class consciousness: Migrant labour in historical perspective in the Ciskei in the 1880s and 1890s. Mimeo. Cape Town: Centre for African Studies, University of Cape Town.

Liebenberg, Alida. 1997. Dealing with relations of inequality: Married women in a Transkei village. In *Culture and the commonplace*, edited by Patrick McAllister, 349–74. Johannesburg: Witwatersrand University Press.

Lincoln, Bruce. 1989. Banquets and brawls: aspects of ceremonial meals. In *Discourse and the construction of society* by Bruce Lincoln, 75–88. New York: Oxford University Press.

Long, Una, ed. 1949. *The chronicle of Jeremiah Goldswain*. Vol. II. Cape Town: Van Riebeeck Society.

Mach, Zadislaw. 1992. Continuity and change in political ritual: May Day in Poland. In *Revitalizing European rituals*, edited by Jeremy Boissevain, 43–61. London: Routledge.

Mandelbaum, David G. 1979. Alcohol and culture. In *Beliefs, behaviours and alcoholic beverages: A cross-cultural survey*, edited by Mac Marshall, 14–30. Ann Arbor: University of Michigan Press.

Marks, Shula and Atmore, A. 1980. Introduction. In *Economy and society in pre-industrial South Africa*, edited by Shula Marks and A. Atmore, 1–33. London: Longman.

Marwick, B A. 1940. *The Swazi*. London: Cambridge University Press.

Mauss, Marcel. 1925. *The Gift*. Trans. Ian Cunnison. London: Cohen and West.

_____ 1979. The notion of body techniques. In *Sociology and psychology: Essays*, by Marcel Mauss, 97-105. Trans. Ben Brewster. London/ Boston/ Henley: Routledge and Kegan Paul.

Mayer, Philip. 1961. *Townsmen or tribesmen*. Cape Town: Oxford University Press.

_____ 1980. The origin and decline of two rural resistance ideologies. In *Black villagers in an industrial society*, edited by Philip Mayer, 1-80. Cape Town: Oxford University Press.

_____ and Mayer, Iona. 1970. Socialization by peers: The youth organisation of the Red Xhosa. In *Socialization: The approach from social anthropology*, edited by Philip Mayer, 109–26. London: Tavistock.

MacAloon, John J. 1984. Introduction: cultural performances, culture theory. In *Rite, drama, festival, spectacle: Rehearsals towards a theory of cultural performance*, edited by John J. MacAloon, 1–15. Philadelphia; Institute for the Study of Human Issues.

McAllister, Patrick A. 1979. The rituals of labour migration among the Gcaleka. M.A.thesis. Grahamstown: Rhodes University.

_____ 1980. Work, homestead and the shades: The ritual interpretation of labour migration among the Gcaleka. In *Black villagers in an industrial society*, edited by Philip Mayer, 205–54. Cape Town: Oxford University Press.

_____ 1981. *Umsindleko: A Gcaleka ritual* of *incorporation*. Grahamstown: Institute of Social and Economic Research.

_____ 1985. Beasts to beer pots: Migrant labour and ritual change in Willowvale district, Transkei. African Studies 44 (2): 121–35.

_____ 1986. Releasing the widow: Xhosa beer drink oratory and status change. African Studies 45 (2): 171–97.

_____ 1989. Resistance to 'Betterment' in the Transkei: A case study from Willowvale district. Journal of Southern African Studies 15: 346–68.

_____ 1993. Indigenous beer in southern Africa: Functions and fluctuations. African Studies 52(1): 71-88.

_____ 1993a. Public oratory in Xhosa ritual: Tradition and change. Ethnology 32 (1): 291–304.

_____ 1994. The Elwandle development research project: Finding alternatives to 'betterment planning' in rural South Africa. In *Case studies in research with a view to implementation*, edited by D. J. Gouws, 114–34. Pretoria: HSRC.

_____ 1997. Ritual and social practice in the Transkei. In *Culture and the commonplace*, edited by Patrick McAllister, 279-310. Johannesburg: Witwatersrand University Press.

_____ 2001. *Building the homestead: Agriculture, labour and beer in South Africa's Transkei*. Aldershot: Ashgate.

_____ 2003. Labor and beer in the Transkei, South Africa: Xhosa work parties in historical and contemporary perspective. Human Organization 63 (1): 100–11.

_____ 2003a. Culture, practice and the semantics of Xhosa beer drinking. Ethnology, 42 (3): 187–207.

_____ 2004. Domestic space, habitus and the practice of Xhosa ritual beer drinking. Ethnology, 43(1): 117–35.

_____ and Deliwe, Dumisane. 1993. Youth in rural Transkei: The demise of 'traditional' youth associations and the development of new forms of association and activity, 1975-1993. Working Paper 61. Grahamstown: Institute of Social and Economic Research, Rhodes University.

Meigs, Anna. 1997. Food as a cultural construction. In *Food and culture: A reader*, edited by Carole Counihan and Penny van Esterik, 95–106. New York and London: Routledge.

Meillassoux, Claude. 1972. From reproduction to production: a Marxist approach to social anthropology. Economy and Society 1(1): 93–105.

_____ 1973. The social organisation of the peasantry. The economic basis of kinship. Journal of Peasant Studies 1(1): 81–90.

Mesatywa, E.W.M. 1954. *Izaci namaqhalo esiXhosa*. Cape Town: Longman.

Moeran, Brian. 1998. One over the seven: Sake drinking in a Japanese pottery community. In *Interpreting Japanese society: Anthropological approaches*, edited by Joy Hendry, 243–58. London and New York, Routledge.

Monnig, H. O. 1967. *The Pedi*. Pretoria: Van Schaik.

Moore, Henrietta. 1986. *Space, text and gender*. New York/London: The Guilford Press.

Moore, M. P. 1975. Co-operative labor in peasant agriculture. Journal of Peasant Studies 1: 270–91.

Netting, Robert McC. 1964. Beer as locus of value among the West African Kofyar. American Anthropologist 66 (2): 375–84.

Niehaus, Isaac. 2001. *Witchcraft, power and politics: Exploring the occult in the South African lowveld.* Pluto Press.

Nyembezi C. L. 1954. *Zulu proverbs.* Johannesburg: Witwatersrand University Press.

O'Laughlin, Bridget. 1973. Mbum beer parties: structures of production and exchange in an African social formation. PhD thesis. Yale University.

Opland, Jeff. 1998. *Xhosa poets and poetry.* Cape Town: David Philip.

Ortner, Sherry. 1984. Theory in anthropology since the sixties. Comparative Studies in Society and History, 26 (1): 126–66.

_____ 1989. *High religion: a cultural and political history of Sherpa Buddhism.* Princeton: Princeton University Press.

Palmer, Robin; Timmermans, Herman and Fay, Derick. 2002. *From conflict to resolution: Nature-based development on South Africa's Wild Coast.* Pretoria, HSRC Publishers.

Painter, Thomas M. 1986. Spontaneous co-operation, introduced co-operation and agricultural development in south-western Niger. In *Anthropology and rural development in West Africa,* edited by Michael M. Horowitz and Thomas M. Painter. Boulder and London: Westview.

Pauw, Berthold A. 1975. *Christianity and Xhosa tradition.* Cape Town: Oxford University Press.

Peires, Jeff B. 1976. A history of the Xhosa. M. A. thesis. Grahamstown: Rhodes University.

_____ 1981. *The house of Phalo.* Johannesburg: Ravan Press.

_____ 1989. *The dead will arise.* Johannesburg: Ravan Press.

Porter, Gina and Phillips-Howard, Kevin D. 1997. Agricultural issues in the former homelands of South Africa: the Transkei. Review of African Political Economy 24 (72): 185–202.

Rappaport, Roy. 1999. *Ritual and religion in the making of humanity.* Cambridge: Cambridge University Press.

Reader, Desmond H. 1966. *Zulu tribe in transition.* Manchester: Manchester University Press.

Rehfisch, Farnham. 1987. Competitive beer drinking among the Mambila. In *Constructive drinking: Perspectives on drink from anthropology,* edited by Mary Douglas, 135–46. Cambridge: Cambridge University Press.

Richards, Audrey I. 1939. *Land, labour and diet in Northern Rhodesia.* London: International African Institute.

Sahlins, Marshall. 1985. *Islands of history*. Chicago and London: University of Chicago Press.

Sangree, Walter H. 1962. The social functions of beer drinking in Bantu Tiriki. In *Society, culture and drinking patterns*, edited by D. J. Pittman and C. R. Snyder, 6–21. New York: John Wiley and Sons.

Sansom, Basil. 1974. Traditional economic systems. In *The Bantu-speaking peoples of southern Africa*, edited by W. David Hammond-Tooke, 135–76. London: Routledge and Kegan Paul.

Saul, Mahir. 1981. Beer, sorghum and women: Production for the market in rural upper Volta. Africa 51: 746–64.

Saville-Troike, Muriel. 1982. *The Ethnography of communication: An introduction*. Oxford: Blackwell.

Sax, William S. 2002. *Dancing the self*. New York: Oxford University Press.

Schapera, Isaac and Goodwin, A. J. H. 1937. Work and wealth. In *The Bantu-speaking tribes of South Africa*, edited by Isaac Schapera, 131–71. Cape Town: Maskew Miller.

Schechner, Richard. 1986. Victor Turner's last adventure. In *The anthropology of performance*, by Victor Turner, 7–20. New York: PAJ Publications.

———— 2002. Performance studies in/for the 21st century. Anthropology and Humanism 26 (2): 158–66.

Schein, Louisa. 1999. Performing modernity. Cultural Anthropology 14 (3): 361–95.

Schieffelin, Edward. 1985. Performance and the cultural construction of reality. American Ethnologist 12(4): 707–24.

———— 1998. Problematizing performance. In *Ritual, performance, media*, edited by F. Hughes-Freeland, 194–207. London: Routledge.

Scott, James C. 1990. *Domination and the arts of resistance*. New Haven and London: Yale University Press.

Searle, John R. 1979. A taxonomy of illocutionary acts. In *Expression and meaning: studies in the theory of speech acts*, edited by John Searle, 1–29. Cambridge, Eng.; New York: Cambridge University Press.

Shaw, Margaret. 1974. Material culture. In *The Bantu-speaking peoples of southern Africa*, edited by W. David Hammond-Tooke, 85–134. London: Routledge and Kegan Paul.

———— and van Warmelo, N. J. 1981. The material culture of the Cape Nguni. Part 3. Annals of the South African Museum 58 (3): 216–445.

Simon, Christian. 1989. Dealing with distress: a medical anthropological analysis of the search for health in a rural Transkeian village. M. A. Thesis. Grahamstown: Rhodes University.

Singer, Milton. 1972. *When a great tradition modernizes.* New York: Praeger.

Snook, Ivan. 1990. Language, truth and power: Bourdieu's *Ministerium.* In *An introduction to the work of Pierre Bourdieu: The practice of theory,* edited by Richard Harker, Cheleen Mahar and Chris Wilkes, 160–79. New York: St. Martin's Press.

Soga, John H. 1931. *The Ama-Xhosa: life and customs.* Alice, Cape Province: Lovedale Press.

South Africa. 1905. South African Native Affairs Commission, Report and Minutes of Evidence. Vols I-V. Cape Town: Government Printer.

Spiegel, Andrew. 1980. Rural differentiation and the diffusion of migrant labour remittances in Lesotho. In *Black villagers in an industrial society,* edited by Philip Mayer, 109–69. Cape Town: Oxford University Press.

Strathern, Andrew and Stewart, Pamela. 1998. Embodiment and communication: Two frames for the analysis of ritual. Social Anthropology 6 (2): 237–52.

Swartz, David. 1997. *Culture and power: The sociology of Pierre Bourdieu.* Chicago and London: University of Chicago Press.

Swindell, Ken. 1985. *Farm labor.* Cambridge: Cambridge University Press.

Tambiah, Stanley J. 1985. *Culture, thought, and social action: an anthropological perspective.* Cambridge, Mass.: Harvard University Press.

Taylor, Charles. 1999. To follow a rule…In *Bourdieu: A critical reader,* edited by Richard Shusterman, 29–44. Oxford: Blackwell.

Theal, George McCall. 1898. *Records of south-eastern Africa.* Vols I - IX. Cape Town: Government of the Cape Colony.

Thompson. John B. 1991. Editor's introduction. In *Language and symbolic power,* by Pierre Bourdieu. Trans. Gino Raymond and Matthew Adamson. Cambridge: Harvard University Press.

Tomlinson, Matt. 2004. Perpetual lament: Kava drinking, Christianity and sensations of historical decline in Fiji. Journal of the Royal Anthropological Institute 10 (3): 653–73.

Turner, J. W. 1992. Ritual, habitus and hierarchy in Fiji. Ethnology 31 (4): 291–302.

Turner, Victor W. 1957. *Schism and continuity in an African society.* Manchester: Manchester University Press.

_____ 1967. *The forest of symbols: Aspects of Ndembu ritual.* Itacha, New York: Cornell University Press.

_____ 1968. Mukanda: The politics of a non-political ritual. In *Local level politics,* edited by Marc J. Swartz, 135-150. Chicago: Aldine.

_____ 1969. *The ritual process.* Chicago: Aldine Publishing Company.

_____ 1974. *Dramas, fields and metaphors.* Ithaca: Cornell University Press.

_____ 1982. *From ritual to theatre: The human seriousness of play.* New York: PAJ Publications.

_____ 1984. Liminality and the performative genres. In *Rite, drama, festival, spectacle: Rehearsals towards a theory of cultural performance,* edited by J. J. MacAloon, 19-41. Philadelphia; Institute for the Study of Human Issues.

_____ 1986. *The anthropology of performance.* New York: PAJ Publications.

_____ 1986a. Dewey, Dilthey, and drama: an essay in the anthropology of experience. In *The anthropology of experience,* edited by Victor W. Turner and Edward M. Bruner, 33–44. Urbana and Chicago: University of Illinois Press.

_____ 1990. Are there universals of performance in myth, ritual, and drama? In *By means of performance,* edited by Richard Schechner and W. Appel, 8-18. Cambridge: Cambridge University Press.

Tyler, Rev. J. 1891. *Forty years among the Zulus.* Boston: Congregational Sunday-School and Publishing Society.

UTTGC. United Transkeian Territories General Council, Proceedings and Reports: 1912, 1914, 1916, 1918, 1927, 1928, 1945, 1955.

Van der Drift, Roy. 2002. Democracy's heady brew: cashew wine and the authority of the elders among the Balanta in Guinea-Bissau. In *Alcohol in Africa: Mixing business, pleasure and politics,* edited by Deborah Bryceson, 179–96. Heineman, Portsmouth (New Hampshire).

Van der Kemp, Johannes T. 1804. An account of the religion, customs...of Caffraria. Transactions of the London Missionary Society 1: 349–505.

Van Gennep, Arnold. 1960. *The rites of passage.* Chicago: University of Chicago Press.

Vilakazi, Absolom. 1962. *Zulu transformations.* Pietermaritzburg: University of Natal Press.

Werbner, Richard. 1977. The argument in and about oratory. African Studies, 36.

Wilson, Monica. 1957. *Rituals of kinship among the Nyakyusa.* Oxford: International African Institute.

_____ 1969. The Nguni people. In *The Oxford history of South Africa,* Vol. 1, edited by Monica Wilson and Leonard Thompson, 116–30. London: Oxford University Press.

_____ 1971. The growth of peasant communities. In *The Oxford history of South Africa,* Vol 2, edited by Monica Wilson and Leonard Thompson, 49–130. London: Oxford University Press.

_____ 1981. Xhosa marriage in historical perspective. In *Essays on African marriage in southern Africa,* edited by Eileen Krige and John Comaroff. Cape Town, Juta.

_____ Kaplan, S., Maki, T., and Walton, E. M. 1952. *Social structure.* Keiskammahoek Rural Survey, Vol 3. Pietermaritzburg: Shuter and Shooter.

Worby, Eric. 1995. What does agrarian wage labour signify? Cotton, commoditisation and social form in Gokwe, Zimbabwe. The Journal of Peasant Studies 23 (1): 1–29.

Zenani, Nongenile Masithathu. 1992. *The world and the word: Tales and observations from the Xhosa oral tradition.* Collected and edited by Harold Scheub. Madison: University of Wisconsin Press.

Index

- A -

administrative area, 85, 151

admonition/s, 125, 157, 281, 283–89, 291, 293–95, 297, 300, 315, 317, 322

agency, 44, 70, 160, 169, 232, 243, 306

agent/s, 44–48, 51, 64, 66, 68, 72, 74, 79, 149, 163–64, 172–73, 187, 244

agnate/s, 38, 121, 125, 136, 139, 154, 160, 176, 179, 188, 202, 205, 217, 224, 265, 289, 296–97

agnatic cluster, 87–88, 99, 236

agnatic group, 112, 116, 160, 187, 224, 269, 271, 273

agnatic kinship, 38, 87, 200, 236

agricultural company/ies, 94, 99, 101–2, 120, 164, 234

agricultural production, 36, 38, 40, 56, 91, 165

agricultural work, 33, 39, 95, 99, 102–3, 120, 234, 238

agriculture, 32, 37–38, 55, 81, 88–89, 95, 188

alcohol, 14–15, 21, 27, 30, 41, 66, 108, 158–59, 179, 240

analogical transfer, 77, 164, 302

analogy, 76, 130–31, 223

ancestor/s, 154, 249, 268

ancestor rituals, 9, 13, 64, 84, 111–12, 114–16, 118, 270, 274

apartheid, 3, 8, 12–13, 16, 40, 49–50, 55–56, 58–60, 62–66, 71, 81, 84, 88–90, 151, 223, 303–4, 308

arranging of the hut, 190, 192, 194, 206–7, 222, 224, 248

avoidance, 136, 188, 200

- B -

Balanta, 158–59

beaker/s, 113, 115, 129, 136, 172, 175–81, 183, 193, 197, 199, 201–22, 224–25, 227–31, 233, 236–37, 240–41, 248–49, 251–56, 259, 271–24, 284–85, 290, 312–13

beer allocation/s, 9, 116, 119–20, 170–72, 177–78, 189, 193–95, 199, 201, 205, 207–8, 211–12, 214, 219, 224, 227–31, 233, 247–49, 251–54, 257–58, 260, 271, 281 beer allocation/s (*continued*)

amasiko, 201, 207–8, 210

igwele, 175, 179, 216, 312

iimvuko, 201, 208–11, 235–37

imifihlo, 179

iminono, 201–5, 216, 224, 227, 232, 272

ingcwele, 177–78, 180, 240

intluzelo, 169, 175–76, 201, 211, 224, 241, 248, 313

intselo, 117–18, 177–78, 201, 211, 220

iqwele, 220–21, 226

isidudu, 179, 221, 311–12

isikhonkwane, 201, 211, 240–41, 252, 254

ivanya, 126, 177, 179, 220–21, 273, 309, 312

ugabu, 212, 275

umcakulo, 201, 211, 224

umlawulo, 212–13, 219–20, 225, 237, 249, 252–53, 255–56, 275, 290

umlumiso, 169, 175–76, 180, 312

umtsho, 180

beer consumption, 13–15, 20–27, 29–30, 66, 88, 107, 109, 111–14, 169–71, 173, 177, 199, 264, 295

beer distribution, 13, 24, 112, 126, 146, 169–70, 172–73, 176–77, 184, 195, 199, 227–28, 230, 232, 234, 240–41, 253, 272, 274, 281, 284, 288

beer for harvest, 95, 99, 118, 188, 201, 224, 228, 234, 238, 244

beer for sale, 22, 30, 37, 42, 90, 104, 110, 120, 173, 227, 239, 241

beer gift/s, 10, 21, 126, 202–3, 216, 227, 233, 239, 271–72, 275, 290

beer lexicon, 37, 171–72, 179

Beinart, 26, 29, 31, 34–35, 37, 39–40, 58, 61, 91, 304, 326

Betterment, 11, 40, 58, 65, 86–87, 92

Bhaca, 26, 153, 167, 331

blessings, 110, 115, 125–26, 141, 146, 166, 260, 271, 277

blood, 22, 110, 130

Bomvana, 7, 22, 112, 121, 200, 266–67

boundary, 161, 164, 191, 211, 222–23, 230, 267

Bourdieu, 13, 43–49, 51–52, 56, 59–60, 62–65, 67–68, 71–73, 76–77, 79–80, 110, 163–66, 186, 188–89, 227, 233, 244–46, 248, 279, 286, 291, 296, 301–3, 305–6

brandy, 6, 26, 107–8, 113–14, 126, 175, 229

brewing, 19–28, 30–31, 107, 109–15, 117–18, 160–61, 206, 221, 224, 233, 239, 241, 267–68, 275, 283, 290, 309–10, 313

bridewealth, 33, 58, 104, 108, 138, 159–60, 167

British Kaffraria, 54

building the homestead, 39, 91, 110, 146, 166, 264, 293

- C -

capital, 43, 45, 55, 222, 245, 286, 304
  capital conversion, 64
  cultural capital, 47, 59, 61, 64–65, 171
  economic capital, 47, 50, 59, 61, 63, 65, 110, 146, 164
  social capital, 47, 50, 61, 63, 146, 291
  symbolic capital, 47, 62, 64, 110, 146, 164, 166, 245, 304
capitalism, 16, 49–50, 164
capitalist production, 50, 62–64, 66, 124, 171, 222, 301
cattle, 25–26, 30, 32, 53–55, 57–58, 63–64, 85, 92–93, 99–102, 104, 130, 137–38, 150, 164, 183, 200, 228, 257
  cattle byre, 57, 95, 108, 112, 115–16, 120, 125–26, 154, 190–91, 197
  cattle-killing, 29, 39, 54, 159–60
chief, 11, 26, 32–33, 54–55, 81, 85–86, 96, 115, 144, 150, 159, 170, 177, 180, 194, 200–1, 210–11, 220, 224, 250, 289
Christianity, 52, 54, 56–57, 80, 84, 297, 337, 339
church, 52, 56–57, 59, 117, 285, 291
clan, 8, 88, 134, 137, 139, 193, 200–2, 208, 211, 224, 236, 238, 250, 261, 265, 269–70, 276, 285, 289, 318
  clan ancestor/s, 120, 125, 132, 279

clan praises, 125
class, 47, 51, 64–65, 107, 113
colonialism, 12, 16, 19–42, 48–50, 62–63, 65–66, 91, 159, 303
colonisation, 61, 72
communication, 22, 67, 69–70, 73, 78, 115, 149, 171, 243–44, 251, 259, 261, 264, 303, 306, 308
communitas, 177, 225
community, 15–17, 21, 23, 38, 57, 65, 77, 96, 110–11, 118–20, 123, 125–26, 131–32, 139, 141–44, 146, 148–49, 153–54, 161–62, 166, 173–74, 181, 183, 195, 239–41, 251, 257, 259, 263, 270–71, 274–76, 279, 281–83, 290–91, 293, 295, 302, 304
conflict, 66, 68, 74, 100–1, 104, 159–60, 162, 208, 236, 238, 299–300
consensus, 66, 68, 86, 100, 243, 246, 248–49, 276, 300
conservatism, 84
convention, 76–77, 90, 193, 197, 241
conversation, 108, 171, 174, 181, 218, 253
co-operation, 32, 40, 95, 100, 103, 110, 158, 164–65, 173–74, 189, 211, 223, 239, 299–300, 303, 307
co-operative work, 14–15, 19, 24, 31–32, 36–37, 41, 61–62, 65, 78, 81, 93, 95, 97, 99, 103, 123, 165, 229, 234, 237, 302

courtyard, 112, 136, 190–91, 242, 285

creativity, 49, 73–74, 260

cultivation, 32, 34, 37, 39–40, 56, 91–92, 94, 100–1, 137, 141

culture, 12, 52, 54, 57–58, 60, 68–69, 80, 98, 185–86

cultural performance, 62, 68, 292, 326, 335, 338, 340

cultural production, 49, 64

- D -

danger, 22, 77, 124, 133, 149, 153–54, 161–62, 164, 222–23, 323, 329

debate/s, 6, 12, 44, 59, 166, 181, 183, 206, 233, 249, 251–52, 256–58, 261, 272–74, 281

domination, 16, 27, 44, 46, 51–52, 63, 245, 301, 303–5

Douglas, 14–15, 148, 161, 179, 222–23, 293, 300

drama, 68, 80, 186, 238, 292–93

dramatization, 196, 292

drinking talk, 169–71, 175, 179

- E -

Eastern Cape, 3–4, 26–27, 50–51, 53, 56, 65, 84, 159, 308

economic co-operation, 299

economic production, 15, 50, 59, 124, 263, 299

economy, 12, 16, 27, 32, 35, 37, 48–49, 51, 58, 61–62, 66, 82, 127, 141, 159, 164, 170, 228, 240, 305

education, 35, 47–48, 52, 54, 56, 59–60, 63–65, 82, 84, 223

employment, 52, 56, 69, 82–84, 89–90, 92, 181

ethnography of communication, 73, 244, 264

etiquette, 9, 21, 24, 56, 170, 246, 251, 258, 274

exchange, 15–17, 21, 24, 98, 103–4, 110, 118, 123, 172–73, 202–3, 225, 240–41, 248, 257, 283, 305–6

experience, 45, 52, 59, 68–69, 96, 100, 141, 148, 162, 165, 257, 270–71, 281, 291–93, 295, 299, 302, 306–7, 309

extended family, 33–34, 37–38, 41, 61, 157–58, 263

- F -

family, 7, 33–34, 37–38, 41, 57–58, 61, 71, 119, 154, 156–58, 180, 185, 198, 200, 238, 263, 283

family size, 33, 61

feast, 108, 114, 180, 199, 309, 329

field/s, 33–36, 40, 43, 45–50, 59–68, 71–73, 76–77, 79, 118–20, 124, 126–27, 141, 150, 163–65, 170–71, 186, 188, 204, 208, 222, 230–31, 235, 238, 240, 243–44, 263, 276, 300, 304–5

fieldwork, 1, 5–7, 12, 36, 45, 52, 81, 88, 104, 120, 127–28, 171, 183, 252, 258, 274

fighting, 26, 29, 59, 133, 136, 287, 317

food, 16–17, 20–23, 27, 33–34,
39–40, 42, 90, 95, 102, 105,
108–9, 113–14, 116, 121, 125,
127, 130–31, 151, 155, 160, 170,
173, 199, 220, 222–23, 229–30,
242, 258, 309
friendship, 97–98, 100, 102, 189,
215, 227

- G -
game, 39, 46, 77–78, 232, 234, 305
garden/s, 33, 36, 39–40, 87, 92–96,
99, 101, 104–5, 118, 120, 229,
263, 288, 309–10, 318
Gcaleka, 54, 81, 194, 200, 286, 315
gender, 47, 56, 96, 110, 127, 165,
176, 185–86, 190, 193, 197, 199,
205, 213, 219, 230, 235, 248,
276, 305
gift/s, 6–7, 10–11, 21, 53, 108,
114, 126, 179, 202–3, 216, 227,
231–33, 239, 241, 249, 271–72,
275, 284, 290, 306
gift exchange, 21, 306
good neighbourliness, 38, 97, 103,
111, 271, 302–3
grazing, 31–32, 85–86, 92–94, 96,
101
greeting, 170, 201, 224
Gwembe Tonga, 23, 37, 42

- H -
habitus, 43, 45–49, 51–53, 59–60,
62–64, 66–67, 69, 72–74, 77,
79, 82, 91, 103, 110, 124, 153,
163–65, 167, 170, 173, 184,
186, 188–89, 201, 222, 227, 232,

243–44, 259, 263, 271–72,
274–75, 278, 281, 295–96,
299–303, 305, 307–8
Hammond-Tooke, 12, 22–23, 26,
31, 34–35, 41–42, 81, 87, 116,
124, 150, 153, 156, 167, 200,
208
harmony, 23, 70, 110, 209, 215,
243, 248–49, 251–52, 257–58,
260, 279, 300, 302
herding, 94–95, 101
hidden beer, 179, 206, 221, 233,
290, 301
hierarchy, 44, 166, 190, 199, 208,
222, 225
history, 3, 44, 48, 51, 53, 56, 60,
63, 72, 81, 208, 227–28, 235–36,
238, 268, 301
hoeing, 93–94, 96, 99, 102, 108,
230
homestead/s, 5, 7–11, 13–14, 23,
31–40, 56–58, 60–65, 81,
85–93, 95–97, 99–104, 109–14,
116–21, 123–27, 129, 131,
138–39, 141–42, 144, 146, 148,
153, 155–61, 163–64, 166,
172–81, 184–91, 197–98,
205–6, 211, 214, 216–17,
227–32, 234–36, 239–43,
246–48, 259–61, 278, 285,
299–301, 303–5, 307, 310,
317–19
building the homestead, 39, 91,
110, 146, 166, 264, 293
homestead head, 10–11, 35, 88,
92, 97, 99, 101, 110, 112–13,
118–20, 161, 170, 173,

homestead head (*continued*)
175–79, 181, 195, 200, 202,
209, 221, 224–25, 232,
239–41, 246, 252, 256, 263,
271, 273, 275–76, 281, 283,
288, 293, 295, 313, 318
homestead size, 31, 34, 36, 38,
40, 123
hospitality group/s, 187, 208, 331
host/s, 10–11, 34, 53, 62, 110, 172,
180, 189, 192–93, 199, 223,
227–29, 231–33, 236–37, 241,
271, 275, 283
host section, 183, 192, 195–96,
202–3, 205–10, 212–13, 216,
220–21, 228–29, 231–33, 251,
254
humanity, 75, 98, 109, 118, 223
Hunter, 7, 22–24, 26, 31, 34–36,
38–39, 42, 104, 153, 156, 160,
167, 179, 214, 220, 225
hunting dog, 130–31, 143

- I -
identity, 12, 47, 52–53, 57–58, 65,
67, 95, 164, 170, 179, 223, 282,
284, 301, 306
ideology, 3, 38, 40, 55, 59, 61, 65,
97, 100, 110, 223, 264
illocutionary act, 74, 292
illocutionary force, 74, 244–45,
271
imbarha, 9, 90, 104, 120–21, 211,
239–41, 249, 254–55
imithombo, 221, 309–12
indeterminacy, 70, 80, 150
indexical, 78–79, 165–66

indexicality, 79–80
individual, 10–11, 13–14, 23, 34,
36, 39, 44, 61, 69, 78, 81,
95–96, 98, 100–3, 110–12, 114,
116, 121, 123–25, 141, 146, 149,
164–65, 173, 176–77, 181, 185,
187–90, 193–95, 205, 207, 214,
223, 225, 227–30, 233–34, 239,
250, 258, 260–61, 271–72, 274,
276, 279, 281, 291, 293, 304–7,
310
individuality, 187, 205
initiation, 27–28, 42, 56, 72, 76,
114, 204, 264, 270, 284, 309
initiation rituals, 9, 108, 112
injoli, 181, 183, 192, 197, 201,
205–7, 209, 213–14, 216,
219–21, 234, 251–52, 273
inkazathi, 112, 121, 239, 241
inkobe, 114, 118–19, 230
inkundla, 112, 190
intercropping, 36, 92
interest, 5, 13, 23, 46, 61, 70, 77,
100, 102–3, 110, 125, 164, 166,
169, 181, 205, 227, 231, 238,
257, 300–1, 305–6
intselo, 177–78, 201, 211, 220
intselo nje, 117–18
invocation/s, 115, 125–26, 142,
144–45, 154, 162, 261
isicelo, 97–99
isichenene, 117, 237, 241, 249, 256

- J -
junior/s, 103, 119, 126, 128, 158,
160–64, 166, 187–88, 198, 200,

216, 220, 228, 245, 252, 256, 269, 274, 296, 299–300

juniority, 191

- K -

Kaffir beer, 28, 30, 42

kava, 173, 179

kin, 6, 8, 17, 22, 24, 32, 37–38, 57, 102, 104–5, 114–17, 120, 126–27, 129, 131, 141–45, 154, 158–60, 175–77, 183, 191, 202–3, 205, 208, 216–17, 221, 224, 232, 246, 257–59, 263, 271, 274–75, 279, 282–84, 297, 310

kinship, 5, 15, 41, 87–88, 98–100, 110, 112, 139, 163–65, 185–86, 188–90, 195, 199–200, 227, 236, 248, 264–65, 299–300, 302, 304–5

Kuckertz, 23–24, 42, 97, 116, 187–89, 200, 208, 220, 271

- L -

labour, 13, 24, 33–43, 47, 49–50, 52, 57–64, 66, 83, 89–96, 98–104, 108, 110, 156–60, 162–67, 171, 177, 211, 222–23, 228–30, 239–40, 245, 259, 263–64, 271, 281, 306, 309–10

communal labour, 24, 61, 123

co-operative labour, 15–16, 37–38, 42, 62, 81, 87, 95, 104, 123, 164, 189, 301

land, 28, 31–36, 47, 53–55, 57, 65, 80–81, 85–87, 89, 91–92, 94, 96, 100–1, 104, 144, 159, 177, 194, 230, 304, 306

land alienation, 50, 55

land shortage, 34–36, 40

language, 12, 170–71, 179, 186, 200, 244–45, 260

liminality, 70, 72, 161, 299

linguistic competence, 244

liquor, 11, 30, 90, 108, 113, 121, 126, 158, 240–41

livestock, 31, 33, 41, 54–55, 57–58, 65, 81, 85, 89–95, 101, 104, 110, 127, 157, 181, 183, 294, 304, 316

Lovedu, 21–22, 24, 42, 258

- M -

maize, 11, 17, 36, 64, 117, 135, 140–41, 144, 170, 173–74, 178

maize beer, 20–21, 27, 30, 42, 90, 95, 102, 104, 107–8, 110, 115, 123, 165, 173–74, 230, 239–40, 306, 309

maize yields, 29, 39, 95, 157

malt, 178, 221, 309

mangumba, 90, 97, 104, 107–9, 113, 120

marriage, 27, 34–35, 42, 58, 78, 114, 159–60, 185, 245, 263, 284, 297

Mayer, 3, 5, 11, 51–55, 57, 59, 223

McAllister, 11, 15, 17, 41, 59, 81, 84, 86, 88, 90, 95, 103, 116, 150, 167, 179, 200, 240, 263, 297

meat, 8, 20, 89–90, 97–98, 105, 115–16, 121, 154, 162, 191, 194, 199, 258, 290 medicine of the home, 111, 115, 125, 131–32

metaphor, 141

Mfengu, 53–55, 104

migrant/s, 13, 42, 76–77, 81, 83–84, 88–92, 95, 104, 113, 118–19, 139, 153–54, 156–67, 170, 175, 183, 211, 281

migrant earnings, 35, 89, 125, 263

migrant labour, 3, 5–6, 27, 31, 35, 37–39, 50, 55, 57–58, 60–64, 81, 89–92, 108, 158–60, 162–65, 167, 211, 222, 228, 245, 259, 263–64, 271, 275, 299, 301, 303–4

milk, 25–26, 29, 33, 39, 41, 89

mine/s, 3, 13, 27–28, 35, 55, 58, 61, 83, 91, 113, 123, 132–33, 153, 267

misfortune, 3, 22, 114, 118, 124, 129, 144, 270, 302

misrecognition, 110, 299, 303, 305

missionaries, 25, 50, 53, 55, 57

money, 11, 24, 39, 58, 89–90, 98, 103–4, 112, 117, 121, 123–24, 127, 129–31, 133, 137–39, 142, 146, 150, 207, 239–42, 256–57, 281

moral, 74–75, 100, 126, 134, 142, 146, 148–49, 157, 161, 163, 165, 193, 205, 223, 227, 241, 259, 293, 300

moral obligation, 98, 110, 117, 172, 229, 307

morality, 78, 103, 188, 209, 299, 304, 306–8

mourning, 14, 112, 114, 119, 172, 198, 212, 261, 275, 281–85, 289–92, 296, 321

Mpondo, 22–23, 25, 34, 38, 97, 104, 153, 179, 186–87, 200, 208, 220

mutual helpfulness, 97–98, 100, 102, 209, 304

- N -

negotiation, 62, 173, 199, 237, 258

neighbour/s, 12, 17, 23–25, 33, 37–38, 41–42, 57, 88, 92, 96–98, 101–2, 105, 108, 112–13, 116, 119, 126, 142, 145, 154, 162, 165, 170, 174–77, 179, 183, 196, 208, 216, 221, 224–25, 233, 238, 240, 265, 275, 283, 291, 300, 310, 312–13

neighbourhood, 8, 15, 32, 35, 41, 87, 96, 98, 100, 116, 118, 121, 161, 189, 193, 225, 231, 265, 299, 302, 304, 310

neighbourliness, 23, 38, 97, 103, 111, 209, 249, 271, 302–3

new homestead, 14, 36, 114, 118–19, 164, 181, 260–61, 263–65, 271–72, 274–75, 278, 281, 300

noise, 183, 219, 249, 255, 258, 261

ntwana nje, 114, 118–19, 196, 204, 248, 263–65, 269–72, 274–78, 300

- O -

objective conditions, 45–46, 48, 53, 56, 165, 302–4

orator/s, 134, 149

oratory, 12, 14, 63, 69, 110, 127,
137, 139, 146, 148–49, 162,
165–66, 199, 243–45, 258, 260,
281, 283, 291–96, 300

oxen, 24, 36–37, 93, 95, 100–1,
118, 123, 140–41, 200

ox-draught, 35, 39, 93

- P -

patriarchy, 29, 39, 218, 281, 296

Pedi, 21

performance, 124, 144, 146,
149–50, 153, 166, 186, 209, 236,
238, 263, 272, 274, 281, 290,
292, 294, 299–301, 306–8

anthropology of performance,
13, 43–44, 67–68, 70, 75,
163

performative, 6, 72, 141, 148,
165–67, 169–70, 194, 201, 205,
245–46, 257, 259–61, 275, 295

performative act, 141, 190

performative effect, 44, 74, 271

performative event, 79, 166

performative force, 74, 125, 248,
259, 271

performativity, 67, 73, 75

perlocutionary, 74, 76, 245, 258,
295

plough, 29, 35–36, 39, 93, 99–101,
120, 140–41, 229

ploughing, 23, 36, 38, 92–96,
99–102, 105, 140, 161, 164,
228–29, 309

ploughing company, 199, 234, 238

Pondoland, 7, 25–26, 31, 34–36,
39–40, 54, 58, 60, 80, 105, 160,
220

polygyny, 35, 157

population, 33–35, 39–41, 57, 84,
88, 93, 103, 151, 303

power, 34–36, 149–50, 158–66,
187, 222, 252, 263, 276, 281–97,
300, 304–7

economic power, 16, 38, 47, 55,
58, 60, 63, 65, 124, 137, 160,
163–64

occult power, 150–63

power differences, 216, 263

power relations, 16, 46, 49, 64,
81, 137, 150, 169, 171, 296,
304

symbolic power, 47, 65, 70, 146,
164, 166, 171, 245, 305

practice, 6, 13–14, 16–17, 30–31,
33, 38, 91, 103, 112, 116, 124,
134, 154–55, 166–67, 169, 172,
174, 184–89, 191, 205, 212–13,
216–18, 223, 227–28, 231–32,
234–36, 238, 241, 263–64, 272,
278, 297, 299–301, 305–7, 312

logic of practice, 47, 163

practice theory, 13, 43–44, 48,
59, 68, 72–73, 163, 191, 305

praise, 120, 136, 150, 201, 206,
217, 261, 279, 297

praise poem, 183, 208, 250, 265

pre-colonial, 31, 33, 36, 39, 86

production, 12–13, 15–17, 19–21,
26, 31, 34–38, 40–41, 49–50,
56–66, 81, 88, 91–92, 95–96,

production (*continued*)
123–24, 153, 157–59, 161,
163–66, 171, 173, 189, 216,
222–23, 263, 299, 301–3, 306

- R -

rainfall, 33, 84, 93

Rappaport, 44, 75–77, 246,
259–60, 292, 306–7

reciprocity, 16–17, 88, 98–100,
103–4, 118, 123, 212, 216, 240,
258, 304–5

red ochre, 57, 284, 323

Red Xhosa, 43, 51–54, 57, 59, 171,
223

Red Xhosa habitus, 62–64, 67,
91, 153, 164, 167, 274

reflexivity, 69–70, 72, 74, 76, 165,
258, 263, 272, 293–94

refrain, 139, 144, 146, 196,
250–51, 265

relations of production, 15–16,
62–63, 96, 153, 157–58, 163,
165, 216, 223

resistance, 3, 16, 27, 29, 47, 51, 53,
58, 60, 63, 65, 71, 164, 223, 303

rites of passage, 13, 112, 114, 258,
281, 284, 302

ritual, 3, 5–8, 13–17, 19, 21–23,
31, 33, 88, 91, 94, 96, 123–25,
127–28, 144–46, 150–51,
157–60, 162–67, 169, 172, 179,
184–87, 189, 191, 201, 205, 228,
232, 238, 248, 252, 256, 272,
276, 278, 281, 284, 290, 292–96,
299–302

ritual change, 43–44, 68, 72–74,
76, 79, 153, 157–58, 166, 260

ritual drama, 80, 293, 340

ritual killing, 22, 41, 77, 114,
119, 151, 154, 163, 264

ritual performance, 14, 44,
67–73, 75–77, 80, 162, 186,
236, 243, 259–60, 294, 299,
306, 308

ritual speech, 44, 75, 78, 148,
243, 245, 260–61, 295

ritual tasting, 8, 115, 154, 284

rule/s, 3, 13, 19, 23–24, 40, 45–46,
50, 70–71, 78, 81, 90, 104, 108,
110, 112–13, 164, 184, 188, 194,
207, 212–13, 223, 231–34, 236,
239, 243–44, 249, 292, 302, 307

rules of speaking, 251, 258

rural disposition, 137

rural field, 62–66, 81–105, 124,
126, 164–65, 171, 222, 300, 305

rural habitus, 63–64, 66, 103,
163–64, 170, 173, 184, 188,
201, 222, 244, 263, 271–72,
274–75, 278, 281, 295, 299–300,
303, 305

rural orientation, 57, 64, 66, 137,
170, 301, 304, 306

rural production, 12–13, 31, 35,
37–38, 56, 62–64, 66, 81, 88,
123–24, 153, 158, 161, 163, 166,
222–23, 263, 301

rural social field, 62–64, 66, 81,
103, 124

rural society, 31, 63, 66, 125–27,
146, 148–49, 156, 158, 161–62,

222, 228, 278, 281, 299–300, 303, 305–6

rural Xhosa habitus, 64, 170, 184, 188, 201, 222, 244, 263, 272, 274, 281, 299–300, 303, 305

- S -

sacred, 111, 125, 131, 136, 178, 191

sacrifice, 21–22, 57, 112, 114, 116, 119, 121, 153, 158, 191, 264, 290, 301

School Xhosa, 43, 51–53, 56, 59

seating places, 10, 116, 169, 189, 191, 193–94, 196, 198–99, 205, 212, 214, 229, 233–34, 236–38

self-interest, 110, 303

senior men, 7, 34, 66, 103, 113, 119, 126, 129, 136, 146, 149–50, 166, 175, 195, 197, 206, 213, 221, 223, 235–36, 245, 251–52, 263, 276, 281

seniority, 29, 108, 110, 159, 161, 185, 188, 200, 220–21, 269, 271, 274

settlement, 31, 54, 81, 84, 87, 185

sharing, 23, 201, 209–10, 214–15, 222, 224, 258, 271, 293

slaughtering, 41, 131, 134, 155–57

snake, 155–57, 160–62, 167

social act, 72, 75, 245, 306

social consciousness, 247, 278

social drama, 68, 80, 186, 238, 292–93

social field, 47–48, 62–64, 66, 71–72, 81, 103, 124

social order, 16, 59–60, 66, 70–71, 74–76, 124, 165, 222, 276, 307

social practice, 14, 17, 43–45, 62, 68–69, 73, 76, 124, 184, 187–88, 236, 238, 260, 272, 278, 299, 301, 306–7

social process, 16, 43–44, 68–71, 73–74, 165, 186, 189, 237–38, 252

social reality, 43, 47, 66–67, 69–72, 169, 173, 186–87, 244, 306

social relations, 15–16, 37, 46, 61, 63, 68, 70, 79, 163, 171, 185, 238, 245, 291, 305–6

social reproduction, 15, 43, 46, 48, 137, 149

social structure, 17, 46, 48, 66, 79, 187–88

sorcery, 124

sorghum, 21, 30, 33, 36, 39, 42, 158

Sotho, 21, 23, 33, 41, 331

space, 49, 61–64, 66, 101, 146, 161, 211–13, 218, 224, 227, 233, 242–44, 248, 271, 276, 281

spatial symbolism, 116, 139, 185, 187, 189, 300

speaker/s, 9–10, 19, 22–23, 25, 30, 33–34, 39–40, 42, 55, 57, 87, 107, 118, 121, 124, 131, 134, 136, 139, 143, 145–48, 150–51, 153, 166, 183–84, 207, 244–52, 257–58, 273, 276, 278, 284, 289

speaking, 8, 14, 31, 46, 50, 79, 104, 136, 139, 141, 146, 148–49, 154–55, 171, 175, 191–92, 200, 204, 213, 234, 243–49, 251–52,

speaking (*continued*)
  254, 258, 260, 268, 291, 294,
  304, 316, 320
speech, 10, 112, 117, 134, 155–56,
  170, 184, 195–96, 238, 283, 289,
  293, 295, 323
  speech act/s, 44, 74–75, 78,
    244–46, 248, 250, 257, 261
spitting, 258, 267–69, 277, 279
strategy/ies, 3, 13, 19, 30, 46–48,
  60, 62–63, 66, 100, 123–24,
  127, 160, 163, 171, 173, 186,
  219, 227, 231, 233, 239, 241,
  293, 301, 303, 305
structure and agency, 44, 169
sub-headman, 7, 85–86, 96, 183,
  193–94, 201, 210, 216, 224, 227,
  232, 241, 289, 302
subjectivity, 46
subsistence, 17, 31–32, 34, 55,
  89–90, 95–96, 239
sub-ward/s, 141, 146, 205, 211
sub-ward sections, 82, 87, 96, 102,
  139, 154, 175, 192–93, 195, 200,
  202–3, 205, 211–13, 220, 227,
  237, 240–41, 272, 285
Swartz, 45–48, 60, 63, 65, 110
symbol/s, 16, 23, 64, 70, 74, 79,
  156, 162, 165–67, 185–87, 197,
  259, 275–76, 292, 295, 302, 306
symbolic structure, 80, 164,
  186–88, 244

- T -
Tambiah, 75, 77–80, 166, 213, 246
taxes, 29, 35, 39, 55, 60

territorial groups, 24, 87–88, 95,
  158, 178, 181, 189, 193, 198,
  202, 205, 219, 230, 240, 252,
  274, 276, 290, 305
territorial organization, 181, 189
territory, 15, 24–25, 31–33, 53, 99,
  112, 116, 177, 189–90, 199, 265,
  304
text, 68–69, 73–74, 231, 243–44,
  286, 289
transformation, 16, 43, 68, 74, 114,
  124, 144, 166–67, 170, 236,
  243, 258, 271, 275, 281, 292,
  299
Transkei, 3, 6–8, 11–12, 24–25,
  28–35, 37, 39–40, 42, 53,
  55–56, 58, 66, 77, 84–87, 92,
  104, 107, 157–58, 160, 167,
  308–9, 311
transposability, 164
Tsonga, 23, 258
Turner, 42–43, 68–74, 77, 79–80,
  150, 173, 185–86, 214, 238, 272,
  278, 292–95, 299

- U -
ubulawu, 111
ubuntu, 98, 117
ukugabu, 211, 213, 230, 290
ukuhlonipha, 188, 200, 218
ukulawula, 193–94, 200–1, 212,
  230, 290
ukungxengxeza, 115, 151, 200
ukuqwela, 201, 220
ukurhabulisa, 201, 210, 214, 227
ukusarha, 213, 229

ukuvana, 102, 175
ukuvumisa, 139, 166, 250–51, 261
umamlambo, 156, 159, 163, 167, 300
umgqibelo, 102, 105, 120, 229
umhlinzeko, 135–37, 154, 158, 160–63, 165, 264
ummango, 32, 87, 225
umphako, 125
umsindleko, 6, 13, 42, 119, 121, 123–25, 127–32, 134, 136–37, 139, 141–42, 144–46, 148–50, 153–55, 157–67, 176, 183, 198, 203, 211, 220, 222, 228, 244, 246–47, 253, 258–59, 264, 281, 299–300, 309–10
urbanization, 50, 88
usipatheleni, 38, 179

- V -
vegetables, 36, 39, 92, 94
verbal exchange, 248

- W -
wage/s, 3, 27, 35, 37, 40, 50, 52, 56–60, 63–64, 82–83, 91–92, 98, 123, 125, 171, 304
war, 52–54, 58, 76, 80, 90, 154, 164
wealth, 33, 39, 56, 156–57, 160, 294
weeding, 36, 39, 100, 102
widow, 112, 119, 198, 261, 272, 275, 281–85, 289–97, 300
Wilson, 31, 34–35, 42, 60, 104, 153, 156, 159, 167
wisdom, 5, 156

witch, 156–58
witch beliefs, 157–58
witch familiar, 156, 300
witchcraft, 124–25, 158–60, 162–63, 236, 297
work party/ies, 7–9, 14–15, 22–23, 36–37, 42, 95–97, 99, 102, 104–5, 108, 111, 120, 123, 188, 211, 217, 219, 227, 229–30, 281–82, 291
work party beer, 23, 37, 105, 120, 188, 217, 219, 227, 229–30, 281–82
world view, 56, 59, 64–65, 78, 84, 222–23

- X -
Xhosa, 12–13, 19, 21–25, 27, 29–31, 34, 39–44, 50–57, 59–60, 62–65, 67, 75–76, 80–81, 85, 87, 91, 95, 104, 108–10, 121, 124, 127, 144, 150–51, 153, 156, 159, 164, 167, 169–71, 173, 175, 177–79, 184–86, 188, 190, 192, 200–1, 214, 220, 222–23, 243–45, 247, 250, 259–60, 263, 272–74, 278–79, 281, 299–301, 303–8, 310–11
Xhosa custom, 57, 64, 95, 144, 153, 184, 192, 250, 273–74, 301
Xhosa identity, 12, 53, 57, 95, 164

- Y -
youth, 59–60, 83, 89, 113, 136–37, 140, 150, 159, 257
youth organizations, 83, 257

1937